Effective Argument

A WRITER'S GUIDE WITH READINGS

Second Edition

J. KARL NICHOLAS

JAMES R. NICHOLL

Western Carolina University

ALLYN AND BACON

Boston   London   Toronto   Sydney   Tokyo   Singapore

Vice President, Humanities: Joseph Opiela
Marketing Manager: Lisa Kimball
Editorial Production Service: Chestnut Hill Enterprises, Inc.
Manufacturing Buyer: Suzanne Lareau
Cover Administrator: Linda Knowles

Library of Congress Cataloging-in-Publication Data
Nicholas, J. Karl (James Karl), 1939–
    Effective argument : a writer's guide with readings / J. Karl Nicholas,
James R. Nicholl. – 2nd ed.
        p. cm.
    Includes index.
    ISBN 0-205-27039-5 (pbk.)
    1. English language–Rhetoric.   2. Persuasion (Rhetoric)
  3. College readers.   4. Report writing.   I. Nicholl, James R.
II. Title.
PE1431.N5   1998
808'.0427–dc21   97-26818
                                                                          CIP

Printed in the United States of America
10 9 8 7 6 5 4 3 2 1   02 01 00 99 98 97

Effective Argument

For
Marguerite and Ted Nicholas
Lil and Elden Nicholl

Contents

5   *Refutation*   88

6   *Putting It All Together*   100

PART TWO: Reading and Analyzing Arguments   119

Speaking Up: Argumentative Essays on Various Topics   132

Taking Sides: Differing Arguments on Important Issues   205

Varying Voices: Multiple Viewpoints on Crucial Questions   285

Selected Classic Arguments   322

Appendix   399

Preface

Now available in a new edition, *Effective Argument: A Writer's Guide with Readings* is a combined rhetoric and reader, created for college-level introductory English courses devoted to argumentative and persuasive writing. The first edition satisfied the needs of many teachers and students across the country; at our own university, we have used it successfully with classes of divergent abilities, ranging from honors students to those who had just completed a remedial English course before beginning their first college writing course.

In revising the book, we worked to retain the relaxed style and thoughtful features that made the original instructional content clear and accessible. At the same time, we modernized the book to meet the needs of students who will begin their professional careers in the 21st Century—by adding, for example, a straightforward but necessary section on citing electronic sources. Finally, we also strove to maintain *Effective Argument's* modest size and open, inviting format. Over the years we have seen too many other books, attempting to become all things to all users, grow more bloated and cumbersome, edition after edition, until their organization became muddled, their pages became too crowded to read comfortably, and the books themselves became virtually too large to carry and handle.

We originally wrote *Effective Argument* in response to the trend to create one or more separate freshman English courses devoted to argumentative writing, a trend that started in the early 1980s and that is still growing. We planned the book as a reader, with minimal apparatus, but in working on it, we quickly realized that students would need additional background, training, and practice in argumentation if they were to use the readings successfully as models for writing arguments of their own. Consequently, the rhetoric section grew, until it is nearly the size of the readings section, which contains 54 essays (28 are new). Even so, that section is not nearly so daunting in size or in content as many competing texts, so that students will feel quite at ease learning from it.

Effective Argument begins with an introduction that reviews the rhetoric of exposition, the kind of explanatory writing that students typically first attempt in high school and usually continue to practice in their first college writing course. It also discusses the value of learning to write effective argumentation and explains key terms, such as argumentation and persuasion.

The rhetoric section consists of six chapters. Chapter One, "The Argumentation Process," defines and illustrates the notions of claim and support. The next chapter, "Supporting the Claim," details strategies for supporting claims of fact, value, and policy. These two chapters, as do the four following ones, contain a number of illustrative examples of the argumentative techniques they describe by such writers as Loren Eiseley, Jesse Jackson, Phyllis McGinley, and John Steinbeck. Exercises are also placed throughout these chapters, keyed both to their examples and to the model essays in the readings section. This feature, not found in competing texts, provides students immediate and timely opportunities to practice and to test the concepts of argumentative writing while they are learning them; it also encourages students to begin examining a variety of written arguments quite early, and to consider the strategies employed by experienced writers.

Chapter Three, "Organizing the Support," begins by presenting inductive and deductive strategies in a manner that will seem familiar to most writing instructors; that is followed by a basic introduction to Stephen Toulmin's modern approach to logic. Chapter Four, "Warrants," continues the treatment of Toulmin's approach, focusing on the strength of the warrant—its logical, ethical, and emotional appeals.

Chapter Five, "Refutation," divides rebuttals into those that attack the opponents' support of a claim (material fallacies), the argument's form (formal fallacies), and the warrant itself. It also introduces the ironic argument and the reduction to absurdity. (A thorough discussion of fallacies is included separately in "A Short Guide to Material and Formal Fallacies" in the Appendix.)

Chapter Six, "Putting It All Together," focuses on the successive drafts of the argument as students work through the phases of the writing process, on the preparation of effective introductions and conclusions, and on the crucial skills students must develop to support the claims of their written arguments by properly documenting their information sources, including such electronic ones as CD-ROMS, on-line databases, and the WorldWide Web.

The readings section of the text begins with an introduction entitled "Reading and Analyzing Arguments," detailing the kinds of careful reading skills that students must develop not only to understand the ensuing essays but also to adapt those essays' techniques for use in their own argumentative writing. To conclude this introduction, we guide students through the analysis of a sample essay.

The readings themselves are divided into four groups. "Speaking Up" (16 essays on diverse topics) consists of four sets of four essays each, to illustrate Claims of fact, Claims of value, Claims of policy, and Refutation. "Taking Sides" (16 essays) presents eight topics, discussed in paired essays which have differing arguments. "Varying Voices" (12 essays) offers three groups of four essays, each group exploring facets of a single issue. "Selected Classic Arguments" provides 10 favorites that are still relevant today. Questions on Content and on Form, plus Suggestions for Writing, are provided for all essays in the readings section. (A separate Instructor's Manual contains answers to the content and form questions, as well as such additional useful information as sample syllabi and other teaching suggestions.)

The book concludes with an Appendix that contains both the guide to fallacies mentioned earlier and a "Glossary of Useful Terms," providing concise explanations of key logical, rhetorical, and argumentative elements and strategies.

Effective Argument owes its inception and continuing existence to the vision, energy, and encouragement of Joseph Opiela, now Allyn and Bacon's Vice-President, Humanities; we are indeed grateful for his efforts on behalf of this book. We also appreciate the professional support provided by Carol Alper and Kate Tolini.

Effective Argument's content, organization, and style were originally improved by the thoughtful, incisive criticism that the manuscript of the first edition received at various stages from these field reviewers: Walter Beale, University of North Carolina at Greensboro; Walter Graffin, University of Wisconsin at Kenosha; C. Jeriel Howard, Northeastern Illinois University; David Jolliffe, University of Illinois-Chicago; Nevin Laib, Franklin and Marshall University; Gratia Murphy, Youngstown State University; John O'Bannion, Robert Morris College; Richard Ramsey, Indiana University, Fort Wayne; Mary Saver, Indiana University, Purdue; Judith Stanford, Rivier College; Gail Stygall, Miami University; Lynn Waller, McLennan Community College; Richard Zbracki, Iowa State University. This second edition has also received valuable outside help, especially benefiting from the thoughtful suggestions of these persons, whose comments were based on their experiences using the first edition with their own students: Barbara E. Ladner, West Virginia State College; Patricia Medieros, Scottsdale Community College; and Toni Stevens, Volunteer State Community College.

We certainly appreciate the time and effort each person gave in order to help make this book better.

We also acknowledge with gratitude the generous assistance we got from Mrs. Nancy De Sain, Office Assistant, Dept. of English, and from the Reference Staff at Hunter Library, Western Carolina University, who several times came to the rescue as we were revising the readings section of this book.

Special thanks are due to our families for their support during the course of yet another Nicholas & Nicholl book project; certainly Veronica and Kathy are glad the revision process has ended, so that we can again share in the household chores. Our final thanks go to our parents, to whom this book is again lovingly dedicated.

J.K.N.
J.R.N.

PART ONE

Effective Argument

Argumentation and the Writing Process

Few human activities are more important or can be more complex than that of persuasion: the art and craft of changing people's minds. When persuasion—or argumentation, if it comes to that—is successful, old beliefs give way to new: our world is understood as round, not flat; it orbits the sun, not vice versa. But when persuasion fails, convictions sometimes clash; then the results can be unpleasant, or even deadly.

For these and other reasons, people began centuries ago to study argumentation, especially in its spoken forms. They wanted to discover what makes some arguments succeed and others fail—which common elements, arrangements, and techniques each includes, and each avoids. The earliest important students of argumentation were the Greeks (such as Aristotle, 384–322 B.C.) and the Romans (such as Cicero, 106–43 B.C.), for in their cultures that skill was especially valued for its immediate influence in their law courts and public assemblies. Scholars of argumentation were called rhetoricians, from *rhetor*, the Greek name for an orator or public speaker. These rhetoricians trained students in the art of effective, persuasive use of language, or *rhetoric*. To do so, they regularly provided their pupils with samples of successful speeches, helped them to analyze their own and others' techniques, and then coached their novice orators to imitate the successful features of the works they had studied.

This book uses a related approach. Much as Greek and Roman students did, you will study models of effective arguments, learning thereby the most appropriate techniques for changing the minds of an audience. However, we will not be concerned with persuasive

1

public speaking in this book, although sometimes the examples that we include appeared first as speeches. (A familiar example is Patrick Henry's emotionally persuasive phrase, "Give me liberty or give me death!", part of a speech he made shortly before the American Revolution to the legislature of colonial Virginia.) Primarily, we provide examples of effective written arguments—or *rhetorical models.*

You understand, of course, that the models we will provide are unique; other people wrote them for purposes and audiences and times different from ours. But just as, hoping to succeed yourself, you might study and imitate a special technique of an athlete on the court or field, or of an artist in a studio or a musician in a concert hall, so also can you learn from imitation of other writers' successes. In fact, the biographies of notable writers consistently describe how their own work was influenced by reading closely the works of their predecessors and contemporaries.

Of course, you also understand that just as success as an athlete (or musician or scientist or accountant or the like) does not come automatically or without practice or effort, so writing successful persuasive prose requires study, thought, and hard work. No piece of writing in this book sprang instantly and perfectly into being; if you could see this introductory essay as we have gone through the process of piecing it together—with its strike-overs, insertions, scratched-out sentences, revisions in three colors of ink, representing numerous writing and revising sessions—you would readily agree with us that no writer is likely to create a perfect argument on the first attempt, or even sometimes on the second or third or fourth.

That declaration leads to this one: Completed writing projects of much complexity are the result of an extended, recursive (looping) process involving certain phases, and the construction of arguments is no exception. Sometimes a piece of argumentative writing will begin with an assignment from a supervisor or a teacher or some other authority figure; sometimes it will start directly from the heart or the mind (perhaps as an apology or as a letter of complaint). In any case, faced with the task, you begin the process. Inevitably that process involves four basic phases, but the process is not usually linear or straightforward. Rather, the phases are often repeated and often overlap, for writing is a messy and plastic activity. Think, for example, of a sculptor working and reworking a mass of clay until a person's facial features emerge in just the right form. Thus, even though we will describe the phases of the writing process in a 1, 2, 3, 4 progression, we do so for convenience and not because that progression exactly represents the normal reality.

The first phase is devoted to prewriting, a period of time before you actually begin to write and during which you call on all your resources, bringing them to bear on the issue or proposition you want your audience to accept. It is during this step that you may seek out and examine actual models (such as those in this book or ones in a library or in the files of your organization) of the kind of writing you plan to do. If you plan to write an editorial condemning a sales tax increase or an article proposing stricter drinking laws, it's always a good idea to examine a few such editorials or articles to see what others have done and how they have solved that particular writing problem. You must also consider all the relevant facts that you know and try to find others that you do not know; you will want to think about how best to reach and convince your probable reading audience, tinker with organizational schemes, test your logic, look for possible fallacies; you'll probably, unless you have an exceptional memory, want to jot down useful examples, write yourself notes, even make an outline in some form. In other words, you will immerse yourself in the subject.

Sooner or later, you will have to select the most likely alternative approach of those considered and begin to write. Then you are starting the second phase, the actual writing of the argument. You may be lucky and discover that your initial strategy or organizational plan works smoothly, with its logic unchallengeable and all of the concrete details you earlier jotted down fitting neatly into their supporting slots. But that rarely happens. More often you will have several false starts, perhaps discarding plans whose promise evaporated as you tried to put them into place. Sometimes new and better ideas occur to you as you write. Or maybe you realize that you have forgotten to take proper account of what your intended audience knows—or doesn't know. Sometimes you must toss away everything and start over again, after a break, a meal, or even a good night's sleep (if the paper's due date permits, that is). If you keep going, however, eventually you will complete your first draft. Then your written work is ready for the third phase: revision of your completed first draft. (Of course, you may not in fact complete the whole first draft before you begin revising, especially with a long and complicated piece of writing. And you may even find that you need to return to phase 1, for instance to examine additional related pieces of writing, to gather additional facts, and the like.)

During revision you will continue to consider your purpose, your intended reading audience, and such matters as organization and supporting examples. Now, during this third phase, you will also finally begin to give special attention to style, as well as to grammar, mechanics, and spelling. Just as important, but often very difficult, is the matter of style. Here the choice is not between the acceptable and the unacceptable; rather, the choice is between several, even many, alternative ways of expressing your ideas and arranging your words, almost all of which are acceptable, but some of which are more effective than others. So you will have to study your sentences to make sure that they say just what you intended in the most effective and most emphatic way. Reading your sentences aloud is one useful strategy at this point. Another is asking peers, at school or on the job, to read and to comment on what you have written. Here, though, you must be sure that those you ask for advice not only understand your writing task, but also that they can give adequate time and serious attention to helping you to revise your work.

With style under reasonable control, it's finally time to make sure that subjects and verbs agree, to insert commas and semicolons, and to check for spelling faults. A standard reference grammar will provide useful guidance in correcting any errors of usage, grammar, and mechanics (such as punctuation) that have slipped into your writing during the preceding step, when you were busily transferring ideas from your mind onto paper. A hardbound dictionary should also be kept handy in your work area, for ease of reference in answering questions of accurate spelling and appropriate word choice.

As you grow more proficient as a writer, you may find yourself able to juggle more stylistic and grammatical considerations while you write your first draft, pausing momentarily to rearrange a sentence for a better effect, to determine the appropriate case of a pronoun, or to decide whether to use either a semicolon or a period. However, in most cases it is best to avoid conscious or extended concern with revision during phase 2—or any time when you are actually creating a piece of writing. Save some time and your serious attention to revision for phase 3, where it naturally belongs.

The fourth and last phase of the writing process is, of course, the creation of a final copy of your revised piece of writing, one you are ready to submit for the judgment of someone else—such as a supervisor, teacher, editor, or government leader. Here you are going "public" with the latest and best version of your work—publishing it, in a figurative and perhaps even a literal sense. Yet even here you may not be completely finished with the writing process, and may find yourself going back to or through the phases of writing, trying always to improve the expression of your ideas.

It should now be clear that the value of this book lies chiefly in the assistance it offers you in the first two phases of the writing process—prewriting (getting ready to compose your argument) and then writing the first draft. Study of this book provides two very obvious benefits, as well as another more subtle one. Obviously you need to have something to write about, some proposition to argue for or against, and this book's diverse reading selections furnish a kind of launch pad for your persuasive flights by providing interesting, often controversial, materials for your consideration and reactions. In addition, these selections, chosen from the work of professional writers, illustrate a variety of argumentative strategies or organizational plans. The shorter selections illustrate clearly the most common argumentative devices and may serve as models for much of your own writing. The longer ones are perhaps most useful for furnishing the ideas that will eventually grow into your own arguments as you read, ponder, and discuss their subject matter with your classmates and teacher.

More subtly, though, any reading that you do—in this book or elsewhere—will have a lasting effect on your abilities as a writer. Every sentence that you read can add to your subconscious mental storehouse of vocabulary, idioms, organizational devices, and stylistic tactics. Similarly, all arguments that you read heighten your awareness of how they are formulated and presented. The advantage of a book such as *Effective Argument* over random reading lies in the careful choice and arrangement of its selections. The readings ensure your wide exposure to writing that demonstrates accurate word choice, mature and clear style, wise rhetorical strategies, and effective persuasive skills in general.

Modes of Writing

Although this book focuses on the writing of effective arguments, we cannot discuss that subject without occasionally referring to other modes or types of writing which sometimes have a part in the construction of arguments. You likely have already studied and practiced such other writing methods as narrative–descriptive and expository, and perhaps have also done literary and expressive writing. But just to be sure we share the same perspective, let's briefly review the modes that are especially useful in argumentative writing.

In narrative–descriptive writing, the writer strives to make the readers think they see and even experience a scene or a series of actions, either real or imagined. To accomplish this, the writer focuses on specific *details*, especially visual ones, as well as on *qualities* (general traits, such as thin, tall, slow, jagged) and *comparisons* (often using *like* or *as*, following the technique of the poetic simile). News and feature articles, character sketches and biographies, short stories and novels, and travel and historical writing provide typical examples of narrative–descriptive writing.

Expository writing often takes even more account of its intended audience, its writer presuming that readers of the work do not know some or all of a particular piece of information and therefore need it explained to them. Here again details, this time in the form of illustrations or examples, are the writer's most successful means of making the readers understand. These illustrations may be organized in a number of different ways, for instance to form classifications, comparisons, analogies, or cause–effect analyses. Of course, a writer will often find it necessary to use narration and description to present most effectively the information needed by the intended audience. Textbooks, essays and reports, technical manuals, and case studies furnish examples of expository writing. It is the most common type of writing in the majority of school and work situations. And just as it may contain narrative–descriptive elements, it may also use argumentative techniques when its author seeks not just to inform but also to persuade a reading audience.

In argumentation, the writer takes a different approach from the other two modes of writing just mentioned. Here the writer presumes that readers already hold an opinion concerning the subject matter. Argumentation's basic purpose is not merely to add new information, although this is sometimes necessary; rather, its purpose is to discuss known information in a way or ways that will persuade readers to change their minds about that information, and to adopt the writer's opinion on the matter. Here also the writer will present key details—this time to support the proposition whose validity is being debated—and of course will also often use narrative–descriptive and expository techniques. Advertisements, scholarly and scientific treatises, editorials, debates, and political speeches provide examples of this kind of writing.

You need to understand these three divisions—narrative–descriptive, expository, and argumentative—because they will help you answer the most important question that will confront you as a writer: What is my purpose in writing? If you basically want to make your audience see or experience a place, person, or circumstance, you will mainly write in a narrative–descriptive mode and use narrative–descriptive techniques. If you want to inform, to educate, to increase your readers' fund of information, then you will depend most on expository techniques. But if you want to change the minds of your readers, you will write persuasively, using the techniques of argumentation.

Some Key Terms

Although you may understand them already, we want to make clear differentiations among three terms that we have already been using, and that we will use even more frequently in the rest of the book. The terms are *persuasion, reasoning,* and *arguing;* we will also briefly discuss some related terms.

"Persuasion" is the broadest of the three main terms, and in fact includes the other two within its general meaning. To persuade is to influence other persons' thoughts, words, or deeds, using virtually any means. People are most often influenced by words, of course. But they may also be persuaded by force (as when they are "coerced") or by rewards, including emotional ones (as when they are "induced"). They may be "prevailed upon," here with the sense that someone or something has used pressure or force, physical or otherwise.

Often reasons, presented by means of spoken or written words, are used to influence others regarding the truth or falsity of something; in such cases, when we use declarative statements linked in a convincing or mind-changing way, we are "reasoning" or "arguing." "Reasoning" and "arguing" are thus synonyms, although not exact ones; unlike "reasoning," the term "arguing" has a connotation (secondary emotional meaning) of the existence of conflict or opposing sides. And both terms lie within the bounds of the more inclusive term, "persuasion."

Another related term, "disputing," suggests, as does "arguing," the presence of controversy or opposing sides, just the sort of situation we have observed in a heated dialogue or a debate between persons holding strongly conflicting viewpoints. (Here you might recall the televised debates between presidential candidates that are now a part of the U.S. political scene every four years.) If such a dispute becomes overheated or angry and rude, we may label it a "quarrel"; at that point the element of reasoning by means of words alone tends to fade or disappear, sometimes being replaced by physical threats or even violent acts. Accordingly, our aim is to help you to use reasoning so persuasively that you will not only cause your good ideas to prevail but that you will also be able to avoid quarrels.

You are now ready to begin to examine in detail the standard features of argumentative writing as well as the writing models in this book, studying how professional writers have organized and presented their materials. Then under the guidance of your instructor and *Effective Argument,* you will learn to adapt these techniques for your own written arguments in English class as well as in your other classes, and for use at work as well as in school.

1

The Argumentation Process

Basic Considerations

If we lived in a perfect world, this book would be unnecessary, for all of us would have everything we need and harmony would be universal. Yet even casual observation of simpler forms of life will show us controversy, creatures taking sides against one another: two ants, perhaps from the same colony, try to tug a beetle's carcass in opposing directions; Garfield the cat tricks Odie the dog out of a comfortable place to rest; one bird species drives another out of a desirable nesting or feeding area. As for us humans, our lives are likewise filled with controversy at home and at school, at work and at play. Sometimes the disputes are relatively trivial, over the last piece of pizza or which television program to watch. But at other times the stakes are much higher, affecting even our survival on this planet, as we argue over mandatory AIDS testing or nuclear weapons control. And as we suggested in the first paragraph of this book's introduction, controversy is as old as humans; presumably, ancient peoples sometimes fought with words or fists over the last piece of mastodon meat, and they argued over whether to share with neighboring clans such valuable innovations as fire or the ability to shape flint into spear and arrow points.

With such a human history and such natural human tendencies (children must be *taught* to share, to wait their turns, and the like), is it any wonder that the Greeks and other earlier humans gave argumentation so much attention? And what would your own life be like if you could not already change others' minds to some extent, or if your ancestors had not been able to do so? Would you be in college, reading this book? Would you have grown up in Ohio rather than in Colorado, or have been reared on a farm rather than in a city's suburb? Would you even exist? How would life be changed for your grandparent or elderly neighbor if Congress had not passed the Social Security Act in the late 1930s, or amended it at intervals since? What if slavery were still legal, or the military draft still existed, or the ten amendments comprising the Bill of Rights had not been added to the U.S. Constitution?

Debating and deciding such issues as those just mentioned will soon to be a responsibility of you and your peers. If you do not learn the basic concepts of argumentation presented in this book, it is likely that you will have little or no influence on the future for yourself and for those who follow you. But presumably you are in college to improve or at least to maintain the quality of life you have experienced so far, and perhaps to try to do the same for others. Furthermore, when you leave college, most of you will go to work.

In your workplace, whether it is in an office, a store, a school, or in a factory, a hospital, or wherever, you will find yourself persuading (and being persuaded) virtually every day, using spoken and written language, sometimes quietly and calmly, sometimes loudly and heatedly. You will get your first job by persuasion, directly or indirectly, and you will keep it by the same means. You will argue often, for or against budget changes, rule interpretations, operating procedures, marketing strategies, or employment practices, among other things. If you argue well, you will thrive; if you argue poorly, you will likely become unsuccessful and unhappy, perhaps even unemployed. Accordingly, we hope by now that you are convinced by *our* argument, that the subject of this book and what it can teach you are crucial to the quality of your life in the future. If so, you will continue to read, to examine with us the argumentative process.

Claims and Support

How many times have you heard people say things like this?

"I know that's so because . . . ."
"I could give you sixteen good reasons why that's so."

Every time that you encounter such declarations, you are face to face with an argument—one that has been stated in its barest possible form. Its bare bones are showing. Let's look more closely.

That's so	Every argument contains at least one of these— an assertion that something is or is not the case,

that it is better or worse than something else, or that it should or should not be done. This component of the argument goes by various names: *position, proposition, supposition, premise, conclusion, assertion,* or *claim.* Here we will call it a *claim.*

Because

For every claim in an argument, there must be at least one of these—a *because*-clause that tells why a claim is factual, preferable, or advantageous. These *because*-clauses we will call *support.*

Most claims are supported by several *because* statements, and, of course, there may be more than one claim in an argument, each with its supporting statements. However, these essential elements often will not be easy to spot. For instance, examine this argument from Dr. Wayne Dyer's book, *Your Erroneous Zones:*

We are conditioned to look for justice in life and when it doesn't appear, we tend to feel anger, anxiety or frustration. Actually, it would be equally productive to search for the fountain of youth, or some such myth. Justice does not exist. It never has, and it never will. The world is simply not put together that way. Robins eat worms. That's not fair to the worms. Spiders eat flies. That's not fair to the flies. Cougars kill coyotes. Coyotes kill badgers. Badgers kill mice. Mice kill bugs. Bugs . . . You have only to look at nature to realize there is no justice in the world. Tornadoes, floods, tidal waves, droughts are all unfair. It is a mythological concept, this justice business. The world and the people in it go on being unfair every day. You can choose to be happy or unhappy, but it has nothing to do with the lack of justice you see around you.   1

Our culture promises justice. Politicians refer to it in all of their campaign speeches. "We need equality and justice for all." Yet day after day, century after century, the lack of justice continues. Poverty, war, pestilence, crime, prostitution, dope and murders persist generation after generation in public and private life. And if the history of humanity can be used as a guide they will continue.   2

The legal system promises justice. "The people demand justice," and some of them even work to make it happen. But it   3 generally doesn't. Those with money are not convicted. Judges and policemen are often bought by the powerful. A President and Vice-President of the United States are pardoned or wrist-slapped for obvious felonies. The poor fill the jails, and have next to no chance of beating the system. It's not fair. But it's true. Spiro Agnew becomes rich after evading his income taxes. Richard Nixon is exonerated, and his yes-men serve a few months in a minimum security prison, while the poor and members of minority groups rot in jail waiting for trial, waiting for a chance. A visit to any local courthouse or police station will prove that the influential have a separate set of rules, although this is relentlessly denied by the authorities. Where is the justice? Nowhere!

Dr. Dyer's argument about justice quite clearly consists of a combination of claim and because-statements, but these elements are not completely obvious. In the first paragraph, the claim appears: "Justice does not exist." There are no because-clauses following, at least literally, but you can certainly supply the *becauses:* [*Because*] robins eat worms, [and] that's not fair to worms . . . , [*Because*] spiders eat flies, [and] that's not fair to flies . . . , and so on. Dyer's first piece of support deals with the natural world. The next paragraph offers further support, this time from our culture. And the final paragraph furnishes still more support, this time from our legal system.

This example, while it does not announce its essential elements with flashing lights or a drum roll, is certainly easy enough to follow. Locating its basic ingredients did not overload your powers of perception. We do not want to mislead you, however. Not all arguments are so straightforward; therefore, it will serve you well to learn to ferret out the essential pieces—claims and their support—from arguments that you encounter. First of all, this practice will enable you to understand arguments better, and, second, it will help you to prepare better arguments yourself.

Another thing is worth mentioning at this point: We will be returning to Dr. Dyer's argument from time to time, using it for examples as we discuss the development of argumentative strategies, so you shouldn't allow that brief argument to fade from your memory; it will crop up again. In fact, you would be wise to reread his essay to prepare yourself now. The same use will be made of other arguments that you will encounter later in this chapter, such as the one we will examine next.

Here is an argument by James Gorman in favor of napping. It makes more than one claim. Try to pick out each claim and then list the support.

American society is not, in general, nap-friendly. It is actually sleepist in the extreme. "There's such a prohibition against admitting that we need sleep!" says David F. Dinges, a nap specialist at the University of Pennsylvania. Nobody wants to get caught napping, to be found asleep at the switch. Even children know that it's bad to be a sleepyhead. To quote an obscure Minnesota proverb worthy of Lake Wobegon, "Some sleep five hours, nature requires seven, laziness nine and wickedness eleven." — 1

Wrong. The way not to fall asleep at the switch is to take naps when you need them. Listen to William Dement of Stanford University, the godfather of sleep research: "We need to totally change our attitude toward napping." Taking a nap, he says, should be viewed as a "heroic" act. "If we see someone taking a nap, we should stand in awe." Our latest hero, leading us all in sleep policy, is none other than President Clinton. According to recent reports, he has begun taking a half-hour nap in the afternoon. — 2

He has science, and me, on his side. Indeed, there is a surge of support for napping these days. Earlier this year, a national commission, led by Dement, identified an "American sleep debt," which one member said was as important as the national debt. The commission was concerned about the dangers of sleepiness: people falling asleep while driving, causing industrial accidents or contributing to disasters like the Exxon Valdez oil spill and the Three Mile Island nuclear accident, both mentioned in the commission report. . . . — 3

The pathologically alert like to think they get more done than nappers. Wrong again. There are scores of stories about successful nappers (successful at something besides napping, that is). Winston Churchill slept every afternoon when he was the wartime Prime Minister of England. Napoleon is said to have napped on the battlefield (a common practice among generals, who don't get a lot of good sack time when a war is on). Alfred Hitchcock slept at parties. Jack Warner, of Warner Brothers, took a nap in his office every afternoon. Once, Bette Davis interrupted his sleep, charging in with complaints about a script. "Without opening his eyes," recounts "The Little, Brown Book of Anecdotes," "Warner reached for the phone and called — 4 his secretary, 'Come in and wake me up,' he said. 'I'm having a nightmare.' "

Calvin Coolidge, Lyndon Johnson and John Kennedy took naps. Ronald Reagan was hardly ever awake. Thomas Edison and Leonardo da Vinci were famous nappers, but in the wrong spirit. They napped to avoid the need to sleep at night. Sleepists!

There are, of course, people who feel they just cannot sleep during the day. These people are the nap-impaired. Fortunately the condition is seldom permanent. Most nonnappers simply lack the opportunity or the knowledge of how to nap, or have been brainwashed since childhood to think that sleeping during the day is like having sex in the kitchen. (I never nap in the kitchen; food keeps me awake.)

In analyzing Gorman's essay to locate its claims and their support, you will find it useful to summarize portions of his argument, stating Gorman's opinions in your own words. The creation of summaries is an invaluable skill when you begin to construct your own arguments. So bear that in mind as we proceed.

First notice that Gorman begins with a claim that he really does not wish to support; that is, many people in America, whom he calls "sleepists," do not think that nap-taking is a good idea. The support that these sleepists usually offer is that taking naps gives a person a bad reputation. You might be thought to be the kind of person who would go to sleep at a railroad switch and derail the train or, in more modern terms, fall asleep while driving and kill yourself or others. Besides, an old proverb associates too much sleep with laziness or even wickedness.

In his second paragraph, however, Gorman states a claim that he *does* wish to support. He says that the first claim is wrong and that he wishes to support its opposite—that napping is a good idea. He does this in two ways. He says that taking naps keeps us alert so that we won't fall asleep at the switch or run off the road. He also gives us two sorts of authorities who share this opinion: Dr. William Dement, of Stanford University, who is a sleep specialist, and the U.S. president, who must share the opinion, since he habitually takes afternoon naps.

Gorman's final claim is related to the last example. He names ten other well-known people—a British prime minister, a French emperor, two movie moguls, and four American presidents, as well as two famous inventors—to support the related claim that nap-takers can get a lot of work done, despite claims to the contrary.

We might reduce Gorman's argument to the following essentials:

Claim	Support	Location
Americans do not approve of napping	Because people regard napping as reckless behavior, "being asleep at the switch."	Para. 1
	Because even a proverb suggests that nappers are lazy or wicked.	Para. 1
Actually, napping is good.	Because it keeps us alert.	Para. 2
	Because Dr. William Dement says so.	Para. 2–3
	Because President Clinton naps.	Para. 2
	Because it prevents industrial accidents.	Para. 3
	Because it prevents falling asleep at the wheel.	Para. 3
Nappers get more work done.	Because productive people such as Winston Churchill and Napoleon napped.	Para. 4
	Because Alfred Hitchcock and Jack Warner also napped.	Para. 4
	Because Calvin Coolidge, Lyndon Johnson, John F. Kennedy, and Ronald Reagan all took naps.	Para. 5
	Because Thomas Edison and Leonardo daVinci also took naps.	Para. 5

To repeat now what you have just seen demonstrated: Every argument consists of two parts: a *claim* and the *support* for that claim. In reading arguments like the two you have just studied, it is obviously important for you to recognize the claims and their support. Why? Being able to recognize the claim and its support enables you to go right to the heart of any argument—to understand it better—and, if you choose, to *summarize* it so that you can use it as a part of an argument of your own. The claim in its barest form will be a statement asserting, or claiming, that something is something else—that is, that X is a Y. Here are some examples of possible claims:

John Smith is a murderer.
Geometry is a waste of time.
Forrest Gump is an excellent movie.
Carol Stone is a better student than Bill Mudd.
Women in Literature is a course that should be offered next year.
Investing in mutual funds is a smart thing to do.

Notice that each of these examples states a position that you could either agree with or disagree with. That is the first condition for a claim: *it can either be affirmed or denied.* It is also easy to see that not all statements of the type X is a Y can be claims, because they do not allow us the option to agree with them or not. Here are some nonarguable claims:

John Smith is a man.
Geometry is a branch of mathematics.
Forrest Gump is a movie directed by Robert Zemickis.
Carol Stone is a student in English 101.
Women in Literature is an English course that appears in the college catalog.
Mutual funds are a type of investment opportunity.

Each of these statements asserts something that no one would care to dispute; such statements are not arguable.

Finding and Stating the Claim

By the same token, just as not all statements that follow the pattern X is a Y turn out to be arguable claims, not all claims are cast in the form X is a Y. The English language furnishes us with a vast array of alternatives; we can make statements in a variety of ways. Each of the claims that were held out as examples could be restated in a form quite different from X is a Y. Here are some possibilities:

Surely, John Smith murdered Bill Jones in cold blood.
I can see no practical value in studying geometry.
Forrest Gump deserved all the Oscars it won.
Carol Stone writes better papers than Bill Mudd.

We should convince the English department chair to include Women in
Literature in next year's schedule.

Mutual funds offer a promising investment opportunity.

We know that each of these statements is a suitable claim because
it conforms to the two criteria we have established:

1. It is reducible to a statement of the type X is a Y.
2. It can be debated.

Keeping these criteria in mind, you should be able to examine the
following list of statements and determine which are legitimate
claims and which are not:

1. The global ecology course discusses six critical dangers to the earth's
   ecosystems.
2. Nursing students usually have a more compassionate view of human
   society than accounting majors do.
3. Bert Biggins has six fingers on his left hand.
4. Allison Edwards really deserves to pass English 102.
5. The Cubs beat the Dodgers yesterday by a score of 9 to 4.
6. The Parkside Restaurant serves the best meals in town.

If you decided that the even-numbered statements represent legitimate claims, or arguable statements, then you were correct. While
a little exercise in syntax would render all of the above sentences in
the form of X is a Y, only the even-numbered ones pose any possibility for serious debate; the others are just not worth arguing about
since their accuracy is so easily verified.

Providing Support

Once you have located the claim, or claims, in an argument,
you will need to find the support. As you have noticed in the arguments cited so far, each claim's support is located nearby, and if we
reduce the supporting statement to its bare essentials, we discover
that the support for any given claim is usually some kind of *because*-
statement:

1. Nursing majors usually have a more compassionate view of human
   society than accounting majors because nurses frequently work directly with ailing humans, while accountants work with computers
   and ledger sheets.

2. Allison Edwards deserves to pass English 102 because she completed all the written assignments and most of the homework with passing grades.
3. The Parkside Restaurant is the best restaurant in town because its tables are regularly filled with satisfied clients and because it receives more catering assignments than any other eating establishment in town.

Now you have had some practice in recognizing claims and support, and you have seen that a combination of the claim and its support—stated in barest fashion—makes a pretty good summary of an argument. Here is another argument for you to examine. Locate the claim that it makes, as well as the support for that claim. Set up a table that shows the claim and supporting data, along with their location. Use the table on page 14 as your model.

No, Let's Keep Them

CULLEN MURPHY

The proposal that the United States get rid of pennies is, like many proposals that smack of cool-headed, cold-blooded pragmatism, one that should be implemented on another planet. It is the kind of apparently sensible yet hugely disruptive reform that a wise society will treat with the same disdain that America has already shown for the metric system and phonetic spelling. [1]

Should we stop making cents? The penny we now have was issued in 1909 to celebrate the centennial of our sixteenth President's birth, and its name and ancestry go back to the eighth century. From the start the penny's biggest foe has been inflation, which has for centuries threatened to render the coin valueless. And yet monarchs and prime ministers have deemed this insufficient cause to rid themselves of it, preferring to let the penny be and to invent higher denominations of currency—as when Edward II established the groat. Indeed, by its continued existence the penny has served notice that the value of money cannot be infinitely debased, that the monetary systems of the English-speaking world have an anchor, albeit a shifting one. As long as the penny exists, there will be things you can buy with one or two or three or four of them. Get rid of it and nothing will cost less than a nickel. [2]

That is the economic defense of the penny. Pennies also serve important social functions. They inform millions of children who [3] may have been exposed to nothing but textbooks that there once was a man named Lincoln who occupied a position of some importance. They are responsible for initiating millions of conversations in stores every day between people who otherwise would complete their transactions in anomic silence. From time to time these transactions are punctuated by mild bleats of satisfaction—"Wait, I have a penny!" Such moments, occurring all across the nation and around the clock, contribute modestly but directly to social comity.

Pennies, moreover, are so deeply embedded in our culture   4
that extracting them would leave small emptinesses in the very substance of life. Pennies help to mark the stages of man. They are the first allowance we receive. Later we put them on railroad tracks, and later still in loafers, and later still in fuse boxes. Inevitably the day comes when a penny falls from the hand and one decides not to pick it up. In the mature adult this prompts a fleeting sense of contentment, for he has acknowledged the fact of his own security. We wish on pennies at fountains and wells, knowing that dimes and nickels won't work. In a pocketful of change pennies serve as an essential garnish, relieving an otherwise drab monochrome like radishes in a salad. And in our language they are called upon liberally when precepts of formidable consequence must be conveyed. "Look after the pennies and the pounds will look after themselves." "A penny saved is a penny earned." Thanks to exhortations like these, it may very well be that if all the pennies hoarded in bowls and jars were taken into account, the often maligned U.S. savings rate would approach that of Japan.

The elimination of the penny might afford some slight phys-   5
ical convenience, but the total social cost exceeds what a liberal democracy ought to countenance. It would be nothing less, one might say, than penny-wise and pound-foolish.

Here is our analysis of the claim and support statements contained in the Cullen Murphy essay, "No, Let's Keep Them." Your analysis may not agree entirely with ours, but there should be considerable similarity.

Claim	Support	Location
Discarding pennies from the U.S. monetary system is a bad idea.	Because it will be a disruptive change like introducing the metric system.	Para. 1

	Because it would debase U.S. money; nothing would cost less than a nickel.	Para. 2
	Because they frequently add warmth to otherwise cold business transactions.	Para. 3
Pennies are important to our culture.	Because they mark the stages of growth and maturity: pennies on railroad tracks pennies in loafers dropped pennies ignored pennies in fountains	Para. 4
	Because some of our proverbs refer to pennies.	Para. 4

Summaries of Arguments

We have emphasized the need for you to be able to locate the claims and support embodied in the arguments that you read because your ability to do so will enable you to understand them and, just as important, to turn them to your use by incorporating them into arguments of your own by summarizing them.

Notice that James Gorman summarized the attitudes of our culture toward nap-taking and that Cullen Murphy did the same for the considerable folklore surrounding pennies, each writer reducing a lengthy statement into a single paragraph and tailoring it to fit his needs—Gorman to show that the public opinion was set against his position, and Murphy to emphasize the importance that our society attaches to pennies.

Like Gorman and Murphy, you will often find it useful to turn to other sources, usually arguments, to find support for your own claims. For that reason, one of the skills you will need to master very early is the ability to write a clear, understandable summary of arguments you have read.

We have taken the first step in showing you how to do that by emphasizing the importance of locating the claims, together with their support, in the arguments that you encounter. Claims and support are the bare bones of an argument, and they are the elements that must necessarily appear in any summary of that argument.

It will be useful at this point to try your hand at some summary writing. The following exercises will direct you to the readings that appear in the next section of this book. (That will also be the practice in most of the exercises that follow.) You will notice that the "Suggestions for Writing" that accompany each of the readings will almost always begin with an assignment to summarize the preceding argument. We have done that because we feel that your ability to read carefully and to prepare summaries of what you have read is the single most important skill a writer of arguments must develop and possess.

EXERCISES

1. Read the article by Gary Turbak, "Plastic: Sixty Billion Pounds of Trouble," on p. 135, and complete the first suggestion for writing. You might begin by listing the claims that you locate, along with their support, the way we did earlier in this section. Just to get you started, we might suggest that the argument could be divided into the following parts: Paragraphs 1–7, 8–11, and 12–15. You might summarize the first part this way:

   > Plastic has become a menace to the natural environment. Birds and marine life are especially victimized by discarded plastic in the form of fish nets, soft drink holders, and even sandwich or trash bags. Plastic does not break down and thus clogs landfills and pollutes beaches. This pollution is often dangerous to humans, particularly when it includes such contaminated items as disposable diapers, hypodermic syringes, condoms, and tampon applicators.

   Now go ahead and summarize the remaining sections in a similar way, producing two more paragraphs. Then try to combine all three paragraphs (ours and yours) into a single paragraph, one that captures in a brief space Turbak's total message.
2. Next read S. I. Hayakawa's argument, "Sex Is Not a Spectator Sport," p. 152, and complete its first suggestion for writing, which calls for a single paragraph summary. How many parts does his argument contain? State each part as clearly and as briefly as you can; then merge those parts into a single paragraph.

Types of Claims

So far we have seen that claims are statements that must be supported if a satisfactory argument is to be made. We have further seen that they are statements that can be debated. Finally, we have seen that the most straightforward way of stating a claim is to assert that something is (or is not) something else, or, more simply, X is (or is not) Y. We have also demonstrated, by presenting several sample arguments, that claims are seldom stated so straightforwardly; they can and, in fact, do appear in a variety of ways.

Claims of Fact

Recall now the sample claims we discussed in the last section.

1. John Smith is a murderer.
2. Geometry is a waste of time.
3. *Forrest Gump* is an excellent movie.
4. Carol Stone is a better student than Bill Mudd.
5. Women in Literature is a course that should be offered next year.
6. Investing in mutual funds is a smart thing to do.

We can begin by examining the first two. These we will call *claims of fact* because they deal with subject matter that can be verified. Either the assertions that they make are so, or they are not so. Either John Smith is a murderer, or he is not. Either geometry is useful or it is not. You might reasonably suppose that a person who makes such claims would be prepared to offer evidence to support them.

The kind of evidence that one might use to support a claim of fact normally will be one or more of these four: physical evidence, facts, reports, or statistical evidence.

To prove that John Smith is a murderer, you will need a signed confession or a photograph of Smith at the murder scene clutching the murder weapon. Lacking these, you might present a hatchet smeared with blood and hair identical with the victim's and bearing Smith's fingerprints. This evidence does not actually prove Smith's guilt, but the set of facts it represents will allow an impartial observer to draw appropriate *inferences* or conclusions based upon them.

If you do not have physical evidence of Smith's guilt, you may be fortunate enough to have an eyewitness who will testify to Smith's violent deed. The reliability of the witness can be called into question, so you will want to take some precautions about the reliability of the witness, making sure that she or he is mentally sound, bears no grudge against Smith, and was not in the pay of someone unscrupulous.

Of course, you may discover that you need to define your terms more clearly. Depending on the level of malice or premeditation, there can be several degrees of murder. Smith may not be guilty of first degree (or premeditated) murder. Rather, he may be guilty of only second degree (or unpremeditated) murder; if so, that is precisely the way the claim should be stated.

Certainly the claim about geometry's being a waste of time suffers from a lack of precision. It is obviously useful to surveying and navigation; indeed, it is the basis of these disciplines. On the other hand, it is not very useful for singers, surgeons, or newscasters. What this claim needs is some redefinition.

Perhaps you might claim that geometry is not useful to you. If, for instance, you happen to be a singer, then you can demonstrate that the skills involved in singing, which you will enumerate and present as evidence—such as pitch, tone, breath control, clarity, and volume—do not depend in any way on an understanding of geometry.

You might even be successful with the somewhat broader claim that geometry is not a very useful skill in this modern age. You might present statistics to show that 87 of the top 100 professions today do not rely on geometry. And you might further demonstrate that most of the 13 professions that do require it, such as marine navigation and air-traffic control, now solve their geometric problems automatically by computers, so that knowledge of the underlying principles is the concern of a limited number of professionals.

Another final point about claims of fact was alluded to earlier. Since these claims deal with verifiable situations, the verification must involve some degree of difficulty, or else the claims are nondebatable and noninteresting statements of this sort:

1. John Smith is a man.
2. Geometry is a branch of mathematics.

These two statements are not claims; they are just facts. You may draw inferences from facts if you have enough of them and if they are in a suggestive arrangement (remember the situation with the victim's hair on the bloody hatchet), but you can't debate them.

Let's have a look now at an argument based upon a claim of fact. This one is by the late Loren Eiseley, one of America's foremost anthropologists and writers. It is part of a larger essay entitled "An Evolutionist Looks at Modern Man." Locate the claim, and then try to enumerate the pieces of support.

Some time ago I had a letter from a professional friend of   1
mine commenting upon the education his daughter was receiving at a polite finishing school. "She has been taught," he wrote

to me a little sadly, "that there are two kinds of people, the tough-and the tender-minded. Her professor, whose science I will not name, informed her that the tough-minded would survive."

This archaic remark shook me. I knew it was not the product of the great selfless masters of the field, but it betrayed an attitude which demanded an answer. In that answer is contained the whole uniqueness of man. Man has not really survived by toughness in a major sense—even the great evolutionists Darwin and Wallace had had trouble with that aspect of man—instead, he has survived through tenderness. Man in his arrogance may boast that the battle is to the strong, that pity and affection are signs of weakness. Nevertheless, in spite of the widespread popularity of such ideas, the truth is that if man at heart were not a tender creature toward his kind, a loving creature in a peculiarly special way, he would long since have left his bones to the wild dogs that roved the African grasslands where he first essayed the great adventure of becoming human.

The professor who growled to his class of future mothers about being tough-minded spent a childhood which is among the most helpless and prolonged of any living creature. If our parents had actually practiced certain of the philosophies that now flourish among us, or if our remote ancestors had achieved that degree of sophistication which would have enabled them to discount their social responsibilities for the day's pleasure, we—you and I and all of us—would never have enjoyed the experience of living.

Man, in the achievement of a unique gift—a thinking brain capable of weighing stars or atoms—cannot grow that brain in the nine months before birth. It is, moreover, a peculiarly plastic brain, intended to receive impressions from the social world around it. Instinct, unlike the case in the world of animals, is here reduced to a minimum. This brain must grow and learn, be able to profit by experience. In man much of that growth and learning comes after birth. The result is that the human infant enters the world in a peculiarly helpless and undeveloped condition. His childhood is lengthy because his developing brain must receive a large store of information and ways of behavior from the social group into which it is born. It must acquire the complicated tool of speech.

The demands of learning thus placed upon the human offspring are greater than in any other animal. They have made necessary the existence of a continued family, rather than the casual sex life of many of the lower animals. Although the family differs in many of its minor features in distinct societies, it is always and everywhere marked by its tender and continuing care of the human offspring through the lengthened period of childhood.

The social regulations of all human groups promote the wel- 6
fare of the young. Man's first normal experience of life involves maternal and paternal care and affection. It continues over the years of childhood. Thus the creature who strives at times to deny the love within himself, to reject the responsibilities to which he owes his own existence, who grows vocal about "tough-mindedness" and "the struggle for existence," is striving to reject his own human heritage. For without the mysteriously increased growth rate of the brain and the correlated willingness of fallible, loving adults to spend years in nursing the helpless offspring they have produced, man would long since have vanished from the earth.

Eiseley's claim of fact occurs most clearly in the second paragraph: "Man has not really survived by toughness . . . instead, he has survived through tenderness." The paragraphs that follow contain the *because*-statements that support this claim. Paragraph 3 might be paraphrased to say that man survives through tenderness because mankind undergoes a prolonged and helpless childhood during which constant care is necessary.

Paragraph 4 asserts that a long childhood is necessary for man's development because the human brain does not develop fully before birth. Eiseley then points out in paragraph 5 that the family unit arises from the need for educating the young during this prolonged period of development, and he concludes in the final paragraph, "The social regulations of all human groups promote the welfare of the young."

Each of these pieces of support—the prolonged childhood, the slowly developing brain, the nuclear family, and the universal attention to child welfare—are facts hardly to be disputed. (Remember those nondebatable claims? They are useful after all.) Arranged as they are, these nondebatable claims form a chain of inference that allows the reader to nod in agreement with Eiseley's claim that tenderness is indeed more crucial to human's development than toughness.

Claims of Value

We live in a world of facts, but we also live in a world of values. This concern with values as well as facts is one of the things that makes us human. We set store by some things and not by others. And quite often we are called upon to justify the evaluations that we make.

One kind of evaluation that no doubt is very much on your mind these days is the one that your instructor will render in your case at the end of this course. According to your performance, you will receive an A, B, C, D, or F. As a rule, students do not challenge instructors to explain themselves over the awarding of an A, but most instructors do brace themselves for certain questions at the end of the term from those who did not make A's: "Why did I flunk?" or more frequently "Why did *you* flunk *me?*" "I thought I deserved better than a C in this course." "Well, what would it have taken to get an A?"

In response to each of these challenges, the beleaguered instructor must make an argument based on *standards* or *criteria*. "You see, there are four things that influence my judgment in assigning grades: the written assignments, class participation, homework, and examinations. You did well on the first two, but as far as . . . ."

It is as though the instructor has *defined* the highest expected level of achievement in terms of these four criteria and then, student by student, measured the performance of each with respect to that highest expected level.

The notion of *definition* is critical to claims of value because in each case, in order to be convincing, the person making the claim, just like the teacher, must define the standards by which the evaluation has been made. At the outset, there's really no other way of organizing support for such a claim. Later on, of course, the teacher may appeal to facts: "You had twelve homework assignments, and you turned in only nine." "You failed to answer two of the questions on the third exam." But when you ask why the third paper received a lower grade than the first one, then the discussion moves right back to standards and criteria again—the kinds of things that are expected to occur in an A paper and which did or did not appear in your papers.

Occasionally, in supporting claims of value such as this one, it is a good idea to appeal to an authority, a lawful source or someone whose judgment is widely known and trusted. The instructor might point to a student handbook that spells out grading policies, especially as they pertain to missed assignments. Or perhaps the instructor might produce a photocopy of an especially good paper, written by a classmate of a complaining student, which exhibits all the qualities of A work.

To review briefly the ways of supporting a claim of value: First, you must ask yourself what the standards are for making such judgments, whether they be about the worth of Porsches, penguins, or pizzas. Once the standards have been identified, the next step is to determine just how the item you are evaluating measures up. For some standards, you may be able to state the facts: Some feature is there, or it isn't. For others, you may not be so absolute: The feature occurs in greater abundance here than there. Finally, you may want to refer to a well-known authority who agrees with your judgment.

Let's look yet again at the six claims we examined at the beginning of this section.

1. John Smith is a murderer.
2. Geometry is a waste of time.
3. *Forrest Gump* is an excellent movie.
4. Carol Stone is a better student than Bill Mudd.
5. Women in Literature is a course that should be offered next year.
6. Investing in mutual funds is a smart thing to do.

By now it should be fairly obvious that claims 3 and 4 represent claims of value. It should be equally obvious that such claims can be supported only if "excellent movie" and "better student" are appropriately defined, each with criteria against which this movie and these students may be measured.

Here now is an amusing argument by American novelist and humorist Phyllis McGinley, one that obviously makes a claim of value. Follow the ways that McGinley supports her claim that women drive cars better than men do. Ask yourself, "What standards is she using to make her judgments?"

Women Are Better Drivers

PHYLLIS MCGINLEY

That men are wonderful is a proposition I will defend to the death. Honest, brave, talented, strong and handsome, they are my favorite gender. Consider the things men can do better than women—mend the plumbing, cook, invent atom bombs, design the Empire waistline and run the four-minute mile. They can throw a ball overhand. They can grow a beard. In fact, I can think of only two accomplishments at which women excel. Having babies is one.

The other is driving an automobile.

Don't misunderstand me. Some of my best friends are male drivers. And they seldom go to sleep at the wheel or drive 90 on a 45-an-hour road or commit any other of the sins of which statistics accuse them. But insurance companies have been busy as bees proving that I don't get around among the right people.

New York State—where I live—has even made it expensive to have sons. Car insurance costs much more if there are men in the family under 25 driving than if there are only women. Obviously the females of the species make the best chauffeurs.

4

They ought to. They get the most practice. Aside from truck- and taxi-drivers, it is women who really handle the cars of the nation. For five days of the week they are in command—slipping cleverly through traffic on their thousand errands, parking neatly in front of the chain stores, ferrying their husbands to and from commuting trains, driving the young to schools and dentists and dancing classes and Scout meetings. It is only on Saturdays and Sundays that men get their innings, not to speak of their outings, and it is over weekends when most of the catastrophes occur.

5

Not that men are responsible for *all* the accidents. Some are caused by women—by the little blonde on the sidewalk at whom the driver feels impelled to whistle. Or by the pretty girl sitting in the front seat for whom he wants to show off his skill, his eagle eye, and the way he can pull ahead of the fellow in the red sports car.

6

But it isn't caution and practice alone which make the difference between the sexes. It's chiefly an attitude of mind. Women—in my opinion—are the practical people. To them a car is a means of transportation, a gadget more useful, perhaps, than a dishwasher or a can opener, but no more romantic. It is something in which we carry the sheets to the laundry, pick up Johnnie at kindergarten and lug home those rose bushes.

7

Men, the dear, sentimental creatures, feel otherwise. Automobiles are more than property. They are their shining chariots, the objects of their affections. A man loves his car the way the Lone Ranger loves his horse, and he feels for its honor on the road. No one must out-weave or out-race him. No one must get off to a better jack-rabbit start. And no one, but no one, must tell him anything while he's driving. My own husband, ordinarily the most good-tempered of men, becomes a tyrant behind the wheel.

8

"Shouldn't we bear south here?" I inquire meekly on our Saturday trips to the country. Or, "Honey, there's a gray convertible trying to pass."

9

"Who's driving!" he snarls like Simon Legree, veering stubbornly north or avoiding, by a hair, being run into.

10

Women drivers, on the other hand, *take* advice. They are used to taking it, having had it pressed on them all their lives by their mothers, teachers, beaus, husbands, and eventually their children. And when they don't know their routes exactly, they inquire at service stations, from passersby, from traffic officers. But men hate to ask and, when they are forced to do so, seldom listen.   11

Have you ever overheard a woman taking down directions on the phone? "Yes," she says affably. "I understand. I drive up that pretty road to the Danbury turn-off. Then I bear left at the little antique shoppe that used to be a barn—yellow with blue shutters. Then right at a meadow with two beech trees in it, and a couple of black cows. Up a little lane, just a tiny way beyond a cornfield, and that's your place. Yes. With a Tiffany-glass carriage lamp in front. Fine. I won't have any trouble." Nor does she.   12

A man has too much pride to take such precautions. "O.K." he says impatiently. "Two point seven miles off the Post Road. A left, a rotary, another left. Six point three to—oh, never mind, I'll look it up on the map."   13

When they don't insist on traveling by car, men travel by chart. I've nothing against road maps, really, except the way they clutter up the glove compartment where I like to keep tissues and sun glasses. But men have a furtive passion for them.   14

When my husband and I are planning a trip, he doesn't rush out like me to buy luggage and a new wardrobe. He shops for maps. For days ahead of time he studies them dotingly; then *I* am forced to study them en route. Many a bitter journey have I taken past the finest scenery in America with my eyes glued to a collection of black and red squiggles on a road map, instead of on the forest and canyons we had come all the way across the country to behold.   15

"Look!" I cry to him as we rush up some burning autumn lane. "Aren't the trees glorious!"   16

"What does the map say?" he mutters. "I've marked a covered bridge about a quarter of a mile along here. That's where we turn."   17

If we should ever approach the Pearly Gates together, I know exactly how the conversation will run. "See all the pretty stars," I'll be murmuring happily. "And, oh, do look over there! Isn't that the City of Gold?"   18

"Never mind your golden cities," he'll warn me sternly, as he nearly collides with a meteor. "Just keep your eye on the map."   19

You cannot miss McGinley's claim; it's in the title and it forms the entire substance of the second paragraph. But what about her support? Notice what she does in the third paragraph. It's a strategy that is well worth copying. She mentions a couple of criteria—staying awake at the wheel and minding the speed limits—only to dismiss them. Men and women drivers are alike in this regard. Some criteria are shared by all good drivers, and we can thus ignore them so that we can concentrate on the really important (and debatable) ones—the ones McGinley wants to call our attention to.

So just what are those criteria? The first is practice. In paragraph 5, McGinley points out that women, as a rule, drive far more frequently than men. The second is caution. In the next paragraph she suggests that women are less likely to become distracted or to show off. The last criterion she describes is an attitude of mind, and she uses the remainder of the essay to characterize that attitude. Briefly, it is the superior patience women exhibit in taking advice and asking directions. She illustrates this preferred behavior through a series of anecdotes.

We hope that you didn't miss what was going on in the fourth paragraph. McGinley was appealing to a very important authority—the state of New York. She calls attention to the fact that the state in its wisdom has made auto insurance more expensive for male drivers than for women. Quite obviously, the state of New York believes that women are better drivers.

Claims of Policy

We have now examined the kind of argument that makes a factual claim—one that is difficult but probable when all the evidence is examined. We have studied arguments that claim that something is better or worse than something else, and we have noted the standards or criteria that were inevitably produced to support such claims.

Now we turn to the final kind of claim—the claim of policy. In this sort of claim, you are usually urging your audience to adopt some course of action: "Vote for candidate X," or "Purchase this brand of shampoo."

Usually you can predict that support for the claim of policy will come in two steps. First of all, you must point out that a state of affairs exists which prompts you to make this urgent appeal. In the case of candidate X, you will want to describe the grand state of the nation: its economy, defense posture, and general well-being, all resulting from the presence of your candidate in office—that is, if your candidate is the incumbent. Conversely, if your candidate is trying to unseat the incumbent, you'll call attention to the deplorable state of the nation, its economy, and so forth. In either case, you will be expected to furnish evidence to confirm that the situation is either as excellent or as grave as you have asserted; you will need to provide statistics, reports of authorities, or facts from which inferences may be drawn.

In the second step of your support you'll need to cite some advantages that will follow if the plan of action you propose is adopted—a vote for the incumbent will be a vote for continuing the desirable conditions that now exist, or a vote for the challenger will spell relief from the terrible conditions that the voters are now enduring. In either case, the more specific instances of good or bad conditions that you can name, the more likely your audience will be to take your advice.

Even the more trivial case of touting a new shampoo follows the same scheme. First, you must make your readers aware of the frightful condition of their hair: lack of body, dinginess, split ends, dandruff. Then you present the effects that the new product will produce: not only a correction for each defect, but the creation of a head of hair that will be utterly irresistible to members of the opposite sex.

Now that you have discovered this much about claims of policy, look one more time at those six original claims that began this section:

1. John Smith is a murderer.
2. Geometry is a waste of time.
3. *Forrest Gump* is an excellent movie.
4. Carol Stone is a better student than Bill Mudd.
5. Women in Literature is a course that should be offered next year.
6. Investing in mutual funds is a smart thing to do.

It hardly comes as a surprise now that the last two claims are ones of policy. And you are now prepared to support each by completing the two necessary steps in presenting a claim of policy:

1. Make the initial claim of fact, describing the situation—either as bad or good.
2. State the recommended policy that will remedy the bad situation or take advantage of the good one.

In these cases, surely the condition of women in literature is a subject that has often been neglected lately, and just as surely the financial marketplace is ripe for just such an investment as mutual funds. There will be benefits arising from each venture: Students will be better informed and less inclined to male chauvinism, and investors will earn sizable dividends.

Recall also the earlier arguments contained in James Gorman's piece on napping and Cullen Murphy's on keeping pennies in the currency. They too posed claims of policy. Napping should be encouraged, and pennies should remain available. Gorman's suggestion that America is suffering from a "sleep debt," which will cause accidents in our factories and on our highways, is certainly the grim situation that his proposal seeks to alleviate. On the other hand, Murphy points to a stable situation that will be maintained if his proposal to keep the penny is adopted.

In general, the procedure that you should follow in presenting a claim of policy is this:

First, describe in some detail the situation that you urge your audience to support or reject. The situation is a fact, so you can be factual, supplying details, evidence, reports, citing authorities.

Next, point out the effects that will follow if your policy is adopted.

Look at the development of this pattern in the following argument by the Reverend Jesse Jackson.

Let me illustrate the point [this] way, using the familiar athletic example, "Runners to your mark, get set, go!" Two world-class distance runners begin the grueling human test of trying to run a sub-four-minute mile. Two minutes into the race, officials observe that one runner, falling far behind, still has running weights on his ankles. They stop the race, and hold both runners in their tracks. The weights are removed from the runner far behind, the officials re-fire the starting gun, and both runners continue from the points where they were when the race was stopped. Not surprisingly, the runner who ran the entire race without the ankle weights comes in with a sizable lead. [1]

The fundamental moral question one could ask about that theoretical race must be, Would anyone call it fair? Again, not surprisingly, the answer would certainly be a simple and resounding No. If one could devise some means of compensating [2] the second runner (for example, comparing the runners' times for the last two laps and projecting them over the entire race), a more accurate appraisal of each runner's ability and performance could be made. And if a reasonable means of compensation could be devised, no one would say that such compensation constituted "reverse discrimination" against the first runner or "preferential treatment" for the second. All would agree that compensation was fair and just.

Everyone can follow this example and see the "reasonableness" and morality of the solution because racial attitudes are not involved. Yet this is similar to the position in which blacks find themselves in the United States. We have been running the race with weights on our ankles—weights not of our own choosing. Weights of "no rights that a white must respect," weights of slavery, of past and present discrimination in jobs, in education, housing, and health care, and more.   3

Some argue that there now are laws forbidding discrimination in education, in public accommodations and employment, in politics, and in housing. But these laws only amount to removing the weights after years of disadvantage. Too often, when analyzing the race question, the analysts start at the end rather than at the beginning. To return to the track-meet example, if one saw only the last part of the race (without knowing about the first part), the compensation might seem unreasonable, immoral, discriminatory, or a form of preferential treatment. Affirmative action programs (in light of the history and experience of black people in the United States) are an extremely reasonable, even conservative, way of compensating us for past and present discrimination. According to a recent publication of the Equal Employment Opportunity Commission (*Black Experience and Black Expectations,* Melvin Humphrey), at the present rate of "progress" it will take forty-three years to end job discrimination—hardly a reasonable timetable.   4

If our goal is educational and economic equity and parity— and it is—then we need affirmative action to catch up. We are behind as a result of discrimination and denial of opportunity. There is one white attorney for every 680 whites, but only one black attorney for every 4,000 blacks; one white physician for every 649 whites, but only one black physician for every 5,000 blacks; and one white dentist for every 1,900 whites, but only one black dentist for every 8,400 blacks. Less than 1 percent of all engineers—or of all practicing chemists—is black. Cruel and uncompassionate injustice created gaps like these. We need creative justice and compassion to help us close them.   5

Actually, in the U.S. context, "reverse discrimination" is illogical and a contradiction in terms. Never in the history of mankind has a majority, with power, engaged in programs and written laws that discriminate against itself. The only thing whites are giving up because of affirmative action is unfair advantage—something that was unnecessary in the first place.

Blacks are not making progress at the expense of whites, as news accounts make it seem. There are 49 percent more whites in medical school today and 64 percent more whites in law school than there were when affirmative action programs began some eight years ago.

In a recent column, William Raspberry raised an interesting question. Commenting on the *Bakke* case, he asked, "What if, instead of setting aside 16 of 100 slots, we added 16 slots to the 100?" That, he suggested, would allow blacks to make progress and would not interfere with what whites already have. He then went on to point out that this, in fact, is exactly what has happened in law and medical schools. In 1968, the year before affirmative action programs began to get under way, 9,571 whites and 282 members of minority groups entered U.S. medical schools. In 1976, the figures were 14,213 and 1,400 respectively. Thus, under affirmative action, the number of "white places" actually rose by 49 percent: white access to medical training was not diminished, but substantially increased. The trend was even more marked in law schools. In 1969, the first year for which reliable figures are available, 2,933 minority group members were enrolled; in 1976, the number was up to 8,484. But during the same period, law school enrollment for whites rose from 65,453 to 107,064—an increase of 64 percent. In short, it is a myth that blacks are making progress at white expense.

In Jackson's argument, the introductory scenario about the unfair foot race served to exemplify the grim situation faced by blacks in today's job market. Enforcement of affirmative action laws would greatly improve that situation without creating reverse discrimination. That is the remainder of Jackson's claim of policy. Let's summarize the way that Jackson sets up his argument.

After setting up his argument with his introductory story, Jackson goes on in paragraph 4 to make his most crucial claim. "Affirmative action programs...are an extremely reasonable, even conservative, way of compensating us for past and present discrimination." The support for this claim has been established by the comparison with the runner. Simply removing the weights was not enough, in the same way that laws forbidding racial discrimination are not enough.

Paragraph 5 constitutes another statement to support the just-stated claim. It asserts that affirmative action programs are reasonable *because* blacks are measurably behind whites in at least three important professions—and by implication in a great many others, if not all.

In the last three paragraphs, Jackson turns to another claim, one regarding "reverse discrimination," the belief that, as a result of affirmative action programs, whites are now being discriminated against. He states this last claim most clearly in the first sentence of paragraph 7: "Blacks are not making progress at the expense of whites . . . " and repeats it in the sentence that concludes his final paragraph: " . . . it is a myth that blacks are making progress at white expense."

What about the support for this claim? Jackson does two things to support it. First, he cites some statistics showing that whites attend law and medical school in higher numbers than before affirmative action plans were put into effect. Next, he calls upon an authority, syndicated newspaper columnist William Raspberry, who, using other statistics, shows that blacks, as a result of affirmative action, have not encroached upon spaces in professional schools formerly reserved for whites. Rather, what has happened is that seats were added for both blacks and whites. As a result, while increasing numbers of blacks (and whites) have gained medical and law school admission, the imbalance favoring whites has been only minimally reduced.

Now that we have introduced the three types of claims, it will be useful for you to study some additional examples. Have a look at the following exercises.

EXERCISES

1. Turn to the readings that begin on p. 132 and reread the Turbak essay, "Plastic: Sixty Billion Pounds of Trouble." How would you label the claim that is made in this argument? Is it a claim of policy or of fact? If it is a claim of policy, does it contain a claim of fact? State these claims as succinctly as possible.
2. Now also look again at S. I. Hayakawa's "Sex Is Not a Spectator Sport." The main claim embodied in this argument is one of value. Where does Hayawaka state it? What criteria does he use to define the things that he considers to be valuable?

3. Cindy Gray's argument, "Elementary Schools Need More Male Teachers," p. 166, is based on a claim of policy. Locate the two parts of the argument: the claims of fact and the policy advocated.
4. If you have completed the exercises in the earlier part of this chapter (p. 20), you have already written brief summaries of the Turbak and Hayakawa articles. Now add a summary of the Gray article to your collection. Since you know it is based on a claim of policy, you should be better able to organize your summary.

2

Supporting the Claim

In the last chapter we examined the types of claims that you might be obliged to support when you argue: *claims of fact, claims of value,* and *claims of policy.* Each calls for its special supporting strategy. We might diagram those strategies as shown in Figure 2.1. As the diagram shows, supporting the claim of fact is the most straightforward procedure. Such claims arc supported by evidence in the form of facts, examples, statistics, or reports of authorities. It is also clear from the diagram that this strategy is repeated in the claim of value, as well as in the claim of policy, once some preliminary organizational matters have been completed.

For claims of value, where the assertion has been made that something is better or worse than something else, the next logical step is to *define* the standards (A, B, and C) by which this kind of evaluation is to be made; that is, we have to know according to what standard, or set of standards, X is better than Y. Once we have determined the standards, then it is a matter of presenting evidence—based on facts, examples, statistics, or reports—to show that X has more of quality A than Y does, more of quality B, and so on.

Similarly, just as the other two sorts of claims do, the strategy for supporting the claim of policy ultimately requires the presentation of factual evidence; however, the organization of the strategy is a little different. Remember that when we claim we should do A about X, we must usually begin with a factual claim about X: That is, X is Y, where X is alleged to be messed up, ineffective, uneconomical, suicidal or the like, and therefore X needs to be changed or corrected. Or maybe X is excellent as it is, and what we should do about X is to preserve it unchanged. Whatever the case, this factual claim gets familiar support: facts, examples, statistics, and reports.

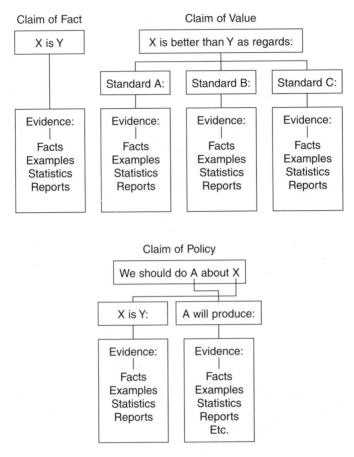

FIGURE 2.1 *Supporting the three types of claims.*

The other step in presenting a claim of policy is to show the benefits that will arise from the recommended course of action. Most often there will be several of these, but for each supposed benefit you will be obliged to show evidence that these kinds of things will indeed occur. The above diagram of a claim of policy suggests that factual evidence must be produced in this case also, and that is true. But you cannot avoid the feeling that this situation is just a bit different; these supporting facts are of a different kind—facts that haven't occurred yet, and supporting those kinds of factual claims surely requires something extra.

That felt need is absolutely correct. First of all, claims of fact can often involve speculations about the future. Second, something extra *is* needed to support these claims. The facts, statistics, and reports must be organized so that special kinds of inferences can be drawn—either by making comparisons or by analyzing causes and effects. But that is something we will need to work up to. Let's begin with a closer, more detailed look at our first formulation of factual evidence: facts, examples, statistics, and reports.

Supporting the Claim of Fact

Using Nondebatable Facts as Support

Remember now those earlier sample claims that were judged to be nondebatable and therefore not interesting as claims:

1. John Smith is a man.
2. Geometry is a branch of mathematics.
3. *Forrest Gump* is a movie directed by Robert Zemeckis.
4. Carol Stone is a student in English 101.
5. Women in Literature is an English course that appears in the college catalog.
6. Mutual funds are a type of investment opportunity.

Undebatable as claims, these are the kinds of materials that can be used to support claims, precisely because they are undebatable. They are facts that everyone can agree about, even opponents in an argument. Furthermore, in the event of disagreement, these claims can be verified easily. As such, undebatable facts such as these form the fundamental support for any argument. Let's examine more closely how such factual support can be marshaled in a convincing way.

Recall the claim that Loren Eiseley made in the last chapter: Mankind has survived not by toughness but through tenderness. Now that's debatable. It challenges the familiar notion of the survival of the fittest. Nevertheless, Eiseley presents some nondebatable facts that tend to support the case for tenderness:

1. Humans require a long period of childhood during which they are dependent and helpless.
2. Human brains do not develop fully during the nine months in the womb.
3. The human brain continues to develop during this prolonged childhood.

4. Learned behavior is more important for humans than it is for other animals.
5. All human groups protect their young.

No reasonable person would seriously dispute any of these facts. They are nondebatable. But each in its way supports the debatable claim that the human race has survived through tenderness:

because humans endure a long and helpless childhood, and
because a thinking brain does not develop prenatally, but develops during that extended childhood, and
because survival depends crucially on learning rather than instinct, and
because of all these things, developing humans must be carefully and cautiously protected.

You will use this sort of procedure time and again in formulating support for the claims of your arguments. You will supply nondebatable facts to support your debatable claims.

Remember how Jesse Jackson supported his claim that affirmative action plans were necessary—a very debatable issue. He first pointed to the undeniable fact that laws prohibiting racial discrimination did not provide compensation for the victims of that discrimination. And, second, he focused upon another incontestable fact—that blacks were measurably behind whites in almost all occupations.

Facts, or nondebatable claims, are obviously useful in supporting your claims of fact, and so are *examples*.

Using Examples as Support

There is a subtle difference, by the way, between facts and examples, and you must be aware of it in order to argue most effectively. Eiseley claims that mankind survives through tenderness and points to the long and helpless childhood that every human endures. That long, helpless childhood is a fact, and the reader can easily supply the connection between the claim and the supporting fact. As someone who survived childhood, you know how it is: You don't get through it without someone to look out for you. The connection is immediate, related, and obvious.

On the other hand, Dr. Wayne Dyer claims that justice does not exist and offers the following support: Robins eat worms. Spiders eat flies. Cougars kill coyotes. Coyotes kill badgers. Badgers kill mice.

Mice kill bugs. The connection between these killings and a lack of justice is neither immediate nor obvious. The reader needs some help to recognize the connection—to understand, that is, the aptness of these *examples,* specifically that the slaughter of worms by robins is not fair to the worms. Each case is an example of a repeated injustice. It is a fact that robins eat worms, and in this case this fact also serves as an example. But while it is a fact that humans have a long and helpless childhood, that is just a supporting fact, not an example. The killing of worms is, however, an *example* of an injustice, and the overall effect of this listing of examples of injustice is to make believable Dyer's claim: Justice does not exist in the face of so many examples to the contrary.

Sometimes examples are numerous, as they were in Dyer's argument. Sometimes they are few. Sometimes it is even necessary to appeal to an example that has never really existed—a hypothetical or fictional example—to illustrate and thus support a claim. That is what Jesse Jackson did at the outset of his argument about affirmative action. You will recall that he sketched a situation involving a race in which the ankles of one runner had been weighted so that lie labored under a severe handicap. Halfway through the race the unfairness was noted and the weights removed, with each runner resuming the race at the exact spot where action had been suspended.

Jackson's initial claim was that the action taken by the judges was unfair because even though the weights were removed, the afflicted runner was not compensated for the adverse effects the weights had caused.

Jackson's example illustrates a number of other principles, each very important for us here. Unlike the numerous examples in Dyer's argument, this narrative presents only one example. It is, however, an *extended example.* Frequently the connection between supporting example and claim is not as readily discernible as in Dyer's argument; in such cases, you must therefore elaborate and expand the example, making it fit the circumstances. Sometimes you may even have to create the example, as Jackson did, producing a theoretical or hypothetical example.

Finally, we must notice that the force of Dyer's examples comes from their abundant quantity, while the force of Jackson's single example comes from its aptness. He was not so much concerned to demonstrate that the race was unfair because the runner's ankles were weighted and because he received no compensation. Rather, he was concerned with another and similar situation—the plight of American blacks after the institution of civil rights legislation. They were *like* the runner whose weights had been removed. Each of them was still far behind in the race, and nothing was done to compensate for the past injustice.

The name associated with Jackson's special use of example is *analogy*. It is a strong and frequently used explanatory device, relying on our human ability to perceive similarities. We can often come to understand difficult and complicated processes or situations by noting that they are in many ways like commonplace, familiar activities.

Analogy, so useful in explanation, is also compelling as an argumentative strategy, as Jackson has just shown us. Having demonstrated the inequity of the hypothetical race, Jackson goes on to point out the similarity between the hypothetical situation and the very real one endured by blacks in modern America. His implication is very clear: What is unfair in a theoretical example is equally unfair in similar settings of real life.

By now you should understand that Jackson's example is three things: (1) an extended example, (2) a hypothetical example, and (3) an analogy. We don't want to be misleading here. It is clear that this kind of example will have a different sort of effect on an audience than the numerous short examples in Dyer's argument. But we also do not want to give the impression that a writer or speaker can use only a single extended example. Certainly multiple extended examples can be used, so long as they can be located or created, and as far as space permits.

Second, you must understand that not all extended examples are hypothetical or constitute analogies. Such was the special virtue of Jackson's example, but it is not the case with every extended example. Recall now just how Phyllis McGinley concluded her argument favoring women drivers. To demonstrate her contention that women's higher degree of patience enables them to perform better behind the wheel, McGinley offers several episodes or extended examples drawn from her own experiences with her husband, involving his typical impatience with elaborate oral directions and overdependence on maps.

McGinley's examples, although more complicated than any Dyer produced, serve the same sort of purpose as his, for each relates immediately to the claim. He says justice does not exist. She says men drivers lack patience. Nothing hypothetical is used in either case, nor is analogy at work.

Using Statistics for Support

Related to the use of facts and examples are *statistics*. Statistics provide a means of condensing many examples or facts into a very small space. Take, for instance, the situation involving the class that you are in right now. The chances are good that it is a freshman class, but if you wished to test the situation, you could inquire of each student, one by one, the status of each: freshman, sophomore, junior, or senior. As each responded, you could record the results, and you could report those results just as they appeared on your clip board, example by example: Mary Greenbaum is a freshman, Bill Shoop is a freshman, etc. However, chances are that you would not resort to such tactics. Rather, you would state the results something like this: "Of the 25 students in my class, all but one are freshmen," or "Freshmen make up 96 percent of my class."

Because statistics represent in a concise way a fairly significant array of facts, they can be quite convincing. Certainly this is the case in Jesse Jackson's argument, where he demonstrates that the representation of blacks is measurably behind that of whites in a number of professions. Specifically he asserts that there "is one white attorney for every 680 whites, but only one black attorney for every 4000 blacks." He repeats this formula for two other professions—physicians and dentists—and then switches to another mode of statistical presentation, pointing out that fewer than 1 percent of the nation's engineers or chemists are black.

While statistics can and often do present a great array of facts or examples in a brief space, we must always be on guard to ensure that they are reliable and correctly interpreted. One way to safeguard both reliability and correctness is to consider the source.

Using Reports as Support

Very few of us conduct our own statistical research. Instead we rely on authorities to accumulate, study, and report the data. When we appeal to such sources, we are obligated to mention them in our writing for two very good reasons:

1. Failure to do so makes us guilty of the crime of plagiarism—using someone else's research or scholarship as though it were our own.
2. Including the name of each source adds the reputation of that source to the force of our argument.

Thus, when the Reverend Jackson provided statistics to show that blacks were measurably behind whites in a number of critical professions in America, he was careful to state that he derived his statistics from a report made by the Equal Employment Opportunity

Commission: *Black Experience and Black Expectations.* He avoided the charge of plagiarism or making up his statistics himself, and he placed the whole reputation of a federal government agency behind his claim.

Similarly, Phyllis McGinley appeals successfully to authority when she points out that auto insurance is cheaper in New York for females under 25 than it is for males of a similar age. The effect is very apparent: It's not just Phyllis McGinley who thinks women are better drivers than men; it's the state of New York's whole insurance industry, which presumably has important economic reasons for carefully determining that this is statistically true.

Note also how James Gorman is quick to point out the fact that his authority, Dr. William Dement, who teaches at Stanford University, is also know as the "godfather" of sleep research. In taking the time to point out these credentials, Gorman is buttressing the support for his claim that napping is necessary. If his claim has the support of such a respected, prominent scientist, then we as readers are inclined to accept the claim as true.

Certainly reputations are important. It makes sense to appeal to authorities who are both knowledgeable and unbiased. Accordingly, however, the speculations of the brilliant physicist Stephen Hawking about religion and philosophy are best viewed as just that: the speculations of a man speaking out of his field—a very wise man to be sure, but one who has ventured beyond his area of expertise.

When Jesse Jackson cites William Raspberry as an authority who supports his claim that blacks are not making progress at the expense of whites, he leaves himself open to the charge that Raspberry, as a popular syndicated newspaper columnist, and not a social scientist, is out of his area of expertise in making such a claim. Furthermore, as a black American, Raspberry is likely to be overly sympathetic with Jackson's claim. In the long run, the worth of Raspberry's testimony will depend on the statistics it contains, facts that he drew from other sources—to which he surely referred in his article—and whose authority and freedom from bias can be subjected to scrutiny.

GIVING CREDIT

With regard to claims of fact that you wish to support, you may use your ingenuity and produce as many facts or examples as you can call to mind, but in the long run, you will often need to resort to outside sources to support your claims. In putting together our own arguments, most of us will need to read a great many arguments just to become familiar enough with a sensitive issue to decide how we really stand. Then we will need to credit those sources that have influenced our judgment, and from which we derive supporting material.

In the last chapter when we emphasized the need for writing summaries, we were also emphasizing the importance of appealing to responsible authorities for both statistics and well-considered opinions. Honest writers do not make up their statistics; neither do they make up the opinions that they use to support their claims. They *borrow* their statistics and their opinions from the reading that they do, they *summarize* that reading, and then they *give credit* to their sources for those borrowings and summaries.

The simplest way to give credit for one's borrowings is to mention the name of the responsible author along with the material that you have borrowed, just as Jesse Jackson did when he summarized the statistics he had found in William Raspberry's column. That is the method most frequently employed by professional writers: they summarize their borrowings and they mention their sources. Sometimes when the information is especially well-stated, writers will quote directly instead of summarizing, but they seldom, if ever, neglect to mention their sources. Certainly you should follow their practices, as a minimum. At other times, your instructor may require or you may voluntarily provide detailed citations (notes and bibliographies) to your sources. Those practices are discussed in detail in Chapter 6.

EXERCISES

1. Read M. G. Lord's "Frats and Sororities: The Greek Rites of Exclusion," p. 138. This argument is based almost entirely on a claim of fact. Try to determine how much of the support for the claims is based on Lord's personal experience and how much is based on reports of authorities. Does Lord give appropriate credit for any borrowed information? Does Lord employ both summaries and direct quotations?

2. Now summarize Lord's basic claim, together with its supporting evidence, in such a way that you might include it as a single paragraph in a paper of your own dealing with Greek life on today's college campuses. Be careful to give appropriate credit to Lord when you compose your summary.

3. Examine Constance Poten's argument "Shameful Harvest," p. 146. It too is based on a claim of fact. What is that claim in its barest form? List the supporting evidence that Poten provides. First, illustrate the claim and support in a diagram similar to the one suggested after the James Gorman article on p. 12. Then turn your diagram into a brief summary of not more than two paragraphs.

Supporting the Claim of Value

The most important thing to remember about any claim of value—the claim that something is good or bad, or better or worse than something else—is that such claims must ultimately be converted into claims of fact before support can be provided.

You cannot present support to show that Nolan Ryan was a great baseball pitcher until you have defined what you mean by a "great" pitcher. In other words, you have to *define* the great pitcher by enumerating the characteristics that you believe one must possess: blazing fast ball, history of strikeouts, low earned run average, successful win–loss record, accumulation of no-hit games.

Now that you have established the criteria by which great pitching is to be measured, all that you need to do is present the facts about Ryan with respect to each of them. His fast ball was consistently between 90 and 100 miles per hour, he struck out over 5000 batters, his lifetime ERA was around 3.00, and he won over 300 games in a career that included six no-hit games. Notice that these supporting data are all nondebatable facts, each supporting the separate subclaims of your overall claim that Ryan was a great pitcher.

Using your criteria, you might even go so far as to show that Nolan Ryan is a better pitcher than Hall of Famer Tom Seaver was, in that Ryan had a consistently faster fast ball, far more strikeouts, a lower earned-run average, more career victories, and more no-hit games. Even Seaver fans could not dispute your facts.

On the other hand, in order to make any progress with the Tom Seaver cause, your opponent would have to take exception to your criteria, charging that you have overlooked some important ones that Seaver exhibited but Ryan does not—things such as complete games, won–lost percentages, effectiveness with men on base, fielding ability, or the prevention of the stolen base. If your man Ryan comes up short on these criteria, it therefore would be wise of you to mention them when you are setting up your standards, stressing that in your estimation these skills are of less importance than the criteria by which you choose to measure great pitching.

Similarly, a careful examination of Phyllis McGinley's argument about women drivers reveals that she too has followed this prescription for supporting a claim of value quite well. She has established three criteria by which she chooses to measure good driving: practice, caution, and patience. Once this has been done, the rest is elementary—just present the facts, examples, statistics, or reports to show that women exhibit more of these than men do. And McGinley does just that.

Women get more practice at driving, she states. But first she carefully and cleverly excepts the legion of male truck and cab drivers. If we don't count these men, then her claim must be judged as true. It would probably be true anyway, since the number of women in the country is certainly greater than the number of males engaged in driving professions, but even so it's good that she points out these fairly obvious groups, if only to discount them.

Next, McGinley presents the facts, or rather the examples, drawing from her experience as a suburban housewife. She asserts that in such circumstances, wives drive five days a week to their husbands' two, completing such driving chores as hauling kids to school, scout meetings, and dance classes, shopping, running errands, and so on. All of these trips are *examples* of the practice that women gain while men are working at nondriving occupations.

Caution is the next criterion, and again McGinley provides examples of men who cause accidents while ogling pretty female pedestrians. This weakness is magnified by the prevailing tendency of men to think of their cars as toys rather than tools, showing off with them rather than merely using them to transport themselves and their passengers.

Finally, the lack of patience that male drivers exhibit, especially in the matter of taking directions, is the subject of the last third of McGinley's essay, where she supplies several extended examples of instances involving her own husband's typical behavior in this regard. These examples, besides being illustrative of typical male behavior, are also highly amusing, and therefore increase the sympathy of her audience for her line of reasoning.

You must measure McGinley's success not only by how well she has supported each of the three criteria she has established for measuring good driving, but by how carefully she chose her standards. Once she had those criteria established and they were accepted, it was simply a matter of supporting each one in the only ways possible for claims of value—with facts, examples, statistics, and reports.

EXERCISES

1. Examine Rachel L. Jones' essay, "What's Wrong with Black English," p. 159. In making her claim of value, what exactly is the kind of language that Jones suggests we should esteem? What criteria or standards does she establish against which language should be measured? What sorts of evidence does she use to support her claims?
2. Summarize Jones's position in a brief paragraph, being careful to give her appropriate credit.

Supporting the Claim of Policy

As we mentioned earlier, the support for the claim of policy usually occurs in two steps, with each step ultimately involving the use of facts, examples, statistics, or reports in order to convince the audience that some suggested policy is to be preferred.

Certainly, this is what Jesse Jackson did when he argued in favor of affirmative action. First of all, he stated that the situation that faced black Americans was an unsatisfactory one, very much like the one faced by the runner in the unfair foot race whose legs had been weighted. The analogy is clear: like the runner, blacks were handicapped by years of repression; therefore, civil rights legislation, which was equivalent to the removal of the weights from the legs of the runner, had been necessary. But those laws had not done—and could not do—anything to enable blacks to regain the ground that had been lost. As a result of this shortcoming on the part of civil rights legislation, blacks have continued to lag behind whites in both educational opportunities and in professional careers. The statistics Jackson produced in paragraph 5 clearly emphasize the advantage that whites enjoy in a number of professional areas. To correct that situation, something more is necessary, and that something more is affirmative action.

That is the second step of Jackson's argument. He must argue for the corrective effect that affirmative action programs would produce. He does this beginning in paragraph 6, but rather than focusing directly on the advantages of affirmative action programs (something that would likely alienate the whites in his audience who felt threatened by such programs), he devotes the remainder of his argument to showing that affirmative action programs are enabling blacks to enjoy progress—but not at the expense of whites. The statistics that he presented in his two concluding paragraphs clearly show that under affirmative action both blacks and whites have progressed in both educational opportunities and in careers. Jackson borrowed the statistics found in paragraph 8 from syndicated columnist William Raspberry, thus buttressing his claim not only with the actual figures but with Raspberry's reputation as well.

EXERCISES

1. Have a look at Ron Green's argument on p. 250, "Paying Athletes? Colleges Do Not Need This 'Cure.' " Unlike Jackson's claim of policy, in which correction is recommended for a prevailing situation,

Green's claim is just the opposite—that a currently existing situation should be preserved. What is the situation that Green wishes to preserve? What good effects does he point to? What bad ones does he suggest are being avoided? What support does he offer for his claim?
2. Prepare a brief summary of Green's argument. Be sure to mention him as the source of the information within your summary.

Using Definitions in Supporting Claims

Earlier, we showed that definition often proved to be a valuable tool in the construction of arguments, specifically in the support of claims. But definition shows up most clearly and often in the support of claims of value, where the criteria or standards by which value judgments are made must be listed or defined.

A definition is basically a statement that something is related to something else. More exactly we might put it in the form of the following formula: x is a y that is z, where x is the thing to be defined and where y is a larger, more general class of things to which x belongs. The final term, z, then is simply a characteristic (or more often a list of them) that distinguishes x from all other members of the class of things contained in y. According to this formula we might define a sextant (x) as a nautical instrument (y) that enables navigators to steer by the stars (z). In other words, the sextant belongs to the more general class of nautical instruments, which also contains such devices as compasses, anchors, and rudders. But we hasten to add the distinguishing attribute of this particular nautical instrument that it enables navigators to steer by the stars, a characteristic not shared by other nautical instruments.

Now you should be able to see clearly just how definitions work in setting up the support for your claims of value. When you argued that Nolan Ryan was a great pitcher or that he was better than Tom Seaver, you were obliged to define what you meant by a "great pitcher": A great pitcher (x) is a ball player (y) who exhibits the following meritorious characteristics (z): blazing fast ball $(z1)$, numerous strikeouts $(z2)$, low earned-run average $(z3)$, impressive won–lost record $(z4)$, and several no-hit games $(z5)$. You could even measure the performance of other pitchers, such as Tom Seaver, against the records established by Ryan with respect to each of these characteristics, thereby determining who is the better pitcher.

Similarly, Phyllis McGinley defined a good driver as one who exhibited the following traits: considerable practice, caution, and patience. Then she went on to show that women drivers demonstrated more of these traits than did their male counterparts. In these cases, as in all arguments involving a claim of value, a definition—and a careful one—must be made so that the assembled facts, examples, and statistics support the (z) element of that definition.

The second use of definition in supporting claims is not quite as central as the one just described, but it is no less important. You must often use definition to make clear the point you are arguing, limiting it in such a way that the supporting facts, examples, and statistics will apply most convincingly. Recall that when we were trying to prove that John Smith was a murderer, we had to determine whether the facts would support the claim of first degree (or premeditated) murder or of second degree murder (where evidence of premeditation is not required). We also saw that it would be foolish to argue that geometry was useless because there is too much evidence to the contrary. Nevertheless, it is possible to restrict or limit the term "useless" in such a way that the claim becomes supportable, and you'll recall that is just what we did when we claimed that geometry was useless to singers.

Similarly, Cullen Murphy, in his argument favoring the retention of the penny, spends his longest paragraph defining it, something that we probably would think a waste of time since we all know what a penny is. Nevertheless, Murphy's treatment of the penny as something that we use to measure the stages of our lives, as something that we use to make wishes, as "an essential garnish" in a pocketful of change—all these definitions help us to see the penny in a way we hadn't before. Therefore, they help us to be more kindly disposed to it—and to Murphy's argument.

EXERCISES

1. In his argument, "Sex Is Not a Spectator Sport," p. 152, S. I. Hayakawa must define what he means by obscenity and pornography. Where does he formulate those definitions, and how are they crucial to his argument?

2. In his essay "A Better Health Plan Goes Rejected," p. 162, Richard Reeves must define what he means by "single payer." Where exactly does he state that definition? Is Reeve's purpose in constructing his definition similar to or different from Hayakawa's in "Sex Is Not a Spectator Sport"? Defend your response to this question.

3. You have read our discussion of the criteria that might be used to define a great pitcher and thereby justify the choice of Nolan Ryan over another pitcher. Now examine how Hayakawa defines pornography in such a way that he can denounce those things that fit his criteria. Now try doing something similar. In a brief essay, define something of your choosing—a good automobile, a successful television com-

mercial, or an Academy Award-winning performance. Then use your definition to demonstrate that one car, commercial, or performance is better than another.

Using Comparison or Analogy to Support Claims

We have already discussed the way in which claims of value may measure one item against another to determine which was better—or worse. We showed how to compare the pitching of Nolan Ryan with that of Tom Seaver by defining what we meant by great pitching—providing a list of several qualities exhibited by big league pitchers—and then went on to examine the performances of each pitcher with respect to the items on that list. That allowed us to make a rather straightforward comparison, point by point; while doing so, we determined who was the most impressive of the two with respect to those points.

This kind of straightforward comparison figures quite prominently in the support of most claims of value, particularly when the relative merits or demerits of several persons or things are being argued: Electrolux versus Hoover vacuum cleaners, Toyotas versus Chevrolets as family cars, George Bush versus Bill Clinton as U.S. presidents.

Regardless of the items to be compared, one thing is certain: you will need to supply a number of points that may be compared for the items. So long as the items to be compared are fairly similar—vacuum cleaners, automobiles, or politicians—those points will be fairly easy to determine.

On the other hand, when the items to be compared are not so similar, the comparison becomes more risky. You often hear someone being accused of comparing apples and oranges. You would not get very far comparing Bill Clinton to a Hoover vacuum cleaner or to a Toyota. You certainly would not expect to find many points in common; in fact, finding any at all would likely strain your imagination. And yet it is just such an exercise that often proves extremely fruitful in argumentation. Such farfetched comparisons, as you should recognize from our discussion in the earlier section, Using Examples as Support, pp. 39–41, are called *analogies*.

You might, for instance, claim that Bill Clinton did not exactly sweep his administration's dirt under a rug, but like a Hoover vacuum, kept it contained and concealed very hermetically within the circle of his closest White House associates. Pressed further, you might even claim that Clinton was like a Toyota, in that his reputation has not depreciated very much despite all the mileage and tough treatment it underwent.

While these analogies may not be terribly compelling, they do help to expand our sense of a couple of the president's characteristics: his secretiveness and his durability.

This human ability to see similarities in essentially unlike things is highly prized. Frequently, in fact, it is a measure of our intelligence. You almost surely will recall being exposed to an "analogies test" at some time in your schooling. You will remember the kind of questions involved: *Farmer is to plow as teacher is to*—and then you are supposed to select one of the following: *student, classroom, book, desk.* In order to succeed in this sort of test, you must try to discover the very limited relationship that exists between *farmer* and *plow* that is shared by *teacher* and one of the items on the list. This may be a bit of a challenge, but after a while you might reason as follows: *The farmer uses the plow as a tool; the teacher uses the book as a tool.*

How, though, is this use of analogy beneficial to those who wish to support claims in an argument? There are two ways.

First of all, analogy is an explanatory device. It helps to make things understandable. That is how the Reverend Jackson used it when he was setting up his argument regarding affirmative action. He realized that his audience was not likely to understand the notion of affirmative action, so he devised a way of explaining it. He used an example, as we noted earlier, but it was a very special kind of example—a hypothetical example of two runners competing in a race. One of the runners, however, was handicapped by heavy weights tied to his ankles. As Jackson recounted this extended example, it became clear that he was doing so for a purpose. The race was like the situation that existed after the passage of civil rights legislation. These laws were like the removal of the weights from the ankles of the handicapped runner, but unless something was done to compensate the runner for the previous handicap, he was still likely to finish last. That, Jackson claims, is the situation of blacks in America. Their handicaps have been declared illegal, but they have not been compensated for the past deprivations they have suffered; consequently, they are still at a disadvantage in competing with whites. He could have stated that claim in just so many words, but its effectiveness is enhanced by the analogy, which says in effect: You may not understand very much about the problems suffered by blacks in America, but you probably are familiar with footraces. Well, if you can understand footraces, you can probably understand this issue. And you can, and you do. Such is the power of analogy.

A second use of analogy occurs quite often in the use of examples. Suppose you were assigned the job of finding a site for a new McDonald's in the area where you live. In order to ensure that the new fast food establishment would be successful, you would probably do some research. You would try to determine just what attributes are shared by successful McDonald's sites. In a nearby town, for instance, there might be a McDonald's that enjoys incredible sales. This store is located near a shopping mall. If, in addition, the successful site sports a sign with a revolving face of Ronald McDonald and if it has a playground with giant bouncy fiberglass hamburgers for children to ride on, you might want to have just such attractions for your new location. And your reasoning would run something like this: The McDonald's in the nearby town is near a shopping mall, it has a revolving Ronald McDonald sign, it has a playground with bouncy hamburgers, and it is successful. Thus there is a chance that if the store I am planning shares these qualities, it too will enjoy success. The principle of analogy used here is simply this: If these stores are alike in a number of key details, then there is the possibility that they will be alike in others as well.

While there is no absolute guarantee that the further key similarity of financial success will materialize, there is certainly a very real possibility that it will. Such is the predictive power of analogy.

EXERCISES

1. To understand better both the explanatory and persuasive power of analogy, turn to "The Right to Bear Arms," by Warren Burger, p. 300. What comparison does Burger make in this essay? What is the effect of that comparison? That is, what does it help you to understand better, and how does it tend to persuade you?
2. In paragraph 3 of his argument, "Ban Paid Political Ads on TV, Radio," p. 190, William Pfaff draws a very convincing comparison. What is the purpose of that comparison? Christopher Hitchens makes a similar one in paragraph 6 of his article "Minority Report" on p. 304. What is it?

Using Cause and Effect to Support Claims

Recall for a moment the argument set forth by Loren Eiseley concerning the importance of tenderness to mankind's survival. We observed that this claim was debatable, but certain facts that Eiseley presented tended to support it quite convincingly: a long and helpless childhood, a brain undeveloped at birth but continuing to develop during childhood, a store of learned behavior that outweighs instinct, and a tendency among all humans to protect their offspring. At the time, we said that these facts were clearly related to the claim that Eiseley was making, but we did not explain exactly what that connection was. Now is the time to do that.

The facts that Eiseley presents to support his claim for the importance of tenderness are *causally connected*. They constitute a *chain of causes and effects* leading logically to Eiseley's conclusion. *Because* humans are born with undeveloped brains, brain growth must continue during childhood. *Because* this period of brain development renders children virtually helpless for a long period, they must be protected in order to survive. *Because* adults must protect children over this period of brain development, Eiseley can claim that tenderness is an absolute ingredient in mankind's survival.

To see the chain of causes and effects more clearly, look at Figure 2.2 below.

The arrangement of facts in this instance to form such a causal chain also serves to highlight another difference between facts and examples. Recall that we observed earlier the connection between facts and the claim that they support, and that we described that connection as immediate, related, and obvious. In other words, the facts are usually *causally* related to the claim that they support. Examples, on the other hand, are not usually so related.

In Dr. Dyer's argument about justice, the examples of spiders killing flies, of mice killings bugs, and of related carnage do not represent either causes or effects of justice or the lack of it; rather they are examples of the kind of things that happen in a world where justice is absent. To put it another way, these killings are not in any way

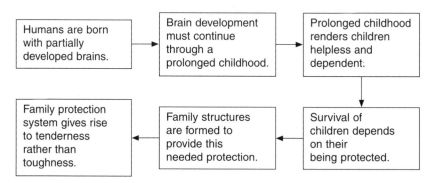

FIGURE 2.2 *A typical causal chain.*

related to one another; one does not cause the other. Neither does a lack of justice bring them about. They are merely bitter facts that serve as examples of a general truth: There is injustice in the world.

Thus we might say that a collection of facts allows one to claim that something resulted because of them. On the other hand, a collection of examples allows one to observe a general truth that each one of the examples illustrates and reinforces.

What we are describing in each of these instances is an argumentative technique known as *inductive proof.* That will be the first subject to examine in the next chapter.

EXERCISES

1. In his argument, "The Other Crisis in Our Schools," p. 172, what does Daniel Singal suggest have been the effects of stressing equality in education? Does he find those effects desirable or undesirable?
2. Reread the causal chains in the essays by Eiseley, p. 22, and Singal, p. 172; then in a brief paragraph construct one of your own. You can probably discover a suitable topic, but if one eludes you, you might try speculating about the chain of events that could arise from failing a crucial exam or from failing to change a car's oil regularly.

3

Organizing the Support

Two Classical Approaches

At the conclusion of the last chapter we introduced the notion of *inductive proof.* It is one of two classical methods of arguing; the other is *deductive proof.* Put very simply, to argue *inductively* means to argue *from the particular to the general;* arguing *deductively* is just the opposite, *from the general to the particular.*

Sometimes labeled the scientific method, *inductive proof* begins with the collection of evidence—facts, examples, statistics, or reports—and, using the data, proposes some general principle that the evidence all points to and supports. *Deductive proof,* on the other hand, begins with a general principle and from it derives specific or particular conclusions or claims, which must be true, provided that the initial principle is true. We might illustrate the two approaches as shown in Figure 3.1. These two classical approaches to argumentation have a long and honored history of use, and for that reason we need to examine them in some detail for what they can show us, especially in light of what we have already learned about claims and support.

Induction

It would be safe to say that almost every argument we have presented so far in this book has been based on an inductive proof. We may need to modify or qualify that statement slightly before we are done but for the time being it is accurate. Certainly it is the case with the selections written by Dyer and Eiseley.

On first inspection it may not seem immediately obvious that these writers proceeded from the specific to the general in their ar-

OUTLINE OF INDUCTIVE PROOF

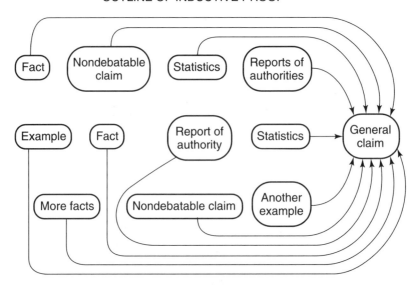

OUTLINE OF DEDUCTIVE PROOF

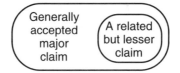

FIGURE 3.1 *Inductive and deductive proofs.*

guments. After all, both began with their general claims (Justice does not exist; Mankind has survived through tenderness) and then demonstrated by the presentation of examples or facts that these claims were true. That appears to be a progression from the general to the particular instead of the other way round.

But notice this. In each case, the *claim to be proved* was the general one—not the particular facts that formed the support. In fact, the supporting facts or examples, as we saw, were nondebatable and needed no support. It was only the general claim that was debatable and which, as a result of the supporting evidence provided by the writer, was rendered less debatable and more credible.

To put it another way, it is not really important which comes first in an inductive proof—the supporting evidence or the general claim—as far as the *arrangement* of your argument is concerned. Of course, you will probably need to do some or even a lot of research in order to *locate* the necessary evidence or support before you are entitled and prepared to make your claim. But having done that research, you may begin with the evidence and work up to the claim, or you may proceed as Dyer and Eiseley did, stating the claim and then presenting your evidence. In either case, if the evidence is convincing—that is, if it is nondebatable, accurate, reliable, and of sufficient quantity—then the audience will be obliged to go along with you as you make what has come to be called the *inductive leap* from the specific support to the general claim.

In Dyer's argument, there is sufficient evidence in the form of examples of slaughter in the animal kingdom, with mice eating insects, and cats eating mice, and so on, to convince us that there is injustice there—certainly to insects and mice and other animals ruthlessly devoured. We nod our heads; we begin to agree that these depredations in the animal world represent gross injustice, and it takes only a slight nudge for us to accompany Dr. Dyer in his inductive leap toward the notion that there is an absence of justice elsewhere. Of course, once Dyer has us leaning, he doesn't stop there; he takes us into our own culture, particularly our legal system. There we witness such notables as Spiro Agnew and Richard Nixon getting away with crimes that would have resulted in jail terms for any of us, and again we agree that Dyer's thesis is less debatable than it was at the outset. We have made the inductive leap.

That was the same leap that we agreed to make with Loren Eiseley when we heard his claim that tenderness and not toughness was responsible for the survival of our species. We were dubious at first, but after examining the nondebatable facts that he presented to us, we concluded that humans with their slowly developing brains are perhaps a special case in evolution and that our survival has not been the product of physical fitness but of moral sophistication—in a word, tenderness. Eiseley, like Dyer, has coaxed us into making the inductive leap.

Another brief example will serve to illustrate the inductive strategy. This one is a paragraph excerpted from the Reverend Martin Luther King, Jr.'s "Letter from Birmingham Jail," which he wrote to the white clergy of Birmingham in response to their charge that his direct action campaign for black civil rights in their city was premature and ill-advised.

We have waited for more than 340 years for our constitutional and God-given rights. The nations of Asia and Africa are moving with jetlike speed toward gaining political indepen-

dence, but we still creep at horse-and-buggy pace toward gaining a cup of coffee at a lunch counter. Perhaps it is easy for those
who have never felt the stinging darts of segregation to say,
"Wait." But when you have seen vicious mobs lynch your mothers and fathers at will and drown your sisters and brothers at
whim; when you have seen hate-filled policemen curse, kick
and even kill your black brothers and sisters; when you see the
vast majority of your twenty million Negro brothers smothering
in an airtight cage of poverty in the midst of an affluent society;
when you suddenly find your tongue twisted and your speech
stammering as you seek to explain to your six-year-old daughter
why she can't go to the public amusement park that has just
been advertised on television, and see tears welling up in her
eyes when she is told that Funtown is closed to colored children,
and see ominous clouds of inferiority beginning to form in her
little mental sky, and see her beginning to distort her personality by developing an unconscious bitterness toward white people; when you have to concoct an answer for a five-year-old son
who is asking: "Daddy, why do white people treat colored people so mean?"; when you take a cross-country drive and find it
necessary to sleep night after night in the uncomfortable corners
of your automobile because no motel will accept you; when you
are humiliated day in and day out by nagging signs reading
"white" and "colored"; when your first name becomes "nigger,"
your middle name becomes "boy" (however old you are) and
your last name becomes "John," and your wife and mother are
never given the respected title "Mrs."; when you are harried
by day and haunted by night by the fact that you are a Negro,
living constantly at tiptoe stance, never quite knowing what to
expect next, and are plagued with inner fears and outer resentments; when you are forever fighting a degenerating sense of
"nobodiness"—then you will understand why we find it difficult to wait. There comes a time when the cup of endurance
runs over, and men are no longer willing to be plunged into the
abyss of despair. I hope, sirs, you can understand our legitimate
and unavoidable impatience.

To help you understand King's organizational (and rhetorical)
strategy, go back through this long paragraph with a pencil and un-
derline each use of the word *when.* Now you can readily see how,
with each of the repeated *when*-clauses, King drives home the point
of his inductive proof—that waiting is no longer tolerable—for the

many reasons he's given, each signaled and emphasized by the repetition of the word *when.*

ORGANIZING THE INDUCTIVE ARGUMENT

It remains now for us to discuss which is the better or more convincing arrangement: to begin with the evidence and then leap to the general truth or claim toward which the induction points, as King did in the preceding example, or to borrow the strategy used by Dyer and Eiseley and state the general principle at the outset and then proceed with the evidence.

We think that in most cases it is more convincing to proceed by first stating the general, debatable concept that you wish your audience to adopt and then presenting the evidence.

However, in making a speech you may gain something by working the other way around; your audience is more likely to keep listening, waiting in suspense for the proverbial other shoe to drop, for you to announce your general claim. Dr. King's ordering of the support before the claim clearly shows his preference for the oral strategy; he was, after all, one of this century's leading orators. Oral strategies are different from written ones, and listeners often appreciate the flash of insight or revelation as the speaker leaps from evidence to generalization, pausing for effect before delivering the clincher, just as you would hold back the punchline of a joke.

But written strategies differ from spoken ones, and we suspect that if we were to complete a survey of all inductive proof rendered in written form, we would find that the tactics adopted by Dyer and Eiseley would be more common by far. It is simply easier to carry your reader along with you if you state your claim at the outset. In that way each piece of evidence tends to reinforce the initial statement, confirming again and again the general claim, so that its debatability begins to drop away bit by bit as each ensuing piece of evidence or each repeated illustration falls into place.

THE STRENGTH OF THE INDUCTIVE ARGUMENT

The strength of the induction, of course, will always depend on the strength of the evidence. If you supply examples, as Dyer did, then you need appropriate ones and a sufficient number of them. If you present facts, then those facts must point directly to the general claim, either because there is a clear causal correspondence, as was the case with Eiseley's facts, or because there is an emerging pattern that admits to no other interpretation. To use a possibly familiar example, if, in playing the board game *Clue,* all the other parties to the crime, their whereabouts, and their access to murder weapons have been accounted for, then we can confidently conclude that Colonel Mustard committed the crime—in the kitchen—with the pistol.

So far we have seen that inductions depend on two kinds of evidence: (1) nondebatable facts and/or (2) examples. These facts or examples are taken as evidence that points toward a general conclusion, either as *causes* for the general claim or as particular *instances* of a general principle. These are the two most prominent types of inductive evidence. There is, however, another but weaker kind of inductive support—analogy.

Analogy is weaker than the other forms of induction that we have seen because, however well constructed our analogy may be, it represents in actual fact an induction based on only one example. Recall our illustration involving the siting of a new McDonald's. You were tempted to locate your new store near a shopping mall and to equip it with a rotating Ronald McDonald head and a playground with bouncy hamburgers, expecting to enjoy the success of the store with similar features in the next county. If you had studied a bit more closely and discovered that the established store had a parking lot that accommodated 200 cars and a drive-through arrangement equipped with a Dolby sound system, you may have decided to copy those features also. But in doing so you would not have increased the likelihood of your success—at least in terms of an inductive proof.

The number of similarities that you can call attention to makes the *analogy* stronger and more convincing, but it does not make the *induction* stronger. In order to do that, you would need to give examples of several other successful McDonald's restaurants, equipped identically with the one in the next county. Only then would the induction be a true one. Inductions based on analogies do not often go to this extreme, but it is well to remember that they should, if they are to be truly convincing.

LOCATING EVIDENCE

Most of the inductive arguments that you will be called upon to write will rely for their evidence on the reading that you have done as you tried to learn enough about the subject so that you could argue intelligently about it. As you read, you probably made some notes, jotting down the bits of information that tended to support the general claim that you felt inclined to favor. What you were doing was gathering *inductive proof* to support your claim.

Because your reading will prove to be the most frequent source for evidence that you will use to support the claims in your arguments, you probably now realize why we earlier emphasized the importance of learning how to write clear, succinct summaries of the arguments that you read. You must be able to reduce these arguments you encounter to their barest form—the claims and their support—and to render these as summary sentences or paragraphs that will be used as part or even all of the evidence or support for your own arguments.

Sometimes it will serve your purposes best to borrow only *facts* or *statistical data* from your reading sources, using them as inductive support for a claim of your own that is perhaps slightly different from the ones urged by the original authors. On other occasions, you may decide to use your summarized facts or anecdotes as *examples* that point inductively to a general claim that you wish to prove. On still other occasions you may wish to borrow the entire argument as an indication that a renowned authority—one whose opinion deserves to be trusted—has argued for a claim similar to yours.

Regardless of how much or how little you borrow from your reading sources, or for whatever purpose the borrowing is done, you must consider carefully how you will give credit to the original author for the borrowed material. Failure to do so will make you liable to the charge of *plagiarism*—literary theft, representing the work of others as your own. To avoid such a charge, we recommend that you cultivate the habit of working the names of your source authors into your summary statements, the way Jesse Jackson did when he referred to government reports or to columnist William Raspberry.

EXERCISES

1. Reread Constance Poten's "Shameful Harvest," p. 146. What makes this an inductive argument? Locate the general claim. What is the support? How many separate pieces of support are there? How much support do you feel it takes to make an induction convincing? Is Poten's induction convincing?
2. Write a concise summary of the induction contained in Poten's article. Be careful to include the author's name in the summary statement.
3. Now have a look at Sarah McCarthy's "Will Jelly Beans Be Illegal?", p. 181. How many pieces of support constitute her inductive support for her claim that politically correct behavior is becoming increasingly absurd? Briefly summarize her argument.

Deduction

In the examples we have analyzed so far, we have not encountered a truly deductive argument. Jesse Jackson's argument in favor of affirmative action does rely on some deductive reasoning, however, and we will point out how he employed that strategy once we have described the elements of a deductive proof.

In this sort of argument, you should remember, the author begins with a *general* principle and proceeds to derive some *particular* principle from it. In most cases it is possible for the author to accomplish this maneuver because the general principle proposed at the outset is nondebatable—something we could not say for the general principles with which Dyer or Eiseley began.

In today's diverse national and world cultures, nondebatable general principles are not so easy to find, and it is perhaps for that reason that such arguments are not used as frequently today as they were in the past. Perhaps you remember your geometry class, where you began with a set of such nondebatable principles: Quantities that are equal to the same quantity are equal to each other, or parallel lines will never meet however far they are extended, or a straight line is the shortest distance between two points. Beginning with such *axioms*—one name for nondebatable principles—you constructed the plane geometry step by step in just the way that Euclid did thousands of years ago. Soon you were demonstrating that side–angle–side was congruent with side–angle–side and all the other convincing theorems, all from that handful of general principles and the proofs that resulted from them. Geometry is a logical system.

What is central in any logical system is a simple device developed by the ancient Greeks and called a *syllogism*. It consists of three steps. The first is the general principle (called a *major premise*) that everyone typically agrees with—for instance, *All fish can swim*. The second is a particular statement (called a *minor premise*) that makes a claim to the effect that something is a member of the general class named in the initial statement: for example, *A trout is a fish*. The third step in the syllogism (called the *conclusion*) is logically inescapable, namely that *A trout can swim*. In other words, if swimming is something nondebatably true about all fish, then it must be true of a particular fish, such as a trout.

While the truths contained in syllogisms are often so immediately obvious that it is difficult to deny them, it is nevertheless difficult for us to reproduce many of these kinds of arguments in our writing nowadays.

In fact, we tend to think of syllogistic or logical reasoning as a bit antiquated or old-fashioned. We are inclined to associate it with the Middle Ages or ancient Greece. We perceive ourselves as citizens of a modern, scientific age, and the reasoning associated with induction—here's the claim or notion and here's the evidence or proof—appeals to us. We don't readily deal in axioms and derived proofs.

If we are patient, however, there is a great deal that we can learn from this sort of reasoning, something that will even allow us to construct better inductive arguments. Let's turn to a truly deductive argument and see how it works. Here is one that you are sure to recognize:

The Declaration of Independence

THOMAS JEFFERSON

When in the course of human events, it becomes necessary [1] for one people to dissolve the political bands which have connected them with another, and to assume among the Powers of the earth, the separate and equal station to which the Laws of Nature and of Nature's God entitle them, a decent respect to the opinions of mankind requires that they should declare the causes which impel them to the separation.

We hold these truths to be self-evident, that all men are cre- [2] ated equal, that they are endowed by their Creator with certain unalienable Rights, that among these are Life, Liberty and the pursuit of Happiness. That to secure these rights, Governments are instituted among Men, deriving their just powers from the consent of the governed. That whenever any Form of Government becomes destructive of these ends, it is the Right of the People to alter or to abolish it and to institute new Government, laying its foundation on such principles and organizing its powers in such form, as to them shall seem most likely to effect their Safety and Happiness. Prudence, indeed, will dictate that Governments long established should not be changed for light and transient causes; and accordingly all experience hath shown, that mankind are more disposed to suffer, while evils are sufferable, than to right themselves by abolishing the forms to which they are accustomed. But when a long train of abuses and usurpations pursuing invariably the same Object evinces a design to reduce them under absolute Despotism, it is their right, it is their duty, to throw off such government, and to provide new Guards for their future security. Such has been the patient sufferance of these Colonies; and such is now the necessity which constrains them to alter their former Systems of Government. The history of the present King of Great Britain is a history of repeated injuries and usurpations, all having in direct object the establishment of an absolute Tyranny over these States. To prove this, let Facts be submitted to a candid world.

He has refused his Assent to Laws, the most wholesome and necessary for the public good. 3

He has forbidden his Governors to pass Laws of immediate and pressing importance, unless suspended in their operation till his Assent should be obtained; and when so suspended, he has utterly neglected to attend to them. 4

He has refused to pass other Laws for the accommodations of large districts of people, unless those people would relinquish the right of Representation in the Legislature, a right inestimable to them and formidable to tyrants only. 5

He has called together legislative bodies at places unusual, uncomfortable, and distant from the depository of their Public Records, for the sole purpose of fatiguing them into compliance with his measures. 6

He has dissolved Representative Houses repeatedly, for Opposing with manly firmness his invasions on the rights of the people. 7

He has refused for a long time, after such dissolutions, to cause others to be elected; whereby the Legislative Powers, incapable of Annihilation, have returned to the People at large for their exercise, the State remaining in the mean time exposed to all the dangers of invasion from without, and convulsions within. 8

He has endeavored to prevent the population of these States; for that purpose obstructing the Laws for Naturalization of Foreigners, refusing to pass others to encourage their migrations hither, and raising the conditions of new Appropriations of Lands. 9

He has obstructed the Administration of justice, by refusing his Assent to Laws for establishing judiciary Powers. 10

He has made judges dependent on his Will alone, for the tenure of their offices, and the amount and payment of their salaries. 11

He has erected a multitude of New Offices, and sent hither swarms of officers to harass our People, and eat out their substance. 12

He has kept among us, in times of peace, Standing Armies without the Consent of our Legislature. 13

He has affected to render the Military independent of and superior to the Civil Power. 14

He has combined with others to subject us to jurisdiction foreign to our constitution, and unacknowledged by our laws; giving his Assent to their acts of pretended Legislation: 15

For quartering large bodies of armed troops among us: 16

For protecting them, by a mock Trial, from Punishment for [17]
any murders which they should commit on the inhabitants of
these States:

For cutting off our Trade with all parts of the world: [18]

For imposing Taxes on us without our Consent: [19]

For depriving us in many cases, of the benefits of Trial by [20]
jury:

For transporting us beyond Seas to be tried for pretended of- [21]
fences:

For abolishing the free System of English Laws in a Neigh- [22]
boring Province, establishing therein an Arbitrary government,
and enlarging its boundaries so as to render it at once an example and fit instrument for introducing the same absolute rule
into these Colonies:

For taking away our Charters, abolishing our most valuable [23]
Laws, and altering fundamentally the Forms of our Governments:

For suspending our own Legislatures, and declaring them- [24]
selves invested with Power to legislate for us in all cases what-
soever.

He has abdicated Government here, by declaring us out of [25]
his Protection and waging War against us.

He has plundered our seas, ravaged our Coasts, burnt our [26]
towns, and destroyed the Lives of our people,

He is at this time transporting large Armies of foreign Mer- [27]
cenaries to complete the works of death, desolation and tyranny,
already begun with circumstances of Cruelty and perfidy
scarcely paralleled in the most barbarous ages, and totally unworthy the Head of a civilized nation.

He has constrained our fellow Citizens taken Captive on the [28]
high Seas to bear Arms against their Country, to become the ex-
ecutioners of their friends and Brethren, or to fall themselves by
their Hands.

He has excited domestic insurrections amongst us, and has [29]
endeavored to bring on the inhabitants of our frontiers, the mer-
ciless Indian Savages, whose known rule of warfare is an undis-
tinguished destruction of all ages, sexes and conditions.

In every stage of these Oppressions we have Petitioned for [30]
Redress in the most humble terms: Our repeated petitions have
been answered only by repeated injury. A Prince, whose character is thus marked by every act which may define a Tyrant, is
unfit to be the ruler of a free People.

Nor have we been wanting in attention to our British [31]
brethren. We have warned them from time to time of attempts

by their legislature to extend an unwarrantable jurisdiction over us. We have reminded them of the circumstances of our emigration and settlement here. We have appealed to their native justice and magnanimity and we have conjured them by the ties of our common kindred to disavow these usurpations, which would inevitably interrupt our connections and correspondence. They too have been deaf to the voice of justice and of consanguinity. We must, therefore acquiesce in the necessity, which denounces our Separation, and hold them, as we hold the rest of mankind, Enemies in War, in Peace, Friends.

We, therefore, the Representatives of the United States of   32
America, in General Congress, Assembled, appealing to the Supreme Judge of the world for the rectitude of our intentions, do, in the Name, and by Authority of the good People of these Colonies, solemnly publish and declare, That these United Colonies, are, and of Right ought to be Free and Independent States; that they are Absolved from all Allegiance to the British Crown, and that all political connection between them and the State of Great Britain, is and ought to be totally dissolved; and that as Free and Independent States, they have full power to levy War, conclude Peace, contract Alliances, establish Commerce, and to do all other Acts and Things which Independent States may of right do. And for the support of this Declaration, with a firm reliance on the protection of Divine Providence, we mutually pledge to each other our lives, our fortunes and our sacred Honor.

Thomas Jefferson begins his argument with a number of general claims that he hopes his audience will accept. He even says as much when he introduces them in this way: "We hold these truths to be self-evident . . . ." Perhaps the most crucial of Jefferson's self-evident truths is that *when governments become destructive of the rights that they were meant to insure, then it is the right of the citizens to replace such a government* (paragraph 2). This statement, or claim, serves as the argument's *major premise* and is the first step in Jefferson's syllogism.

His next step is to show that *the government of the American colonies has become destructive of the rights it was meant to insure.* This is the second step in Jefferson's syllogism, his *minor premise.* Notice that while Jefferson's major premise was nondebatable, his minor premise was highly debatable; therefore, he had to go to great lengths to establish *inductively* the truth of it. And he this did by supplying 28 separate pieces of evidence, as facts to be "submitted to a candid world" (paragraphs 3–31).

After enumerating all of these facts, Jefferson feels that he has amply demonstrated the truth of his minor premise and can go on to the incontrovertible third step or *conclusion:* Then *it is the right of the American colonists to replace the government imposed on them by the British crown.* That, of course, is the substance of his final paragraph, which you notice uses the word that normally introduces all deductive conclusions, *therefore.*

Let's return now to Jesse Jackson's argument in favor of affirmative action. Remember that he began by showing that African Americans lag demonstrably behind other Americans in educational and career opportunities. He did this by arguing inductively through the use of statistical examples, showing that in the black community there were proportionally fewer lawyers, dentists, and engineers than in the white community. He also constructed an analogy, showing that contemporary blacks are like the runner in a foot race who has to wear ankle weights, and that the unfairness of the situation is not alleviated simply by removing the weights. In each of these instances, Jackson's approach was essentially inductive. He then suggested that affirmative action programs were needed to remedy the unfair situation that he had described. In doing so, he was arguing deductively.

In essence, Jackson stated his argument this way: We need to remedy the unfair situation in which American blacks find themselves. This statement actually contains a syllogism's conclusion (we need to remedy the situation in which American blacks find themselves) and its minor premise (the situation in which American blacks find themselves is unfair). However, Jackson has not stated his major premise, containing the general principle that he feels certain his audience will find undebatable; nevertheless, we can easily supply it: Unfair situations should be remedied.

We can now state the complete syllogism in its simplest form:

(Unfair situations should be remedied.)

This situation is unfair.

This situation should be remedied.

Like Jefferson, Jackson in his major premise has appealed to a general principle, one that he feels his audience will accept intuitively. Also like Jefferson, he has supplied inductive proof for his minor premise, showing by analogy and by statistics that American blacks find themselves at an unfair disadvantage in education and career opportunities. And Jackson's conclusion, like Jefferson's, is undeniably logical—that this unfair situation ought to be remedied. He must, of course, go on to show that affirmative action programs are an effective way to remedy that unfairness. Jackson next uses another deductive proof to do just that.

He says that affirmative action programs should be maintained because they have removed the unfairness of the blacks' situation without disadvantaging whites. Again we can rephrase this claim in such a way that two premises of a syllogism can be clearly seen. The conclusion is that affirmative action programs should be maintained. The minor premise is that affirmative action programs correct an unfair situation for blacks without disadvantaging whites. The major premise is now quite clear, and it is one that Jackson expects his audience to accept, namely: Any program that corrects the unfair situation of blacks without disadvantaging whites is a program that should be maintained. We might streamline that syllogism and restate it this way:

> Programs that remedy unfairness to blacks should be maintained.
> Affirmative action remedies unfairness to blacks.
>
> Affirmative action should be maintained.

The major premise in the streamlined version takes up where the conclusion of our earlier syllogism left off. Recall that its conclusion was this: *This situation should be remedied.* Recall also that *this situation* might be restated as "unfairness to blacks." Note that in streamlining Jackson's syllogism, we removed an important qualification to the major premise, i.e., that remedying unfairness to blacks should not be at the expense of whites. The qualification is an important one because it makes the major premise acceptable to everyone in Jackson's audience, particularly whites.

Let's go back now to the two bare-bones claims of Jackson's argument:

> We need to remedy the situation in which American blacks find themselves because it is unfair.
> Affirmative action programs should be maintained because they remedy the unfair situations in which American blacks find themselves (without at the same time disadvantaging whites).

These statements are called *enthymemes.* That term is used to describe a syllogism that has one of its premises implied or unstated rather than stated overtly. Usually that implied or unspoken premise, as we have seen in the preceding examples, is the major premise, the one that contains the general, undebatable principle to which the audience is expected to give its whole-hearted support.

That is usually the form that most deductive proofs take—an enthymeme consisting of a conclusion and a *because* statement that turns out to be a minor premise. The remaining part of the syllogism, the general claim, or major premise, is implied rather than stated. And that is why most people, especially students in writing classes, have such a difficult time in creating and manipulating syllogisms. It's hard to see the syllogism when only part of it is stated.

It is because of this difficulty that most modern approaches to argumentation have shunned the classical treatment of deductive proofs in favor of other approaches. In the next section we shall examine one such approach that has gained much popularity in recent times.

EXERCISES

1. Have a look at Peter Drucker's essay, "What Employees Need Most," p. 155. It is based on a deductive argument or syllogism. What is that syllogism? If you have trouble formulating that syllogism, you can find our rendering of it in Question 2 under "Questions of Form" on p. 158. Complete the remainder of that question by locating the paragraphs that contain each of the premises of that syllogism.
2. Next, look at Rachel Jones's "What's Wrong with Black English," p. 160. In setting up her claim of value, Jones creates a definition (or set of criteria) by which value may be measured. She does this in paragraph 6, and then in the following paragraph, she actually conducts the measurement. Can you state the procedure that she is using in terms of a syllogism? *Hint:* The definition to be derived from paragraph 6 will serve as the major premise.

The Toulmin Approach

Because the study of classical logic has not been much emphasized in recent times, we do not expect you to feel comfortable in dealing with syllogisms or enthymemes. It has been our experience that when we oblige students to deal with these kinds of things, the results are less than impressive. Here is one such effort:

Some dogs have fuzzy ears.

My dog has fuzzy ears.

Therefore, my dog is some dog.

Of course, there are rules for the construction of syllogisms and logical systems, but this poor attempt violates so many of them that it is hard to know where to begin to assist its perpetrator.

Modern students, we find, respond more eagerly—and with better understanding—to the inductive approach. Its straightforward method of accumulating evidence in support of a general claim constitutes a much more familiar procedure for them—something akin to the scientific method that they encounter in their chemistry and physics classes, where repeated demonstrations convince the observers that certain chemical elements will always bond in predictable ways, or that bodies will fall with predictable accelerations.

Accordingly, you quite likely were convinced by Dr. Dyer's argument from early in Chapter 1 that justice was nonexistent because spiders killed flies and robins killed worms, and so on. The accumulation of evidence in the form of repeated examples urged you to make the inductive leap to his conclusion that justice could not exist in a world where such killings occurred. For us, this sort of reasoning works better than a syllogism.

Very often it has seemed in our classrooms that the coming of the scientific revolution had banished classical logic for good. We and our students had much difficulty fathoming just how those old logicians managed to use their syllogisms to tease the particular out of the general. But at the same time, we also felt that something was missing, that we were giving up something worthwhile in our focus on a strictly scientific method of persuasion.

This is where British philosopher/logician Stephen Toulmin comes in. Toulmin began by noting that classical enthymemes generally consisted of a combination of claim and support—the very stuff with which we began our discussion of the argumentation process back in Chapter 1. You'll recall these arguments:

Justice does not exist because robins eat worms.
Mankind has survived through tenderness because it endures a
    long, helpless childhood.
Affirmative action is necessary because civil rights laws do not
    provide compensation for the victims of past discrimination.
Women are good drivers because they are patient.

In each of these cases Toulmin would claim that the argument is convincing because the audience is inclined to accept the unstated connecting link between claim and support—that unstated element that will turn the enthymeme into a syllogism, as shown in the combinations that follow.

(In a world where justice exists, robins will not eat worms.)

But robins eat worms.

Therefore, justice does not exist.

(No one can survive a long, helpless childhood without tender treatment.)

Mankind endures a long, helpless childhood.

Therefore, mankind has survived through tenderness.

(Victims should be compensated for their distresses.)

But civil rights laws do not provide compensation for the victims of past discrimination.

Therefore, affirmative action plans, which do provide compensation, are necessary.

(Good drivers have patience.)

Women have patience.

Therefore, women are good drivers.

Each of the parenthetical statements in the above syllogisms is what we have earlier called a major premise. They are also what Toulmin would call a *warrant*. The warrant is what makes the support for the claim acceptable to the audience.

The enthymemes we have listed above are apparently logically sound, as well as persuasive, and for that reason they can readily be expanded to syllogisms. Toulmin's contribution to the study of argumentation is not so much his modern recasting of the syllogism as it is his blending of the classical and the modern. That blending allows us to observe in the most common of argumentative forms—the claim and support statement—the rudiments of a logical system: pieces that can be connected by a *warrant—a belief that we accept as true, often without proof.*

Look, for instance, at the underlying syllogism of the Declaration of Independence:

Governments that are destructive of the rights of their citizens should be overthrown.

This government is destructive of the rights of its citizens.

Therefore, this government should be overthrown.

Thomas Jefferson certainly felt that his audience was predisposed to accept his major premise, because he included it in a list of truths that he declared were self-evident. If the prerogative of citizens to overthrow governments that are destructive of their rights is indeed self-evident, as well as inalienable, then Jefferson certainly has a very strong warrant for claiming that this government ought to be overthrown.

Deductive arguments or syllogisms in the classical world had to be valid, had to conform to rules. But in Toulmin's world of the here and now, claims and support may be linked by warrants that appeal to the audience's sense of logic, or of ethics, or of emotions. The *strength of the warrant*—either logically, ethically, or emotionally—will determine just how convincing the argument proves to be. The strength of warrants is the subject of our next chapter.

EXERCISES

1. Glance back at the set of exercises following the discussion of deductive arguments on p. 69. You were asked to construct the syllogism contained in paragraphs 6 and 7 of Rachel Jones's "What's Wrong with Black English." What did you determine the major premise of that syllogism to be? Does that major premise satisfy the definition we have given for a warrant? That is, does it require support, or is it a general claim that most audiences will accept without support? Look also at the syllogism you constructed for Peter Drucker's "What Employees Need Most." Does the major premise of this syllogism qualify as a warrant? Why? Why not?
2. Reread the excerpt from Martin Luther King's "Letter From Birmingham Jail," pp. 57–58. Reduce this paragraph to its claim and support. How would you state the warrant that connects the claim with its supporting evidence?

4

Warrants

Strength of the Warrant

A *warrant*, as we have seen, is an underlying assumption, a belief rooted deeply in the minds of an audience. If we are aware of such a relevant belief, then we have a distinct advantage in supporting the claims of an argument.

If, for example, we can count on our audience's tendency to value blazing fast balls, win–loss records, strikeouts, and earned-run percentages as the measure of great pitching, then we can be sure that we will have a strong argument in favor of Nolan Ryan's greatness as a pitcher when we recount his amazing achievements in each of these categories. If, on the other hand, the audience is not inclined to value these types of achievements, but rather places more stock in fielding, defense against the stolen base, or stinginess with bases on balls, then such an audience is likely to be less impressed with Ryan's accomplishments, and the argument is accordingly weaker.

Consequently, it is important in every argument to assess the attitudes of the audience, just as you would be wise to check the temperature outside before deciding which coat to wear to the movie theater on a night in November. Presumably, that is what Thomas Jefferson did when he composed the Declaration of Independence. He quite correctly gauged the prevailing sentiment among the majority of American colonists, that tyrannical governments ought to be overthrown. Similarly, Phyllis McGinley, writing in a lighter vein, examined her probable audience and determined that the overwhelming majority would favor patience as one of the defining characteristics of a good driver. Having made these determinations about their audiences, Jefferson could take the next step and present supporting evidence to show that King George's government in 1776 was tyrannical, and McGinley could go on to demonstrate that women drivers consistently exhibit patience.

The kind of warrant we have just described is one that will work quite well with an audience that is not hostile to your beliefs. A neutral audience—one with no firm convictions about a claim one way or the other—will be frequently swayed by the amassing of factual or statistical support, so long as the underlying warrant does not conflict with some deep-seated conviction.

But what is to be done about a hostile audience? How can a useful warrant be found? Although such a prospect seems impossible, there are ways. Study the following brief argument by Nobel prizewinning novelist John Steinbeck. It is clear from his argument that Steinbeck is offended by the frequent obscenities that he has seen in print during the campus free speech movement of the middle 1960s. It is also clear that he would not likely have gotten very far by rebuking the students at Berkeley or Columbia or Wisconsin for their foul language, telling them that their words were not consistent with decency or decorum. Look at what he does instead.

In a way I hated to leave America last December. Every day was interesting, some of it dangerous, I suppose, but all of it fascinating to me. For instance, the student organizations and picketing and even rioting. It's not so long ago that the biggest and best smash our college students could manage was a panty raid on a girls' dormitory. Serious people despaired of them. Foreign students were politically alive while ours barely managed to swallow goldfish or see how many could get into a telephone booth. 1

Well, that's all changed, you must admit. A goodly number of our students are raring to go. It's a relief to see. They'll march and picket and tip over automobiles with the best students anywhere. I'd back them against the medieval scholars who tore up the Ile de la Cite in the day of Aucassin. I admire rebellion—any time and against anything. Besides, it passes the time. And it takes energy to study and to riot at the same time. 2

The Berkeley students who struck a blow for freedom of speech are particularly to be praised. I hope when they get it themselves, they will allow it to others. And I think they should certainly have the right to speak or print four-letter words on the campus as well as off it. 3

My only reservation about this doesn't come from a censorious impulse, but one of conservation. We don't have many 4 four-letter words of sturdy quality and, when you use them up, there's no place to go. Also, overuse milks all the strength out of them. One of our middle-aged young writers has worn out his stock so completely that a simple English sentence would shock his readers to death.

No, if you crowd a window with diamonds, they become un- 5 interesting. It is the single jewel centered on black velvet, alone and glorious, that jars us into appreciation. Obscenities are too valuable to waste and, if one can combine with another to explode like a star-spangled sky rocket, that is true art and, like all true art, rare and precious.

I may tell you that once long ago, when I was working on a 6 ship, a seaman of Irish extraction dawdled his hand into a winch drum and the steel cable snipped off three of his fingers. For a moment he looked at the wreck which hadn't yet started to bleed and then softly, slowly and sweetly he came up with the greatest curse I have ever heard. It had everything—vulgarity, obscenity, irreverence and sacrilegiousness, all precisely placed in one short staccato burst of prose that peeled the paint off the deck machinery and tattooed itself on the deck engineer's chest. I have cherished this oath ever since, but I wouldn't think of using it. I have never said it aloud, even alone. I am saving it for the time when I need it. But it will have to be an enormous need, a tomwallager of a need, but I am content that when it comes I am equipped for it. Imagine the waste if I had piddled it away on some picayune crisis.

If I am stern about this, it is because I know that overexpo- 7 sure withers the rich bloom of our dear heritage of obscenity.

Since Steinbeck is at odds with his audience (or at least that portion of it that represents the free speech movement), he cannot appeal to a warrant that calls for good manners in speaking, especially the avoidance of shocking obscenities, because it is the right to use just such words that Steinbeck's youthful adversaries are supporting so staunchly. So he looks around for some common ground—something that he and his audience can agree upon. And he finds it in the notion of *conservation*.

In addition to being against the Vietnam War, the radical students of the nineteen-sixties were quite vocal in their support of conservation practices, branding capitalistic and industrial America as a careless and wasteful giant that would, in its pursuit of ever larger profits, soon deplete our rich continent of its natural resources.

Knowing this, Steinbeck can state his warrant with confidence, and he does in the fourth paragraph, where he says: "My only reservation about this doesn't come from a censorious impulse, but one of conservation." The remainder of the argument is quite straightforward: We mustn't waste the power of our obscenities through overuse because they are very limited in number and hence quite precious.

Any educated Greek contemporary of Aristotle could have expanded the enthymeme embedded in Steinbeck's statement into a full-blown syllogism.

> Precious things should not be wasted. (major premise)
>
> Obscenities are precious things. (minor premise)
>
> Therefore, obscenities should not be wasted. (conclusion)

Notice, too, how the major premise of this syllogism neatly states the warrant that Steinbeck was at pains to discover. He doesn't need to offer support for it, because he has carefully measured his audience and has determined that it is a premise that they will accept.

The second or minor premise is not quite so obvious, so Steinbeck has to supply some support for it. First, he compares an obscenity to a diamond, commenting that diamonds in great abundance do not dazzle, but a single one, properly displayed, will capture an onlooker. Second, he provides the extended example of the Irish sailor's curse, which he describes as very valuable and very comforting and thus not something to be squandered foolishly. By the time Steinbeck has recounted these examples, the audience can well understand his seemingly curious claim that obscenities are precious, as well as his conclusion that they should not be wasted.

Steinbeck's argument works because it has a strong warrant. And the strength of that warrant depends on three things: its logical appeal, its ethical appeal, and its emotional appeal.

Logical Appeal

A warrant has logical appeal if it accurately expresses the generalization that is appealed to by the enthymeme. Now, what does that mean? It's what we have been talking about all along. The enthymeme is nothing more than the combination of a claim and its support:

> Affirmative action is needed because civil rights laws do not require compensation for past discrimination.

Obscenities should not be wasted because they are precious.
Women are good drivers because they are patient.

What generalization is appealed to by each of the foregoing claim-plus-support statements (or enthymemes)? Look at these related statements:

People who have been oppressed should be compensated.
Precious things should not be wasted.
Good drivers are patient.

Each of these statements is a *warrant*—a justification for making each of the claims contained in the foregoing enthymemes. The logical appeal of each of these warrants can be illustrated and determined by a simple diagram, called by logicians a *Venn diagram:* Take the first term of each warrant above—*oppressed people, precious things, good drivers*—and draw a circle around each as shown in Figure 4. 1. Next, draw a larger circle around each of these circles, and label that circle with the second term of the warrant—*people who should be compensated, things to be preserved, patient people* (see Figure 4.2). The test now is to see if the third element, the one that appears in the claim-plus-support statement or enthymeme (but not in the warrant) can be placed within the innermost circle. If it can, then it must necessarily and logically be a part of the larger circle (see Figure 4.3). People for whom civil rights laws were enacted are among the members of the class of oppressed people; that is, they belong inside the innermost circle. As such, they also belong inside the larger circle of people who should be compensated. Therefore, the logic holds, and the warrant has a strong logical appeal.

FIGURE 4.1

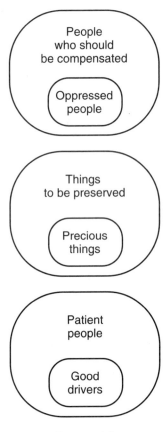

FIGURE 4.2

Steinbeck's warrant is also logically strong (Figure 4.4). Because they belong in the class of precious things, at least according to Steinbeck, obscenities also belong to the larger class of things that ought to be preserved. Now let us examine McGinley's enthymeme and its underlying warrant, arranged as in Figure 4.5. It would be incorrect to include the class of women completely within the circle of good drivers because McGinley's claim is not that all women are good drivers but that they are patient. You can draw the circle representing women in several ways within the outermost circle. Some will intersect the circle of good drivers, and others will not. The logical appeal of McGinley's claim comes from the inverse of the claim that women are patient; that is, that men are not patient. So if we draw the men's circle, it must appear outside the circle of patient

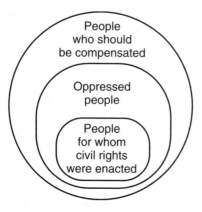

FIGURE 4.3

people and thus certainly outside the inner circle of good drivers (Figure 4.6).*

As Figures 4.5 and 4.6 show, the case for women being good drivers is not as logically compelling as were the three cases represented in the earlier diagrams. Nevertheless, there is certainly logical appeal for the claim that women drive better than men, and that after all was McGinley's contention.

Ethical Appeal

McGinley's claim about women drivers not only has logical appeal, but it also has what we shall call *ethical appeal*; that is, it appeals to a sentiment that underlies the beliefs, customs, or practices of a person or society.

---

*This, of course, puts a whole new complexion on the argument. Since all the adult humans in the world who constitute the potential set of drivers are either men or women—and nothing else, since there are no other sexes—and if all men are excluded from the ranks of patient people, then that effectively makes women and patient people the same set, since there are no other kinds of people who can be patient. Now all drivers must form a subgroup of people who are both patient and female. The new diagram would look like this:

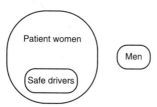

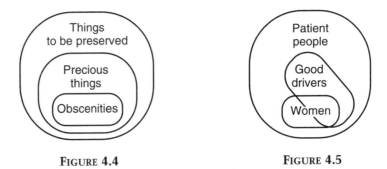

FIGURE 4.4   FIGURE 4.5

The ethical appeal of McGinley's claim rests upon the strength of the warrant that patient people make good drivers, but it goes even deeper—to another warrant that most, if not all, members of our society would subscribe to: As a rule, women are more patient than men.

Similarly, the ethical appeal that lends strength to Jackson's claim about affirmative action is our abiding belief, as a people, that wrongs should be righted—that people who have sustained an injury should be compensated for that damage.

Steinbeck's claim that obscenities ought to be preserved and used sparingly because they are precious appeals to a similar sense of ethics. It was Steinbeck's special genius that enabled him to discern just that portion of our society's ethical heritage which was still being observed by young radicals of the 1960s. While they had rejected prudery as something puritanical or conservative—labels they would have considered bad—they still believed in the conservative practice of avoiding waste, especially as it applied to limited or endangered natural resources. Steinbeck took advantage of this remaining bias to point out that obscenities were truly precious things that ought to be preserved, particularly because they were in danger of losing their potency and thus their very being.

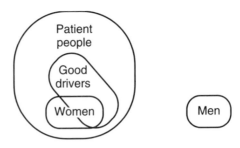

FIGURE 4.6

What is at stake here is the need to examine the values of the audience to determine what sorts of claims will work and which ones won't. Those that match the deeply felt convictions of the audience will succeed more readily than those that do not. The lesson from Steinbeck is just this: Claims that conflict with the underlying beliefs or principles of the audience are likely to be doomed, however logically we frame them, *unless* we discover some way to couch those claims so that they have an ethical appeal as well.

Determining the ethical or cultural convictions of your audience and then fashioning your argument to take advantage of them is just one element of what we mean by ethical appeal. There is yet another—what the ancient Greek rhetoricians called *ethos*. This is the character of the person doing the arguing—you. It is of utmost importance that you establish yourself as someone whose views are worth listening to; in a word, you must be *credible*.

ESTABLISHING CREDIBILITY

Surely you have noticed that public speakers frequently begin a speech or an argument with a joke. While the joke does not necessarily increase their believability in the eyes of the audience, it does tend to make them seem to be the kind of person that the audience will want to believe.

We believe people for two reasons:

1. They are our friends.
2. They are authorities.

For the time being we will deal with the first of these—the appearance of friendship, because it is certainly the case that one does not get to be an authority by telling jokes; nevertheless, it is a *friendly* thing to do.

The point here is simply this: You will make your audience more kindly disposed to your claims if you show that you have a sense of humor. People who keep their sense of humor are less inclined to be threatening, or boring, or overly technical—modes of behavior that tend to repel the average audience.

The ancient rhetoricians also had a name for this tactic; they called it *transfer* and considered it one of the sorts of argumentative flaws they called material fallacies, along with hasty generalizations and false cause. What they would find troublesome about transfer, especially in our modern multimedia society, is that it works, despite its fallacious nature.

Think of any five television commercials that you have seen recently; the chances are pretty good that transfer is involved. For instance, willowy blonds in suggestive dress are often seen in automobile ads; they are desirable, at least to the young male target audience, and that desirability is psychologically "transferred" to the featured automobile.

Similarly, the dazzlingly beautiful young woman on the moonlit beach who bites into that chocolate–coconut candy bar awaits with cool and total assurance the approach of the handsome young man bounding through the surf. The physical beauty, the romantic opportunity—these are things that few of us will possess very often, if at all. But the candy may be had for fifty cents. There is no claim in this advertisement that the candy will make you attractive to the opposite sex or lead to romance; the opposite effects, in fact, are more likely. Nevertheless, the romantic spell is *transferred* along with the candy.

The measure of transfer's success is easily gauged by the frequency of its use. And for that reason it is certainly worth your attention in planning your approach to your audience, whether it be imitating Phyllis McGinley's disarming humor in broaching the subject of women drivers or recognizing the cleverness of John Steinbeck's praising nonconformity in order to stake out a piece of common ground that he could share with his audience of rebellious students. Both were establishing themselves as friendly figures, using time-honored means of establishing their credibility.

Another method of rendering yourself believable, as well as agreeable, is to concede at least some portion of your opponent's argument. As we will note in the next chapter, when we discuss refutation strategies, it is always important to examine views opposing your own, with an eye toward countering them. You are unlikely ever to cause your opponents to discard all of their views and take up all of yours, but if you can bring about at least a partial compromise by giving over some claim that you do not feel is too crucial to your cause, you can score several small victories. First of all, you can draw the opposing sides a bit closer to agreement by narrowing the gap between them. Second, you can win some measure of goodwill from your opponents. Third, you can make yourself appear to be a most agreeable and sensible person in the eyes of the larger, uncommitted audience, toward whom most of your claims are directed.

Phyllis McGinley did not lose anything by admitting that men as a rule were very capable representatives of the human species and that they were, as a rule, quite good at a number of things. That generous concession at the outset of her argument helped both to establish her credibility and to make her male audience less hostile toward her.

You needn't, however, become a jokesmith or give away half your argument to establish yourself as a friendly, nonthreatening figure. But you must always be conscious of the *tone* of your writing. By tone we mean your attitude toward your audience as revealed by your writing. With a turn of a phrase you can reveal yourself either as superior and condescending or as concerned and helpful. Compare the following sentences:

Don't be so stupid as to neglect your audience.
Always keep your audience in mind.

Of the two pieces of almost identical advice, we feel sure that you are more inclined to heed the second one, because it is couched in a more friendly tone. And it's good advice; be a friend to your audience, not an adversary. First, study the audience and determine what its concerns and interests might be; then ensure that your approach—whether it relies on humor, shared concerns, or the like—features subject matter that will be appealing and nonthreatening.

If the tone of your argument establishes you as a friendly figure, then the structure of the argument, including its grammar and spelling, will help to establish you as an *authority*. As John Steinbeck once observed, the wisest philosopher could utter the profoundest of truths with absolutely no effect on his audience if he had neglected to zip up his trousers. Your credibility suffers in exactly the same way with every misspelling and every grammatical blunder.

In the final analysis, however, the authority of your argument quite often will depend on more than good spelling and grammar, on more than the form and the structure of the argument, and on more than the audience's acceptance of you as an authority figure. Quite often, as we have seen, you need to appeal to other authorities. If Dave Thomas, the founder and chief executive officer of Wendy's, tells you in a television commercial that his newest sandwich is the most delicious ever and then backs up that claim with a money-back offer if you are not satisfied, then you feel a real temptation to try one. You know that he is in a position to deliver on such an offer and that he must feel pretty strongly about his new sandwich if he is willing to put his money where his mouth is. Similarly, if Charles Schwab tells you that he can save you money on your stock investments, you also feel that he speaks with authority because the brokerage firm that he is representing on television bears his name.

In contrast, while you may marvel at the feats of Michael Jordan and Emmet Smith, you are not inclined to believe claims about the athletic shoes associated with their names; indeed, Jordan and Smith seldom make outright claims, because they know as surely as we do that their amazing feats are mainly the result of their special talents and not the by-product of their equipment. If we are disposed to buy the shoes they endorse, it is because we *transfer* our admiration for Jordan and Smith onto the shoes and not because we judge them to be authorities in the same way that we do Thomas and Schwab.

Thus, when we produce authorities in support of our claims, it is always well to analyze exactly what we are doing. We can gain something by way of transfer simply by name-dropping, hoping that the pleasant feelings of admiration associated with the names of our sources will tend to influence the audience. But such a strategy lacks the credibility of using an authority whose credentials are impeccable, one who is a genuine authority on the subject at hand—not someone who was chosen because his or her name has become a household word.

Emotional Appeal

While we respond to claims that we consider logical, we are also moved to agree with them if they have ethical appeal as well—if they correspond to some deeply felt sentiment that we, as members of a special group, organization, religion, people, or civilization hold to be true—or if they come from a source that we feel we can trust. We are also moved by arguments that lay claim to our emotions.

In his discussion of tragic dramas, the Greek philosopher Aristotle observed that those tragedies were most effective which appealed to our strongest emotions: fear and pity. We can return to Jesse Jackson's argument to see how such emotional appeals work.

We have already examined the logical appeal of Jackson's argument. Let us look briefly at its ethical appeal as well. When he says that the "fundamental moral question one could ask about that theoretical race must be 'Would anyone call it fair?' " he is making an ethical appeal. He calls it a "moral" question and asserts that the situation was "not fair." These are ethical concerns. But when he goes on to cite the EEOC report which predicts that without affirmative action "it will take forty-three years to end job discrimination," then he is appealing to something else—not to ethical ideals but to *fear* that unless something is done soon in the way of affirmative action, many who are suffering will not live to gain relief. And when he describes the situation of blacks in the job market as running with weighted ankles—"weights not of our own choosing," "weights of slavery, of past and present discrimination," he is appealing to another emotion—pity.

In a more modest way, Steinbeck's argument also appeals to fear—fear that our language's few and precious obscenities will be lost or weakened for all time through trivial and excessive use. We may respond to the logical appeal of the enthymeme and to the ethical strength of the warrant that precious things should be protected, but we also are likely to find urgency in the fear that Steinbeck stirs up.

Besides fear, Steinbeck also appeals to pity. We are moved by the suffering of the maimed Irish sailor, and we judge his response to that suffering—his great and priceless curse—to be justified or warranted. Similarly, we are moved to pity the runner in Jackson's opening illustration, forced to compete with heavy weights on his ankles. And it is to Jackson's credit that he contrived his example so as to appeal to his audience's sense of pity.

Contriving to instill fear or pity in the audience is something that obviously can be done. We can point out dire results or we can hold up sympathetic models. We can also take advantage of the language itself to convey such emotions. By paying attention to the *connotations* (emotional meanings) as well as to the *denotations* (dictionary meanings) of words we can actually tilt the language in our favor. Such a tactic is called *slanting*. Take, for example, the second paragraph of the Declaration of Independence. Jefferson uses several words to describe the behavior of the English crown toward the colonies: *despotism, usurpations, tyranny*. Besides what these words actually mean (their denotations), there is an emotional power or appeal that attaches to them (their connotations) that goes beyond their actual meanings. It is this second aspect of words that has the power to arouse an audience's emotions, and Jefferson was well aware of this impact.

The use of emotion-charged words can be quite effective, as it obviously was in the Declaration of Independence. Quite frequently, however, such a practice can be overdone, as it admittedly has been in recent presidential elections, where the word *liberal*, the so-called "l-word," was used without regard for its denotation, thereby creating a sense of fear associated with higher taxes, wasteful spending, and permissive treatment of criminals. Clearly, the unbridled use of emotionally charged language can give argumentation a bad name. In point of fact, it perhaps already has. Such language practices often are labeled as *rhetoric*, a word that originally meant the effective use of language, particularly in the construction of arguments, but which now is often taken to mean exaggerated, emotion-packed language, usually associated with dishonest or hypocritical politicians or demagogues.

Back to Warrants

We have just seen that the strength of a warrant—that is, the predisposition of the audience to yield to its claim—will be dependent on several factors:

1. Its logical appeal. How does your claim relate to the warrant? Is it a logical part of some pervasive belief that the audience holds?

2. Its ethical appeal. Is the warrant really a part of the audience's system of beliefs—of its culture? Also, how does the audience feel about you? Have you presented yourself as a friendly and credible authority? As the writer, have you given the audience sufficient reason or warrant to be persuaded?

3. Its emotional appeal. Is the audience's warrant based on a fear of dire consequences? Is the audience moved to pity? Has either of these primary emotions been stirred by the slanted use of language?

EXERCISES

1. In earlier exercises you were asked to state the claims contained in certain essays in the Readings section. Return now to three of those essays and, having extracted the claim, determine the nature of the warrant that underlies that claim. To what predisposition or attitude on the part of the audience is the author of each of the following essays appealing?
   a. "Plastic: Sixty Billion Pounds of Trouble."
   b. "Shameful Harvest."
   c. "Frats and Sororities: The Greek Rites of Exclusion."
2. How would you describe the connection between the claim and the warrant in each of the above essays? Try drawing a Venn diagram to illustrate the logical relationship.
3. With what sort of appeal does Turbak begin his essay, "Plastic: Sixty Billion Pounds of Trouble"? What about the appeal that is implicit in the opening paragraphs of B. J. Phillips' "Irresponsible to Allow Companies to Push Credit Cards at Young" p. 133? Do you detect any slanted or emotion-charged language in the two approaches? What specific words carry an emotional charge?
4. Examine Molly Ivins' "Ban the Things. Ban Them All." on p. 303. What is the attitude that Ivins displays toward those opposing gun

control? What word choices reveal that attitude? What do those choices of words have to say about Ivins' attitude toward her audience. What exactly seems to be the makeup of that audience? What portion of the reading public has she ruled out as unlikely to be affected by her claim? With what audience will she enjoy the strongest appeal?

5. Who is the chief audience of Lord's "Frats and Sororities"? Upon what evidence would you rely to justify your answer?

5

Refutation

Up to this point we have devoted our attention to composing sound, logical, well-constructed arguments. We have examined claims of fact, value, and policy, and demonstrated how to provide sufficient support for them. In each instance we were arguing *for* a position, a belief, a course of action.

While it is important to know how to argue in support of a claim, it is also important to know how to argue against one. Such counterarguments are what rhetoricians call *refutation* or *rebuttal.* When you refute an opponent's claim, you can attack the support, you can attack the argument's form, or you can attack the warrant. We will examine these three kinds of refutation one at a time. As we do so, keep in mind that these strategies of refutation should also be considered even as you formulate arguments of your own; you should be constantly aware of how your opponent is likely to respond to your claims. If you do that, the result will almost certainly be the strengthening of your own argument, as you determine how best to counter any potential rebuttal. Therefore, as we examine the three refutation strategies, we will also discuss ways in which you can anticipate and neutralize the refutations of your opponents.

Attacking the Support

Remember the way that claims of fact are most often supported. They can be supported inductively by amassing a number of pieces of evidence that tend to support the claim. If the pieces of support are not numerous enough, the argument often fails to be convincing. Such was the case of the foolish mathematician who concluded that all odd numbers were prime (divisible only by themselves or by one) on the basis of his examination of the first odd numbers—1, 3, 5, and 7. If he had examined only the next odd number, 9, he would have noted that it was the product of 3 times 3 and would have seen the error of his ways. His generalization had been made too hastily, on the basis of too little evidence. This is the refutation strategy most frequently employed against claims of fact—an accusation that the opponent has failed to examine all the evidence and hence has made a "hasty generalization." Classical rhetoricians are responsible for that name; furthermore, they contend that the hasty generalization is but one of a large number of "material fallacies," so called because they represent failures of the *material*, or the supporting data necessary to prove a claim. We will examine other material fallacies momentarily, but we have introduced this one first because of its frequent occurrence. (For a concise discussion of all the common sorts of fallacies, see "A Short Guide to Material and Formal Fallacies," in the Appendix.)

Perhaps the surest safeguard against hasty generalization is to provide a great deal of evidence, enough to convince your reader that you have examined a very large quantity indeed, so much so that any opponent would find it difficult to present a greater number of opposing examples.

Recall how Martin Luther King contended that African Americans were justified in their impatient desire for justice and equality. He immediately produced nine pieces of evidence—vivid and poignant examples of injustices and inequities that would certainly have tried the patience of any member of his audience. His audience would have been hard-pressed to produce a greater number of examples to the contrary.

Remember also how Thomas Jefferson contended that George III was a tyrant and then went on to support that claim by producing 28 concrete instances of the king's tyrannical behavior. The sheer number of instances made Jefferson's claim an impressive one because no opponent would be apt to argue that Jefferson had not examined enough instances—that he had reached a *hasty generalization.*

Other inductive strategies for supporting claims of fact, you will recall, involved analogy (or comparison) and causal analysis. The underlying assumption in all analogies is this: If two situations can be shown to be similar in a number of ways, it is likely that they will be similar in an additional one. That additional one, of course, is the one that you seek to prove.

You might, for example, reconsider the argument we posed earlier concerning the location of a McDonald's restaurant. The supposed success of the new operation was based on the similarity it bore to another, already established and successful one: its location near a shopping mall, its flashy revolving sign, and its playground for small customers. An opponent of the project could well appeal to the material fallacy of *false analogy* by demonstrating that, while these similarities do exist, there are also dissimilarities that have not been examined, such as the presence of two other chain fast food restaurants within 100 yards of the proposed site and the presence of a ten-store ethnic food court inside the shopping mall—competitive factors not present at the successful location.

The surest way to guard against the fallacy of false analogy is to draw the comparison very carefully, pointing out as many kinds of similarity as possible while anticipating possible points of dissimilarity. That is what Jesse Jackson did when he likened affirmative action to the compensation given a runner whose ankle weights had been removed part-way through a race. The situations in which black workers found themselves were similar to that of the runner in several ways. They were as handicapped by racial prejudice as the runner was handicapped by the weights. The inequities in both cases— the prejudice and the weights—had been recognized and outlawed. And in both cases compensation was justified.

At this point Jackson could have dropped the analogy and argued for the compensation that was due blacks who had suffered discrimination in the job market. However, he would have left himself open to the charge of false analogy. Job searches and foot races are, after all, quite unlike, and given no more points of similarity than the ones we have enumerated, the audience might view the analogy as a weak or false one. Fortunately, Jackson did not stop at that point. He anticipated that most readers would agree that the most logical way of compensating the aggrieved runner would be to have him compete again on another day without the ankle weights. Such a suggestion, while eminently fair in the case of the foot race, would have no counterpart in the job market, where adjustments can often be made but where starting all over again is an impossibility. Even to suggest such a prospect would be to court the charge of false analogy.

So Jackson quite cleverly added another point of comparison to his analogy, one that he called "reasonable compensation," which is, after all, what affirmative action purports to be. "If one could devise," Jackson suggests, "some means of compensating the second runner (for example, comparing the runners' times for the last two laps and projecting them over the entire race), a more accurate appraisal of each runner's ability and performance could be made."

By this additional step, Jackson's argument has gained considerable strength, and he has successfully avoided a charge of false analogy.

Causal analysis, another method of support for claims of fact, is frequently subject to charges of fallacy. The most common fallacy has an impressive Latin name: *Post hoc, ergo propter hoc,* which translates, "After this, therefore because of this." A more common name for this fallacy, and the one that we will use, is *false cause.* This fallacy asserts that just because one event follows another does not mean that the first one caused the second. A normal human reaction to significant events is to seek backward for their cause. But a black cat's crossing your path will have nothing to do with your subsequent auto accident, particularly if you encountered the cat at the beginning of your trip while the accident occurred an hour later and 50 miles away. More likely causes for the accident are sure to be discovered—especially by insurance adjusters.

Similarly, we might also contend that, in addition to making a false analogy, the argument concerning the location of the new McDonald's suffers from false cause as well. The causes advanced for the success of the first McDonald's—location near a mall, attractive sign, and attached playground—all no doubt contributed to the success of the operation. All other things being equal, they could very well have been sufficient cause for the success. But, as we have seen, all other things were not equal; there was another relevant cause that we did not even notice until we examined the site for the new McDonald's and determined that it would encounter stiff competition from two other fast food restaurants and an ethnic food court within the mall—competition that the first location did not experience.

In short, we had not determined the *actual* cause of the first McDonald's success; rather, we had seized upon several possible *false* causes for its success—a tendency that you will do well to guard against.

For a more successful handling of causes in support of a claim, we have only to look once more at Loren Eiseley's argument that tenderness rather than toughness is responsible for humanity's survival. No one is likely to deny the claim that human prominence on the planet is the result of an advanced brain. But a long period of development *after birth* is required in order for that brain capacity to be achieved—a period during which the child is vulnerable and requires the tender protection of parents.

So while brain power is responsible for humanity's survival and rise to power, that added mental capacity was not without its price—a long and relatively helpless growth period—and to overlook that while pointing to mental ability alone is to make a mistake as grave as Eiseley's opponent, who had singled out toughness as the key factor in humanity's ascendancy. In reality, as Eiseley has demonstrated, both toughness and increased brain power (traits that humans surely have) were false causes. They were sufficient reasons for survival if all other things had been equal. But as with the Mc-Donald's locations, all other things were not equal, and these two causes had to bow to the necessary cause that Eiseley convincingly demonstrated—tenderness.

Turning now to claims of value, we must focus upon the usual strategy employed in supporting such claims. We determined that the best way to support any claim of value was to *define* what we meant by value (such as excellence) in the thing or activity being considered, and then to go about showing how the thing or activity meets or exceeds the definition. That is what we did when we claimed that Nolan Ryan was a sensational pitcher. We set up some criteria by which we asserted that good pitching should be judged, and then we measured Ryan's accomplishments against them.

That too is what Phyllis McGinley did when she discussed good drivers; she established three criteria that good drivers must exhibit, and then she demonstrated that women exhibited them more often than men.

Those who wish to refute claims of value frequently point out that not all the facts have been examined—that based on the established criteria, another person or product has a better claim, with accomplishments or characteristics of greater value than those that you have enumerated. This would be an appeal to the fallacy of hasty generalization.

But more often the strategy used in refuting a claim of value is to point to a different material fallacy, that of *special pleading,* often called *card stacking.* We have already alluded to this tactic in connection with the discussion of Nolan Ryan's pitching. The person who grants that by your criteria Ryan was a sensational pitcher will build a case for a different pitcher by alleging that you have called attention to just those traits of a good pitcher that your favorite exhibits, while ignoring those that he lacks. In doing so you were "stacking the cards" in Ryan's favor.

McGinley's argument about women being better drivers than men is also vulnerable to the charge of special pleading; in selecting as important only the traits of practice, caution, and patience, she is ignoring other traits that good drivers ought to have as well, such as quick reflexes and good vision. The person who would most easily and successfully refute her argument would need to focus attention upon those traits she ignores.

Finally, claims of policy, because of their special strategies, are open to several avenues of rebuttal. Remember that in a claim of policy attention must be called to an existing condition—one that is to be acted upon. If it is a bad condition, then the proposed policy would remedy it. If it is a good condition, the proposed policy would preserve it.

First of all, an opponent might well claim that the existing condition has been misjudged—that it is not as good or as bad as it has been represented. In other words, the existing situation has been the victim of special pleading.

Second, the opponent might argue that the course of action recommended will not produce the desired effect—that the thinking involved in predicting the success is based on a false cause, a false analogy, or a hasty generalization.

Let us examine a concrete example, the argument advanced by Jesse Jackson for affirmative action programs. Remember that Jackson claimed first that the situation in which African Americans found themselves was deplorable: in both education and job opportunities, they were like runners with weighted ankles, demonstrably behind their white competitors and not likely to catch up despite the enactment of civil rights laws. This was so because civil rights laws, although they had the effect of removing the weights of oppression, did nothing to compensate for the ground that had been lost during that oppressed period. He then argued that affirmative action programs would allow blacks to make up that lost ground, while at the same time not disadvantaging whites.

To attack this claim of policy, an opponent would need to attack Jackson's assessment of the existing situation, showing that the condition of blacks in education and in the job market is not nearly so distressing as he claims, that in fact the conditions experienced by the two races are very nearly equal.

Or, granting Jackson's claim that blacks suffer a serious disadvantage in competing for education and jobs, an opponent might argue that the affirmative action programs that Jackson champions will not have the effects that he promises—that they will not produce equality of opportunity or, more likely, that they will do so by seriously disadvantaging whites.

Attacking the Argument's Form

Another approach to refutation is to attack an argument's form. However, it is difficult to find fault with the form of most arguments. Most arguments consist, as we have seen, of a claim supported by a *because*-statement or perhaps several of them. Usually, the more *because*-statements you can provide, the better your claim will be supported. Accordingly, your argument will be stronger and less vulnerable to refutation.

Nevertheless, at least in studying classical rhetoric, a great deal of attention is devoted to *formal fallacies*; these fallacies are mistakes that can be made in the construction of syllogisms, mistakes that render the syllogism, and thus the argument, invalid. To see how formal fallacies occur, recall that arguments consist of a claim plus at least one *because*-statement for support. This combination usually results in what classical rhetoric calls an enthymeme:

> Obscenities should be preserved because they are precious.
> This government should be overthrown because it is tyrannical.
> Women are good drivers because they are patient.

To convert each of these ethymemes into a complete syllogism, it is necessary to supply a general claim, which we have called a warrant, that will show the connection between the claim and its support. The general claim (warrant or major premise) appears below in parentheses.

> (Precious things should be preserved.)
> Obscenities are precious things.
>
> Therefore, obscenities ought to be preserved.

We have also shown how the relation between the claim and support within the syllogism can be illustrated in a Venn diagram, such as that in Figure 5.1. Because precious things belong to the class of things that should be preserved, and because the class of precious things also contains within itself the still smaller class of things we call obscenities, then obscenities must exist within the larger class of things that should be preserved. As the diagram shows, the syllogism is correctly formed; it is thus free of formal fallacies and is *valid*.

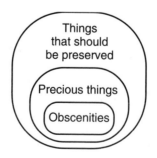

FIGURE 5.1

The same is true of the syllogism contained in the Declaration of Independence:

(Tyrannical governments ought to be overthrown.)
This government is tyrannical.
Therefore, this government ought to be overthrown.

You can draw the Venn diagram for yourself and thereby determine that the syllogism is correctly formed and that the conclusion is therefore valid.

On the other hand, you will recall that the Venn diagram that underlies the enthymeme *Women are good drivers because they are patient* looks like Figure 5.2. While women belong to the larger group of patient people, and while it is also true that good drivers also belong to the larger group of patient people, there is no guarantee that all women belong to the group of good drivers. Some women may be good drivers while others may not. This syllogism is said to be guilty of the formal fallacy of *undistributed middle* and is thus invalid. Without going into a detailed explanation of this fallacy, we can simply state that the syllogism does not succeed because it fails to capture accurately the relationship between the claim and its support: Women are good drivers because they are patient. The only salvation for McGinley's argument lay in the fact that she had excluded all men from the class of patient people, so that they had no chance of belonging to the smaller class of good drivers contained within the larger group of patient people. At least that portion of her argument was formally valid.

The conclusion to be drawn from the foregoing discussion is simply this: It's always a good idea to test out each of your claim and support statements by sketching a mental Venn diagram (or a real one if you have a hard time visualizing these things), so that you won't leave yourself open to the kind of refutation that depends on the appeal to formal fallacies.

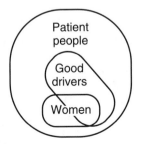

FIGURE 5.2

Attacking the Warrant

We have just seen how the argument of Phyllis McGinley was at least partially flawed by reason of formal fallacies in the way that it was constructed. Steinbeck's argument about the preciousness of obscenities, on the other hand, issued from a perfectly valid syllogism. It had the added virtue of having a major premise (or warrant) that coincided fairly well with the feelings of the audience toward whom it was directed, namely the radical college students of the 1960s Free Speech Movement—people who would not likely be swayed by the appeal to clean up their language, but who might find some common ground in an appeal to conservation practices. In other words, Steinbeck's audience would not be likely to challenge his warrant that precious things should be preserved.

Although Steinbeck's argument has a sound warrant, such is not the case with Jefferson's. Recall that Jefferson's enthymeme *This government ought to be overthrown because it is a tyranny* rests on the warrant *Tyrannies ought to be overthrown.* The colonists of Jefferson's time certainly found that warrant most agreeable. They found it to be a "self-evident truth," as did Jefferson, so altogether the argument was a very convincing one.

But not every audience would have been so agreeable. Students of Plato will remember that the subject of the dialogue called *Crito* is that the duties of a citizen include the obeying of laws—even those that are unjust or tyrannical. In his prize-winning novel *The Caine Mutiny,* Herman Wouk makes the same case for the much despised Captain Queeg, whose warship's crew mutinied against his crazed and tyrannical command. It was the duty of the *U.S.S. Caine*'s crew, according to the naval lawyer Barney Gruenwald, to support and assist the deranged captain, not to overthrow him.

When James Gorman suggested at the outset of his argument that our culture does not look favorably on napping, he was describing a warrant that he wished to challenge, namely the frequently held belief that napping is a bad thing, indulged in by lazy people. To his credit, Gorman challenged this warrant fairly successfully by demonstrating that people who nap are apt to be more alert rather than less so.

The insight here is just this: Warrants can be challenged, even those as hallowed as the ones in the Declaration of Independence. Claiming that truths are self-evident doesn't make them so.

If, like Steinbeck, you can find a warrant that is agreeable to your audience, then you will not need to support it. Certainly Jefferson was well enough aware of the prevailing sentiments at the time of the American Revolution that he did not feel compelled to justify the notion that tyrannies ought to be overthrown. But you should be aware that warrants may be challenged.

Stephen Toulmin, too, was aware of this possibility, and he proposed two methods of bolstering or supporting warrants. One method is to supply what he calls *backing*. Backing is nothing more than the kind of support that you are obliged to provide for any claim that you might make: evidence in the way of factual data, statistics, or appeals to authority—arranged either inductively or deductively.

To spend much time and space trying to support a warrant, however, tends to undercut the appeal of that warrant. You are better off to use Steinbeck's strategy and try to find one that will not be rejected or refuted—at least not by its intended audience. If the warrant appears weak as a general claim, it is better in the long run to qualify it in some way so that it can be stated succinctly without calling too much attention to its weakness. That is the second of Toulmin's strategies for support: *qualification*.

For instance, Steinbeck could have used that qualification strategy; he would not have sacrificed too much by claiming that *almost all* precious things should be preserved, nor would Jefferson have by admitting that *nearly all* tyrannies should be overthrown. Such qualifications allow you space to maneuver, without providing your opponents room to attack the warrant.

Another and the perhaps most frequent attack upon a warrant is the challenging of its authority. Recall how Jesse Jackson appealed to two authorities: a report by the Equal Employment Opportunity Commission and a column by William Raspberry. The underlying warrant involved here is that these are reliable sources; therefore we can accept their data. However, an audience is under no obligation to accept such sources as reliable.

When you appeal to a source, you are issuing (and depending on) an unspoken warrant: This source is reliable. In effect, the warrant is only as strong as the reputation of the authority. While it is perhaps strategically unwise to spend much time advertising the reputation of each authority whose information or opinions you introduce, it is always wise to remember that such authorities are subject to attack and may therefore need to have their reputations emphasized or even defended.

Another Effective Method of Refutation

There is still another often used method of refutation, but one that does not depend upon attacks against the support, the form of the argument, or the warrant. That is the *reduction to absurdity*. In this approach you pretend to agree with your opponent's claims, but your purpose in doing so quickly becomes apparent as you point out that acceptance of the opponent's claim will lead to some pretty unpleasant consequences, which, of course, your opponent has conveniently overlooked.

Suppose, for example, your opponent argues in favor of animal rights, pointing out that furriers cruelly kill wild animals and that using their pelts for coats is a senseless waste, since other types of clothing provide equal warmth. You might respond by agreeing with these claims but adding that leather shoes and belts should also be outlawed, and perhaps even the eating of meat.

Or suppose your opponent champions the war on drugs, claiming that a significant reduction in the drug traffic will make our city streets safe again for children. You could respond by agreeing that the reduction in drug traffic will be a very good thing indeed—especially for the drug lords, since drugs, like any other commodity, will enjoy a price increase when there is a shortage, and that the crime rate will inevitably rise as pushers and users scramble to get money to pay the higher prices.

In both these cases the opponent's argument has been reduced to an absurdity because of ill effects that had been overlooked.

So how does one prevent having one's argument reduced to an absurdity?

Both arguments we have cited above are victims of the material fallacy *dicto simpliciter,* the unqualified generalization. The killing of animals is wrong. Stopping the drug traffic will promote safety in our cities. These are unqualified generalizations. Remember that Toulmin's logic emphasized the need to qualify one's generalizations.

It should be clear now how the above generalizations might be qualified so as to avoid the reduction to absurdity. If you had to defend such claims, you might argue that killing animals *for their pelts* is wrong and that curtailing the drug traffic will *eventually* lead to safer cities. You would be prepared to concede that slaughtering animals for food, provided that it is done humanely, is not a violation of your principles. And you would also admit that there would be hard times ahead—both for racketeers, as well as many innocent victims—if the war on drugs is to be prosecuted to its ultimate conclusion; you would contend, however, that the price is worth it.

EXERCISES

1. Examine April Armstrong's "Let's Keep Christmas Commercial," p. 184. It is a classic example of refutation, attacking the common

complaint that Christmas is overcommercialized. Armstrong appeals to at least two material fallacies in her refutation. Study the list of material fallacies in "A Short Guide to Material and Formal Fallacies" in the Appendix and then determine which she is using to refute her opposition's claim.

2. In her refutation Armstrong finds it necessary to attack a commonly held warrant: Religious things are sacrosanct and should not be cheapened. What strategy does she employ in attacking this warrant?

3. In "Motherhood: Who Needs It?", p. 193, Betty Rollin must attack the almost universally held warrant that motherhood and everything connected with it are sacred and not to be tampered with. How does she go about attacking such a universally held belief?

4. McCarthy uses a reduction to absurdity refutation in her "Will Jelly Beans Be Illegal?", p. 181. How many times does she use this tactic, and where does it occur?

6

Putting It All Together

Up to this point we have been discussing the essentials of argumentation: claims and the strategies for supporting and refuting them. This is properly the *middle* of an argument, but it is ordinarily the part you will compose first. After you have framed the basics of your argument, then comes the time for you to work up an introduction for it and to figure out an appropriate conclusion. So let's begin where we ought to—in the middle.

Arranging the Claim and Support

In Chapter 3 we stated our preference for arrangement of claim and support. We believe that it's most advantageous for a writer to begin with a claim and than follow it up with supporting evidence, rather than doing it the other way around (beginning with the evidence and working up to the claim). The latter approach is more often better suited to oral than to written presentations.

One good way to begin preparing an argument is with a brainstorming session, probing your memory, attempting to determine what you really think about the issue, and which side you will take. Sometimes you will know at the outset which side you will choose; in other cases that initial decision will be more difficult. Your conscience and memory alone may not be enough to help you make that decision. You may need to do some background reading—perhaps quite a bit.

But the time will come to assemble your evidence—the facts, statistics, examples, and comparisons that have guided you to the position you occupy on one side or the other of an issue. Now you must examine the evidence and arrange it in the best order possible.

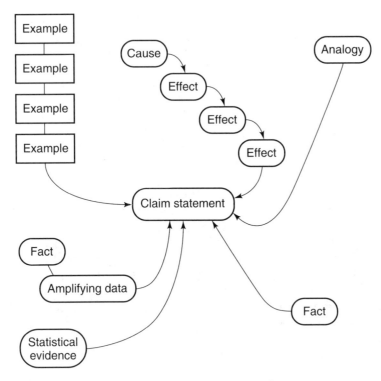

FIGURE 6.1 *Schematic diagram of an argument.*

This is especially crucial if you intend to organize your argument using such modes as cause–effect, classification, comparison–contrast, or process analysis.

One device that we have always found useful is the schematic diagram. It appeared in Chapter 3, but it's worth repeating here. Begin by simply stating your claim. Write that down in the middle of a blank page. There—you've begun. Now around that claim, start assembling your supporting evidence. Some pieces of evidence will need additional support; others, perhaps cause–effect sequences, will need to be linked together because they form a connected line of reasoning. Soon your jottings might begin to look something like Figure 6.1.

The First Draft

Once you have assembled the supporting evidence for your claim, you are ready to begin a first draft. (In composing your drafts, it's a good idea to leave wide margins—at least 1½" left and right—and to double- or triple-space between lines, thus leaving plenty of room for notes and additions along the way.) Right now, don't bother with an elaborate introduction; just start by stating your claim. Then work your way around your diagram, turning your cryptic jottings into sentences. If you can't think of a good transition between one of your pieces of support and another, forget about that need for the time being and press on. After all, a different order may suggest itself later on. Now you are writing, and you need to stick with the central task of converting your initial impressions into sentences.

At this stage fascinating and surprising things start to happen. Often you won't know exactly where you stand on an issue until you actually begin the process of writing down the supporting data. Some evidence you may reject, and other evidence may occur to you as you write. *Just becoming engaged in the writing process is an important method of discovery,* every bit as important as the initial step of schematically arranging what you thought you knew. That's why it's important to press on to the completion of that initial effort. You needn't bother with a conclusion, or with matters of tone or credibility. All that can come later—after you've gotten the basic pieces of your argument down on paper in sentence form.

Subsequent Drafts

If you double- or triple-spaced your first draft and left generous margins, you can now begin the process of coaxing your initial ideas into something approximating a final form. The whole procedure may require several drafts, each addressing a special concern or group of concerns.

Certainly, one thing you'll want to analyze in that first draft is the *order* of presentation. Sometimes the absence of a suitable transition between two key parts (that is, if one did not occur to you right away) is really a clue or suggestion that a better order might be found.

As you ponder the order of your evidence, drawing arrows from one paragraph to an earlier or later one, or cutting and pasting, either manually or else electronically on a computer, you will begin to tackle the necessary task of providing transitions. Phrases such as *besides that* or *more importantly,* and even enumeration devices such as *first, next,* and *last* will come to mind. You'll take advantage of those wide margins and spaces between the lines to insert transitions, along with amplifying and clarifying information. Sometimes whole paragraphs will grow from these interlinear insertions.

You may, of course, discover during this process that you will need to drop some support that has proved to be less convincing than you originally judged it to be. Or you may need to search for something to fill a gap that you suddenly notice. Often the order of presentation will be dictated by matters of warrants—just what will the attitude of your audience be toward your claim, as well as toward the evidence? You may need to supply *backing* for warrants that your audience may not initially favor. Alternatively, you may wish to restructure your approach to take advantage of an inclination or leaning that you have perceived on the part of your audience. Such things happen as you work with the supporting data, crafting it into its best form.

Once your draft has arrived at that *best form* stage, where all the supporting data has been included and you are reasonably certain that it appears in the most appropriate order, you are ready to attend to beginnings and endings (which we deal with in the final part of this chapter), and you'll need to check for grammatical and mechanical correctness. Such concerns are usually relegated to the last draft, although as you become a more practiced writer, you may attend to such matters almost automatically, along with more important concerns. The crucial point about grammar and mechanics is just this: Do not allow concern for these matters to interfere with the major ones, such as providing adequate support in an effective arrangement.

Using Sources

As mentioned earlier, the brainstorming session that often precedes the composition of an argument requires, more often than not, a good deal of reading. As you read, you will need to take notes, recording relevant material as you find it. Sometimes it will be useful to copy down brief passages word for word, particularly if the information contained in the passage is especially appropriate or well phrased. More frequently, you will find it useful to summarize what you read. Such summaries will prove to be more useful to you than will directly quoted passages, for several good reasons:

1. Summarizing information that you read helps you to understand the material better, forcing you to incorporate the information into your own fund of knowledge.

2. It allows you to impose your own order on the information you are borrowing, adjusting it slightly to serve your purpose rather than the purpose of the original author.

3. It allows you to compress a great deal of the original source's information into a brief space, appropriately adapted to your needs.

We have found that the best place to copy these summaries and briefly quoted passages is on note cards. In addition to the summarized or quoted material, each note card should include the source of the information, that is, the author's name and the work's title, together with the page number and where the borrowed information appeared. On a separate card to identify each source used, you will need to record not only the author and title but also relevant publishing data, plus a note about where you located the source (library call number, Internet address, or the like).

Once you have the necessary information recorded, you will find that it serves much the same purpose as the schematic diagram. You can organize your note cards into related groups that will begin to suggest an order of presentation. Such a practice may never completely replace the need for a schematic or outline, but you can derive a great many benefits from shuffling and reorganizing your note cards. They are an invaluable tool in organizing an initial draft. You can also sort and arrange the identification cards prepared for each source, using this as an efficient way to manage the customary requirement to list your sources at the end of a paper or report.

Citing Sources

If you are an effective note taker, you will be careful not to include too much information on a single card. In that way you will end up with a great many bits and pieces of information that you can arrange in a variety of ways. To do otherwise, copying down long passages of directly quoted material or writing overly long summaries of borrowed argument or supporting data, will simply impose too much of the original authors' organization and phrasing on your own presentation, vastly limiting the alternatives that are open to you in stating your case your way.

One reason that most note takers prefer small note cards (either 3 by 5 or 4 by 6 inches) is that the very size limits the amount of material it is possible to include on a single card. If you find yourself needing to use more than one card to complete a quotation or a paraphrase, that is a fairly good sign that the information should be cut or further condensed—or divided into two independent pieces of information, capable of being used in separate locations.

Furthermore, each note card represents a separate borrowed piece of information, each of which must be acknowledged by a *ci-*

tation. A citation is simply a prescribed method of indicating that the material has been borrowed. It is a matter both of accuracy— showing the source of your information—and of scholarly honesty— avoiding the charge of *plagiarism,* the academic crime of presenting the ideas of others as though they were your own, just as you would not present something that you had bought as if it were a personally made gift for a friend or relative. Furthermore, as a matter of simple courtesy, you should tell your readers where you found the information that you are using, so that if they want to do some research on the same subject themselves, they can follow your lead.

There are several prescribed methods for citing borrowed information. The one that we use here was developed by the Modern Language Association, an organization of college English and foreign language teachers. It is the prescribed method for citing sources in articles appearing in that association's journal, *PMLA: Publications of the Modern Language Association.* Many other journals and periodicals that treat literary topics also use the MLA method of citation. Other organizations specify slightly different citation practices: the American Psychological Association, the Linguistic Society of America, the American Medical Association, and so on. In the course of a college career you may be obliged to use several citation methods. Regardless of their differences in detail, all methods have two things in common:

1. Each provides for a method of citing borrowed information within the text of an article.
2. Each provides a method of recording, at the end of the essay, article, or report, the list of sources from which material was borrowed.

Using the MLA method of citation, we will describe each of these parts of the citation procedure. (Your instructor or supervisor is the final authority, of course, for any documentation matters in a paper or report that you must submit for a class or in a job situation; she or he should be willing to advise you concerning the desired procedures and format.)

CITING SOURCES IN THE TEXT

As we mentioned earlier, borrowed information may take two forms: directly quoted material or summarized material. We will look first at direct quotations.

Directly Quoted Material. Quotations that run less than five lines may be included within a paragraph of the text. Such quotations are almost always introduced by some lead-in like the following: *Janis Brown recently observed* or *William Green, writing for the local newspaper, stated the case in this way.* The quotations then follow these lead-ins and, of course, are enclosed in quotation marks and, unless obviously shortened, begin with a capital letter.

Sometimes it is useful to customize the quotation so that it fits the lead-in's syntax better. Often you will save considerable space and also gain clarity by doing so. Ordinarily omissions are signaled with ellipsis dots (three spaced periods . . .), while additions, changes, or insertions are placed in square brackets [added].

Long quotations (five lines or more) are indented ten spaces from the left margin and double-spaced. Such quotations must also be introduced by an appropriate lead-in, but they should not be indicated by quotation marks.

Each of these three types of quoted borrowings must be followed by a page number (or numbers) in parentheses, indicating the page(s) where the borrowed material originally occurred. Here are illustrations of these three techniques, with quotations drawn from Drucker's "What Employees Need Most."

Short Quotation

According to Peter Drucker, "Ours has become a society of employees" (155).

Long Quotation, with lead-in

Peter Drucker has observed that our world is changing:

Ours has become a society of employees. A hundred years or so ago only one out of every five Americans was employed, i.e., worked for somebody else. Today only one out of every five is not employed but working for himself (155).

Quotation, abbreviated to fit the syntax of the lead-in

Peter Drucker notes that we are now "a society of employees . . . [where] only one out of every five . . . work[s] for [her]self" (155).

(Note here how the ellipsis marks serve to show where deletions from the original have occurred. The information enclosed in brackets [   ] indicates minor adjustments that have been made to the original.)

If the lead-in to the quotation does not include the author's name, and it is not therefore clear who made the quoted statement, then the name should precede the page number that appears at the quotation's end, as in this example:

> One observer has noted, "Ours has become a society of employees" (Drucker 155).

(**Note:** MLA form does not use either a comma or the abbreviation p. between the author's name and the source's page number.)

CITING SUMMARIZED INFORMATION

Summaries of borrowed material are more useful and thus more frequently used than directly quoted borrowings. Here are two examples of ways that the above passage from Drucker might have been summarized and cited:

> Drucker claims that we are increasingly becoming a nation of employees, where only about twenty percent of the people work for themselves (155).

or

> Today we have become a nation of employees, where, according to one leading authority, only twenty percent of the people work for themselves (Drucker 155).

(Note that even in summarized material lead-ins are expected, and page citations are required.)

Occasionally, you may be directed to "suppress documentation." This expression, used by the editors of newspapers and of some magazines, means to avoid the use of parenthetical or other page citations, as well as the usual listing of sources at an article's end. Such is the case in a number of articles in this book; for instance, look at Turbak's "Plastic: Sixty Billion Pounds of Trouble," in which facts, quotations, and summaries appear without parenthetical page citations. If you are directed to suppress documentation, then it is all the more important that you employ your tags or lead-ins effectively to indicate the sources of your borrowings—as Turbak did. You might even go so far as to elaborate the tag this way:

> As early as 1952, Peter Drucker, writing in *Fortune* magazine, noted that we have turned into "a society of employees."

Such a tactic incorporates into the lead-in most of the facts usually documented in the works cited listing at the end of the article.

THE LISTING OF WORKS CITED

The listing of works cited, also called "bibliographical entries," appears at the end of a documented article under the heading "Works Cited." There should be one entry for each separate work from which you have borrowed information, and these entries are double-spaced and arranged *alphabetically* according to the last names of their authors. (If the name of the author is not known or is not included with the article, the article is listed alphabetically according to the first major word in its title.)

Bibliographical entries usually contain the following information:

1. For books: author's name (last name first), title (underlined), place of publication, publisher, and date of publication.
2. For magazine articles: author's name (last name first), title (in quotation marks), name of magazine (underlined), volume number, date of issue, and the article's inclusive page numbers.
3. For newspaper articles: author's name, if available (last name first), title (in quotation marks), name of the newspaper (underlined), date of issue, and inclusive page numbers.

Here are some typical entries that illustrate these three most frequently occurring types:

Books

Holmes, Charlotte. <u>Gifts and Other Stories</u>. Lewiston: Confluence, 1994.

The author's last name begins the entry, so that alphabetical listing may be based on last names. The title is underlined in typescript (or italicized in printed works). The place of publication is separated by a colon from the publisher's name, and the publication date appears after a comma; the entry ends with a period. This information is normally all found on the book's title page, except for the date, which appears on the reverse of that page.

Finegan, Edward, and Niko Bisnier. <u>Language: Its Structure and Use</u>. San Diego: Harcourt, 1989.

Here there are two authors. Notice that only the name of the first one appears last name first. The subtitle, *Its Structure and Use,* is separated from the major title, *Language,* by a colon. Only the first place of publication listed on the title page is used in the entry, together with a shortened version of the publisher's name, Harcourt Brace Jovanovich, Publishers. The second line is indented five spaces so that the authors' names, used for placing the citations in alphabetical order, can be more easily scanned when a reader is seeking to locate particular citations.

Magazines

Barnett, Rosalind, and Caryl Rivers. "Look Who's Talking About Work and Family." <u>Ms.</u> July/Aug. 1996: 34-36.

Headden, Susan. "Danger at the Drug Store." <u>U.S. News & World Report</u> 26 August 1996: 46-51, 53.

Snow, Robert L. "From Gumshoe to Gamma Rays." <u>The Writer</u> March 1994: 16-18.

The title of the article is enclosed in quotation marks; the name of the magazine is underlined. The inclusive page numbers follow the colon after the date.

Scholarly Journals

1. Journals with continuous pagination

Wells, Susan. "Rogue Cops and Health Care: What Do We Want from Public Writing?" <u>College Composition and Communication</u> 47 (1996): 325-41.

For articles from scholarly or professional journals, you must notice whether the pagination of the issue you are using begins with page 1 or with some higher number. In this case, even though the Wells article is the first in this issue, page 1 of this journal occurred two issues earlier, at the beginning of Volume 47. Because the pagination continues throughout the volume, which contains four separate issues, you need not mention either the number of this issue (3) or the month it appeared (October).

2. Journals that begin each issue with page 1

Laabs, Jennifer S. "Sexual Harassment." <u>Personnel Journal</u> 74.2 (1995): 36-46.

Although this is the second issue number in Volume 74, each issue of *Personnel Journal* begins with page 1; consequently, the issue number must appear with the volume number in this entry to identify the source sufficiently.

Newspapers

Pincus, Walter. "Intelligence Agency Chiefs Report Advancement on Bias Issue." <u>Washington Post</u> 21 Sept. 1994: A18.

Tyson, Ann Scott. "US Companies Move to Curb Sexual Harassment on Job." <u>Christian Science Monitor</u> 30 May 1996: 1.

Electronic Sources

The rapidly expanding availability of an array of electronic sources for information makes both using and citing them an increasing probability for most users of this book. At the same time, these electronic resources seem to be changing on an almost daily basis, driven by technological innovations. In general, when using these resources to add facts and insights to your own writing, you must provide essentially the same information in the same order and form that would be required if the work cited had been in printed form. However, you must add three more elements of information: (1) the medium of the source (CD-ROM, on-line database, WorldWide Web, etc.); (2) any publisher or vendor's name (Infotrac, ERIC, First Search, etc.); and (3) the date either of electronic publication (for CD-ROMs and other portable databases, such as diskettes, that do not change) or of access (for on-line sources that can or do change, such as databases, List Servers, and Web Sites).

The most familiar and accessible printed general guide to citing electronic sources for many of you is probably in Sections 4.8 ("Citing CD-ROMS and Other Portable Databases") and 4.9 ("Citing On-line Databases") of the *MLA Handbook for Writers of Research Papers*, 4th ed., edited by Joseph Gibaldi (New York: MLA, 1995). The publisher of this textbook also has available the *Allyn and Bacon Guide to Using and Documenting Electronic Sources*, which not only covers a wider range of possible citation circumstances but also provides specific guidance on accessing electronic resources for research purposes.

If you have WorldWide Web access, there are two particularly good sites for getting help with electronic citation. One is Purdue

University's On-line Writing Lab (or OWL), with its "Citing Electronic Sources" (http://owl.english.purdue.edu/Files/110.html). It also has a link to the most complete list we have found for getting more information on citations. This is the International Federation of Library Associations' "Citation Guides for Electronic Documents" (http://www.nlc-bnc.ca/ifla/I/training/citation/citing.htm).

Here are examples of how to cite the two basic forms of electronic resources, followed by guidelines for each form.

1. CD-ROMs and other portable databases, such as diskettes

```
Gibbs, Nancy. "'Til Death Do Us Part." TIME 18 Jan.
    1993: 38+. TIME Almanac. CD-ROM. Washington: Compact,
    1994.
```

For portable electronic databases, provide the following information in this order, normally separating each numbered element by periods, except 3 and 4, which are separated by a colon plus one space:

1. Name of author (if available)
2. Title of material used (in quotation marks, except underlined if the item would have been separately published in printed form, such as a pamphlet or book)
3. Date (if available)
4. Number of pages or paragraphs (if available)
5. Publication medium (CD-ROM, diskette, etc.)
6. City of publication (if available, then followed by a colon instead of a period)
7. Publisher (if available, then followed by a comma and the year of publication, as in the example above)
8. Year of publication

2. Online sources (computer databases, Internet, etc.)

```
Krugman, Paul. "Two Cheers for the Welfare State." For-
    tune 1 May 1995: 41 (2 pp.). Infotrac: Expanded Acade-
    mic ASAP. Online. 17 Oct. 1996.
Singleton, Dan. "Gun Control Laws Betray Intent of Consti-
    tution." The Oklahoma Daily Online 2 April 1996:15 par.
    Online. Internet: WWW. http://www.uoknor.edu/okdaily/
    issues/spring1996/apr-02/gun-processed.html. 3 Nov.
    1996.
```

For online sources, provide the following information in this order, separating each numbered element by periods, except 3 and 4, which are separated by a colon plus one space:

1. Name of author (if available)
2. Title of material used (in quotation marks, except underlined if the item would have been separately published in printed form, such as a pamphlet or book)
3. Date (if available)
4. Number of pages or paragraphs (if available)
S. Database title, underlined (if applicable)
7. Publication medium (use the word Online here)
8. Name of computer network or service or electronic address
9. Date of computer access

We will end this list of example entries here with this warning: We have not attempted to provide you with an exhaustive list of every possible entry. In your search for source materials you will surely encounter books, magazines, and newspapers that will require you to include other types of documentation that we have not illustrated here: names of editors, translators, edition numbers, volume numbers, and the like. We make no apologies for these omissions; rather we encourage you to consult a standard reference grammar or handbook for a more exhaustive list of illustrated entries. You should own such a book, just as you should own a hardbound dictionary; they are a writer's basic tools.

We do not apologize either for limiting our discussion to the MLA style of documentation. Other formats exist, and it will be your task to become familiar with the ones that are required of you. Here we have sought to provide you with a general idea of the following:

1. the sorts of borrowed information that should be cited
2. the use of tags or lead-ins and parenthetical notes for
   a. directly quoted material
   b. summarized borrowings
3. the bibliographical entries in lists of works cited.

Furthermore, we realize that one of the reasons for using a book such as this is to save a certain amount of trouble that is involved in library research, locating materials to consult during your brainstorming process. We have provided you with a generous number of readings ranging over many controversial issues, articles that you may read and ponder to sharpen your opinions or to provide you with opinions where you held no deep prior convictions. Furthermore, after the discussion questions which follow each cluster of related essays in the "Varying Voices" readings section, we have provided a short list of additional essays on the same general topic, with their bibliographic information in MLA form.

In the spirit of helping you to save the time and effort of doing library research while you concentrate on the more important skills involved in organizing and executing an argumentative essay, we thus have provided you with enough source materials to support a great many claims that you might wish to make.

That concludes our treatment of how you should construct the middle portion of your arguments. Now let us examine how to make good beginnings and good conclusions.

Background

How many times have you glanced at the "Letters to the Editor" section of your local newspaper's editorial page and seen something like this:

> I don't know where Bill Champion thinks he will get the money to support this latest bit of idiocy, but if he has any intention of raising taxes, then he can start right now hunting for another job next year, because those of us who know better are going to see that he won't misuse any more of our hard-earned money.

Crank letters like this one are written every day by people who are convinced that everyone in the world shares their innermost concerns. They do not, therefore, bother to inform their readers about Bill Champion's identity or exactly what his "latest bit of idiocy" might be. As the letter unfolds, we can begin to deduce that Champion must be a local politician and that the "idiocy" must involve some expenditure of taxpayers' money. Beyond that, the message is limited to Bill Champion (he might understand) and the crank's closest friends—and perhaps not even to them.

To avoid the label of "crank," everyone who argues a point owes the audience a suitable *background*. That is, the audience must be provided with sufficient information, so that they will be able to understand fully the claim that is being made, as well as the support for it. In this case, we, the audience, deserve to know just what Bill Champion's claim of policy is and how he intends to support it. We must also be reminded who Champion is, just in case we are not as informed on local current events as the letter writer. Then, and only then, do we need to learn the crank's reasons for believing the plan to be unworthy of our support.

Considerations like the ones we have just mentioned are what background is all about, and without background information most arguments are doomed, because no audience, however well informed, is likely to be warmly receptive to an argument that begins abruptly with the claim.

Even Jesse Jackson, who begins his argument with the extended analogy of the runner with the weighted ankles, hastens at once to draw similarities between this unfair foot race and the situation in which African Americans find themselves as they compete for education and jobs. Without this background information, readers would not be able to follow the line of reasoning suggested by the analogy.

Similarly, Loren Eiseley begins by sharing a friend's letter, which contained a note of concern over the supposed survival of the tough-minded. This approach allows Eiseley to introduce references to the evolutionists Darwin and Wallace and to reassure the audience that the popular notions of survival of the fittest associated with evolution are poorly understood. Having introduced us to the problem, Eiseley is ready to resolve it.

A good rule of thumb to use in preparing background for your argument is simply to ask yourself, "What information would a reasonably intelligent person need to know in order to understand my claim?" You are certainly not obliged to direct your argument to the most foolish or ignorant members of your audience, but you are better off veering in that direction than in supposing that your audience knows as much as you do about the subject.

Gaining Attention

In addition to providing background information, the introduction to an argument should get its readers' attention. It's always a good idea to remember that in most writing situations your audience is under no obligation to read your argument. You are much more likely to succeed if you can provide a "hook" or "grabber" that will capture the readers' interest, keeping them turning the pages until you've had your say.

Here are a number of attention getters that usually work:

1. Tell a story. (Remember how effective Jesse Jackson's story about the race proved to be.)

2. Ask a question. (Should America quit using pennies?)
3. Pose a paradox. (Mankind has survived through tenderness, not toughness.)
4. Make a startling statement. (As an ex-prisoner of war, it hurts me to see our country's flag burned, but I part company with those who want to punish flag burners.)
5. Make lists. (That's what we're doing here.)
6. Use humor. (I can think of only two things that women do better than men: having babies is one; driving is the other.)

Telling a story is a good strategy because all of us are susceptible to stories: we simply like them. Of course, the story should not be so long and detailed that it detracts from the purpose it serves. Jackson's story about the unequal foot race and Eiseley's reference to his friend's concern over his daughter's schooling are about the right length to serve as a hook without getting in the way of the argument. Additionally, each serves in a most effective way to provide background information.

The question, the paradox, and the startling statement are all part of the same strategy: They get your reader to thinking about the claim you are prepared to support. If the reader is uncertain about the answer to the question or perplexed by the paradox or the unexpected statement, then your hook has served its purpose; you have the reader's attention.

Using a list is another especially effective attention getter. Besides providing the reader with a highly organized capsule of the forthcoming argument, it is *visually* effective. The reader's eye is drawn to the list because it is different from other things on the printed page—as are illustrations, charts, or graphs. Once the eye is attracted, the mind is likely to follow, and the audience is "hooked" into reading further.

Finally, humor is useful as a hook for the same reason that the story is: Most of us enjoy a good chuckle. If the humor is directed toward or associated with the claim you are about to make and support, so much the better. Perhaps, though, you have listened to speakers who began by telling the latest joke they had heard, with little regard for how appropriate it was to the subject of their speech. While such jokes fail as "hooks" or attention grabbers, they do serve another purpose, and that is why they are so often part of speeches: they help to make the audience more at ease and favorably inclined toward the speaker. They are a first step toward *gaining credibility*, which you have already seen lends *ethos*, or ethical appeal, to your argument.

Conclusions

All good things must end, and so must the arguments that you construct. While there is something to be said for shutting up when you have had your say, it is not good to conclude too abruptly. Conclusions are, as a rule, the place for two sorts of things: summaries and appeals, either to ethics or to emotions.

A summary is an excellent way to tie up the scattered ends of an argument, reminding the audience briefly of the ground that has been covered—the claim or claims and their pieces of support. Creating summaries is something that you should be fairly good at by now, having summarized several arguments—or parts of them—to support your own. It should be a pleasant change to begin a conclusion by summarizing your *own* argument. That, you will recall, is precisely what Loren Eiseley did in his concluding paragraph:

> Man's first normal experience of life involves maternal and paternal care and affection. It continues over the years of childhood. Thus the creature who strives at times to deny the love within himself, to reject the responsibilities to which he owes his own existence, who grows vocal about "tough-mindedness" and "the struggle for existence," is striving to reject his own human heritage. For without the mysteriously increased growth rate of the brain and the correlated willingness of fallible, loving adults to spend years in nursing the helpless offspring they have produced, man would long since have vanished from the earth.

It is all there: the repeated claim that tenderness outweighs toughness because of the extended human childhood needed for increased brainpower, with the resulting need for paternal and maternal care and affection. Eiseley manages to restate his argument with great economy, and that too is important. Like the background statement, the summary should not be so long that it's tedious. Besides, you may wish to follow the summary with an ethical or emotional appeal.

Cicero, the famous Roman orator, insisted that the concluding portion of a speech should be reserved for those kinds of appeal that would earn the speaker the sympathy of the audience. We have already touched upon such appeals—ethical and emotional—as effective means of gaining support for your claims. You may choose to use them in the main body of your argument, or, like Cicero, you may decide to save them for your conclusion.

Certainly Cullen Murphy makes an ethical appeal when he concludes his plea to save the penny with these words: "Elimination of the penny might afford some slight physical convenience, but the total social cost exceeds what a liberal democracy ought to countenance." It is an ethical appeal because it reminds us of our obligations as citizens of a democracy—to work for and protect the common good, the *ethos* of our civilization.

If that reminder to our consciences touches our hearts as well, so much the better. Ethics and emotions—*ethos* and *pathos*—are for most of us inextricably entwined; thus it would be quite difficult for us to decide whether Jefferson's concluding appeal in the Declaration of Independence is ethical or emotional: "And for the support of this Declaration, with a firm reliance on the protection of Divine Providence, we mutually pledge to each other our lives, our fortunes and our sacred Honor."

Even Phyllis McGinley's amusing treatment of men and women drivers manages to strike an emotional chord in its conclusion, where she takes a bittersweet glance into the future and imagines an afterlife adventure in which her husband's persistent bad driving habits underscore her claim one last time.

We'll conclude here by summing up our basic advice: State your claims, organize your support, cite your sources, and consider your audience, measuring the logical, ethical, and emotional appeal that your case will need to produce.

You're now prepared to construct effective arguments. We hope you convince a lot of people.

PART TWO

Reading and Analyzing Arguments

Reading arguments is not completely new to you, of course. However, you probably have listened to and otherwise participated in spoken arguments much more often. This is particularly true if you like to watch televised talk shows or court room dramas. In fact, because so many persuasive situations involve speaking and listening, it might be ideal if we could provide a demonstration videotape, so that we could also help you learn how to listen to and analyze spoken arguments in an immediate, fairly realistic way.

However, we must necessarily limit ourselves to providing samples of written arguments (a few originally presented as speeches), and to putting emphasis on reading and analyzing those written arguments. Most of these samples will be complete essays, although sometimes we will provide shorter pieces, such as single paragraphs or excerpted groups of paragraphs from longer arguments. It should be obvious, by the way, that as you learn to read and analyze written arguments, and to write and revise your own arguments, you will become more proficient in listening carefully and analytically to spoken arguments, as well as in responding to them through spoken or written words.

As for the actual tasks of reading and analyzing written arguments, you already know that we all must make special efforts to understand anything of much complexity, whether it is a concrete object (such as a mechanism or a living organism) or an abstraction (such as a religious belief or a psychological condition—or a written argument). Understanding arguments and the arguing process, whose complexity has already been examined earlier in this book, is therefore generally not a simple or an easy task; doing so will demand mental alertness and persistent effort on your part. Even more of that alertness and effort will be required when you are putting your own arguments in written or spoken form.

Nevertheless your efforts to understand argumentation, as audience, critic, and creator, will provide significant, even crucial, rewards both to you and to others. Ignoring, standing idly by, or turning your back on human challenges, especially moral ones, can put you in undesirable circumstances, such as those described by the German Lutheran pastor, Martin Niemoeller. Speaking of the Holocaust perpetrated by the Nazis under Adolf Hitler's leadership before and during World War II, Pastor Niemoeller recalled, "They came first for the Communists, and I didn't speak up because I wasn't a Communist. Then they came for the trade unionists, and I didn't speak up because I wasn't a trade unionist. Then they came for the Jews, and I didn't speak up because I wasn't a Jew. Then they came for the Catholics, and I didn't speak up because I was a Protestant. Then they came for me, and by that time there was no one left to speak up." As a result of Pastor Niemoeller's reluctance to get involved in what always seemed to be other people's problems, he was indirectly responsible for the suffering and death of some of those other people, spent four years himself in the Dachau concentration camp, and was indeed fortunate to survive when millions of others perished or were executed. Although none of us expect a return to that hellish time, clearly the human stakes of declining to be involved in controversy, or of being ineffective even when actively involved, can become too high before we realize it.

There are two sorts of suggestions we want to make that will help you to read and to analyze arguments most effectively. While they really work together and often overlap, for instructional purposes you are likely to understand and apply them better if we discuss the two separately. The first sort deal with the physical conditions under which you read any argument, and the second sort focus on mental approaches that will improve your reading.

Physical Aids to Reading Arguments

Some of the suggestions concerning physical aids to reading arguments most effectively are commonsense ones; if you are already successfully reading serious pieces of writing, you are likely already applying some or all of them. But for the benefit of those who are struggling to read difficult selections, and therefore probably aren't using these aids, we are going to review them. We'll start with the most obvious suggestions and move to more subtle or uncommon ones.

1. Get rid of or away from all distractions as much as possible. This suggestion perhaps needs little or no comment, but clearly if you cannot focus on your reading because of distracting sounds, lights, views, smells, living creatures (pets, family members, roommates, friends, and the like), and other interruptions, you will have trouble concentrating on—and thus comprehending—the complex features of many arguments. The real difficulty may be, of course, "getting away from" or "rid of" a particular distraction. If the distraction must remain or if you must stay near it, try to at least reduce the degree of distraction. This may mean working out a schedule of quiet or study times with others who live near you, buying earplugs or even a telephone answering machine, or making various other adjustments. In fact, you may have to use the arguing skills you presently have in order to set up the conditions under which you can best improve those skills.

2. Don't get too comfortable. This is another obvious suggestion. But if you are too relaxed, perhaps lying down on a bed or lounging in an overstuffed chair, the mental effort of following an argument may be overwhelmed and you'll find yourself daydreaming—or even asleep, really dreaming. You will be better off at a desk, in a chair that makes you sit up, with good light on what you are reading, and in a room that is cool rather than warm.

3. Read with a pencil or pen in your hand. The only exception to this suggestion is if you are reading an argument in materials that are not your own, such as books or periodicals belonging to a library or another person. Otherwise, you should be actively marking the text, especially in the margins, to indicate key features of the argument, sections that you find confusing or questionable, words that you do not know or understand. It is especially effective to write comments and questions as if you are having a dialogue with the author, for then you are truly engaged or involved with the argument and its subject.

A related hint that some readers find helpful is to let the writing instrument (or your finger) move like a pointer along the line in front of your eyes, leading them through the text; this will tend to keep your attention focused on your reading better, which will improve the efficiency, and therefore the overall speed, with which you complete a piece of reading. You may also find that if you move the pointer at a pace that is a little faster than your normal reading rate, the result will not only be more speed but even better concentration.

4. Have a full-sized dictionary within reach. Dictionaries are the storehouses for meanings of words, of course, and words are the

building blocks of all arguments (all writing, for that matter); you must understand the words a writer uses if you are to understand her or his message. Don't stop to look up words as long as you believe you are getting the gist of the writing. However, you will likely find it useful to make a special marginal mark beside troublesome words in your reading, and then go through later and look up the meanings for any words that are still unclear. Neglecting to perform this task may cause you to misunderstand part or all of an argument.

A related hint: Make a single tick mark in your dictionary beside any word you look up; when you open the dictionary to a word that already has two such marks, go ahead and memorize its meaning, for the word clearly is appearing in your reading often enough that you should learn its meaning for efficiency's and understanding's sake.

Mental Aids to Reading Arguments

Clearly the preceding physical suggestions numbered 3 and 4 also have a mental aspect, thereby furnishing a sort of transition to the following suggestions for improving your mental approach to the reading of argumentative samples of writing. As you consider these suggestions, and as you begin to apply them, you may find it helpful to notice how the suggestions influence you to consider more carefully a reading selection's *content* (what it says), as well as its *form* (how it presents its content).

1. Get an overview of the selection *before* you begin reading it. Do this by considering the piece's title (if it has one), since the titles of many works are attempts to put in capsule form the main subject and thesis. For instance, such titles as "In Defense of Voluntary Euthanasia," "Death Penalty's False Promise: An Eye for in Eye," and "The Dangers of Disarming" all not only reveal their basic subjects but even indicate their authors' attitudes toward those subjects; thoughtfully considering such titles, then, can make your job as a reader easier from the start. (All titles are not so helpful, of course; consider what the subjects might be for these, all used for argumentative essays: "Facing Reality," "In the American Grain," and "Sharing the Land and the Legacy.")

Also consider any information provided about the author or authors, or any information that you already have. For instance, if you read newspaper editorial pages regularly, you soon will come to recognize the normal political stance of most syndicated columnists; thus you will expect Ellen Goodman and David Broder to take a liberal position on such questions as abortion rights or welfare reform, while Linda Chavez and George Will typically take conservative positions. Furthermore, consider the author's real or probable expertise concerning the subject she or he is discussing; for instance, a Nobel prize-winning physicist may be too far out of his realm of knowledge in discussing cures for AIDS, and a great heart surgeon may have little worthwhile to add to a debate on nuclear arms control. Of course, there is a natural human tendency to assume that a person with notable skill or expertise in one realm of activity should be accepted as a knowledgeable authority in another realm; hence, we frequently see media personalities, such as actresses, pop singers, and sports stars, in advertisements where they promote all sorts of consumer products, as if they were experts on fashion, nutrition, or transportation. You will recall, though, that in an argument this is the fallacy of *transfer*.

After considering the title and any author background, look for summaries of the work in such places as the table of contents (for some periodicals and collections of essays), the introduction (for both books and essays), the dust-jacket covers and flaps (for books). If you are reading a book, look at the table of contents and chapter headings in particular, and if reading an essay, flip through it, paying attention to any subheadings or section titles. All of the foregoing can give you a good sense of what you are likely to find in the work itself, especially with regard to its subject, the author's stance on that subject, and the discussion's organization.

2. Pay particular attention to the introductory paragraph or paragraphs of the work, especially when reading essays or single chapters; if the work is a book, give its preface full attention. Do so because it is in these places that authors often explain the purpose and scope of an essay, a chapter, or a book in brief, clear language, no matter how long and complex the work itself may be. Using such clues, try to figure out the author's thesis or main point. It's also a good idea at this time to try writing that thesis down in your own words, which leads to the next suggestion.

3. As you read an argument, pause occasionally to make a concrete record of your reading and understanding of the previous portion. Here you are trying to understand the work better by doing something with it, going beyond merely reading the words. The textual and marginal notes you make (see Physical Suggestion 3) are tied to this suggestion, of course. In particular you may find it useful to mark some or even all transitional words (such as *because, also, but, therefore*) and transitional phrases (such as *on the one hand, not only, in conclusion*), since these typically are clear signals

of steps or phases of the argument. You may also find it useful to number the key parts of the argument in the margins, perhaps using traditional outlining notation (I, IA, IB, II, III, IIIA, IIIB, and so on) as a concrete aid to understanding the argument's structure.

Beyond those notes you will find that creating some written record of your reading on a separate sheet of paper, perhaps also in outline form, will be of great value in comprehending the argument more fully, in being able to analyze its strengths and weaknesses, and in later recalling the basic features of the argument without going to the time and trouble of rereading it.

Your outline may be formal, with the customary groupings using Roman numerals, capital letters, Arabic numerals, and the like, or it may be informal, just a series of phrases and key words, perhaps clustered or webbed in patterns that will help you recall the main points and their means of support. The actual note-taking format is less important than the fact that you have made a permanent record of your reading and your understanding of that particular argument.

4. Stay mentally alert and inquisitive as you read an argument by constantly recalling the kinds of questions journalists ask: *Who? What? When? Where? How? Why?* To read, understand, and analyze arguments you cannot be passive, as we all generally are when we watch television and even as we do much of our reading, especially that of a recreational sort (newspaper sports pages, celebrity gossip columns and magazines, popular novels). Rather, you must have an inquiring mind, of the active, probing sort that a good investigative reporter or a detective needs for success at her or his work. Now let's examine in some detail the use of those six one-word questions (investigators call them "basic interrogatives") that you should keep asking mentally as you read; you need to understand the sorts of information about content and about form that you are likely to gain by asking these six questions.

When you ask "Who?", you are going to be seeking two kinds of information. The first is about the author (as discussed earlier in Mental Suggestion 1): his or her expertise concerning the subject of the argument, biases that she or he holds, and the like. The second is about the basic audience for whom the argument was originally intended. As you should probably realize already, writers (and speakers) adapt their language, their styles, their tones, and their supporting examples according to their intended or target audiences. Certainly you would adjust all of these in a dramatically contrasting fashion if you were going to speak on the dangers of drugs to two quite different groups, perhaps today to a first grade class at a nearby elementary school, and tomorrow to a campus group to which you belong. Sometimes the adjustments for a particular audience will be much more subtle, of course, but in any case you should be especially alert for those audience adjustments, since they affect so many aspects of the presentation of the argument.

When you ask "What?", you are focusing on the subject of the argument, figuratively putting it under a strong light for close scrutiny, almost as if you were some sort of research scientist. You want to be aware of every aspect of that subject; here is where your analytical powers really come into play, and where you depend on close, careful reading and other useful resources for better understanding, such as the dictionary. You are trying to ensure that you comprehend as fully as possible both the topic being presented and the author's attitude toward that topic.

When you go on to ask "When?" and "Where?", you will again be considering aspects of audience, for here you want to know the time and place in which this argument was first presented. For example, an argument made in favor of universal military service (the "draft") for young American males changes its basic character when it is made today rather than in 1862 or 1941 or 1967, and it also changes when its principal audience is intended to be members of the U.S. Congress, or the readers of the *New York Times*, of *Business Week*, or of *Rolling Stone*. Ignoring such changes—or even their possibility—puts you at a disadvantage as a reader.

The foregoing questions relate mainly to the content of the piece of writing. But you must also consider its form. When you ask "How?", you are posing an analytical question about the organization and other rhetorical and logical devices of the argument itself. This is probably the most important question of these six as far as improving your own ability to *write* arguments is concerned, for by asking it you will be trying to determine how the author constructed (in every sense of that word) her or his argument. You will be trying to spot the key elements of success and failure in this piece of writing, hoping to adapt the good and avoid the bad as you craft your own arguments.

As you analyze each argument, you are disassembling it, separating it into its components, just as you might do with any mechanism, such as a bicycle or an automobile. Your intent is to figure out how the argument was put together, or assembled, so that through that analysis you can understand not only how it works as a unified piece of writing, but also how it creates its rhetorical effects, for good or ill, on its audience. Accordingly you will look at the argument's organization, which is analogous to the frame of a bike or a car, and its sentences, which move the argument forward, propelling it just as drive trains and wheels and engines and pedals and chains move other mechanisms. You will even look closely at such smaller parts as transitional devices and even individual words; these are in some ways analogous to a vehicle's paint and chrome trim, which may affect our positive or negative opinion of a vehicle that moves flawlessly.

On the other hand, and just like a car or a bike, if something is faulty or out of tune or badly adjusted, the mechanism will falter or perhaps not even move at all, no matter how flashy or impressive it looks. Thus you will need to determine what argumentative strategies are being used in the reading selection, and whether or not they are being used correctly. You will, for instance, want to determine what claims the writer is making, and how those claims are supported. Which is the writer using, induction or deduction?

As you gain experience in doing this sort of disassembly, learning to spot more quickly any flaws anywhere, you will become not just a better reader but also a better writer. For when you go to create or assemble your own argumentative mechanisms, you will have a much better sense of which parts fit where and how they should be adjusted to run most smoothly. Instead of analysis, you will then be performing even more complicated acts. You will be synthesizing content and form, joining your ideas and their supporting facts with the other pieces of writing (words, phrases, sentences, grammar, punctuation, organization, argumentative techniques, and the like), checking their fit and adjustment (revising and rewriting), performing road tests (reading the argument aloud or to others, or having them read it and react), before you take the argument on a trip to meet the public, which may consist of your instructor, a supervisor, a committee, or some other audience—perhaps thousands of miles away.

When you move on and reach the last of the investigator's questions, you will ask "Why?" Here you are again considering the author, especially his or her purpose in writing this particular argument. What personal stake might she or he have in this subject? Was she or he paid by some special interest group for writing this argument? Why did he or she choose to publish it in this particular periodical, when it clearly might have appeared elsewhere?

You will also want to consider the argument's warrant, and you must try to determine the sorts of appeals being used: ethical, emotional, or logical. Then you must ask why you or any member of the piece's reading audience should accept the writer's argument. For instance, is there some universal warrant present, to which the writer is appealing? Is the strength of that warrant determined by its logical appeal, or by ethical or emotional considerations?

The answers to questions such as these will help you determine any biases the author may have, and thus will help you decide whether to accept part, all, or none of the writer's argument. You must not become too suspicious of motives, of course, or you will likely lapse into a cynicism that will destroy your ability to trust any other human beings. On the other hand, you certainly cannot read arguments analytically by accepting them at their face value, with your rose-colored glasses in place; then you and your innocence will get steamrolled by the world's realists and hypocrites, who often end up in positions of power and leadership.

Practicing the Suggestions for Reading Arguments

Now the time has come to practice the four physical and four mental suggestions for reading and analyzing arguments. If you haven't already done so, try right now to make all of the physical adjustments that we suggested: get rid of distractions, get somewhat uncomfortable, read with a pencil or pen in your hand, and have a dictionary nearby. Recalling the four mental suggestions, get an overview of the essay that follows before you read it, by considering its title and its author's background, plus any other useful surface information. Then remember to notice in particular the opening paragraphs and also to make some notes in the margin and the text of the essay. Most importantly, you should try to answer the journalist's six questions, giving careful attention to what those help you learn about the essay's content and its form.

The following essay appeared in the August 7, 1989, issue of *Air Force Times*, a civilian-owned weekly newspaper whose principal readers are active, reserve, and retired U.S. Air Force commissioned and enlisted personnel. The author, James H. Warner, is a Washington, DC, lawyer. As a Marine Corps pilot, Warner was a Vietnamese prisoner of war from October 1967 to March 1973.

Freedom—Even for Those Who Burn Flag

JAMES H. WARNER

In March 1973, when we were released from a prisoner of war   1
camp in North Vietnam, we were flown to Clark Air Base in the Philippines. As I stepped out of the aircraft, I looked up and saw the

flag. I caught my breath; then, as tears filled my eyes, I saluted it. I never loved my country more than at that moment.

Although I have received the Silver Star and two Purple Hearts, they were nothing compared with the gratitude I felt then for having been allowed to serve the cause of freedom.   2

Because the mere sight of the flag meant so much to me after 5½ years as a prisoner, it hurts me to see other Americans willfully desecrate it. But I have been in a communist prison and looked into the pit of hell. I cannot compromise on freedom. It hurts to see the flag burned, but I part company with those who want to punish flag burners.   3

Early in the imprisonment, the communists told us that we did not have to stay there. If only we would admit we were wrong, we could be released early. If we did not, we would be punished. A handful accepted, most did not. In our minds, early release under those conditions would amount to a betrayal of our comrades, of our country and of our flag.   4

Because we would not say the words they wanted us to say, they made our lives wretched. Most of us were tortured, and some of my comrades died. I was tortured for most of the summer of 1969. I developed beriberi from malnutrition. I had long bouts of dysentery. I was infested with intestinal parasites. I spent 13 months in solitary confinement. Was our cause worth all of this? Yes, and more.   5

Rose Wilder Lane, in her magnificent book *The Discovery Of Freedom*, said there are two fundamental truths that men must know in order to be free. They must know that all men are brothers, and they must know that all men are born free. Once men accept these two ideas, they never will accept bondage. The power of these ideas explains why it was illegal to teach slaves to read.   6

One can teach these ideas, even in a communist prison camp. Marxists believe that ideas are merely the product of material conditions; change those material conditions, and one will change the ideas they produce. They tried to "re-educate" us. If we could show them that we would not abandon our belief in fundamental principles, then we could prove the falseness of their doctrine. We could subvert them by teaching them about freedom through our example. We could show them the power of ideas. I did not appreciate this power before I was a prisoner of war.   7

I remember one interrogation where I was shown a photograph of some Americans protesting the war by burning a flag. "There," the officer said. "People in your country protest against your cause. That proves that you are wrong."   8

"No," I said. "That proves that I am right. In my country we are not afraid of freedom, even if it means that people disagree with us."   9

The officer was on his feet in an instant. He smashed his fist onto the table and screamed at me to shut up. I was astonished to see pain, compounded by fear, in his eyes. I have never forgotten the satisfaction I felt at using his tool against him.

Aneurin Bevan, former official of the British Labor Party, once   10 was asked by Nikita Khrushchev how the British definition of democracy differed from the Soviet view. Bevan responded that if Khrushchev really wanted to know the difference, he should read the funeral oration of Pericles.

In that speech, recorded in the Second Book of Thucydides' *His-*   11 *tory of the Peloponnesian War,* Pericles contrasted democratic Athens with totalitarian Sparta. Unlike the Spartans, he said, the Athenians did not fear freedom. Rather, they viewed freedom as the very source of their strength. As it was for Athens, so it is for America.

We don't need to amend the Constitution in order to punish   12 those who burn our flag. They burn the flag because they hate America and they are afraid of freedom. What better way to hurt them than with the subversive idea of freedom? Spread freedom; it is the best weapon we have.

Warner's essay was short enough that you shouldn't have fallen asleep, and we hope you had no major—or even minor—distractions while you were reading it. As you look over the essay again, you may notice that you marked a few words whose meanings weren't made clear by their contexts, such as *desecrate* in paragraph 2, *beriberi* in 5, *subvert* in 7, plus perhaps a few more. For any puzzling words, now use your dictionary, remembering to put a tick mark beside each problem word you look up.

Review the notes you made in the essay's margins, plus any you made separately. (You may even want to reread the essay and make more notes or even a summary, often a necessary task for analyzing and understanding arguments, especially ones that are longer and more complex than Warner's.) First, let's consider some things you should have noticed about its content when you tried to get an overview of the essay. You learned from the title that the general subject was burning the flag, and that Warner supported freedom for those who do so. His attitude may have struck you as surprising, since as a former prisoner of war Warner might be expected to be an especially fervent patriot. You may recall, too, that in recent years federal courts have ruled that American citizens have the Constitutional right to burn and otherwise desecrate their nation's flag without punishment. Such legal decisions have not only provoked strong criticism from a range of persons across the country, from U.S. presidents and members of Congress to ordinary citizens, but many military veterans and their organizations such as the American Legion have also campaigned vigorously for an amendment to the Constitution to prohibit and punish such behavior.

Yet here is Warner, who spent 5½ years in a North Vietnamese prison (paragraphs 1, 3) and was decorated for bravery (2), announcing in his essay's title that he supports other citizens' freedom to dishonor the flag that brought tears to his eyes when he first saw it after his release from prison (1). You should also have noticed that Warner is a lawyer, and thus professionally trained to comment on legal questions. Furthermore, he lives and works in our nation's capital, where he should have a heightened sense of government, laws, and patriotism. After all, the executive, legislative, and judicial branches of our government are headquartered there, and monuments to such great national leaders as Washington, Jefferson, and Lincoln are prominent landmarks in the city.

What did you notice when you took our suggestion to examine closely the opening paragraphs of this essay? You may have been a little surprised at Warner's organization of his material, the form that he chose for presenting it to us. He goes back in time, to report an episode over sixteen years earlier, and spends his first two paragraphs discussing that experience before announcing his thesis in the last two sentences of paragraph 3. As you analyzed or disassembled his argument further, you should have noticed that twice more (paragraphs 4–5, 8–9) Warner goes back in time, to his prisoner of war experiences. Why do you suppose he goes back so often, and what does his argument gain by his recounting of those earlier times?

As we look at another aspect of his essay, you will recall that earlier in this book much was said about using authorities to provide support for arguments. Certainly Warner, after 5½ years of sickness and torture, including 13 months in solitary confinement, should be an expert on what freedom means, since he was without it so long. Did you notice, though, that he also uses references to others that he considers authorities on freedom? First, he goes so far as to use the label "magnificent" for Rose Wilder Lane's book *The Discovery of Freedom* before he summarizes one of her main points (6); then he uses that point in explaining how it took his prisoner of war experiences to help him learn the real power of ideas, such as freedom. Next Warner describes an episode involving representatives of British democracy and Marxist communism (10). Their discussion, too, turned to freedom and Aneurin Bevan, the British speaker, used a classical work of history to make his point, that in democratic

Athens freedom was thought to create strength rather than to undermine it (11). Finally Warner compares America to Athens, before wrapping up his argument in the following paragraph. Why does he refer to these other authorities? And what does he expect to gain by comparing today's America to the Athens of over 2000 years ago? These are the sorts of reporter's questions that you need to be constantly asking, ones that will lead you to a fuller understanding of and appreciation for a written argument's content and form.

We now need to consider the strongest portion of Warner's argument, paragraphs 8 and 9, where he describes a Communist interrogating officer's futile attempt to break Warner's commitment to democracy and freedom by showing him a photograph of American antiwar demonstrators burning the flag. Here for the first and only time Warner reports the words spoken in their dialogue, giving the episode a heightened sense of drama and realism, and making this a particularly effective use of narration. Then in four short, emphatic sentences Warner describes his psychological conquest of his captor, when "pain, compounded by fear" invaded the officer's eyes (paragraph 9) and Warner had won their argument about freedom. Warner has wisely organized his material to present his strongest supporting example toward the essay's end, planning there to clinch his point with us readers if he had not already done so.

We will leave this essay after raising two more questions that you also should probably have asked: Why would Warner want his essay published in *Air Force Times,* and why would they want to publish it? Here you must carefully consider the newspaper's audience, just as you should always do, usually as one of your first and most important moves when creating your own arguments.

You are just about ready now to move on to the readings sections of this book. There you will notice that these essays are followed by questions on content and form, much like those we have just asked about Warner's essay on flag burning. You will also find there a variety of suggestions for writing tasks, sometimes directly based on the reading, sometimes on related subjects. You are likely to find it useful to read through those content and form questions, as well as the writing suggestions, *before* you read the essays to which they refer. By doing so, you will get even more of an overview of the essays and will also give yourself additional direction as you read, particularly as you search for answers to the questions. We hope, of course, that you will be trying to apply our four physical and four mental suggestions for improving your reading as you read those essays and any other serious pieces of writing. Most of all, as you read, you should be asking: Who? What? When? Where? How? Why?

Speaking Up: Argumentative Essays on Various Topics

This first collection of reading selections consists of unrelated example essays that concentrate their arguments on topics of current or continuing interest. The order of the essays in this collection is from least to most difficult; length is a secondary arrangement factor, so that typically the early essays are shorter than the later ones.

Each essay in this section should be considered separately, unless your instructor directs you otherwise, and you should concentrate your energies on these aspects of each essay:

1. Understanding the *content* or subject matter, including the words or vocabulary used and any allusions (references) made to current, historical, or literary persons, places, and events.
2. Understanding the essay's *form*, including the organization and the argumentative and rhetorical strategies used.
3. Special features of *language*, such as use of concrete rather than abstract (and specific rather than general) words and phrases, use of foreign or unusual words and phrases, level of difficulty of diction or word choice.
4. Special features of *tone*, particularly in relation to the essay's apparent intended audience.
5. Special features of *style*, such as sentence and paragraph length, sentence variety and complexity, ease and grace of expression, use of figurative language, and the like.
6. *Other features* of the essay that enhance or detract from the essay's effectiveness as a written argument, such as presence or absence of specific, relevant, and clear examples.

As mentioned earlier in the text, your own writing will automatically and naturally be strengthened by your careful and attentive reading of other writers' arguments, especially when you give thoughtful attention to content and form. The questions that we have placed after each essay are therefore a starting place for analytical thought and constructive discussion, while the writing suggestions there may lead either to classroom discussions or to writing assignments for individuals or groups, as your instructor directs. Examining all of each assigned essay's questions and writing suggestions beforehand is a useful way to get ready to read the essay itself most purposefully, thoroughly, and efficiently.

CLAIMS OF FACT

Irresponsible to Allow Companies to Push Credit Cards at Young

B. J. PHILLIPS

All the other credit-card peddlers do the same thing, so the brochure from Citibank—stuffed into the plastic bag with every purchase from the college book store—can be considered typical. 1

On the front are photographs of Citibank Visa and MasterCard credit cards and, in bold print, the reassuring words: NO FEE. NO WORRIES. 2

Just in case an unemployed 18-year-old with no credit history and no visible means of support was doubtful about the wisdom of taking on credit-card debt, the brochure promises that his new Citibank card "makes life simpler . . . [so] you can concentrate on the important parts of college life." 3

It's unclear exactly what a credit card does to simplify math tests and the study of English poetry, but getting the card is certainly a piece of cake: "Applying is as easy as writing your name. There's no co-signer or minimum income required. All you need is a minute and an unchewed pen." 4

Once that's done, students are urged to "just relax. Do what comes naturally at college." 5

The sound you hear is the parents of college students falling over in a dead faint. 6

They know good and well that "what comes naturally" to college students is spending every dime they get their hands on. 7

No sooner do parents take out a second mortgage to send their kids to college than along comes the country's largest bank hawking a four-figure credit line to inexperienced and impulsive freshmen. 8

Make life simpler, the bank says. NO WORRIES. 9

No worries, that is, as long as the student cardholder pays interest rates that "start" at 18.4 percent. If he or she falls behind on payments and the account isn't kept in good standing, the rate can be increased by another 3.5 percentage points. 10

Though there are no firm statistics on how many students are   11
hooked on credit cards, experts who counsel debtors say the inci-
dence is rising.

For students and families, easy credit can mean individual hard-   12
ship. But we all pay a price for their debt.

Meanwhile, the Federal Deposit Insurance Corp. says the 77   13
banks that control four-fifths of the credit-card business more than
doubled their earnings between 1991 and 1996.

QUESTIONS OF CONTENT

1. The apparent impetus for this article was a brochure advertising a
   credit card. Where was the brochure found, and what does this suggest about the scope of the marketing tactics of the U.S. banking industry today?
2. What sort of interest rates are typically required of credit card holders, and how do those compare with those required by Citibank for
   its student credit cards?
3. In paragraph 12, Phillips suggests that credit cards frequently lead to
   financial hardship for students and their families. He concludes by
   saying, "But we all pay a price for their debt." What does he mean
   by that statement?
4. Just how lucrative is the credit card business? Where does Phillips
   indicate this?

QUESTIONS OF FORM

1. Phillips' strategy in this argument is largely one of educating the audience, providing—through claims of fact—information that the audience is not likely to know. How many distinct claims of fact can
   you locate in this brief essay?
2. How would you characterize this argument's tone (i.e., the attitude
   of the writer toward the subject matter and toward the audience)?
   What evidence prompts your judgment? Who seems to be the intended audience for this piece?
3. Does this argument rely on any ethical or emotional appeals? If so,
   how does Phillips accomplish them?

SUGGESTIONS FOR WRITING

1. Are you aware of any other national marketing appeals that are, like
   this one, directed toward college audiences? Write a brief argument,

similar to Phillips', in which you inform your audience about any dangers inherent in one of these other marketing appeals.

2. You return home for a weekend visit to discover that your sister has just recently fallen prey to a television marketing scheme involving the sale of exercise equipment. She now wishes that she had never made the purchase, but she is in a quandary what to do next. She still has ten payments to make. She asks you to help her write a letter to the manufacturer detailing her reasons for returning their product instead of continuing the payments. Try to couch the reply in claims of fact, as Phillips did.

Plastic: Sixty Billion Pounds of Trouble

GARY TURBAK

On a California beach, a seal flops ashore entangled in a section of nylon fishing net. The plastic has cut into the animal's neck, exposing raw and festering flesh. The seal futilely tries to bite through the tough material. Starving and weary from struggling against its man-made tormentor, the mammal lies down to die.

From the high seas to the Rocky Mountains, plastic is killing wildlife, clogging landfills and disfiguring America's natural beauty. The miracle material of yesteryear has evolved into a significant environmental problem that no one really knows how to solve.

"Plastic consumes precious resources, creates toxic chemicals, does not decompose and is generally not recycled. It's a huge problem," said Brian Lipsett, science adviser for the Citizens Clearinghouse for Hazardous Waste.

First used in 1868 as a substitute for ivory billiard balls, "plastic" is now the generic term for thousands of different polymers which are synthesized primarily from petroleum. Now more common than steel, aluminum and copper combined, plastic appears in everything from artificial hearts to Army helmets; it can be as strong or soft, rigid or flimsy, transparent or opaque as scientists want it to be. Above all else, the stuff endures. The plastic you throw in the trash today may still be there 400 years from now.

As litter, plastic is unsightly and deadly. Birds and small animals die after getting stuck in plastic, six-pack beverage rings. Pelicans accidentally hang themselves with discarded plastic fishing line. Turtles choke on plastic bags or starve when their stomachs become clogged with hard-to-excrete, crumbled plastic. Sea lions poke their heads into plastic rings and have their jaws locked permanently shut. Authorities estimate that plastic refuse annually kills up to 2 million birds and at least 100,000 mammals.

The worst killers of all are plastic drift nets—the strong, two-inch mesh used by commercial fishing fleets. Buoyed at the top, weighted at the bottom and extending for up to 40 miles, the nets become lethal, sea-bound roadblocks that entangle and drown a teeming menagerie of victims. Tens of thousands of seals and a host of sea-going birds, turtles, dolphins and other animals die each year in the nets. When a net is lost or discarded, which happens thousands of times each year, it may travel the seas indefinitely as a silent, phantom killer. 6

Often, seaborne plastic trash comes ashore in the form of everything from AIDS-contaminated medical waste to condoms to disposable diapers. On some beaches, plastic tampon applicators are so ubiquitous they're referred to as "Jersey seashells." In 1987, volunteers cleaned 157 miles of Texas beach and collected more than 200 tons of plastic litter. A one-day scouring of 150 miles of Oregon shoreline yielded 26 tons of plastic. 7

Who's to blame? 8

"When plastic becomes a nuisance in the marine environment, the problem usually lies with people and the way they use plastic and not with the material itself," said Wayne Pearson, executive director of the Plastics Recycling Foundation, a group of about 50 plastic-packaging companies. Ships dump about 100 million pounds of plastic in the oceans each year, and U.S. Navy vessels contribute four tons per day to that total. 9

Even when plastic is disposed of properly, it can cause problems. Plastic is the fastest-growing component of a solid waste deluge clogging the nation's landfills, one-third of which are expected to reach capacity in the next five years. Manufacturers produce about 60 billion pounds of plastic annually, and we promptly cast more than one-third of it into the environment. Measured by volume, nearly one-third of the nation's garbage is plastic, and some of it—such as fast-food containers—has a useful lifespan of about two minutes. 10

"This is really a situation where we have met the enemy and it is us," said Michael Bean, senior attorney with the Environmental Defense Fund. "We all use plastic because it's tremendously convenient. There is no single villain." 11

Not even the most ardent environmentalist suggests that all plastic be outlawed. The material is simply too useful. Some areas have, however, banned certain kinds of plastic. For example, New York's Suffolk County prohibits plastic grocery bags, and Berkeley, 12

Calif., will soon allow only biodegradable fast-food containers. About 20 states are considering similar measures. In January 1989, the United States and 28 other nations banned the dumping of plastics at sea. The Navy is working to comply by its 1993 target date, but it will take years to clean up what's already there, and enforcement will be difficult.

Another approach is to create plastic that degrades when exposed   13 to sunlight or bacteria. One technique is to mix plastic with cornstarch, which can easily be broken down by microorganisms. Biodegradable plastic garbage bags are available, and 16 states already require that all six-pack rings be degradable. Degradable plastic cannot be used, however, in food containers or long-lived products, and most experts see a limited potential for this solution.

Plastic is, however, a good candidate for recycling—at least in   14 theory. Recycled plastic can be turned into new fencing, flower pots, boat docks, patio furniture and other items. Five two-liter plastic soda bottles will yield a ski jacket, and 36 bottles will provide filling for a sleeping bag. "Within five years we'll be recycling half of all plastic beverage containers and in a decade maybe half of all plastic," Pearson predicts. Currently, though, plastic recycling is a problem-plagued infant, and only 1 percent of the material gets a second life.

In the end, the best solution may simply be to use less plastic.   15 Although glass, paper and other alternatives are often less convenient, they are available. "The big question," said Bean, "is whether we're ready to pay the outrageous environmental price for a little extra convenience, or whether we'll act responsibly to solve the problems associated with plastic."

QUESTIONS OF CONTENT

1. What is plastic made of? When was it first used and for what purpose? Name three plastic items not mentioned by Turbak.
2. What plastic item does Turbak label as the "worst killer" of sea life? Why is it so deadly?
3. What are some of the more repugnant forms of plastic litter that Turbak describes?
4. Who or what is responsible for this inundation of plastic?
5. According to Turbak, why do environmentalists hesitate to argue that all plastic use should be outlawed?
6. What four measures does Turbak mention that are possible ways to reverse this dangerous situation?

QUESTIONS OF FORM

1. In paragraphs 5–7 Turbak makes a claim of fact and supports it inductively. What is that claim? What are the elements of his induction?
2. Turbak quotes two authorities in paragraphs 9 and 11. What is the purpose of their testimony?
3. In paragraph 12, before commencing his policy recommendations, Turbak makes a concession. What is that concession, and what effect does it produce?

SUGGESTIONS FOR WRITING

1. State Turbak's argument as briefly as possible. Try to limit your summary to a single paragraph.
2. What products other than plastic threaten our environment? Think of additional threats to forests, streams, rivers, and oceans; to wild life, both terrestrial and aquatic. Focus on a single harmful product, such as dioxins, nuclear waste, acid rain, carbon dioxide, or chlorofluorocarbons. Then proceed in two steps. Demonstrate that this product or substance indeed poses a threat. You may find it helpful to consult a subject index in your library, such as the *Readers' Guide to Periodical Literature* or, if available, a computer data base, such as Infotrac. Next state your suggestions for remedying the problem. Be sure to give proper credit to any sources that you use.
3. You (or a group of classmates) operate a factory that manufactures Styrofoam plates, cups, and sandwich cartons. Clearly you do not want fast-food chains to return to paper plates, cups, and wrappers. What sort of case can you build for your products? Examine some recent reports on the specific hazards of Styrofoam before responding. While you will not want to propose that outlets use less Styrofoam, you might want to follow Turbak's lead and champion one of his other recommendations. Do so in a concise, well-supported essay describing your solution(s) to the problem.

Frats and Sororities:
The Greek Rites of Exclusion

M. G. LORD

My interest in fraternities began innocently, on a balmy night last fall, when a friend and I attempted to drive across the campus of the University of Michigan at Ann Arbor, where, after ten years as a journalist in New York City, I was back in school on a fellowship. We were heading to a movie that people said had great special effects. I couldn't say. Due to the special effects on the street, we never made it to the theater.

Hundreds of white women swarmed along Hill Street—our route and the university's fraternity row. They huddled in packs, hugging and squealing and sometimes singing, defiantly stopping traffic. The crowd reeked of money: pearl necklaces and the effects of orthodontia were everywhere in evidence. According to statistics on sorority membership at Michigan, there must have been a few blacks and Asians present, but I didn't see any. Just four blocks of blond people—Kewpie doll faces, retroussé noses—a living Leni Riefenstahl tableau.

I've since learned that what I witnessed was part of "Rush," the process by which fraternities and sororities select new members, but I had no words for it at the time. My companion, an associate professor of anthropology, was not at a similar loss. She called their strange rites "codified white exclusionary ritual."

About one in four of Michigan's undergraduates participates in this "white exclusionary ritual" each fall, according to Jo Rumsey, the assistant director of housing information. This year 779 new members were inducted into fraternities, almost twice the number that joined in 1975. "We lost 30 to 40 percent of the fraternities in the late sixties and early seventies," Rumsey said, "but since 1975, at least nine chapters—including three which are predominantly Jewish—have come back. They're certainly a strong influence on undergraduate life."

Michigan is not alone in its Greek revival. From the late 1960s to the early 1970s at the University of California, Berkeley, the number of women rushing sororities had dwindled to about 150 per year; now it's five times that. On campuses where chartered sororities never existed—Yale, Princeton, the University of Chicago—new chapters have been "colonized," an interesting choice of verb by a group almost entirely of white Protestants. Even at Amherst College, where fraternities were abolished in 1984, they continue to thrive unofficially off campus. In the past ten years, fraternity membership has doubled—even though the full-time undergraduate population has increased only by 20 percent, from 5 million to 6 million. And undergraduate sorority membership has grown by about 30 percent, from 180,000 in 1975 to 240,000 in 1985.

If any one thing is emblematic of the difference between the class of '87 and the class of '77, I think it's the resurgence of these organizations. During the 1960s and 1970s, students sought alternative social activities that promoted integration and discouraged racism and sexism—activities that many of today's college students consider comical. "We don't have to pay attention to that stuff," an undergraduate quipped only half-facetiously. "Back then they were all on drugs."

Not only have fraternities been resurrected, they've also been   7
cosmetically retouched. Crude proscriptions against blacks and Jews are out. Occasional black members are in, showcased to counter charges of racism. But nothing, in fact, has changed.

These clubs are "racist and anti-Semitic by way of pure dele-   8
tion," explains Wendy Martin, a recent Michigan graduate who rushed a sorority her senior year as fieldwork for an anthropology course. "It's not so much 'us' and 'them'; they're not even articulated as another. if they don't rush your sorority, they simply don't exist."

And when a few organizations at Michigan ostensibly made a   9
play for minority membership, it backfired. "First I see a Tri-Delt with a sweatshirt on and she never speaks to me, then they send fly-ers around saying they want their sorority to be more 'diverse.' I think it's a bunch of bullshit," says Mary Walker, a black junior at Michigan. "I can't see joining a white organization if they don't make an effort to get to know me in class. It's hypocritical. It's to-kenism. They're just trying to look good."

Add alcohol to the system (which members regularly do) and the   10
tacit racism becomes overt. At the University of Pennsylvania, "Black students regularly report that they are subjected to verbal racial abuse when they walk down Locust Walk," the university's fraternity row, says Jaqui Wade, director of the Afro-American stud-ies program. "It becomes worse on Thursday or Friday or Saturday nights when they're having their parties." And at Michigan this spring three members of Alpha Tau Omega, a predominantly white Christian fraternity, stole a mock jail cell built on campus to publi-cize the plight of Soviet Jews. Their excuse? "We did so while drunk, without malicious intent."

Ironically, racism was very much a concern at Michigan last   11
winter. Two incidents—the distribution of a racist leaflet in a dor-mitory and the broadcast of racist jokes by one of the campus radio stations—attracted national media attention. Some students took advantage of the publicity to criticize the low number of minority students on campus and the lower number of minority faculty members.

At no point, however, was the racist behavior of the Greek sys-   12
tem challenged. This struck me as odd—particularly since at least one of the incidents, the radio broadcast, seemed almost innocuous when compared with the jarring ritual I'd witnessed on the street the previous fall. Although the contents of the broadcast were re-pugnant and inappropriate, they were no more revolting than what

Manhattan disc jockey Howard Stern—on whom the student host's program was modeled—airs regularly in the undergraduate's hometown. For what the young disc jockey apologetically termed "ninety seconds of bad judgment," he was blasted by *The New York Times*, *Newsweek* and National Public Radio. Yet when 5,000 undergraduates participate in the month-long white exclusionary rites of Rush, it isn't considered a problem. When I suggested to Michigan president Harold Shapiro that it may be, he responded, "The fraternities are all integrated now."

Violence against women, another component of fraternity life, is more difficult behavior to ignore. Once again the distinction involves language: was the victim "willing" or "raped"? And, as in the case of racially motivated vandalism, alcohol blurs the distinction. 13

According to Bernice R. Sandler, director of the Association of American Colleges' Project on the Status and Education of Women and co-author, with Julie Kuhn Ehrhart, of *Campus Gang Rape: Party Games?* at least fifty documented gang rapes have occurred in fraternities in the past two or three years. "Fraternity members have a word for gang rape: they call it 'pulling train,'" says Sandler. "Charts of how many beers it took to seduce various sorority women are common in fraternity houses." And if a woman actually does press charges against a fraternity, "their excuse is, 'She asked for it'—even if she was unconscious." 14

Often women are reluctant to report rapes because they fear they'll be stigmatized, which is what usually happens, Sandler says. "Fraternity brothers harass them, say they deserved it because they'd been drinking. Well, that's like saying because there's money in your purse you deserve to be robbed." And, adds Sandler, to protect someone accused, "Brothers will remain silent or even lie." 15

In a paper published last April, Mary Koss, a psychologist at Kent State University, concluded that 15 percent of all college women (a startling one in seven) had had a forced-sex experience that met the legal definition of "completed rape." According to Koss's data, one-on-one acquaintance rape is not restricted to fraternities but, she told me, "We found that a significant predictor of a male's sexual aggression was the extent to which he involved himself in a peer group that sexually objectified women, that discussed women in sexual terms, that created a climate of 'scoring.'" 16

"Studies have shown that men who join fraternities have a much greater need to dominate than those who don't," says Andrew Merton, associate professor of English at the University of New Hampshire, who has written about fraternities and rape since 1979. "I think these men are scared of women, scared of dealing with them in any way approaching a basis of equality. They see women 17 only in a sexual context, in a context where men are rule-makers. And there's a tremendous pressure to drink in fraternities. Drinking allows the guys to act upon the sexual stereotypes in their heads and then say, 'Oh, it wasn't really my fault. I didn't know what I was doing.'"

He adds, "If the fraternities constituted a state of the union, it would be a very small one, with about half the population of Vermont. If, in a state that size, fifty confirmed gang rapes took place within two or three years, impartial observers might begin to wonder about the place." 18

Of course, not all fraternity members swashbuckle their way through college, raping and pillaging. But any group that sets itself up as elite, discriminates on the basis of race, religion and gender, posts lewd and degrading charts relating to the opposite sex and conspires to protect members from the consequences of criminal activities performed while drunk seems less likely than other campus clubs to promote sympathy between individuals of different race, religion and sex. 19

"As a black person, I begin to worry whenever groups—particularly groups of whites—permit themselves a kind of thuggish behavior as a group that they'd never dare to think about as individuals," says James Snead, an assistant professor of English at Yale. "When these kids were growing up, white male America was seen as a country on its way to wimpdom. It was possible to infer that everyone was picking on the white male and that he had no recourse—except to band together and revert to a more primitive kind of behavior." 20

Jaqui Wade concurs: "These white males who have been socialized to believe that the world was theirs—and they didn't have to compete with black men and women and white women—now feel the tensions of that competition. They're very, very threatened and they're acting out." 21

Four years ago, the Michigan chapter of Sigma Alpha Mu, a predominantly Jewish fraternity, held a "jungle party" at which three members painted their bodies black, wore tribal paint and rings through their noses. After *The Michigan Daily,* the campus newspaper, ran photographs of the event, blacks protested. The group's president claimed to be stunned. "It is difficult to know how minorities feel about certain practices," he said. "There is a lack of knowledge in general as to what those sensitivities are." 22

Historically, Jews and blacks have responded to white Protestant exclusion by forming their own support groups. In addition to three predominantly Jewish fraternities in the National Interfraternity Conference, and two predominantly Jewish sororities in the 23

National Panhellenic Conference, there is also a black Greek system, the National Pan-Hellenic Council, made up of eight black men's and women's organizations. The oldest black fraternity, Alpha Phi Alpha, was founded at Cornell University in 1906, and its members have included Thurgood Marshall, Martin Luther King, Jr., and Andrew Young. Although membership is selective and confers status, black Greek organizations are different from their white counterparts. They rush at different times, and on white campuses they are havens from white exclusion. They also preserve minority culture and prevent dilution of minority identity. In the late 1960s and early 1970s, when white Greek membership plummeted, black Greek membership remained about the same as it is now.

One reason colleges tolerate fraternities is that they can't afford 24
not to. "The reason fraternities don't get abolished in smaller schools is that the trustees are generally terrified of offending the alumni and cutting off large, essential contributions," said G. Armour Craig, acting president of Amherst in 1984, the year fraternities were abolished there. Another is the fiction that if Jews and blacks are allowed to form their own organizations, white exclusiveness is acceptable—the old "separate but equal" refrain.

This leads to packs socializing with packs rather than individu- 25
als with individuals. At Michigan, members of Alpha Phi Alpha complain that when they play a "friendly" game of basketball with a white fraternity, it is often anything but. "If the game is close, a white referee will call it their way," says Marcus Webster, former president of Alpha Phi Alpha. "But when we play other black fraternities, the referees let us beat each other up. They don't call anything."

Fraternities are not the same on every campus. For example, half 26
the members of the Yale chapter of the Kappa Kappa Gamma sorority are either Jewish, Hispanic, Asian, American Indian or black. In the Yale environment, the group could almost be described as anti-elitist—the response of public-school girls who couldn't find a place in other organizations. Some members, however, received a rude shock when they stayed on vacation at a Kappa house at the University of California, Los Angeles. "It was another world," said Jennifer Maxwell, a founding member of the Yale chapter. "An immense house with Kappa things everywhere—Kappa jewelry, Kappa clothes, everything. It was supposedly one of the most selective groups. . . . Everyone was gorgeous and had blonde hair." She paused, "I would never have been accepted into a group like that." Would anyone in the Yale chapter? "Probably not."

Yet establishing a chapter at Yale—like having a token black— 27
is a public relations coup for the sorority. Like eighteenth-century

European empire builders, fraternities must "colonize" to survive. "Most of the interest in them is generated from the outside," said Lloyd Suttle, associate dean of administrative and student affairs at Yale. "We don't give them a room to meet in. They put an ad in the newspaper and rent a room at the Holiday Inn."

And the students clearly want what the organizations have to offer. "It's a cold cruel world out there and you need friends," says Jon Baruch, a member of Alpha Epsilon Pi at Michigan. "A fraternity provides instant friendship." It also provides scholarships, low-interest loans and lodging when one travels. Members talk incessantly about networking with alumni. They point out that twenty-one Presidents, including Ronald Reagan, were in fraternities, not to mention fifty-two current members of the Senate and 33 percent of the House of Representatives. They talk about the time they volunteer to social service and the money they raise for charity. They make fraternities sound like a force for good. 28

But they're not telling the whole story, which is more along the lines of the following open letter from the grand president of Kappa Alpha Theta (the oldest women's fraternity) to her sisters: 29

> We still have alumnae who are reluctant to recommend anyone other than the traditional white, Anglo-Saxon Protestant. And this is their right: The purpose of the recommendation system is to give alumnae the opportunity to highlight personal friends and the daughters of friends, not to provide a "ticket" for everyone. . . . Last year, one of our chapters pledged the first black woman on a campus with traditionally "all-white" sorority membership. This year, another Theta chapter on an all-white Greek campus affiliated the first black woman. Both chapters are to be congratulated for not being afraid to take risks. And there were risks. Why? Because there were people who warned the chapters that if they pledged these women, they would not receive recommendations or pledges in the future. And some men's fraternities told the chapters they would not continue to "party" with Thetas at these two schools.

The use of the word "ticket" should dispel any lingering doubts about the practice of "white exclusionary ritual" among fraternal organizations. According to *Webster's Third New International Dictionary,* the word means "a certificate or token of a right . . . as of admission" or "a means to something desirable." It's an unusually vulgar and explicit word—a word that a member would not be likely to use with outsiders; a word that smacks of the 1950s, of a world in which even tokenism is a "risk." 30

"This is elite ritual practice, not redneck ritual practice," explains Susan Harding, the associate professor of anthropology at the 31

University of Michigan with whom I first glimpsed the rites of Rush. "It's tacky to be verbally racist but perfectly acceptable to discriminate through your behavior, through your choices. Elite racism is implicit, acted-out, behaved—not expressed in language. And fraternities are a training ground for that kind of elite racial practice."

I'm not advocating the abolition of fraternities. It doesn't work   32
—they spring up unofficially off campus. Nor am I sneering at the impulse to join selective organizations. I remember what it was like to be an adolescent—insecure and character deficient—and although I didn't solicit invitations to belong, I didn't refuse them either. Ironically, though, the secret society I joined at Yale turned out to be exclusionary only in number. Some clever members in the 1960s revamped the organization so that it was half black and Hispanic— and thus could never revert to its original, all-male, all-white status. It was the only fully racially integrated environment I'd ever experienced—considerably richer, I discovered, than being sequestered with Xeroxes of myself. But many kids with my character deficiencies, which I suspect is the majority, won't have the chance to make that discovery. They'll join fraternities instead.

Fraternities invest white bread with cachet. It's an impressive   33
sleight of hand. "They work on your soul," explains Clayton Eshleman, National Book Award-winning poet and translator, who pledged Phi Delta Theta at the University of Indiana in the 1950s. "There were motifs of Greek mythology in the rituals and lots of Greek words in the bylaws. It was a way to give a kind of old, fake European feel to a dull, safe Hoosier life."

QUESTIONS OF CONTENT

1. On what university campus did Lord make her initial observations about fraternities and sororities? What other campuses does she use for examples? How useful are the added examples?
2. Although her major thesis seems to be the racism that is inherent in many Greek organizations, Lord pauses (paragraphs 13–19) to discuss another troublesome issue. What is it?
3. What are some of the reasons that Lord suggests for this rise of racism among fraternities and sororities?
4. Are black fraternities and sororities immune to these problems? How are they like white Greek organizations? How do they differ?
5. Based on Lord's essay, what seem to be some of the risks involved for Greek organizations that attempt to overcome racist trends and extend their membership to members of other races?

QUESTIONS OF FORM

1. Lord is making a complicated claim of fact, but before doing so she provides what sorts of supporting evidence? Which sort seems more convincing to you, and why?
2. How does she expand on his first claim of fact, regarding racism and anti-Semitism, made in paragraph 7?
3. How has Lord used comparison and contrast to make a claim of policy late in her essay? Why might she have delayed so long?
4. The conclusion of Lord's essay is flat and anticlimactic, especially in comparison with the detailed anecdotal support she has consistently used. How might she have ended more forcefully?

SUGGESTIONS FOR WRITING

1. Summarize Lord's attitudes toward Greek organizations. Prepare your summary for a general audience consisting of young adults, some college trained, some not.
2. Now make the same summary, but this time address an audience of fraternity or sorority members.
3. Assume that you are a new pledge of a white Christian fraternity or sorority, somewhat disturbed by Lord's essay. Draw upon your personal experience to do one of the following:
   a. Refute Lord's claims of racism and sexism by pointing out that such abuses do not exist on your campus.
   b. Support Lord's position by pointing out similar disturbing situations that you have personally witnessed and then call for corrective measures.
4. Our society has many exclusionary organizations, of course, other than Greek-letter ones. Recall those you have belonged to or encountered, perhaps in high school or in college, and then write a letter to Lord, suggesting that she consider reporting on one whose faults you describe in enough detail so that she might be encouraged to investigate it. If possible, use one or more means of support that she employed. (Your instructor may want you to try this in groups rather than alone.)

Shameful Harvest

CONSTANCE J. POTEN

Dark clouds float over the ranch town of Wibaux, Mont. An illegal hunt is under way, and a number of people are waiting for their   1 payoff at the Palace Hotel. I am in a pickup truck a block away with "Roy," Montana's lone undercover wildlife agent.

Two voices rise from the metal suitcase between us: wildlife agents on loan from another state, body-wired. We see them emerge from the hotel. Behind them is Neal Atkinson, a 47-year-old "outfitter" from Florida, who has allegedly taken 23 people on illegal hunts in Montana this fall alone. He thinks the agents are genuine clients.

Roy picks up his radio mike. "They're leaving. Let's take 'em down." Fourteen Montana game wardens hear this. In moments Atkinson is surrounded by vehicles, and he and his partners are frisked and handcuffed.

A little more than a year later, Atkinson is found guilty of 21 federal counts of organizing illegal hunts and helping to transport the spoils across state lines. He is ordered to pay $21,000 restitution to the state of Montana and serve 37 months in prison. He has appealed the conviction.

Global Demand. Atkinson is but one player in a lucrative American industry—poaching. While no one knows the bottom line, U.S. Fish and Wildlife Service (FWS) officials estimate the illegal trade of U.S. animals is a $200-million-a-year business and growing. The industry attracts rich and poor—even organized crime—because the return is high, the risk of getting caught is low and, until recently, the penalties have been minimal.

Nationwide, the illegal kill of animals equals or exceeds the legal kill, FWS officials say. Feeding a global demand for American wildlife, poachers every year destroy hundreds of thousands of protected birds, reptiles, fish and game animals. Unscrupulous outfitters purchase illegally trapped mountain lions and endangered jaguars for hunters willing to pay substantial trophy fees. Collectors cross over into national parks and shoot elk, deer, mountain goats, grizzlies and bighorn sheep for the record book, wall mounts, photograph albums.

To protect wildlife, we have fewer than 200 federal agents and 7000 state officers—about half the Chicago police force—guarding the entire United States. Increasingly, wildlife officers rely on undercover operations like the one in Wibaux to penetrate networks of poachers and buyers. There is a 94-percent conviction rate for those caught, but only a fraction of the violators are apprehended. "Knock one bad guy down and ten step forward," says FWS agent Terry Grosz. "I think Custer had better odds."

Grisly Toll. "We have a war going on," says FWS agent Dave Hall. "And as long as enormous profits are attached to wildlife, wildlife loses."

The following is just a sampling of the illegal slaughter taking   9
place:

Bears in dumpsters. I ask the manager of an apothecary shop in   10
New York City's Chinatown if she sells bear galls, or gallbladders,
and she asks where I'm from. "Montana," I say. "Can you get me
bear galls?" she asks. We're discussing a felony, but getting caught
is unlikely.

"For the Asian gentleman who has everything," says Montana   11
Assistant U.S. Attorney Kris McLean, "present a bear gall in a nice
case. A grizzly gall is even better." Diced and mixed with liquor,
galls are believed to cure a host of ailments, including blood toxins,
backaches and eye problems. For a five-ounce Alaska grizzly gall, a
hunter can make $1300. In South Korea, galls sell for as much as
$18,300 each.

Game wardens in Washington State and Idaho are finding   12
butchered bears stuffed in dumpsters. Their parts are sold like those
of a stripped-down car. Bear meat and bear-paw soup, special-occa-
sion foods in Asia, are gaining popularity as exotic foods in America.

Since the sale of bear parts is legal in some states, merchandise   13
from poached bears is very difficult to track. "Until we have standardized laws throughout the United States and Canada, trade in illegal bear parts will flourish," says Washington State wildlife
enforcement officer Ron Peregrin.

Beheaded walruses. In Alaska's Bering Sea, walrus tusks have   14
become the focus of a frantic, escalating trade. The Marine Mammal Protection Act of 1972 makes it illegal for non-Native Americans to hunt or sell walruses, seals, sea otters, sea lions or polar
bears. So, many dealers use Alaskan natives to disguise unlawful
ivory trade.

To kill walruses for ivory, natives drive motorboats out to ice   15
floes, shoot the animals with semi-automatic weapons and behead
those they can retrieve. Half the animals sink, washing to shore in
the spring. In 1988 a thousand walrus bodies washed up on St.
Lawrence Island, nearly all headless.

Though raw ivory is illegal to sell to nonnatives, it changes   16
hands like currency, buying gas, groceries, drugs, liquor, even air
fare. "Some people have turned subsistence into unrestricted
slaughter," says FWS special agent Gary Mowad.

Vanishing birds. Four major fly-ways funnel migratory water-   17
fowl from the Arctic to Mexico and South America, and from beginning to end, illegal killings are withering populations. In 1988,
after a three-year investigation on the Gulf Coast of Texas, FWS
agents brought charges against over 200 people for more than 1300
violations in the biggest waterfowl undercover operation in history.

"The hunters and their guides did everything illegally," says one 18
agent. "Shot too early and too late in the day, used lead shot and
electronic callers, left crippled birds to die, and herded birds with
airboats." When 88 geese fell in one large volley, one of the guides
complained, "It could have been better." He happened to be one of
the justices of the peace who handle wildlife cases.

Meanwhile, an international fascination with Native American 19
artifacts fashioned from feathers has focused a demand on eagles,
hawks, owls, scissortails, anhingas, flickers, bluebirds and magpies.
A golden-eagle tail may go for $260; kestrel and flicker hatpins, $10;
a scissortail fan, $700.

"We have an annual million-dollar black market in eagle feath- 20
ers in the West right now," says FWS agent Joel Scrafford. "Most of
them go to Japan, Germany, Britain and Eastern Europe."

During a four-year undercover operation, federal agents pene- 21
trated a black market of endangered peregrine falcons, gyrfalcons,
goshawks and Harris' hawks that stretched from the Alaskan Arctic
to Saudi Arabia. Although more than 50 people have been convicted
in Operation Falcon, those accused of being the key figures in a
worldwide smuggling network are still at large: members of the
Ciesielski family of Cologne, Germany; they have been indicted for
conspiring to buy, sell and export raptors outside of the United
States.

Fish frenzy. Depletion of the paddlefish became a concern in the 22
1980s when the supply of beluga sturgeon caviar from Iran was cut
off. Tennessee fishermen learned to prepare caviar from paddlefish
eggs, and profits from this "black gold" went beyond fantasy. For this
rare fish that can produce ten pounds of caviar—worth as much as
$500 a pound on the retail market—it amounted to a death sentence.

In 1985 low water in Missouri's Table Rock Lake exposed 15 23
dead paddlefish, their stomachs split open, their heads and tails tied
together, and the carcasses weighted down with rocks. Two undercover agents joined paddlefish poachers in 1987 and found that at
least 4000 paddlefish were killed that year. One poacher boasted of
clearing $86,000 in five nights. A year later, 23 people faced 200 state
and federal charges. But the market for such roe continues to grow.

Glory Hunters. Profit is only one motive behind this traffic. 24
Where big-game animals are concerned, another motive is the ob-
session by some to possess, at any cost, these symbols of power and
freedom.

During a fall hunt, Pennsylvanian William Heuer pressured his 25
Montana guide for an under-the-table hunt and illegally bought a
resident's license. He didn't know the salesman was Montana's undercover agent, Roy. At dark, in a no-hunting area on the edge of Yel-

lowstone National Park, Heuer set his gun on the hood of Roy's truck and aimed at a huge bull elk. The shot rang out.

Months later, Roy's tape blasted the gunshot through the quiet of a federal courtroom. The jury's decision was quick: three years' probation, $13,300 in fines and 200 hours of community service.   26

"Trophy hunting does not appreciably affect wildlife populations," says Lawrence Means, executive director of the Boone and Crockett Club, a prestigious hunting club that publishes a record book of trophy animals.   27

FWS agent Scrafford disagrees. "Seventy percent of my caseload involves trophy poaching," he says. "They're killing off the biggest, the best of the gene pool." And they are using any means necessary, say FWS officials, including aircraft, laser night scopes, one-million-candlepower spotlights to transfix deer, two-way radios, silencers, poison and all-terrain vehicles.   28

Trophy-size animals have become so rare in the wild that "people are hitting the parks hard now," says Scrafford. In his zeal to acquire a Roosevelt-elk trophy, one man contacted an outfitter about hunts in Washington's Olympic National Park. "He wanted to skip the hunt and just have the elk delivered to the Seattle airport," says an FWS agent.   29

"Hunters invest in record-book trophies like art collectors collecting Remington bronzes," adds Scrafford. "Hold one for five years, and it can be worth $50,000. People poach on speculation now."   30

There are success stories, however. Creatures have survived illegal pillage and made strong comebacks. Poaching threatened the survival of the American alligator two decades ago, but law-enforcement operations and closely monitored harvest and trade controls brought it back.   31

Poaching hot lines have become major information sources. States are working to strengthen penalties and standardize laws to prevent the smuggling of animal products.   32

"New Frontier." A hope for the future is the National Fish and Wildlife Forensics Laboratory, which is dedicated to suppressing world wildlife crime. In Ashland, Ore., top scientists in chemical analysis, serology and morphological studies, such as feather identification, work together for what they call "a new lab in a new frontier." By the end of the decade, they hope to be able to trace a tanned, dyed and glued leather purse back to the animal; identify cut and frozen meat; trace a bloodstain to a specific deer. The lab's mission is to strengthen legal cases; in the past the difficulty of providing the origins of animal products has stymied the prosecution of cases.   33

Poachers take away more than the animals. They take beauty,   34
leave waste and undermine an already precarious natural balance.
Says one federal judge, "The time has passed when we can allow people to wipe out natural resources in the name of short-term profits."

QUESTIONS OF CONTENT

1. What types of wildlife are the chief victims of poachers? Why?
2. Poten contends that the risks involved in poaching are quite low but
   the financial rewards are high. Why is this so?
3. What does Poten mean by "trophy poaching," and why does she find
   it particularly offensive?
4. What new development of the National Fish and Wildlife Service
   does Poten see as becoming especially useful in the war on poaching
   during the twenty-first century?

QUESTIONS OF FORM

1. What purpose is served by the brief narrative with which Poten begins this argument?
2. Poten appeals both to statistics and to authorities in this article. To
   what purpose?
3. Is the thrust of Poten's appeal essentially logical, ethical, or emotional?
   Justify your response by citing instances from the text of the article.
4. Examine Poten's attitude toward her audience. How might Poten
   have adjusted her approach to address a hostile audience?

SUGGESTIONS FOR WRITING

1. Write a summary of Poten's position, suitable as an illustration in an
   argument favoring government regulation of American life.
2. For three generations members of your family have been hunters,
   and you fully plan to continue the tradition. How would you go
   about refuting Poten's case against trophy hunters? Compose a well-
   ordered response in which you attack the portion of her argument
   that you find especially vulnerable.

CLAIMS OF VALUE

Sex Is Not a Spectator Sport

S. I. HAYAKAWA

In current discussions of pornography and obscenity, there is 1
widespread confusion about two matters. First there is sexual behavior and what it means to the participants. Secondly there is the
outside observer of sexual behavior and what it means to him. When
a man and a woman make love, enjoying themselves and each other
unself-consciously, a rich relationship is reaffirmed and made richer
by their lovemaking. However beautiful or sacred that love relationship may be to that man and woman, it would have an entirely
different significance to a Peeping Tom, secretly watching the proceedings from outside the window. The sexual behavior is not itself
obscene. Obscenity is peculiarly the evaluation of the outside observer. Theoretically the actors may themselves be made the observers. If, for example, unknown to the man and woman, a movie
were to be made of their lovemaking, and that movie were to be
shown to them later, that lovemaking might take on an entirely different significance. What was performed unself-consciously and
spontaneously might be viewed later by the actors themselves with
giggling or shame or shock. They might even insist that the film be
destroyed—which is entirely different from saying that they would
stop making love.

What I am saying is that obscenity and pornography can happen 2
only when sexual events are seen from the outside, from a spectator's point of view. This is the crux of the pornography problem.
Pornography is sexual behavior made public through symboliza-
tion—by representation in literature, by simulation or enactment in
a nightclub act or on stage, by arts such as painting, photography, or
the movies. To object to pornographic movies or art is not, as some
would have us believe, a result of hang-ups about sex. One may be
completely healthy and still object to many of the current representations of sexual acts in the movies and on the stage.

Standards of morality are one thing. Standards of decorum are 3
another. There is nothing immoral about changing one's clothes or

evacuating one's bowels. But in our culture people as a rule do not change their clothing in the presence of the other sex, excepting their spouses. Men and women have separate public lavatories, and within them each toilet is in a separate compartment for privacy. Love too needs privacy. Human beings normally make love in private, whether that love is socially sanctioned, as in marriage, or unsanctioned, as in a house of prostitution.

The trouble with sexual intercourse as an object of artistic or literary representation is that its meaning is not apparent in the behavior. Hence serious writers have historically been reticent in their description of sex. In Dante's *Divine Comedy* Francesca tells of her tragic love for Paolo. They were reading an ancient romance and, as they read, their passions suddenly overcame them. What happened? Dante simply has Francesca say, "That day we read no further." The rest is left to the reader's imagination—and the reader cannot help feeling the power of that on-rushing, fatal passion. 4

Men and women couple with each other for a wide variety of reasons. Sometimes the sexual encounter is the fulfillment of true love and respect for each other. Sometimes one of the partners is using sex as an instrument of exploitation or aggression against the other. Sometimes sex is a commercial transaction, with either party being the prostitute. Sometimes sex is the expression of neurosis. Sometimes it is evidence of people getting over their neuroses. However, to the movie camera, as to a Peeping Tom, they are all "doing the same thing." To concentrate on the mechanics of sex is to ignore altogether its human significance. 5

Today movies do not stop at exhibiting copulation. Every kind of aberrant sexual behavior and sadomasochistic perversion is being shown. The advertisements in the newspaper before me announce such titles as *Nude Encounter, Too Hot to Handle, Deep Throat, The Devil in Miss Jones, The Passion Parlor, Hot Kitten,* and *Honeymoon Suite,* as well as " 16 hours of hard-core male stag." The only purpose of movies such as these, from all I can tell from advertisements and reviews, is, as D. H. Lawrence expressed it, "to do dirt on sex." Let the American Civil Liberties Union fight for the right of these movies to be shown. I will not. 6

QUESTIONS OF CONTENT

1. Hayakawa draws a careful distinction in the opening paragraph. What distinction does he make and why?

2. Besides lovemaking, Hayakawa alludes to two other human acts that are customarily accomplished in privacy. What are they, and how are all three related to what he calls "standards of decorum"?
3. Who are Francesca and Paolo, and what purpose is served in the essay by Hayakawa's literary allusion to them?
4. Hayakawa does not claim that all sexual unions are an expression of love. For what other reasons does he suggest that people have sexual encounters? Why does he bring up these reasons as part of his argument?
5. What kind of organization is the American Civil Liberties Union? Why and on what basis might the ACLU fight for the right to show pornographic movies, as Hayakawa implies?

QUESTIONS OF FORM

1. Hayakawa's argument is essentially a claim of value. It consists of drawing a definition of what is to be valued and showing how some things correspond to that definition and should, as a consequence, be valued, while others do not correspond to it and should thus not be valued. Where exactly does Hayakawa make that definition?
2. Hayakawa appeals to two authorities. Who are they, and what purpose does each appeal fulfill?
3. In paragraph 5 Hayakawa restates his claim of value in different terms. Where exactly do you find that restatement? Compare it with the earlier claim.

SUGGESTIONS FOR WRITING

1. Summarize Hayakawa's argument in a single well-constructed paragraph.
2. Assume that the psychology department on your campus regularly offers a course entitled "Human Sexuality." It is quite popular among the students because it reportedly features several films that demonstrate techniques of lovemaking. You are scandalized by the use of such films, especially by the whispered comments you have overheard about them. Using Hayakawa's argument as a starting point, write a letter to the campus newspaper objecting to the practice of using such films in the Human Sexuality course.
3. You are a psychology major and you work for the professor who teaches Human Sexuality. Sometimes it is your responsibility to show the films that the student in Suggestion 2 objects to. Write a response to that student's probable complaint, defending the practices of the psychology professor. You may also wish to use Hayakawa's argument in defending your position.

What Employees Need Most

PETER DRUCKER

Most of you . . . will be employees all your working life, work-　1
ing for somebody else and for a pay check. And so will most, if not
all, of the thousands of other young Americans . . . in all the other
schools and colleges across the country.

Ours has become a society of employees. A hundred years or so　2
ago only one out of every five Americans at work was employed, i.e.,
worked for somebody else. Today only one out of five is not employed but working for himself. And where fifty years ago "being
employed" meant working as a factory laborer or as a farmhand, the
employee of today is increasingly a middle-class person with a substantial formal education, holding a professional or management job
requiring intellectual and technical skills. Indeed, two things have
characterized American society during these last fifty years: the
middle and upper classes have become employees; and middle-class
and upper-class employees have been the fastest-growing groups in
our working population—growing so fast that the industrial worker,
that oldest child of the Industrial Revolution, has been losing in numerical importance despite the expansion of industrial production.

This is one of the most profound social changes any country has　3
ever undergone. It is, however, a perhaps even greater change for the
individual young person about to start. Whatever he does, in all likelihood he will do it as an employee; wherever he aims, he will have
to try to reach it through being an employee.

Yet you will find little if anything written on what it is to be an　4
employee. You can find a great deal of very dubious advice on how
to get a job or how to get a promotion. You can also find a good deal
on work in a chosen field, whether it be metallurgy or salesmanship,
the machinist's trade or bookkeeping. Every one of these trades requires different skills, sets different standards, and requires a different preparation. Yet they all have employeeship in common. And
increasingly, especially in the large business or in government, employeeship is more important to success than the special professional knowledge or skill. Certainly more people fail because they
do not know the requirements of being an employee than because
they do not adequately possess the skills of their trade; the higher
you climb the ladder, the more you get into administrative or executive work, the greater the emphasis on ability to work within the
organization rather than on technical competence or professional
knowledge.

Being an employee is thus the one common characteristic of   5
most careers today. The special profession or skill is visible and
clearly defined; and a well-laid-out sequence of courses, degrees, and
jobs leads into it. But being an employee is the foundation. And it is
much more difficult to prepare for it. Yet there is no recorded information on the art of being an employee.

The first question we might ask is: what can you learn in col-   6
lege that will help you in being an employee? The schools teach a
great many things of value to the future accountant, the future doctor, or the future electrician. Do they also teach anything of value
to the future employee? The answer is: "Yes—they teach the one
thing that it is perhaps most valuable for the future employee to
know. But very few students bother to learn it."

This one basic skill is the ability to organize and express ideas   7
in writing and in speaking.

As an employee you work with and through other people. This   8
means that your success as an employee—and I am talking of much
more here than getting promoted—will depend on your ability to
communicate with people and to present your own thoughts and
ideas to them so they will both understand what you are driving at
and be persuaded. The letter, the report or memorandum, the ten-
minute spoken "presentation" to a committee are basic tools of the
employee.

Of course . . . if you work on a machine your ability to express   9
yourself will be of little importance. But as soon as you move one
step up from the bottom, your effectiveness depends on your ability to reach others through the spoken or the written word. And the
further away your job is from manual work, the larger the organization of which you are an employee, the more important it will be
that you know how to convey your thoughts in writing or speaking. In the very large organization, whether it is the government,
the large business corporation, or the military, this ability to express oneself is perhaps the most important of all the skills a [per-
son] can possess.

Of course, skill in expression is not enough by itself. You must   10
have something to say in the first place. The popular picture of the
engineer, for instance, is that of a man who works with a slide rule,
T square, and compass. And engineering students reflect this picture in their attitude toward the written word as something quite
irrelevant to their jobs. But the effectiveness of the engineer—and
with it his usefulness—depends as much on his ability to make
other people understand his work as it does on the quality of the
work itself.

Expressing one's thoughts is one skill that the school can really   11
teach, especially to people born without natural writing or speaking
talent. Many other skills can be learned later—in this country there
are literally thousands of places that offer training to adult people at
work. But the foundations for skill in expression have to be laid
early: an interest in and an ear for language; experience in organizing ideas and data, in brushing aside the irrelevant, in wedding out-
ward form and inner content into one structure; and above all, the
habit of verbal expression. If you do not lay these foundations during your school years, you may never have an opportunity again.

If you were to ask me what strictly vocational courses there are   12
in the typical college curriculum, my answer—now that the good
old habit of the "theme a day" has virtually disappeared—would be:
the writing of poetry and the writing of short stories. Not that I expect many of you to become poets or short-story writers—far from
it. But these two courses offer the easiest way to obtain some skill
in expression. They force one to be economical with language. They
force one to organize thought. They demand of one that he give
meaning to every word. They train the ear for language, its meaning, its precision, its overtones—and its pitfalls. Above all they force
one to write.

I know very well that the typical employer does not understand   13
this as yet, and that he may look with suspicion on a young college
graduate who has majored, let us say, in short-story writing. But the
same employer will complain—and with good reason—that the
young [people] whom he hires when they get out of college do not
know how to write a simple report, do not know how to tell a simple story, and are in fact virtually illiterate. And he will conclude—
rightly—that the young [people] are not really effective, and
certainly not employees who are likely to go very far.

QUESTIONS OF CONTENT

1. Drucker claims that during the past century our country has undergone a most profound social change. What is the nature of that change?
2. What, according to Drucker, is the present ratio of employees to employers? What was the ratio a century ago? Why has this change occurred, and will it affect you?
3. In paragraph 6 Drucker asks the following question: "What can you
   learn in college that will help you in being an employee?" What answer does he supply?

4. Name three occupations in which writing and speaking ability are crucial to success. How important are these abilities in your likely vocation?
5. What courses found in most college curricula does Drucker suggest for students who wish to improve their communication skills?

QUESTIONS OF FORM

1. In the opening paragraph, Drucker makes a claim. What is that claim, and how does he support it?
2. Drucker's essay begins with a syllogism that we might state in this way:

   All employees must be able to communicate effectively.

   You will be an employee.

   Therefore, you must be able to communicate effectively.

   Where does Drucker state the major premise of this syllogism? Where does he state the minor premise?
3. If we think of Drucker's major premise, as stated in question 2, as a warrant, then we see also that it is not one that Drucker expects his audience to accept without some support or backing. What kind of backing does he supply?
4. Examine paragraph 3, specifically its last sentence. It contains several instances of sexist diction: that is, use of the masculine pronoun to refer to both men and women—a practice that many modern readers find confusing and even offensive. How might you rewrite that sentence to clearly include both sexes?

SUGGESTIONS FOR WRITING

1. Summarize Drucker's argument in a paper that does not exceed three paragraphs. When you make your summary, do not take over Drucker's argument as though it is your own; be careful to mention him as the source of your information.
2. Using the same argumentative strategy employed by Drucker in this essay, create your own argument advocating another essential skill or attitude that all employees should strive to develop. Alternatively, you might argue for a skill that a specific profession would find indispensable, for example, a teacher, coach, restaurant manager, computer scientist, or lawyer. Argue for the development of this skill and, as Drucker does, recommend a course of action that will enable the reader to achieve the skill.
3. You are applying for a job. Write a letter arguing that the communications skills you have developed through both formal and informal

education make you an ideal candidate. To complete this assignment, you will also need to furnish a brief description of the job for which you are applying.

What's Wrong with Black English

RACHEL L. JONES

William Labov, a noted linguist, once said about the use of black   1
English, "It is the goal of most black Americans to acquire full control of the standard language without giving up their own culture." He also suggested that there are certain advantages to having two ways to express one's feelings. I wonder if the good doctor might also consider the goals of those black Americans who have full control of standard English but who are every now and then troubled by that colorful, grammar-to-the-winds patois that is black English. Case in point—me.

I'm a 21-year-old black born to a family that would probably be   2
considered lower-middle class—which in my mind is a polite way of describing a condition only slightly better than poverty. Let's just say we rarely if ever did the winter-vacation thing in the Caribbean. I've often had to defend my humble beginnings to a most unlikely group of people for an even less likely reason. Because of the way I talk, some of my black peers look at me sideways and ask, "Why do you talk like you're white?"

The first time it happened to me I was nine years old. Cornered   3
in the school bathroom by the class bully and her sidekick, I was offered the opportunity to swallow a few of my teeth unless I satisfactorily explained why I always got good grades, why I talked "proper" or "white." I had no ready answer for her, save the fact that my mother had from the time I was old enough to talk stressed the importance of reading and learning, or that L. Frank Baum and Ray Bradbury were my closest companions. I read all my older brothers' and sisters' literature textbooks more faithfully then they did, and even lightweights like the Bobbsey Twins and Trixie Belden were allowed into my bookish inner circle. I don't remember exactly what I told those girls, but I somehow talked my way out of a beating.

I was reminded once again of my "white pipes" problem while   4
apartment hunting in Evanston, Illinois, last winter. I doggedly made out lists of available places and called all around. I would immediately be invited over—and immediately turned down. The thinly concealed looks of shock when the front door opened clued

me in, along with the flustered instances of "just getting off the phone with the girl who was ahead of you and she wants the rooms." When I finally found a place to live, my roommate stirred up old memories when she remarked a few months later, "You know, I was surprised when I first saw you. You sounded white over the phone." Tell me another one, sister.

I should've asked her a question I've wanted an answer to for   5
years: how does one "talk white"? The silly side of me pictures a rabid white foam spewing forth when I speak. I don't use Valley Girl jargon, so that's not what's meant in my case. Actually, I've pretty much deduced what people mean when they say that to me, and the implications are really frightening.

It means that I'm articulate and well-versed. It means that I can   6
talk as freely about John Steinbeck as I can about Rick James. It means that "ain't" and "he be" are not staples of my vocabulary and are only used around family and friends. (It is almost Jekyll and Hydeish the way I can slip out of academic abstractions into a long, lean, double-negative-filled dialogue, but I've come to terms with that aspect of my personality.) As a child, I found it hard to believe that's what people meant by "talking proper"; that would've meant that good grades and standard English were equated with white skin, and that went against everything I'd ever been taught. Running into the same type of mentality as an adult has confirmed the depressing reality that for many blacks, standard English is not only unfamiliar, it is socially unacceptable.

James Baldwin once defended black English by saying it had   7
added "vitality to the language," and even went so far as to label it a language in its own right, saying, "Language [i.e., black English] is a political instrument" and a "vivid and crucial key to identity." But did Malcolm X urge blacks to take power in this country "any way y'all can"? Did Martin Luther King, Jr. say to blacks, "I has been to the mountaintop, and I done seed the Promised Land"? Toni Morrison, Alice Walker and James Baldwin did not achieve their eloquence, grace and stature by using only black English in their writing. Andrew Young, Tom Bradley and Barbara Jordan did not acquire political power by saying, "Y'all crazy if you ain't gon vote for me." They all have full command of standard English, and I don't think that knowledge takes away from their blackness or commitment to black people.

I know from experience that it's important for black people,   8
stripped of culture and heritage, to have something they can point to and say, "This is ours, we can comprehend it, we alone can speak it with a soulful flourish." I'd be lying if I said that the rhythms of my people caught up in "some serious rap" don't sound natural and right

to me sometimes. But how heartwarming is it for those same brothers when they hit the pavement searching for employment? Studies have proven that the use of ethnic dialects decreases power in the marketplace. "I be" is acceptable on the corner, but not with the boss.

Am I letting capitalistic, European-oriented thinking fog the issue? Am I selling out blacks to an ideal of assimilating, being as much like whites as possible? I have not formed a personal political ideology, but I do know this: it hurts me to hear black children use black English, knowing that they will be at yet another disadvantage in an educational system already full of stumbling blocks. It hurts me to sit in lecture halls and hear fellow black students complain that the professor "be tripping dem out using big words dey can't understand. " And what hurts most is to be stripped of my own blackness simply because I know my way around the English language.

I would have to disagree with Labov in one respect. My goal is not so much to acquire full control of both standard and black English, but to one day see more black people less dependent on a dialect that excludes them from full participation in the world we live in. I don't think I talk white; I think I talk right.

QUESTIONS OF CONTENT

1. What is the attitude of Jones toward black English? How does her attitude compare with James Baldwin's? With William Labov's?
2. Growing up as she did in a lower middle-class family, how does Jones account for her command of standard English?
3. How does she define standard English or "talking white"?
4. What advantage does Jones see for blacks who do have a command of standard English?

QUESTIONS OF FORM

1. Claims of value, such as Jones's, typically consist of a definition of the thing to be valued. Then there is a measurement of other items that are less valued against that definition (or set of criteria). Where and how does Jones actually do this?
2. For whom is this argument intended? Is its audience most likely to be blacks or whites? What response could be expected from each of these groups?
3. Where and how does Jones use her references to authorities like William Labov, James Baldwin, Malcolm X, Martin Luther King, Jr., and others in support of her claim?

4. In paragraph 9, Jones begins by asking two rhetorical questions. What do you think the answers might be? What makes that strategy effective?

SUGGESTIONS FOR WRITING

1. Summarize Jones's position as fairly and as accurately as you can.
2. You are a black American, and you have experienced many of the doubts and travails that Jones describes. But you are convinced that apartments are frequently unavailable to black persons (as Jones describes in paragraph 4) because of their race and not because they speak a nonstandard dialect. You even suspect that prejudiced white people exaggerate the supposed backwardness of black English as an excuse for behaving the way they do. Write a brief refutation of Jones's position by calling attention to these speculations, as well as to any other sentiments that you might feel.
3. You are a young teacher, assigned to an inner city high school. Many of the school's black students are quite vocal in their disdain for the English that they are expected to use in the classroom and in their writing assignments. They claim that standard English is the language of the white shopkeeper, the landlord, the politician—and yes, even the teacher, white or black. Its one purpose is to keep them down. How do you respond to this argument? Write an essay addressed to these students, suitable for publication in a high school newspaper.

A Better Health Plan
Goes Rejected

RICHARD REEVES

Every couple of weeks or so I get a call from a friend or colleague   1
in Canada saying something like: "How can they lie the way they
do about our health-care system? Almost every Canadian thinks we
have a much, much better system than you do."

"I know, I know," I answer. "But everyone from Bill Clinton on   2
down is afraid that if we talk 'single-payer,' the insurance companies
and the doctors will start screaming 'socialized medicine' again."

The screaming from the insurance companies begins because   3
they could be eliminated if the United States did what everyone else
in the world does: use government as the single-payer to guarantee
universal health care. To avoid that, President Clinton has proposed
a middleman system with insurance companies providing universal
care on a competitive basis.

I am certain that he rejected single-payer—knowing it would   4
cost less and probably work better—because he believed Americans
would never accept anything like the Canadian system. He is a professional politician who believes in double-talk and half-loaves—
even if his wife and most of the people around him say single-payer
is the only way to guarantee universal care without raising the overall cost of health care.

Now, amazingly, the American College of Surgeons has become   5
the first big player (60,000 member surgeons with an average annual
income of $244,000) in the health-care game to say single-payer is
better. As their friends at The Wall Street Journal put it on Friday,
perhaps a bit grudgingly: "A single-payer system is attractive to the
surgeons today because it would preserve patients' rights to choose
their physicians, reduce bureaucracy more than any other health-re-
form proposal, and best foster the autonomy of physicians to make
their own medical decisions."

Wow! The truth, the whole truth and nothing but the truth—   6
something that has been in short supply from all sides in the "health
crisis" confrontation.

It was only a week ago that new surveys indicated that Ameri-   7
cans pay 60 percent more for the same medication than do the
British with their single-payer system. Valium, for instance, costs
10 times more in the United States (where it was developed) than
in the United Kingdom. Pharmaceutical company spokesmen immediately said the studies were irrelevant because you can't compare prices in "the best health-care system in the world" to "one of
the worst."

But you can try. That "worst" system in Great Britain, accord-   8
ing to the latest available figures, costs $711 per capita, accounting
for a little more than 6 percent of gross national product, and produces average life expectancy of 75 years and an infant mortality
rate of nine deaths per 10,000 births. The "best" system, ours, costs
$1,926 per capita, accounting for more than 11 percent of GNP, and
produces the same life expectancy, 75 years, and a higher infant
mortality rate, 11 per 10,000 births.

The Canadian system, by the way, costs $1,370 per capita, ac-   9
counting for 8.6 percent of GNP, and produces a life expectancy of
77 years and an infant mortality rate of only seven per 10,000 births.

So that makes us the best? It does at the very top of the line. If   10
you can afford it, the U.S. private medical system has the highest
technology and the best-trained physicians in the world—for example, the 60,000 members of the American College of Surgeons.

Having said that, here is a Canadian view friends have been urg-   11
ing on me, written by Diane Francis in McLean's magazine:

"Canada is a caring country with a superior society and, in many   12
ways, more opportunities for its people. By contrast the United
States, the wealthiest country on earth collectively, condemns millions of its citizens to ignorance and poverty because of regressive
social structures . . . It is only a matter of time before Americans realize what Canadians realized long ago. If expenses are spread across
the entire society, as is the case here and in virtually every other industrial country, unit costs would drop dramatically and society can
provide efficient and relatively cheap care for all."

Well, some smart Americans have realized that now. Real brain   13
surgeons. Maybe we'll all wise up soon.

QUESTIONS OF CONTENT

1. Name at least three ways in which, according to the author, the
   Canadian health care system is superior to the U.S. system.
2. According to Reeves, what is the major obstacle that prevents the
   United States from adopting a Canadian-style health care system?
3. A Valium capsule costs 10 times more in the United States than it does
   in Great Britain, despite the fact that the capsules must be exported
   from their place of manufacture in the United States. Why is this so?
4. Why does the American College of Surgeons prefer a "single-payer"
   health care delivery system?

QUESTIONS OF FORM

1. Reeves' argument is essentially a claim of value. What exactly is his
   claim; in other words, what does he claim is to be preferred—or valued more highly than some other thing?
2. By what criteria is the preference in the preceding question to be determined? What sorts of evidence does Reeves produce?
3. At the outset Reeves must define the term "single-payer." Where exactly does he do that?
4. What special force does the paragraph dealing with the American
   College of Surgeons lend to Reeves' argument?

SUGGESTIONS FOR WRITING

1. Try to summarize Reeves' argument in a single paragraph.
2. Think about advertisements that you have seen recently in newspapers, magazines, or on television in which two products are com-

pared, such as headache remedies, automobiles, soft drinks, diet plans, and the like. Write a brief essay in which you restate the original claim of value favoring one of these products over another. As far as possible, follow Reeves' pattern of development in defining terms, appealing to authority, and measuring the products according to specific criteria.

3. How do you suppose a small-town insurance agent, a general practice medical doctor, hospital administrator, an emergency room nurse, or an elementary school teacher with two small children would each respond to Reeves' argument? Select one of these identities and from that person's point of view, write an argument for or against U.S. adoption of the Canadian health care system.

CLAIMS OF POLICY

Elementary Schools Need
More Male Teachers

CINDY GRAY

Last week was Fire Prevention Week, and I tagged along as a 1
crew of volunteer firemen visited some local second-graders. The
firemen looked huge and impressive in their insulated coveralls and
yellow, visored helmets.

Early in the presentation, a couple of boys got rowdy, elbowed 2
each other and sniggered disruptively. A fireman stepped forward,
pointed a long finger, and roared authoritatively, "Hey, you boys!
Pay attention!" The guilty parties looked lightning-struck. The rest
of the assembly proceeded without their disruptions.

This is something we don't see too much of anymore, I thought 3
to myself, watching the big men lecture sternly on how to behave
in emergencies, how to save lives how to care for one's family and
one's neighbors. The firemen's words were earnest, the expressions
on their faces concerned as they looked into the eyes of the little
ones sitting cross-legged on the gymnasium floor. The children's
faces showed awe, and not a little bit of fear.

I glanced around the gym, noticing not a single male teacher. 4
Asking later, I discovered that there is, in fact, one man who teaches
there. "He's really strict," was one child's opinion of him. Other
teachers told me, "The kids just love him."

Too few children have men in their lives, it occurred to me. Men, 5
that is, who are intensely involved with helping children, who care
about children's education, who make children their top priority.
Sadly, more and more children are coming into the world who will
never know, or have any involvement with, their biological fathers.

And what *about* fathers? What role should they (or stepfathers 6
or boyfriends) play in children's lives? Is it merely to wield the
"hickory" or the belt? It seems to me that in this era of two-income
and single-parent families, the excuse that men are the "breadwin-
ners" can no longer be used to get them off the hook of child-rearing responsibilities.

Should we try to force men who impregnate women to behave   7
as fathers, even if this coercion makes them angry and defiant? Are
angry, defiant men really what our children need? Or are there other
ways to meet children's needs for positive adult male role models?

The firemen got me thinking, and to reading. In Europe, there is   8
a strong tradition of men as teachers and child-care providers. Two
hundred years ago, a Swiss educator named Johann Pestalozzi wrote,
"Teaching is by no means the essence of education. It is love that is
its essence. Without love, neither the physical nor the intellectual
powers of the child will develop."

Another of my readings took me to interviews with recent   9
"Teacher of the Year" winners. A man who had won said he's been
a successful businessman for more than a decade. But after raising
his own children he went back to college and became a teacher.

After the safety lecture the firemen took the children out to   10
show them the fire truck. The little ones clamored to be lifted up,
to be bounced on the firemen's laps, to thumb-wrestle and get "noo-
gies" from the big men. The fire truck paled in comparison to their
interest in gaining the attention of the firemen who drove it.

I asked one of them, "Do they pay you much to do this?" And   11
he replied, "Are you kidding? I'm a volunteer."

"Well, you ought to think about becoming a teacher," I sug-   12
gested to him. "The pay's not much better, but the kids really need
you."

QUESTIONS OF CONTENT

1. What occasion prompted the author to ponder the need for more
   male teachers, especially in elementary schools?
2. What useful purpose does Gray feel will be served by increasing the
   number of male teachers? Where in the article does she articulate
   that purpose?
3. What is necessary to attract more men into the teaching profession?
   Where does Gray hint at a solution to this problem?

QUESTIONS OF FORM

1. We have included this essay in the section devoted to claims of policy. Such claims are usually organized by first declaring that a situation exists which deserves either to be remedied or maintained.
   Then a policy is offered which will remedy the situation or else pre-

serve it. Does Gray follow that organization plan in her essay? Where does she describe the existing situation? Where does she introduce the policy that is to remedy or to preserve that situation?
2. How does Gray use anecdotes to bolster her argument?
3. Gray appeals to authorities in her essay. What is her purpose in doing so; i.e., what part of her argument are the appeals to authority designed to support?
4. Does Gray use any ethical or emotional appeals? If so, where?

SUGGESTIONS FOR WRITING

1. Examine your own experiences in elementary school. Did you have any male teachers? What effect do you think their presence or absence had on your education? On your goals or outlook? If, like Gray, you are persuaded that there should be more male teachers, construct your own argument in which you support a similar claim of policy, drawing on your own experiences.
2. After you have recalled you own school experiences, you may be convinced that, as a rule, men make better teachers than women—or that the reverse is true. Construct an argument in which you support this claim of value, drawing on your own experiences for support.
3. You have just received a letter from a high school friend who is now in college also. He informs you that he plans to change his major next semester to pursue a teaching career. What is your response? Write a letter in which you encourage him in this plan, or alternatively, write a letter in which you state the reasons why you feel that his decision is a bad one.

Perils of Prohibition

ELIZABETH M. WHELAN

My colleagues at the Harvard School of Public Health, where I studied preventive medicine, deserve high praise for their recent study on teenage drinking. What they found in their survey of college students was that they drink "early and . . . often," frequently to the point of getting ill.

As a public-health scientist with a daughter, Christine, heading to college this fall, I have professional and personal concerns about teen binge drinking. It is imperative that we explore why so many young people abuse alcohol. From my own study of the effects of alcohol restrictions and my observations of Christine and her friends' predicament about drinking, I believe that today's laws are unrealistic. Prohibiting the sale of liquor to responsible young adults creates an atmosphere where binge drinking and alcohol abuse have become a problem. American teens, unlike their European peers, don't learn how to drink gradually, safely and in moderation.

Alcohol is widely accepted and enjoyed in our culture. Studies show that moderate drinking can be good for you. But we legally proscribe alcohol until the age of 21 (why not 30 or 45?). Christine and her classmates can drive cars, fly planes, marry, vote, pay taxes, take out loans and risk their lives as members of the U.S. armed forces. But laws in all 50 states say that no alcoholic beverages may be sold to anyone until that magic 21st birthday. We didn't always have a national "21" rule. When I was in college, in the mid-'60s, the drinking age varied from state to state. This posed its own risks, with underage students crossing state lines to get a legal drink. 3

In parts of the Western world, moderate drinking by teenagers and even children under their parents' supervision is a given. Though the per capita consumption of alcohol in France, Spain and Portugal is higher than in the United States, the rate of alcoholism and alcohol abuse is lower. A glass of wine at dinner is normal practice. Kids learn to regard moderate drinking as an enjoyable family activity rather than as something they have to sneak away to do. Banning drinking by young people makes it a badge of adulthood—a tantalizing forbidden fruit. 4

Christine and her teenage friends like to go out with a group to a club, comedy show or sports bar to watch the game. But teens today have to go on the sly with fake IDs and the fear of getting caught. Otherwise, they're denied admittance to most places and left to hang out on the street. That's hardly a safer alternative. Christine and her classmates now find themselves in a legal no man's land. At 18, they're considered adults. Yet when they want to enjoy a drink like other adults, they are, as they put it, "disenfranchised." 5

Comparing my daughter's dilemma with my own as an "underage" college student, I see a difference—and one that I think has exacerbated the current dilemma. Today's teens are far more sophisticated than we were. They're treated less like children and have more responsibilities than we did. This makes the 21 restriction seem anachronistic. 6

For the past few years, my husband and I have been preparing Christine for college life and the inevitable partying—read keg of beer—that goes with it. Last year, a young friend with no drinking experience was violently ill for days after he was introduced to "clear liquids in small glasses" during freshman orientation. We 7

want our daughter to learn how to drink sensibly and avoid this pit-
fall. Starting at the age of 14, we invited her to join us for a glass of
champagne with dinner. She'd tried it once before, thought it was
"yucky" and declined. A year later, she enjoyed sampling wine at
family meals.

When, at 16, she asked for a Mudslide (a bottled chocolate-milk-   8
and-rum concoction), we used the opportunity to discuss it with
her. We explained the alcohol content, told her the alcohol level is
lower when the drink is blended with ice and compared it with a
glass of wine. Since the drink of choice on campus is beer, we contrasted its potency with wine and hard liquor and stressed the importance of not drinking on an empty stomach.

Our purpose was to encourage her to know the alcohol content   9
of what she is served. We want her to experience the effects of liquor
in her own home, not on the highway and not for the first time during a college orientation week with free-flowing suds. Although
Christine doesn't drive yet, we regularly reinforce the concept of
choosing a designated driver. Happily, that already seems a widely
accepted practice among our daughter's friends who drink.

We recently visited the Ivy League school Christine will attend   10
in the fall. While we were there, we read a story in the college paper
about a student who was nearly electrocuted when, in a drunken
state, he climbed on top of a moving train at a railroad station near
the campus. The student survived, but three of his limbs were later
amputated. This incident reminded me of a tragic death on another
campus. An intoxicated student maneuvered himself into a chim-
ney. He was found three days later when frat brothers tried to light
a fire in the fireplace. By then he was dead.

These tragedies are just two examples of our failure to teach   11
young people how to use alcohol prudently. If 18-year-olds don't
have legal access to even a beer at a public place, they have no experience handling liquor on their own. They feel "liberated" when
they arrive on campus. With no parents to stop them, they have a
"let's make up for lost time" attitude. The result: binge drinking.

We should make access to alcohol legal at 18. At the same time,   12
we should come down much harder on alcohol abusers and drunk
drivers of all ages. We should intensify our efforts at alcohol education for adolescents. We want them to understand that it is perfectly OK not to drink. But if they do, alcohol should be consumed
in moderation.

After all, we choose to teach our children about safe sex, in-   13
cluding the benefits of teen abstinence. Why, then, can't we—
schools and parents alike—teach them about safe drinking?

QUESTIONS OF CONTENT

1. What is Elizabeth M. Whelan's background, and why should her arguments in favor of lowering the drinking age carry more weight than most other people's?
2. Whelan notes that while drinking is forbidden in the United States until age 21, a number of other behaviors associated with responsible adults may be legally undertaken before that age. What are they.?
3. According to Whelan, what is the chief reason why young people in the United States engage in binge drinking?
4. Why does Whelan feel that teens today are more at risk with respect to drinking than members of her generation were at a similar age?
5. What course of action did Whelan and her husband undertake to help their daughter cope with the problems of teenage drinking?
6. Whelan provided two examples of tragedies that occurred when students were unprepared to drink responsibly. What were they?

QUESTIONS OF FORM

1. The usual arrangement of an argument containing a claim of policy is the description of a situation that should be altered. Whelan's is essentially a claim of fact. This description is then followed by the policy that will remedy the situation just described. How does Whelan's argument fit this arrangement? Where does she describe the situation? Where does she state her remedy?
2. Early in her argument and later in her conclusion, Whelan uses comparison. What purpose does each comparison serve?
3. In paragraph 10 Whelan uses the device of cause and effect. She presents two effects that she claims are the result of a cause that she later describes. What is that cause, and where does she state it? How does this tactic help to support her claim of policy?

SUGGESTIONS FOR WRITING

1. Examples like those Whelan cites in paragraph 10 are all too common on college campuses today. Surely you are familiar with some that you might add. Rewrite her paragraph 10 with one of your own, drawing on your experience.
2. You are chair of a fraternity or sorority rush program. You are convinced that your organization will be able to attract excellent members while at the same time offering the opportunity to abstain from alcohol or, at least, to drink responsibly. How will you present your views to the membership?
3. Think of other situations that exist on your campus, in your residence hall, or in a specific class that are in urgent need of some sort

of remedy. Argue for that remedy using the technique Whelan follows in her argument.

The Other Crisis in Our Schools

DANIEL SINGAL

A few years ago two unusually capable juniors in my college history class came to ask me, what is this thing called the New Deal? I had mentioned it during a lecture, assuming that everyone would be acquainted with Franklin Roosevelt's domestic program. I was wrong. The two said their friends had never heard of the New Deal either.

For most Americans, mention of the crisis in education centers on wretched conditions in ghetto schools. But another crisis is stalking American education. Half the country's students, the group referred to as "college-bound," are entering college so badly prepared that they perform far below potential—a fact with grave implications for our ability to compete with other nations in the future.

Look at what has happened on the Scholastic Aptitude Test (SAT). In 1972, of the high-school seniors taking the SAT, 11.4 percent had verbal scores over the bench mark of 600; by 1983 the number had dropped to seven percent, and it remains in that vicinity. The percentage scoring over 600 in math dropped from 17.9 in 1972 to 14.4 by 1981. (Since then, the math scores have climbed back, largely due to an influx of high-scoring Asian-American students.) The available information, including my own research, suggests that a typical bright high-school senior in 1991, compared with one in 1970, might score roughly 55 points lower on the verbal section and 25 points lower on the math part.

According to Herbert Rudman, a professor of educational psychology at Michigan State University and a co-author of the Stanford Achievement Test for more than three decades, students in the bottom quartile have shown steady improvement on standardized educational tests since the 1960s. *Average* test scores, however, have gone down, primarily because of the performance of those in the top quartile. This "highest cohort of achiever," Rudman writes, has shown "the greatest declines."

People who dismiss those declines as insignificant haven't seen a college term paper lately. It's not that freshmen are unable to read or write. Most high-school seniors possess what the National Assessment of Educational Progress considers satisfactory skills. But do they have sufficient command of English to comprehend a college text or express a reasonably sophisticated argument on paper? In the early 1970s the overwhelming majority of freshmen at the more selective colleges arrived with such "advanced" skills. Now only a handful do.

Missing Scaffold. Emilia da Costa, who has taught history at   6 Yale for the past 19 years, estimates that while 75 percent of her students can pick out the basic theme of a book, only 25 percent come away with deep comprehension. David Hollinger, professor of history at the University of Michigan, has had to ease up on assignments. Even a journalist like Walter Lippmann is too hard for most underclassmen, he finds.

Students who don't read at advanced level can't write well either.   7 According to Richard Marius, director of expository writing at Harvard, "freshmen's vocabulary and the forms by which they express themselves are very, very limited." Schools like Harvard get the cream of the crop. Teachers at less elite institutions get mangled sentences and writing that can't sustain a thought for more than half a page.

Along with impoverishment of language comes a downturn in   8 reasoning skills. R. Jackson Wilson finds this to be the greatest change he has observed during a quarter-century of teaching history at Smith College. "Students are ready to tell you how they feel about an issue, but they have never learned how to construct a rational argument to defend their opinions."

Finally, they have an extraordinary dearth of factal knowledge.   9 Paula Fass, a professor of history at the University of California at Berkeley, is astonished that sophomores and juniors are often unable to differentiate between the American Revolution and the Civil War.

A direct connection exists between this deficit in factual knowl-   10 edge and the decline in verbal skills. No matter how fascinating a new detail might be, it is almost impassible to hold in memory unless it can be placed in the context of previous knowledge. Providing that intellectual scaffold used to be a major function of year-long survey courses in history and literature. Yet not enough high schools today teach that kind of curriculum.

The few schools that have kept test scores stable or even rising   11 share two characteristics. One is that academics receive priority over every other activity. These schools require semester- or year-long courses in literature and encourage rigorous math classes, including geometry and advanced algebra.

The other key factor is the practice of grouping students by abil-   12 ity. The contrast is stark, as pointed out in a 1978 study by the National Association of Secondary School Principals. Schools that had "severely declining test scores" mixed students of differing abilities in the same classes, while "schools that have maintained good SAT scores" tended "to prefer homogeneous grouping."

Literary Junk. Why have these high-quality schools become so 13
rare? The answer lies in the cultural ferment of the 1960s. Educational gurus of the day called for essentially nonacademic schools,
whose main purpose was to maximize spontaneity, creativity and
affection for others. To the extent that logic and acquired knowledge
interfered with that process, they were devalued.

This populist tidal wave receded by the late 1970s, but the medi- 14
ocrity remains. Students are all too often given works that, as the
English department at one highly ranked independent school puts
it, are "age-appropriate" assignments "that reflect their interests as
adolescents, that they can read without constant recourse to a dictionary, and from which they can take whatever they are inspired to
take." Feed a student the literary equivalent of junk food and you
will get a lackluster command of English.

As for writing, the tendency is to call for first-person narratives 15
that describe what the student has seen, felt or done. Essays in
which the writer marshals evidence to support a coherent, logical
argument are all too rare.

In sum, this is a generation whose members may be better 16
equipped to track the progress of their souls in diaries than any
Americans since the Puritans, but not at all equipped for writing papers in college, or for later producing documents that get the world's
work done.

Students headed for college used to get a solid grasp of Ameri- 17
can and European history in high school. Now they pass through so-
cial-studies courses designed to impress upon them the central
values of the '60s, including concern for the environment, respect
for different racial and ethnic groups, and women's rights. These values are important, but teaching them in a superficial manner, de-
void of historical context, deprives students of that vital base of
knowledge they must have to succeed as undergraduates.

Accompanying this dumbing-down of the curriculum has been 18
a wholesale change in school philosophy. In place of "stretching"
students, the key objective in previous eras, the goal has become not
to stress" them. But the stress they avoid in high school only comes
back to haunt them in college.

Perhaps most crucial, the '60s mentality has shifted the locus 19
of concern from high to low achievers. Educators judge themselves
by how well they can reach the least able student. Programs to
help the culturally disadvantaged and the learning-disabled have
proliferated, while those for the gifted receive no more than token
interest.

The prevailing ideology holds that it is much better to give up 20
the prospect of excellence than to take the chance of injuring any

student's self-esteem. So teachers invest their energies in making sure that slow learners do not think of themselves as failures. One often senses a virtual prejudice against bright students.

In adopting this posture, educators have simply been carrying   21
out their social mandate in the wake of the '60s, to produce equality rather than excellence. To restore academic quality, we must make clear to teachers and administrators that we want to move toward social equality *and* academic excellence.

Action Plan. To restore excellence to our schools we should take   22
four concrete steps:

1. Dramatically increase the quality and quantity of assigned   23
reading. By the senior year of high school, college-bound students should be reading the equivalent of at least 12 books a year for class, not counting textbooks, along with six to eight additional books in independent study and summer reading. In the preceding grades, students should become accustomed to reading more and more each year.

This sort of reading load, which was standard in our best schools   24
a quarter-century ago, is still standard in some. At McDonogh, an independent school outside Baltimore that enrolls college-bound students from a wide range of ability levels, 15 to 20 assigned books a year in English class is not unusual for 11th- and 12th-graders. College admissions officers I know rave about how well-prepared McDonogh graduates are, and how enthusiastic they are about learning.

2. Bring back survey courses. They would ensure that students   25
enter college with a firm knowledge of how the world has developed. One year of history and English might focus on the United States, another year on Europe and a third year on the non-European world. Issues of race and gender would naturally arise; it is hard, for instance, to cover American literature without including black and women writers, or to discuss our past without spending time on slavery and segregation.

3. Institute flexible ability grouping in elementary and sec-   26
ondary schools. A student might begin in the fast group in math but the slow one in English, with the placements changing from year to year depending on his or her progress. The guiding principle is not to give special treatment to any one group, but to provide instruction tailored to the learning needs of each child.

At the Waynflete School in Portland, Maine, for example, an in-   27
tensive section in English entails a heavier than normal load of reading in more advanced texts, more sophisticated writing assignments, and faster-paced instruction. Since the curriculum includes the same core material covered in a regular section, students unable to handle the demands can drop back at any time during the school year.

Administrators at Waynflete report that a number of kids of   28
middle-range academic ability perform well in intensive sections
because they enjoy the challenge.

4. Attract more bright college graduates into teaching. The av-   29
erage verbal SAT score of the young people drawn into teaching has
hovered around 400 for more than a decade. Clearly, if we want top-
notch instruction for college-bound students, we must find a new
supply of capable teachers.

To the familiar prescriptions of higher pay and better working   30
conditions I would add abolishing certification requirements for
teachers, at least above the elementary-school level. Future teachers spend far too much time taking Mickey Mouse courses on how
to construct a lesson plan. Most private schools do not require certification, yet they still attract a teaching corps of much higher quality—even when paying lower salaries than public schools. "Our
teachers never learned how to teach, which is why they teach so
well," quips Laurance Levy, the former head of McDonogh's first-
rate English department.

In the words of education analyst Paul Copperman, "For the   31
first time in the history of our country, the educational skills of one
generation will not surpass, will not equal, will not even approach
those of their parents." This failure will bring a lower sense of professional fulfillment for our youngsters as they pursue their careers,
and will hamper their ability to stay competitive with European and
Asian countries. As the United Negro College Fund aptly puts it, a
mind is a terrible thing to waste. It's time to recognize that we have
been wasting far too many good ones.

QUESTIONS OF CONTENT

1. In his introduction, Singal complains that his students were ignorant
   of the New Deal. Here he is using an *allusion* to a historical event.
   (If you are not familiar with this word, look it up in this book's Glossary of Useful Terms.) When did the New Deal era exist, and what
   was its importance to U.S. history?
2. Singal mentions the general decline in SAT scores during the last two
   decades. What aspect of these statistics does he find most alarming?
3. Singal claims that many of his students encounter difficulty in placing newly learned information within the context of previous knowledge. Why does he think that this difficulty exists, and how does he
   think it can be resolved?
4. Does Singal favor grouping students by ability? Why or why not?

5. Instead of stressing excellence in education, what does the author feel the schools are stressing? Why does he believe this is so?
6. How many books a year does Singal think a high school junior or senior should be required to read in a typical English class?

QUESTIONS OF FORM

1. In this claim of policy, Singal begins by describing a dismal state of affairs. Summarize that situation.
2. What policies does he propose to remedy this bad situation? Where does he state them?
3. Why does Singal recommend emphasizing survey courses? What part of the bad situation would their reinstitution serve to remedy?
4. When he discusses ability grouping as a possible remedy, Singal introduces an important *qualification.* What is this qualification, and why is Singal wise to use it?

SUGGESTIONS FOR WRITING

1. If you recently graduated from high school, do you find yourself in complete agreement with Singal's assessment of American education? If you do not, write a brief rebuttal, attacking the point or points with which you disagree.
2. Perhaps you feel that Singal's recommendations do not go far enough. In a brief essay, summarize his position and then add your own proposals.
3. You are a student in the College of Education who hopes some day to become a teacher. How do you feel about Singal's essentially unsupported claim about what he calls "Mickey Mouse" education courses? Write a brief response in which you justify the kinds of instruction that you are receiving or that you expect to receive. You may want to consult with one of your instructors or with your academic advisor about the content of your response.

Don't Swamp Parks with Ad Money

DONELLA H. MEADOWS

Most Americans haven't heard of the government's plan to commercialize the national parks. To the few who have, it seems like proof that we have gone much too far with our national experiment in shifting from public to private responsibility.

The park proposal is not an invitation for corporations to plas- 2
ter their logos across Half Dome, the Lincoln Memorial or the
Grand Canyon. Rather, it is an opportunity for 10 or so selected
companies to contribute around $15 million apiece each year to the
national parks.

In return, the companies can use in their advertising a special 3
symbol—like the Olympic rings—to proclaim themselves "official
sponsors" of the national park system. Under the National Parks
Commercialization Act, corporate logos would not appear within
the parks.

The sponsorship millions certainly could be put to good use. An- 4
nual budgets for our 369 national parks, memorials, battlefields, historic sites and recreation areas have been cut by more than $200
million since 1983, while the number of visitors in that time has increased 30 percent, from 207 million to 270 million a year. For lack
of funds, some campgrounds had to be closed this summer, and
there were 900 fewer park rangers. Research programs have stopped.
Paint is peeling. Roads are potholed. The Park Service says it would
take $4 billion to catch up with all the postponed maintenance.

There is precedent for the private sector paying for what the gov- 5
ernment will not do. In 1986, corporations contributed to a $300-
million drive to refurbish the Statue of Liberty and Ellis Island. In a
burst of ads, the companies took credit for the restored Miss Liberty.

That experience engendered plenty of criticism. The essence of 6
charity is anonymity, some said. If you have to brag about it—especially if you spend more bragging about it than you gave in the first
place—that isn't charity, it's marketing. Furthermore, it's marketing
based on false claims. The corporate contributions (and ads) were
tax-deductible, so in fact they were taken from taxpayers' hides.
And twice as much money was contributed by individuals and fraternal, ethnic and community groups as by corporations.

The bill in Congress aims to turn sporadic infusions of corpo- 7
rate money into regular practice. In the current plan, companies will
cover only 8 percent of the Park Service's annual budget. But one
only has to contemplate the Olympics to imagine a slippery slope
that could carry the parks into a commercial swamp.

There may be a soul somewhere who believes that the Golden 8
Arches or Mickey Mouse will not follow the money into the parks,
but there is no such innocence in the advertising world. There are,
of course, other ways to fund the national parks.

In most cases, entrance fees haven't gone up since the parks 9
were established. There is another bill before Congress that would
not only allow parks to raise fees, (a car entering Yellowstone, for
example, might pay not $10 but $25), but also would let each park

keep the money instead of, as at present, passing it to the general treasury.

Greater sums also could come from park concessions. More than 650 private companies earn a total of $700 million a year operating campgrounds, restaurants, hotels and other enterprises in the parks. They pay $19 million a year for their monopoly licenses, which are granted for 10 to 30 years and are renewed automatically. 10

Here's a place where market principles could benefit our parks. But bills to open park concessions to competitive bidding passed Congress overwhelmingly last year only to be held back by the Republican leadership, so they never reached the president for signature. 11

Another way to pay for the parks is—shocking thought!— through our taxes. Doubling the current $1.5 billion National Park Service operating budget would cost $5 per American per year—call it $15 per family. 12

If we, the least-taxed people in the industrialized world, feel too poor to raise our taxes that much, we could get the money by building one less B-2 bomber. 13

Generations of Americans poorer than we somehow managed to maintain the parks, commonly owned, commonly supported. We inherited them, the crown jewels of our citizenship. Is there really something different about us, something less wise, something weaker or cheaper or meaner, that prevents us from passing to our children these beautiful lands, well-kept, publicly supported, refuges from the commercialism that dominates every other part of our world? 14

QUESTIONS OF CONTENT

1. Meadows says that the proposal to commercialize the national parks would mean that "ten or so selected companies [would] contribute around $15 million apiece to the national parks," in return for which they would become "official sponsors of national parks," a title they can use in their advertisements. This seems innocuous enough; what does Meadows find alarming about it?
2. Meadows proposes at least four alternate ways of providing additional support for our national parks, none of which involve commercialization. What are they?
3. Meadows admits that there is already a precedent for seeking private sector support for national parks. What instance does she have in mind, and why does she feel that it is not a very convincing example?

QUESTIONS OF FORM

1. If we look upon Meadows' argument as one involving support for a claim of policy, what is that claim of policy, and what precisely is her support for it?
2. What exactly is Meadows doing in paragraph 4 that is crucial to supporting all claims of policy?
3. While supporting her own claim of policy, Meadows is *refuting* another claim of policy. What claim is that, and how does she go about it?
4. Meadows makes good use of both ethical and emotional appeals in her argument. Where exactly does she do this?
5. In paragraph 7 Meadows uses the term "slippery slope." Look it up in this book's "Short Guide to Material and Formal Fallacies." How is she using the term—as an appeal to a particular failure of logic on her opponent's part or as a description of her own belief about the likely effects of commercialization? Might you argue that her use of the term might constitute a weakness in her approach?

SUGGESTIONS FOR WRITING

1. Briefly summarize the two points of view revealed in this argument regarding the funding of national parks.
2. If you feel that the situation described in question 5 above really does represent a serious weakness in Meadows' argument, then do one of two things:
   a. Rewrite that portion of her argument, strengthening it appropriately.
   b. Write a refutation of Meadow's position.
3. Do library research in *Fortune* magazine and pick a corporation from its most recent "Fortune 500" list that you believe would or would not benefit especially from the proposed national park sponsorship program. Write a letter to that corporation's Chief Executive Officer in which you give your reasoning as if you were a corporate stockholder.

REFUTATION

Will Jelly Beans Be Illegal?

SARAH J. MCCARTHY

An irate consumer in Salem, Ore., not long ago phoned the De- 1
partment of Housing and Urban Development (HUD) to complain
of an offensive photo in the real-estate section of the local newspaper, the *Statesman Journal*. HUD agents were mobilized to action.
An investigation revealed that the photo had indeed run, and the
Journal promised it would not happen again.

Did the photo show a half-naked woman? A rock star swallow- 2
ing a live chicken?

Hardly. It depicted the Easter Bunny. The caller, you see, was an 3
atheist who felt that the egg-toting rodent promoted religion and
was therefore discriminatory.

Having refused to make the holiday switch from white choco- 4
late crosses—suddenly a form of "religious harassment" in some
quarters—to chocolate rockets and bowling balls, I am moved to
wonder: Will jelly beans be next?

Not as crazy as it sounds. The *New York Times* reports that a 5
School-Parent Association in Voorhees, N. J., warned parents to
avoid jelly beans and purple and yellow decorations at their spring
parties (which, of course, used to be known as Easter parties). Seems
it has become unacceptable to expose the MTV generation to an
Easter basket.

When President Bush signed the 1991 Civil Rights Act, later up- 6
held by the Supreme Court, he made it possible for punitive damages in the hundreds of thousands of dollars to be levied on those
guilty of permitting a religiously "hostile environment"—and that
can be interpreted to mean almost any religious expression at all.
This intolerance has now been extended to include holiday celebrations and song, except for the most bland and generic. Americans
who once embraced diversity and celebrated the rich texture of different cultures have allowed themselves to be straight-jacketed by
legal challenges from the blandness police, who want everything to
be gray and "equal."

Jack-o'-lanterns and flying witches are considered by some to be   7
a celebration of "Satanic rituals." A school or workplace that displays such decorations over objections from employees or customers may be found guilty of promoting—you guessed it, a hostile
environment. Punitive damages can reach $300,000 per pumpkin.
Amid a legal climate that rewards plaintiffs for coffee spills and "na-
palm" apple-pie burns, schools and employers are twice shy.

What's more, the Iowa City Community School District has   8
compiled a list of offensive Halloween costumes. The district's Equity Affirmative Action Committee suggests that children not dress
as hobos, old men or women, witches, the devil, Indians, Africans
or gypsies. Marian Coleman, the committee director, recommends
that kids trick-or-treat dressed as Abraham Lincoln or Robin Hood,
demonstrating her own insensitivity to those who think Robin
Hood was a Marxist.

Atheist Jon Murray argues that an employee should be able to   9
sue the boss if another employee—get this—hums *Amazing Grace.*
Murray is not to be taken lightly, though. He's the son of Madalyn
Murray O'Hair, who successfully sued to have prayer removed from
public schools. O'Hair, other atheists and the ACLU are responsible
for much of the purge of religious expression from American life.

These activities, of course, reach a fever pitch around Christmas   10
Season—uh, make that Holiday Season. A 1989 Supreme Court decision known as the "reindeer rule" held that a Nativity scene on
public property is acceptable only if it is diluted by more commercial personae, such as Santa and Rudolph. But wait—doesn't the
court know that Santa Claus is itself a derivative of Saint Nicholas,
and therefore is brimming with religious overtones? Clearly, anyone
with a name beginning with Saint should have no legitimate part in
a culturally sanitized holiday. "The Holiday Person Is Coming To
Town" may be a preferable, less exclusionary alternative.

You laugh? The word "virgin" was expunged from *Silent Night*   11
and replaced with the less judgmental "caring mother" in a Unitar-
ian Church in Massachusetts, perhaps to avoid offending any vir-
ginally challenged persons in the congregation. This, by the way, is
the same church that published a hymnal of politically correct
songs, disallowing the word "Amen" because it contains the word
"men."

In Pittsburgh, the Christmas season has been renamed Sparkle   12
Season so as not to step on any toes. *Silent Night* is banned from
many schools, but *Jingle Bells* is okay. Snowpersons are safe, as long
as they don't offend "people of gender." In some classrooms in suburban Pittsburgh, teachers and students have been told not to wear
Christmas sweaters, and children's homemade Christmas calendars

were removed from bulletin boards. Even red and green cookie sprinkles have raised eyebrows.

Are you one of those people who derives a special smile from Holiday Season commemorative stamps? Then expect to be smiling less from now on. After more than three decades of issuing such stamps, the U.S. Postal Service also has become wary of permitting "a hostile environment." Last year, the Post Office announced there will be no more traditional Christmas stamps, religious or secular. (A public outcry now has that decision under review.) In post offices this year, no signs reading "Merry Christmas" are to be displayed—though it's unclear whether they hope to avoid offending non-Christians, or just people who aren't merry. In any case, Postal Service spokeswoman Robin Minard says there has been much discussion about whether "the C-word will be allowed to exist on a stamp." 13

The fact is, regardless of its intentions, the so-called Civil Rights Act of 1991 has unleashed an *attack* on civil rights and given rise to cultural repression. Huge windfalls should not be awarded to people who say they've been offended by a Madonna stamp. Term limits seem in order for a Supreme Court that lacks the foresight to see the effect these laws have on a free people. 14

Writes Richard Harwood, former ombudsman at the *Washington Post*, "This is the nuttiness that passes for 'political correctness' and finds itself very often incorporated into laws more appropriate to a police state than a democracy founded on principles of freedom." 15

QUESTIONS OF CONTENT

1. McCarthy begins this essay with an example of the Easter Bunny coming under attack as an instance of "religious harassment." What other instances of alleged religious harassment does she point to?
2. Why does she believe such attacks must be taken seriously?
3. What do you understand by the term "political correctness," and how does the term apply to the topic of this essay?

QUESTIONS OF FORM

1. Read the section of Chapter 5 entitled "Another Effective Method of Refutation." How is the refutation contained in this essay a reduction to absurdity? In how many specific instances does McCarthy employ this device?

2. What other types of refutation might be made in response to those who, in the name of political correctness, object to traditional celebrations of Easter or other religious holidays?
3. Does McCarthy appeal to authorities? Does she use emotional or ethical appeals? If so, where? And how effective are those uses?

SUGGESTIONS FOR WRITING

1. Examine another refutation in this section. How might you subject the claim that author is refuting to a reduction to absurdity?
2. Your younger brother or sister has just returned from elementary school in a tearful state because a Valentine's Day party had just been canceled owing to a complaint that it was a celebration of St. Valentine, a Christian saint. Write a letter to the school principal stating your support for or opposition to this decision.
3. You are a teacher in an elementary school and have been made chair of this year's Christmas pageant planning committee. You have some reservations about the pageant because you know that there are at least three Jewish children in your class and there are a number of Middle Eastern and Oriental children whose religious beliefs are unknown to you. What will you do? Write a memo to the principal outlining the course of action you prefer to take.

Let's Keep Christmas Commercial

APRIL OURSLER ARMSTRONG

Every year right after Halloween, the world becomes Christmas-conscious—and people begin deploring. if only we could have a *real* Christmas, they say. The good old kind. Quiet, inexpensive, simple, devout. If only we could retrieve the holy day from the hands of vulgar moneygrubbers, they say. They say, with earnest horror, that the price tag has become the liturgical symbol of the season.

As a Christian, I do find facets of the Christmas season ridiculous, offensive or disturbing, but I believe most complaints about the commercialization of Christmas are unconsciously hypocritical nonsense. I'm afraid that often the complainers are kidding themselves, striking spiritual poses. I'm not ashamed to admit that if I had to spend Christmas somewhere far from the crowd and the vulgar trappings, I'd hate it. I love the lights, the exquisite ones in *boutiques,* the joyful ones in village centers, even the awkward ones strung on drugstores and filling stations. I love the Santa Clauses, including those on street corners, the intricately animated windows, the hot bewilderment of the bargain basement, the sequins of the dime store. Cut off from the whole wild confusion, I'd not be holier. I'd be forlorn. So, I suspect, would most of us.

What's supposed to be wrong with a commercialized Christmas?   3

For one thing, it's usually said that Christmas has become the   4
time of parties where people drink and eat too much. ("Turning Yuletide into fooltide"—that exact phrase was used to describe the holiday in Merrie Olde England, so those who yearn for the "good old Christmas" should carefully define their terms.) Oddly enough, it seems to me that often the people who most loudly criticize this holiday partying are those folks who acquire Christmas hangovers and indigestion. And they deplore it as if no one ever had to avoid hangovers, indigestion or exhaustion at any other time of the year.

They say that commercialization has made the buying of Christ-   5
mas presents a rat race. God knows, most of the gifts we peddle to each other have nothing to do with the infant of Bethlehem. For my part, I enjoy gawking in the catalogues at the new luxuries for people who have everything. My imagination romps over items for my private Ostentatious Wastefulness list: silver-plated golf clubs, hundred-dollar dresses for little girls to spill ice cream on. Dime and department stores are crammed with gifts no wise man would bring anyone. Things like stuffed dinosaurs twelve feet high and replicas of the *Pietà* that glow in the dark.

With rare exceptions it is foolishly pompous to get scandalized   6
and accuse manufacturers, advertisers and vendors of desecrating Christmas by trying to sell what you or I may think is silly junk. Obviously some people like it and buy it, and that's their business. It's said to be the fault of the commercializers that parents buy overpriced, unnecessary toys for children. And that's a fancy alibi. If you don't like what's being hawked this Christmas, you don't have to buy it. And if you're a sucker, your problem isn't seasonal.

Christians began giving presents to each other to celebrate Jesus'   7
birthday in imitation of the Wise Men who came to Bethlehem. The basic idea was and is to bring joy, to honor God in others, and to give in His name with love for all. But in our social structure, with or without the blessings of the Internal Revenue Service, Christmas presents serve many purposes. Gift givers are, in practice, often diplomats, almoners, egoists, or investors. A shiny box with gold ribbon may be a guilt assuager, a bribe, a bid for attention, or merely payment for services past or future. And what is in the box must look rightly lavish, conveying subliminal impact while not costing too much. That kind of petty ugliness we all know about. And we know that often, too, gift givers play Santa Claus against their will, badgered by cozy reminders in the parking lot about how the boys

wish you Season's Greetings, or by collections taken up in offices, clubs, Sunday schools, Scouts and third grades.

But are extortion, begging, status seeking and advantage taking so unusual among us that they occur only once a year? Isn't it more realistic to admit that whatever is sleazy about Christmas isn't seasonal? 8

After all, the instinct and art of commercialization are neither good nor bad. People normally, naturally, make a living from every kind of want, aspiration and occasion. We exploit births, weddings, deaths, first communions, bar mitzvahs, the wish to smell nice, the craving for amusement, and the basic desires for housing, clothes, love and food. Is anything more commercialized than food? But no one complains when millions cash in on our need to eat. 9

Do we assume that eating is so earthy and undignified that commercialization upgrades it, while celebrating Christmas should be so totally ethereal a process that it shouldn't be treated in a human way? If so, we are both pretentious and mistaken. We are creatures who both eat and worship, and God doesn't want us as split personalities. When Christ once raised a little girl from death, the next thing He did was to tell her mother to feed her. 10

Simony is a sin, the sin of trying to buy or sell what is sacred. But this is not simony or sin, this peddling of manger sets, this pitchman heralding the season. No one can buy or sell Christmas. No one can steal it from us, or ruin it for us, except ourselves. If we become self-seeking, materialistic, harried and ill-willed in this Christmas melee, that's our problem, not the fault of the world in which we live. 11

Some people are dismayed today in a different way, because they honestly fear Christmas is being de-Christianized, made nonsectarian. They are upset when someone who does not share their faith sets up a tree and exchanges gifts and wishes them "Season's Greetings" instead of naming the holy day. They resent the spelling "Xmas." Others fret over the way Santa Claus and snowmen crowd out the shepherds. Put Christ back into Christmas, these offended people cry. 12

As far as I know, Christ never left it. He could never be cut out of Christmas, except in the privacy of individual hearts. I don't care if some people designate Xmas as the Time for Eggnog, or Toys. Let them call it the Time to Buy New Appliances, the Time to Use the Phone, or the Time for New Loans. The antics of the rest of the world can't change Christmas. Why on earth should we expect everyone to share our special joy our way? 13

Actually, what bothers most people who decry the vulgar American Christmas is a matter of taste, not of morals or of religious commitment. Taste is a very personal matter, relative, changing and worldly; we're all a rather tacky lot anyway, religious or not. Some Christians like those new stark liturgical Christmas cards, and 14 some dote on luminous plastic crèches, and I hate both, and the Lord doesn't care a bit. Maybe you can't stand Rudolf, are bored with the same old carols, and cringe at Santa in a helicopter. But don't blame your discomfort on commercialization and become righteous and indignant. After all, if your taste is better than that of most other people, you're probably proud of it, and you should be willing to suffer the consequences in kindly forbearance.

I believe the root of complaints about commercialized Christmas is that we're falling into the dangerous habit of thinking that religion is somehow coarsened by contact with real people. I suspect that unconsciously we're embarrassed at the prospect of trying to live with God here and now. At times we modern Christians seem to have a neurotic refusal to embrace reality in the name of the Lord who was the supreme realist, and maker of the real.   15

It's always easier, if you're not doing very well religiously, to insist that the secularizing world prevents you from devotion. Christmas is meant to be lived in the noisy arena of the shopping day countdown, amid aluminum trees, neckties and counterfeit French perfume. If all the meditation I get around to is listening to Scrooge and Tiny Tim, or begging heaven for patience to applaud a school pageant, I'm a fool to blame anyone but myself. Census time in Bethlehem was distracting too.   16

I know a man who confides that he learns more about patience and love of his neighbor in post-office lines than anywhere else. More than one mother has learned that Christmas shopping on a tight budget can be a lesson in mortification, humility, willpower and joy. There's grist for meditation in the reflection of tree lights in a sloshy puddle. Families have their own customs, their private windows on glory. And families that are honest and relaxed find that the commercially generated atmosphere of goodwill hinders them not at all in their celebration. God works in wondrous ways still, even among assemble-it-yourself toys.   17

Christmas is a parable of the whole Christian venture. The Christian's attitude toward it, his willingness to make it relevant repeatedly in his own time and space, is a symptom of his whole encounter with God. The first Christmas happened, so Christians believe, because God lovingly plunged Himself into human nature to transform it. He is not honored by men and women who want to disown other people's human nature in His name.   18

Let's not make the mealy-mouthed error of complaining that paganism threatens Christmas today. Christmas has already absorbed and recharged the vestiges of Druid feasts, Norse gods and sun worship. Christmas took the world as it was and built on it, and it's still doing just that.   19

To those who fear that Christmas is prostituted by the almighty   20
dollar, I suggest that it's remarkable and beautiful that Christmas is
publicly touted at all. Nor do I make that suggestion, as some might
suspect, in a tone of meek appeasement to groups that object to
Christmas celebrations in public schools, or crèches in town squares.
Realistically, I know that in our society what is important to people
and concerns them deeply, whether it's cancer or get-rich-quick
schemes, patriotism or religion, is talked about and exploited.

If Christmas becomes for some people primarily a subject for   21
commercials, at least God is getting equal time with toothpaste. If
people didn't care about Him, He wouldn't even get that.

In good taste or bad, by your standards or mine, the fact of Christ,   22
the good news of the meeting of heaven and earth, the tidings of love
and peace for human nature, are announced everywhere. It is still
true that he who has ears to hear will hear.

QUESTIONS OF CONTENT

1. In paragraphs 4 through 8, according to Armstrong, people who deplore the commercialization of Christmas usually claim that the real
   meaning of Christmas has been undermined by three kinds of
   human activity. What human activities are these?
2. Armstrong suggests in paragraph 14 that the source of much criticism of America's commercialization of Christmas is that it offends
   our sense of good taste. She disagrees with this claim and suggests
   that it is not really commercialism that we find distasteful but
   something else. That something else is pivotal to her argument;
   what is it?
3. In order for her argument to succeed, Armstrong must demonstrate
   two things: her religious background and her knowledge of Christian
   traditions surrounding Christmas. Where in her essay does she
   demonstrate these things?
4. What does Armstrong mean when she says in paragraph 18 that
   Christmas is a parable of the whole Christian venture?
5. Why does Armstrong consider the commercialization of Christmas
   a hopeful rather than a dreadful thing?

QUESTIONS OF FORM

1. Paragraph 2 contains both a *concession* and a *claim*. Identify each.
2. Armstrong calls attention to the material fallacy of *false cause* in refuting the claim that the commercialization of Christmas tempts

people to buy overpriced, unnecessary junk. She says that such a claim is a fancy alibi—that if people are suckers, their problem isn't seasonal; the real cause of their problem is human nature and not Christmas and its attendant commercialism. She appeals to the same fallacy in paragraphs 7 and 8. Explain how that appeal is made.

3. *Special pleading* is the fallacy of examining only part of the evidence (the part that suits one's purposes) while ignoring or minimizing other evidence. In paragraph 9 Armstrong accuses her opponents of this kind of pleading. How exactly does she do this? Where is she guilty of the same fallacy?

4. In arguing for the commercialization of Christmas, Armstrong finds it necessary to attack a warrant that is practically unopposed in the Christian world: Religious things are precious and should not be cheapened. In order to prevail, she must call attention to a warrant whose appeal is even stronger. What warrant is that?

SUGGESTIONS FOR WRITING

1. In a concise essay, state the basic elements of Armstrong's position.
2. Think about your own campus culture. What are some claims that you take for granted, that you've heard repeated over and over? Consider these:

> The humanities are useless for career seekers.
> Athletics are overemphasized.
> The drinking age should be lowered.
> Residence hall life is too restrictive.
> The cafeteria food is awful.

Now take your cues from Armstrong and attempt to refute one of these often accepted claims—or another college-related one of your own devising. Consider Armstrong's use of the material fallacies of false cause and special pleading and try to show that your opponents have been victimized by them.

3. Choose another unpopular stand and defend it as Armstrong does in "Let's Keep Christmas Commercial." First, determine the warrant that makes the claim unpopular. Then attack that warrant either by (a) showing that it has insufficient support or backing or by (b) locating another and stronger warrant, one supportive of your claim, that your opponents can share.

4. Now try something really difficult. Refute Armstrong's argument from either a Christian or a non-Christian point of view. Examine the evidence that she presents, and demonstrate that she has misrepresented the situation. Consider such questions as these as you prepare to write: Suppose you are a non-Christian—does her argument have the same force for you? How much of it is dependent on Christian ideals and doctrine?

Ban Paid Political Ads on TV, Radio

WILLIAM PFAFF

I suppose this is a hopeless cause, but in an election season any-   1
thing can happen, and certainly this year's has been the most sordid
American election campaign yet.

Americans do not have to put up with this. There is a way to   2
change the country's political campaigns for the better. It is by eliminating paid political advertising on television and radio.

Nearly every other democracy bans paid broadcast political   3
advertising and enforces an impartial use of the airwaves by political candidates and parties. It can be done—and is, in nearly every
other advanced society. The United States is the only serious democracy that allows its politics to be dominated by a system that compels people to raise hundreds of thousands of dollars—sometimes
millions—in order to have a chance to be elected to public office.

The system corrupts and demeans candidates, corrupts the polit-   4
ical system because of the influence it gives to those who contribute
the money and corrupts the debate by driving out the discussion of issues, substituting emotional appeals, image-mongering and character
assassination—the last a particular feature of this year's campaigns.

The advantage the present system gives not only to special in-   5
terests but to incumbents is obvious, at a time when there is a massive (if not particularly rational) movement of voter opinion against
incumbents.

The argument also is made that this system provides officehold-   6
ers with an unconstitutional advantage, since no challenger can expect to enjoy the same cash favors from special interests as the man
already in Washington, or in the state legislature or Statehouse. It certainly is a system that defies the spirit of the American constitutional
system, in which citizens—and candidates—are supposed to be equal.

Money corruption is a factor in all democracies, as currently or   7
recently and blatantly is demonstrated in Italy, France, Britain and
Japan. But why must Americans positively encourage corruption by
the way we run our elections?

Paid political broadcasts should be banned. A system of equi-   8
tably distributed broadcast time for rival candidates and parties
should be substituted. Nearly everyone else in the democratic world
does this. Why can't we?

In principle, one would think this time should be contributed by   9
broadcasters and cable companies as part of their public service
obligation, but that undoubtedly is too much to ask. The time will
have to be paid for from public funds. But since the overall cost of

campaigns will have drastically been reduced by this reform—together with the consequent demands on federal matching money—the public will undoubtedly still come out ahead.

Certainly the present system amounts to a machine for transferring the public funds granted candidates into the bank accounts of the broadcasting companies. That, of course, is one reason the opposition to what I propose is so virulent.   10

The benefits of reform nonetheless are clear: The influence of special-interest campaign contributors and PACs would be greatly reduced. The power of lobbyists in Washington and in the state capitals would be cut, as they would no longer hold a money threat over officeholders. The political field would be opened up to new candidates. Television would (partially, at least) be depolluted during campaign time. Journalists would be forced to stop covering campaigns as campaigns and go back to covering politicians as politicians and even to discussing issues.   11

There is something more that could be done. There could be rules about what goes into a political broadcast. Certain kinds of appeals could be banned. The emotionally loaded image could be excluded. Politicians could be forced to talk to voters in their broadcasts, be interviewed, debate one another, be challenged.   12

No doubt this would make the campaigns much more boring than they are now, but in the governance of a democracy, boring reality would seem preferable to fiction, fantasy and fabrication. No doubt this reform would also be attacked as limiting free speech. It would in fact encourage and even require free speech, in place of lying images and demagogic manipulation.   13

If politicians and pundits can seriously talk about term limits, which solve nothing, or mandated budget balancing, which is economic nonsense, or any other half-baked nostrum in current American public debate, we can certainly talk about installing in the United States the campaign rules and limitations that prevail in most of the rest of the democratic world.   14

We can eliminate from the United States a practice that most of the world's democratic citizens see as a scandalous subversion of representative government, benefiting only demagogy and special interest. Who among our politicians would take the lead?   15

QUESTIONS OF CONTENT

1. Pfaff claims that our current system of paid political ads favors the incumbents. Why is that? He also says that it gives office holders an unconstitutional advantage. Explain this claim.

2. What sort of alternative does Pfaff suggest to our system of paid ads?
3. Who reap the financial rewards from the current system?
4. What are three of the benefits that Pfaff suggests would follow if his alternative plan were to be adopted, and which seems most important?
5. Pfaff states in two places his strongest reason for favoring campaign reform. What is it and where does he state it?

QUESTIONS OF FORM

1. We have included Pfaff's argument in the section illustrating refutation because he is arguing *against* the status quo, i.e., our current system for conducting political campaigns. Nevertheless, his argument may be construed as making a claim of value, as well as a claim of policy. How might you state each of them?
2. In paragraph 11, Pfaff states the benefits that will result from the adoption of his plan. What sorts of claims are these?
3. Where does Pfaff detail the disadvantages that result from the present plan?
4. Does Pfaff's refutation involve the challenging of a warrant? If so, what is that warrant?

SUGGESTIONS FOR WRITING

1. Summarize Pfaff's argument in two paragraphs. In the first, state the disadvantages of the present system of campaign advertising, and in the second, state Pfaff's plan for reform along with its advantages.
2. Your older sister is running for chair of the school board in your home county. She has just called to tell you that her campaign woes have just ended because she has been offered a sizable political contribution, one that will allow her to pay for all the radio ads that she had planned to get her message out to the electorate. When you ask the source of this assistance, you discover that it comes from a wealthy sporting goods manufacturer who has been very vocal in past years about making the high schools' athletic teams more competitive—even at the expense of lowering academic standards. After you have hung up, you are troubled and feel that you need to write to your sister and explain to her the risks that she is running. Write that letter.
3. You discover that your congressional representative has just accepted a rather large donation from a political action committee which favors clear-cutting large tracts of national forests. You have been very interested lately in preserving natural resources, especially through recycling paper products. Write a letter to this representative in which you express your concerns. Focus as Pfaff did on the disadvantages of one plan and then upon the advantages of your alternative plan.

Motherhood: Who Needs It?

BETTY ROLLIN

1   Motherhood is in trouble, and it ought to be. A rude question is long overdue: Who needs it? The answer used to be (1) society and (2) women. But now, with the impending horrors of overpopulation, society desperately *doesn't* need it. And women don't need it either. Thanks to the Motherhood Myth—the idea that having babies is something that all normal women instinctively want and need and will enjoy doing—they just *think* they do.

2   The notion that the maternal wish and the activity of mothering are instinctive or biologically predestined is baloney. Try asking most sociologists, psychologists, psychoanalysts, biologists—many of whom are mothers—about motherhood being instinctive: it's like asking department store presidents if their Santa Clauses are real. "Motherhood—instinctive?" shouts distinguished sociologist/author Dr. Jessie Bernard. "Biological destiny? Forget biology! If it were biology, people would die from not doing it."

3   "Women don't need to be mothers any more than they need spaghetti," says Dr. Richard Rabkin, a New York psychiatrist. "But if you're in a world where everyone is eating spaghetti, thinking they need it and want it, you will think so too. Romance has really contaminated science. So-called instincts have to do with stimulation. They are not things that well up inside of you."

4   "When a woman says with feeling that she craved her baby from within, she is putting into biological language what is psychological," says University of Michigan psychoanalyst and motherhood-researcher Dr. Frederick Wyatt. "There are no instincts," says Dr. William Goode, president-elect of the American Sociological Association. "There are reflexes, like eye-blinking, and drives, like sex. There is no innate drive for children. Otherwise, the enormous cultural pressures that there are to reproduce wouldn't exist. There are no cultural pressures to sell you on getting your hand out of the fire."

5   There are, to be sure, biologists and others who go on about biological destiny, that is, the innate or instinctive goal of motherhood. (At the turn of the century, even good old capitalism was explained by a theorist as "the *instinct* of acquisitiveness.") And many psychoanalysts will hold the Freudian view that women feel so rotten about not having a penis that they are necessarily propelled into the child-wish to replace the missing organ. Psychoanalysts also make much of the psychological need to repeat what one's parent of the same sex has done. Since every woman has a mother,

it is considered normal to wish to imitate one's mother by being a mother.

There is, surely, a wish to pass on love if one has received it, but   6
to insist women must pass it on in the same way is like insisting that every man whose father is a gardener has to be a gardener. One dissenting psychoanalyst says, simply, "There is a wish to comply with one's biology, yes, but we needn't and sometimes we should-n't." (Interestingly, the woman who has been the greatest contributor to child therapy and who has probably given more to children than anyone alive is Dr. Anna Freud, Freud's magnificent daughter, who is not a mother.)

Anyway, what an expert cast of hundreds is telling us is, simply,   7
that biological *possibility* and desire are not the same as biological *need*. Women have childbearing equipment. To choose not to use the equipment is no more blocking what is instinctive than it is for a man who, muscles or no, chooses not to be a weight lifter.

So much for the wish. What about the "instinctive" *activity* of   8
mothering? One animal study shows that when a young member of a species is put in a cage, say, with an older member of the same species, the latter will act in a protective, "maternal" way. But that goes for both males and females who have been "mothered" them-selves. And studies indicate that a human baby will also respond to whoever is around playing mother—even if it's father. Margaret Mead and many others frequently point out that mothering can be a fine occupation, if you want it, for either sex. Another experiment with monkeys who were brought up without mothers found them lacking in maternal behavior toward their own offspring. A similar study showed that monkeys brought up without other monkeys of the opposite sex had no interest in mating—all of which suggests that both mothering and mating behavior are learned, not instinc-tual. And, to turn the cart (or the baby carriage) around, baby ducks who lovingly follow their mothers seemed, in the mother's ab-sence, to just as lovingly follow wooden ducks or even vacuum cleaners.

If motherhood isn't instinctive, when and why, then, was the   9
Motherhood Myth born? Until recently, the entire question of ma-ternal motivation was academic. Sex, like it or not, meant babies. Not that there haven't always been a lot of interesting contraceptive tries. But until the creation of the diaphragm in the 1880's, the birth of babies was largely unavoidable. And, generally speaking, nobody really seemed to mind. For one thing, people tend to be sort of good sports about what seems to be inevitable. For another, in the past, the population needed beefing up. Mortality rates were high, and agricultural cultures, particularly, have always needed children to

help out. So because it "just happened" and because it was needed, motherhood was assumed to be innate.

Originally, it was the word of God that got the ball rolling with "Be fruitful and multiply," a practical suggestion, since the only people around then were Adam and Eve. But in no time, super-moralists like St. Augustine changed the tone of the message: "Intercourse, even with one's legitimate wife, is unlawful and wicked where the conception of the offspring is prevented," he, we assume, thundered. And the Roman Catholic position was thus cemented. So then and now, procreation took on a curious value among people who viewed (and view) the pleasures of sex as sinful. One could partake in the sinful pleasure, but feel vindicated by the ensuing birth. Motherhood cleaned up sex. Also, it cleaned up women, who have always been considered somewhat evil, because of Eve's transgression (" . . . but the woman was deceived and became a transgressor. Yet woman will be saved through bearing children . . . ," I Timothy, 2:14–15), and somewhat dirty because of menstruation.

And so, based on need, inevitability, and pragmatic fantasy—the Myth *worked*, from society's point of view—the Myth grew like corn in Kansas. And society reinforced it with both laws and propaganda—laws that made woman a chattel, denied her education and personal mobility, and madonna propaganda that she was beautiful and wonderful doing it and it was all beautiful and wonderful to do. (One rarely sees a madonna washing dishes.)

In fact, the Myth persisted—breaking some kind of record for long-lasting fallacies—until something like yesterday. For as the truth about the Myth trickled in—as women's rights increased, as women gradually got the message that it was certainly possible for them to do most things that men did, that they live longer, that their brains were not tinier—then, finally, when the really big news rolled in, that they could choose whether or not to be mothers—what happened? The Motherhood Myth soared higher than ever. As Betty Friedan made oh-so-clear in *The Feminine Mystique*, the '40's and '50's produced a group of ladies who not only had babies as if they were going out of style (maybe they were) but, as never before, they turned motherhood into a cult. First, they wallowed in the aesthetics of it all—natural childbirth and nursing became maternal musts. Like heavy-bellied ostriches, they grounded their heads in the sands of motherhood, only coming up for air to say how utterly happy and fulfilled they were. But, as Mrs. Friedan says only too plainly, they weren't. The Myth galloped on, moreover, long after making babies had turned from practical asset to liability for both individual parents and society. With the average cost of a middle-class child figured conservatively at $30,000 (not including college), any parent

10

11

12

knows that the only people who benefit economically from children are manufacturers of consumer goods. Hence all those gooey motherhood commercials. And the Myth gathered momentum long after sheer numbers, while not yet extinguishing us, have made us intensely uncomfortable. Almost all of our societal problems, from minor discomforts like traffic to major ones like hunger, the population people keep reminding us, have to do with there being too many people. And who suffers most? The kids who have been so mindlessly brought into the world, that's who. They are the ones who have to cope with all of the difficult and dehumanizing conditions brought on by overpopulation. They are the ones who have to cope with the psychological nausea of feeling unneeded by society. That's not the only reason for drugs, but, surely, it's a leading contender,

Unfortunately, the population curbers are tripped up by a romantic, stubborn, ideological hurdle. How can birth-control programs really be effective as long as the concept of glorious motherhood remains unchanged? (Even poor old Planned Parenthood has to euphemize—why not Planned Unparenthood?) Particularly among the poor, motherhood is one of the few inherently positive institutions that are accessible. As Berkeley demographer Judith Blake points out, "Poverty-oriented birth control programs do not make sense as a welfare measure . . . as long as existing pronatalist policies . . . encourage mating, pregnancy, and the care, support, and rearing of children." Or, she might have added, as long as the less-than-idyllic child-rearing part of motherhood remains "in small print." 13

Sure, motherhood gets dumped on sometimes: Philip Wylie's Momism got going in the '40's and Philip Roth's *Portnoy's Complaint* did its best to turn rancid the chicken-soup concept of Jewish motherhood. But these are viewed as the sour cries of a black humorist here, a malcontent there. Everyone shudders, laughs, but it's like the mouse and the elephant joke. Still, the Myth persists. Last April, a Brooklyn woman was indicted on charges of manslaughter and negligent homicide—eleven children died in a fire in a building she owned and criminally neglected—"But," sputtered her lawyer, "my client, Mrs. Breslow, is a mother, a grandmother, and a great grandmother!" 14

Most remarkably, the Motherhood Myth persists in the face of the most overwhelming maternal unhappiness and incompetence. If reproduction were merely superfluous and expensive, if the experience were as rich and rewarding as the cliché would have us believe, if it were a predominantly joyous trip for everyone riding—mother, father, child—then the going everybody-should-have-two-children 15 plan would suffice. Certainly, there are a lot of joyous mothers, and their children and (sometimes, not necessarily) their husbands reflect their joy. But a lot of evidence suggests that for more women than anyone wants to admit, motherhood can be miserable. ("If it weren't," says one psychiatrist wryly, "the world wouldn't be in the mess it's in.")

There is a remarkable statistical finding from a recent study of Dr. Bernard's, comparing the mental illness and unhappiness of married mothers and single women. The latter group, it turned out, was both markedly less sick and overtly more happy. Of course, it's not easy to measure slippery attitudes like happiness. "Many women have achieved a kind of reconciliation—a conformity," says Dr. Bernard,   16

> that they interpret as happiness. Since feminine happiness is supposed to lie in devoting one's life to one's husband and children, they do that; so *ipso facto*, they assume they are happy. And for many women, untrained for independence and "processed" for motherhood, they find their state far preferable to the alternatives, which don't really exist.

Also, unhappy mothers are often loath to admit it. For one thing, if in society's view not to be a mother is to be a freak, not to be a *blissful* mother is to be a witch. Besides, unlike a disappointing marriage, disappointing motherhood cannot be terminated by divorce. Of course, none of that stops such a woman from expressing her dissatisfaction in a variety of ways. Again, it is not only she who suffers but her husband and children as well. Enter the harridan housewife, the carping shrew. The realities of motherhood can turn women into terrible people. And, judging from the 50,000 cases of child abuse in the U.S. each year, some are worse than terrible.

In some cases, the unpleasing realities of motherhood begin even before the beginning. In *Her Infinite Variety*, Morton Hunt describes young married women pregnant for the first time as "very likely to be frightened and depressed, masking these feelings in order not to be considered contemptible. The arrival of pregnancy interrupts a pleasant dream of motherhood and awakens them to the realization that they have too little money, or not enough space, or unresolved marital problems. . . ."   17

The following are random quotes from interviews with some mothers in Ann Arbor, Mich., who described themselves as reasonably happy. They all had positive things to say about their children, although when asked about the best moment of their day, they all confessed it was when the children were in bed. Here is the rest: 18

Suddenly I had to devote myself to the child totally. I was under the illusion that the baby was going to fit into my life, and I found that I had to switch my life and my schedule to fit him. You think, "I'm in love, I'll get married, and we'll have a baby." First there's two, then three, it's simple and romantic. You don't even think about the work. . . .

You never get away from the responsibility. Even when you leave the children with a sitter, you are not out from under the pressure of the responsibility. . . .

I hate ironing their pants and doing their underwear, and they never put their clothes in the laundry basket. . . . As they get older, they make less demands on our time because they're in school, but the demands are greater in forming their values. . . . Best moment of the day is when all the children are in bed. . . . The worst time of the day is 4 P.M., when you have to get dinner started, the kids are tired, hungry and crabby—everybody wants to talk to you about *their* day . . . your day is only half over.

Once a mother, the responsibility and concern for my children became so encompassing. . . . It took me a great deal of will to keep up other parts of my personality. . . . To me, motherhood gets harder as they get older because you have less control. . . . In an abstract sense, I'd have, several. . . . In the nonabstract, I would not have any. . . .

I had anticipated that the baby would sleep and eat, sleep and eat. Instead, the experience was overwhelming. I really had not thought particularly about what motherhood would mean in a realistic sense. I want to do *other* things, like to become involved in things that are worthwhile—I don't mean women's clubs—but I don't have the physical energy to go out in the evenings. I feel like I'm missing something . . . the experience of being somewhere with people and having them talking about something—something that's going on in the world.

Every grownup person expects to pay a price for his pleasures, but seldom is the price as vast as the one endured "however happily" by most mothers. We have mentioned the literal cost factor. But what does that mean? For middle-class American women, it means a life style with severe and usually unimagined limitations; i.e., life in the suburbs, because who can afford three bedrooms in the city? And what do suburbs mean? For women, suburbs mean other women and children and leftover peanut-butter sandwiches and car pools and seldom-seen husbands. Even the Feminine Mystiqueniks—the housewives who finally admitted that their lives behind brooms (OK, electric brooms) were driving them crazy—were loath to trace their predicament to their children. But it is simply a fact that a childless married woman has no child-work and little housework. She can live in a city, or, if she still chooses the suburbs or the country, she can leave on the commuter train with her husband if she wants to. Even the most ardent job-seeking mother will find little in the way of great opportunities in Scarsdale. Besides, by the time she wakes up, she usually lacks both the preparation for the outside world and the self-confidence to get it. You will say there are plenty of city-dwelling working mothers. But most of those women do additional-funds-for-the-family kind of work, not the interesting career kind that takes plugging during childbearing years.

Nor is it a bed of petunias for the mother who does make it professionally. Says writer-critic Marya Mannes: 20

> If the creative woman has children, she must pay for this indulgence with a long burden of guilt, for her life will be split three ways between them and her husband and her work. . . . No woman with any heart can compose a paragraph when her child is in trouble. . . . The creative woman has no wife to protect her from intrusion. A man at his desk in a room with closed door is a man at work. A woman at a desk in any room is available.

Speaking of jobs, do remember that mothering, salary or not, is   21
a job. Even those who can afford nurses to handle the nitty-gritty still need to put out emotionally. "Well-cared-for" neurotic rich kids are not exactly unknown in our society. One of the more absurd aspects of the Myth is the underlying assumption that, since most women are biologically equipped to bear children, they are psychologically, mentally, emotionally, and technically equipped (or interested) to rear them. Never mind happiness. To assume that such an exacting, consuming, and important task is something almost all women are equipped to do is far more dangerous and ridiculous than assuming that everyone with vocal chords should seek a career in the opera.

A major expectation of the Myth is that children make a not-so-   22
hot marriage hotter, or a hot marriage, hotter still. Yet almost every available study indicates that childless marriages are far happier. One of the biggest, of 850 couples, was conducted by Dr. Harold Feldman of Cornell University, who states his finding in no uncertain terms: "Those couples with children had a significantly lower level of marital satisfaction than did those without children." Some of the reasons are obvious. Even the most adorable children make for additional demands, complications, and hardships in the lives of even the most loving parents. If a woman feels disappointed and

trapped in her mother role, it is bound to affect her marriage in any number of ways: she may take out her frustrations directly on her husband, or she may count on him too heavily for what she feels she is missing in her daily life.

"... You begin to grow away from your husband," says one of the Michigan ladies. "He's working on his career and you're working on your family. But you both must gear your lives to the children. You do things the children enjoy, more than things you might enjoy." More subtle and possibly more serious is what motherhood may do to a woman's sexuality. Often when the stork flies in, sexuality flies out. Both in the emotional minds of some women and in the minds of their husbands, when a woman becomes a mother, she stops being a woman. It's not only that motherhood may destroy her physical attractiveness, but its madonna concept may destroy her *feelings* of sexuality.

And what of the payoff? Usually, even the most self-sacrificing of maternal self-sacrificers expects a little something back. Gratified parents are not unknown to the Western world, but there are probably at least just as many who feel, to put it crudely, shortchanged. The experiment mentioned earlier—where the baby ducks followed vacuum cleaners instead of their mothers—indicates that what passes for love from baby to mother is merely a rudimentary kind of object attachment. Without necessarily feeling like a Hoover, a lot of women become disheartened because babies and children are not only not interesting to talk to (not everyone thrills at the wonders of da-da-ma-ma talk) but they are generally not empathetic, considerate people. Even the nicest children are not capable of empathy, surely a major ingredient of love, until they are much older. Sometimes they're never capable of it. Dr. Wyatt says that often, in later years particularly, when most of the "returns" are in, it is the "good mother" who suffers most of all. It is then she must face a reality: The child—the appendage with her genes—is not an appendage, but a separate person. What's more, he or she may be a separate person who doesn't even like her—or whom she doesn't really like.

So if the music is lousy, how come everyone's dancing? Because the motherhood minuet is taught freely from birth, and whether or not she has rhythm or likes the music, every woman is expected to do it. Indeed, she *wants* to do it. Little girls start learning what to want—and what to be—when they are still in their cribs. Dr. Miriam Keiffer, a young social psychologist at Bensalem, the Experimental College of Fordham University, points to studies showing that

> at six months of age, mothers are already treating their baby girls and boys quite differently. For instance, mothers have been found

to touch, comfort, and talk to their females more. If these differences can be found at such an early stage, it's not surprising that the end product is as different as it is. What is surprising is that men and women are, in so many ways, similar.

Some people point to the way little girls play with dolls as proof of their innate motherliness. But remember, little girls are *given* dolls. When Margaret Mead presented some dolls to New Guinea children, it was the boys, not the girls, who wanted to play with them, which they did by crooning lullabies and rocking them in the most maternal fashion.

By the time they reach adolescence, most girls, unconsciously   26
or not, have learned enough about role definition to qualify for a master's degree. In general, the lesson has been that no matter what kind of career thoughts one may entertain, one must, first and foremost, be a wife and mother. A girl's mother is usually her first teacher. As Dr. Goode says, "A woman is not only taught by society to have a child; she is taught to have a child who will have a child." A woman who has hung her life on the Motherhood Myth will almost always reinforce her young married daughter's early training by pushing for grandchildren. Prospective grandmothers are not the only ones. Husbands, too, can be effective sellers. After all, they have the Fatherhood Myth to cope with. A married man is *supposed* to have children. Often, particularly among Latins, children are a sign of potency. They help him assure the world—and himself—that he is the big man he is supposed to be. Plus, children give him both immortality (whatever that means) and possibly the chance to become more in his lifetime through the accomplishments of his children, particularly his son. (Sometimes it's important, however, for the son to do better, but not *too* much better.)

Friends, too, can be counted on as myth-pushers. Naturally one   27
wants to do what one's friends do. One study, by the way, found a correlation between a woman's fertility and that of her three closest friends. The negative sell comes into play here, too. We have seen what the concept of non-mother means (cold, selfish, unwomanly, abnormal). In practice, particularly in the suburbs, it can mean, simply, exclusion—both from child-centered activities (that is, most activities) and child-centered conversations (that is, most conversations). It can also mean being the butt of a lot of unfunny jokes. ("Whaddya waiting for? An immaculate conception? Ha ha.") Worst of all, it can mean being an object of pity.

In case she's escaped all those pressures (that is, if she was   28
brought up in a cave), a young married woman often wants a baby just so that she'll (1) have something to do (motherhood is better than

clerk/typist, which is often the only kind of job she can get, since little more has been expected of her and, besides, her boss also expects her to leave and be a mother); (2) have something to hug and possess, to be needed by and have power over; and (3) have something to *be*— e.g., a baby's mother. Motherhood affords an instant identity. First, through wifehood, you are somebody's wife; then you are somebody's mother. Both give not only identity and activity, but status and stardom of a kind. During pregnancy, a woman can look forward to the kind of attention and pampering she may not ever have gotten or may never otherwise get. Some women consider birth the biggest accomplishment of their lives, which may be interpreted as saying not much for the rest of their lives. As Dr. Goode says, "It's like the gambler who may know the roulette wheel is crooked, but it's the only game in town." Also, with motherhood, the feeling of accomplishment is immediate. It is really much faster and easier to make a baby than paint a painting, or write a book, or get to the point of accomplishment in a job. It is also easier in a way to shift focus from self-development to child development—particularly since, for women, self-development is considered selfish. Even unwed mothers may achieve a feeling of this kind. (As we have seen, little thought is given to the aftermath.) And, again, since so many women are underdeveloped as people, they feel that, besides children, they have little else to give—to themselves, their husbands, to their world.

You may ask why then, when the realities do start pouring in, 29 does a woman want to have a second, third, even fourth child? OK, (1) just because reality is pouring in doesn't mean she wants to *face* it. A new baby can help bring back some of the old illusions. Says psychoanalyst Dr. Natalie Shainess, "She may view each successive child as a knight in armor that will rescue her from being a 'bad unhappy mother.'" (2) Next on the horror list of having no children, is having one. It suffices to say that only children are not only OK, they even have a high rate of exceptionality. (3) Both parents usually want at least one child of each sex. The husband, for reasons discussed earlier, probably wants a son. (4) The more children one has, the more of an excuse one has not to develop in any other way.

What's the point? A world without children? Of course not. 30 Nothing could be worse or more unlikely. No matter what anyone says in *Look* or anywhere else, motherhood isn't about to go out like a blown bulb, and who says it should? Only the Myth must go out, and now it seems to be dimming.

The younger-generation females who have been reared on the 31 Myth have not rejected it totally, but at least they recognize it can be more loving to children not to have them. And at least they speak of adopting children instead of bearing them. Moreover, since the new nonbreeders are "less hung-up" on ownership, they seem to recognize that if you dig loving children, you don't necessarily have to own one. The end of the Motherhood Myth might make available more loving women (and men!) for those children who already exist.

When motherhood is no longer culturally compulsory, there   32 will, certainly, be less of it. Women are now beginning to think and do more about development of self, of their individual resources. Far from being selfish, such development is probably our only hope. That means more alternatives for women. And more alternatives means more selective, better, happier, motherhood—and childhood and husbandhood (or manhood) and peoplehood. It is not a question of whether or not children are sweet and marvelous to have and rear; the question is, even if that's so, whether or not one wants to pay the price for it. It doesn't make sense any more to pretend that women need babies, when what they really need is themselves. If God were still speaking to us in a voice we could hear, even He would probably say, "Be fruitful. Don't multiply."

QUESTIONS OF CONTENT

1. In paragraph 1 Rollin introduces the Motherhood Myth. What exactly is this?
2. If women have neither the need nor the instinct for motherhood, then why does society demand it of them; in other words, why is there a Motherhood Myth?
3. According to Rollin, why are birth control programs usually ineffective?
4. Rollin goes so far as to claim that there is a connection between the Motherhood Myth and drug use. What precisely is that connection?
5. Rollin claims that childhood all too often bring unhappiness rather than fulfillment. What are some reasons that she cites for this unhappiness?
6. What alternative to motherhood does Rollin offer?

QUESTIONS OF FORM

1. In posing the Motherhood Myth, Rollin is attacking two warrants. What are they?
2. Paragraphs 11 and 15 serve important structural functions in this argument. What purpose does each serve?
3. Rollin appeals to a number of authorities in her article. What claims does she support with these appeals?

4. Rollin asserts that, as a rule, childless marriages prove to be happier than those with children. What evidence does she produce in support of her claim?

SUGGESTIONS FOR WRITING

1. Try to summarize Rollin's essential claims in an essay of no more than three paragraphs. It's a long essay, so you will have to gloss over supporting details in order to devote space to the claims.
2. You are a young woman, engaged to be married. Your parents are quite pleased with your spousal choice and have more than once expressed that satisfaction to you. They have also confided to you their eagerness to become grandparents. However, you and your fiancé have discussed having children and have decided to wait. You wish to pursue a career, and depending on the rewards that could very well materialize, you may even decide to opt against motherhood. Explain your feeling to your parents in a letter. You may very well borrow some points from Rollin's argument.
3. As the youngest in a family of five children, you feel more than a little indignant with the position that Rollin has taken in her article. This is especially true since your childhood memories are very pleasant ones; your parents may not have always been deliriously happy, but theirs was always a stable and caring household, one that you remember fondly. What do you say in response to Rollin's debunking of the Motherhood Myth? Write a paper in which you challenge at least one of her assumptions.

Taking Sides: Differing Arguments
on Important Issues

This readings section provides a series of pairs of essays, each pair focused on the same basic subject. While both essays are on the same subject, each author has a different perspective on that subject and argues for his or her own ideas regarding it. Sometimes the two authors are at opposing poles, but just as often their ideas are closer, comparing more than they contrast. Therefore you should watch not just for places where the ideas of the two essays differ, but also where they share some common ground. By reading the related essays in pairs, you should be able to improve your ability to notice both small and large differences in opinions and arguments, and therefore you should learn how to increase the subtlety and the effectiveness of your own arguments.

As in the previous section, we have furnished questions of form and of content, as well as suggestions for writing; these appear after the second essay of each pair. Again, we encourage you to look over the questions and writing suggestions *before* reading the two essays, and to refer to them as needed *while* you read, so that you'll comprehend more fully the essays' subject matter and their argumentative strategies.

CENSORSHIP

Right and Wrong Way to Get Involved

MICHAEL GARTNER

Isn't there enough in this world to worry about—war in Chechnya and bombings in Iraq, perhaps—without worrying about "Huckleberry Finn"? 1

Isn't there enough in this world to worry about—starvation in Asia and disease in Africa perhaps—without worrying about "Of Mice and Men"? 2

Isn't there enough in this world to worry about—drug emperors in South America and poverty in the United States, perhaps—without worrying about Shakespeare? You'd think so. 3

But that is not the case. 4

Again last school year, parents and legislators and school-board members across the nation tried to censor what our children—our children, not just their children—can read and learn in the public schools. It's all documented in the 14th annual report "Attacks on the Freedom to Learn," a sad compilation put out last week by People for the American Way. 5

The group chronicles 475 attacks on textbooks and library books and curricula and student speech. That's a record, yet the American Library Association estimates that there are four or five attempts at censorship for every one that is reported. 6

That would put the real number at somewhere between 1,900 and 2,400—or one for every six or seven public-school districts in the United States. 7

In Eureka, Kan., the school board banned "The Canterbury Tales" from a 12th-grade college preparatory literature class; parents said it was too racy. In Jacksonville, Fla., a grandparent objected to Alice Walker's "The Temple of My Familiar," saying it was vulgar and sexual, so now students can check it out of the library only with parental permission. In San Jose, Calif., the school board removed 8

"The Adventures of Huckleberry Finn" from required reading lists in high schools because it contains the word "nigger."

There were, too, the usual petitions to teach creationism in the schools, to put prayer into the classroom and to keep all talk of homosexuality out of it. 9

This is bad—but not all bad. 10

Every study and every educator will tell you that your children will do better in school if you get involved. You are supposed to talk to your children about school, go over homework with them, discuss current events, meet the teachers and join the parent associations. 11

There is nothing wrong with questioning the curriculum—no school board or superintendent is infallible. There is nothing wrong with challenging texts—some are outdated and others are lacking. There is nothing wrong with confronting teachers—some are inexperienced and others may not know the special needs of your son or daughter. 12

Getting involved with the education of your child is good. But getting involved in the education of mine is bad. 13

You can tell the teacher you don't want your child to read Maya Angelou, and the teacher probably will find an alternate assignment. But don't tell the teacher that my child shouldn't read "I Know Why The Caged Bird Sings." 14

There is a difference between involvement and censorship. 15

One is being a good parent. 16

The other is being a bad citizen. 17

My Rap Against Rap

NATHAN MCCALL

I'll never forget the first time I went with some buddies in the early '70s to see "The Godfather." I don't know how many violent films I'd seen before that one, but for me "The Godfather" was the serious joint. Gangsters, guns and violence have always held a fascination among Americans, and blacks like me are no different. I was mesmerized by "The Godfather," mainly because its machine gun shootouts and retaliatory murders among competing "families" took the thrill of gang warfare to another level. 1

I was most impressed by the ruthless code of principles that governed the gangsters' lives. They had a way of resolving conflict 2 that was appealing to a teenager trying to work through the murky rites of manhood. The message I picked up was, if somebody double-crosses you, he deserves to die. I remember sitting in the theater and thinking, *Yeah, that's right. He deserves to die.*

After "The Godfather" ended, I concluded that was the hippest   3
flick I'd ever seen. My buddies and I stepped outdoors, inspired and hyped, so hyped that we bopped down the sidewalk talking loud and intentionally bumping into people, hoping somebody would protest and give us an excuse to do a bare-knuckled version of what we'd just seen on the movie screen.

Clearly, we were young and impressionable and less able to fil-   4
ter fantasy from fact. "The Godfather" was fantasy, but to us—a bunch of spirited boys trying to define ourselves and identify with a group—it was a celebration of machismo, a celebration that elevated the glory and glamor of gang life.

I eventually got my chance to do the Godfather thing when an   5
older guy in the neighborhood threatened my girl. Because that dude had offended my lady and, by extension, disrespected me, I concluded: *He deserves to die.*

I was 19, and it didn't take much more than that emotion, at   6
that age, to push me into reckless action. When I ran into that guy, I gunned him down. From the moment I pulled the trigger, it was like one great fantasy, as glorious as the gangland slayings in that movie I'd seen. After he collapsed, I stood over him, proud that I'd properly dispensed street justice and upheld the code of Godfather principles that I'd embraced. Later that night, I wound up sitting in a police station, being fingerprinted and booked. That's when fantasy faded. That's when the *real* me resurfaced. That's when I shed my pseudo-gangster persona and discovered what I really was: a silly, scared teenager who was mixed up in the head.

Lucky for me, the guy lived. I went to court and got off with a   7
light sentence.

But I never stopped thinking about the shooting and the influ-   8
ences that had led me to do such things. I thought about it again recently while following reports of efforts by Attorney General Janet Reno and others to press for restriction on TV and movie violence. Their efforts are a reminder of a child-rearing truism that seems to have been lost on too many of us: Young people bombarded with images of sex and violence often find it hard to separate fantasy from fact. And some can't resist the temptation to act out what they've seen.

With public support swelling for voluntary or mandatory con-   9
trol, it's probably inevitable that concrete steps will be taken. That's

encouraging, but there is something about the campaign that's un-
settling to me: If Reno and others succeed, it will ensure that white
kids get less exposure to graphic images that may influence them;
but any controls may overlook a volatile area that's specific to blacks.
The truth is, white kids are more plugged into TV, and black kids
nowadays are more into music, especially rap.

Of course, not all rap is bad; in fact much of it is so brilliant that   10
it makes me shout. But more and more, the good stuff is being over-
shadowed by a torrent of obscene lyrics and graphic videos.

Especially troubling are the lyrics in "gangsta rap," which be-   11
came the dominant strain in the late 1980s. It often denigrates
women and glorifies guns and gangs. Consider a catchy piece of advice from popular rapper Dr. Dre and imagine how it sounds to a
young boy's ears: It says "never hesitate to put a nigga on his
back . . . " Plain and simple, that is a boastful call for black men to
kill each other. Lyrics like these have become so pervasive that
they're the accepted norm.

On its face, it may seem crazy for someone to tie music to be-   12
havior. But the history of African Americans shows that, from the
days of slavery to the present, music has always played a monu-
mental role in what we think and do. It has always been an agent of
change.

Anyone who really understands the nature of rap knows that it's   13
more than mere rhyming words. It's a phenomenon, the central part
of an unorganized but powerful cultural movement—hip hop—that
influences the way young blacks walk, talk, dress and think.

The key element is aggression—in rappers' body language, tone   14
and witty rhymes—that often leaves listeners hyped, on edge, angry
about . . . something

Perhaps the most important element is gangsta rap is its mes-   15
sages, which center largely around these ideas: that women are no
more than "bitches and hos," disposable playthings who exist
merely for men's abusive delight; that it's cool to use any means
necessary to get the material things you want; and most importantly, it's admirable to be cold-blooded and hard. . . .

When rap music first surfaced, many blacks—including me—   16
overlooked the harsh lyrics because they were viewed as gritty
urban political expression—outrage at a hostile white world.
Then, over time, the language changed. Rappers who once sang
about being oppressed began sounding oppressive and hateful
themselves. . . .

Gangsta rappers often defend their themes by saying they reflect   17
a reality that they're not responsible for. The rappers' justification

would be more persuasive if the brutality they toast had always been part of our reality. But this is more a case of life imitating art in the worst of ways.

Apparently, many rappers believe their own hype, and some 18 don't hesitate to act on what they sing about. Look at:

> Tupac Shakur, arrested in Atlanta earlier this month for shooting two cops.
>
> Flavor Flav, shooting at a guy he suspected of having sex with his girlfriend.
>
> Snoop Doggy Dogg, charged in connection with a murder, who says he packed two guns as "a protection thang."

Other rappers have faced charges for rape, shootings and assorted other crimes. I can't condemn them for getting into trouble, 19 because I've been there myself. But I keep worrying about those kids who can't tell the difference between music and reality, and how this may affect them.

"It's not rap itself, it's the messages that some of the popular rap 20 generates," says William Byrd, a clinical psychologist who works with black children in Washington. "When you bombard someone with [those] messages, it causes conflict, even within those who may have been taught other values. With the messages, not only are they being bombarded with radio, they get video. So it's what you hear *and* what you see."

Obviously, gangsta rap does not inspire every young listener to 21 pick up a gun, but what, I wonder, is the impact of all this on people already at risk?

"While the vast majority of kids are able to take negative rap and 22 put it in perspective, some of our most vulnerable ones are influenced," says Melvin Williams, intern commissioner for the D.C. Commission on Mental Health Services. "Those young people who have faulty parenting or no parenting at all are particularly vulnerable to influences such as rap."

When it comes to the violence around us, it's undoubtedly true 23 that other complex social factors—public apathy, parental neglect, the allure of drugs and guns—are also to blame. And even the most hard-edged gangsta rap, when isolated from those factors, is probably harmless.

But given all the other forces messing with black folks' minds, 24 negative lyrics are an addition that we just don't need.

Many have been reluctant to speak out against such material 25 because they aren't convinced of its influence. Or, they say, there's nothing new—music has always had its share of violent themes. Furthermore, they say, there's no empirical proof, no hard data that shows a direct relation between, say, gangsta rap and drive-by shootings.

What they leave out is that never before have young people 26 been bombarded non-stop by such violent language and imagery. The fact is that, more than anything else—their mamas, their daddys, their preachers and teachers—the minds of many young blacks seem to be homed in on rap, to the tune of $700 million annually.

Social scientists say that while they can't measure the degree to 27 which constant exposure to violent images in music and on TV affect young people, they're sure that it has some impact.

Na'im Akbar, a psychologist who often writes and lectures 28 about such matters, acknowledges that the effect of negative messages on young people is not something that can be quantified. Yet he contends, " 'You can't prove that it's causative, but it certainly is correlational."

Here are some correlations that I've been mulling over: 29

Black-on-black violence—especially in juvenile violence—has 30 escalated sharply only since the late 1980s, when the popularity of gangsta rap was on the rise. In Washington in a three-year period (1988–90), the number of juvenile homicide arrests almost tripled (from 26 to 67). Those numbers correspond with nationwide statistics, which suggest that the number of juvenile killings has almost doubled in the last 10 years and that the rate of juvenile violent crime has risen by more than 40 percent.

Even if you make the argument that black-on-black drug wars 31 account for many of the murders, and even if you concede that there are a lot more guns on the street—a condition of the crack economy—that still doesn't wholly explain the sharp rise in random violence.

The sudden, unexplained change in the values and behavior of 32 young blacks in rural American towns is another development that has only taken place in recent years. Earlier generations, who were cut off geographically from violent urban influences, now have ready access to hip-hop music and videos. Now we've begun hearing more about random violence in places such as Kansas and North Carolina, where a few murders a year were once big news.

What all this means to me is that while we've been searching 33
for complex sociological explanations for the sudden surge in violence afflicting young blacks, part of the answer may be quite simple, something dangling right under our collective noses—and ears.

It's not hard to imagine that young blacks look to rappers— 34
many of whom are only kids themselves—as people they want to
emulate. Hero-worship and fantasy is a big part of young people's
lives. Basketball legend Michael Jordan is paid millions to endorse
sneakers because advertisers know that many kids—and young
adults—buy them to indulge their fantasy to "be like Mike." By the
time Jordan reached the height of his fame, young black men all over
America were fantasizing—shaving their heads, wearing black
sneakers and even trying to walk pigeon-toed, just like him.

Nobody fantasizes more than young black men. When you live 35
in a world that limits your hopes, reality is often too much to bear.
Because they are largely invisible, black males fantasize about becoming professional athletes—stations they think will make the
world acknowledge them. Because they are powerless, they are consumed with the symbols of power—guns and gangstas.

They imagine themselves as godfathers and, sadly, some actu- 36
ally get up the nerve to act out such roles. So they spray gunfire into
crowded swimming pools, as happened in Washington last summer; or they gun folks down on a recreation field, like the men
whose stray bullets killed a 4-year-old girl. Too often, reality does-
n't kick in until the handcuffs are slapped on, just as it happened
to me.

When a policeman told my stepfather and me that the guy I shot 37
might die, I became mired in the weirdest illogic: It was clear that
if he died, I'd be charged with murder, yet I would have denied to
the end that I was a murderer.

Why wasn't I prepared to accept the consequences of my actions 38
or concede to being branded a killer if I took someone's life? Because, on some level, I was certain that the person who shot that
guy was not really me—it was some person I'd *thought* I wanted to
be. I'd been fantasizing, and fantasies don't deal with consequences.

If asked, I couldn't have explained why I shot that dude. I was 39
completely unaware of the forces driving me. Likewise, many of
these young killers today can't tell you why they did what they did.
They don't have a clue.

You have only to look at juvenile assailants' faces during some 40
of these televised arrests to see the utter confusion in their eyes. At
those moments, they're like I was, frightened, mixed-up, suddenly
facing felony charges more serious than they can comprehend.

As people whose young are bearing the brunt of the murder and mayhem, you'd think blacks would have moved decisively to stop it. In the 1960s, we mobilized when white police, dogs and hoses were our most immediate threat. But several complex factors seem to have stumped our collective logic and made us second-guess ourselves. In the civil rights struggle, it was clear that there were institutions that we were taking on. And if there was some doubt about exactly which institutions we were up against, we at least knew that the enemy was white. Now we're confused and ambivalent because the faces of the triggermen are black. 41

We've also been reluctant to take part in anything that could be seen as censorship. But, as Akbar says, "Freedoms have come to be used as a justification of anarchy. Someone has got to monitor civilized life." 42

There are lots of things that we can do to stop the violence assaulting our eyes and ears. We can, for starters, declare war on recording companies that produce this garbage, and try to hit them where it hurts—in their pockets. As police groups showed when they took on Time-Warner over Ice-T's "Cop Killer" album, the power of embarrassment is immense. 43

One black station, KACE-FM in Los Angeles, recently decided to counter what it said is a "disturbing trend in black music" by banning airplay of records that glorify drugs, sex, abuse of women and violence. Other black stations should follow suit. We should also denounce misguided rappers who spread messages of hate. 44

These are only first steps toward addressing a crisis in which African-American adults must confront the ways we're hurting ourselves. "So many of us adults are in denial and we pay a heavy, heavy price," says Jan Hutchinson, director of child and youth services for the D.C. Mental Health Commission. "We have to confront these issues with these kids." 45

Because the hip-hop movement is so totally black (notwithstanding sales in white suburbia), this may not be a battle that Janet Reno and others can easily join; the discussion would quickly become sidetracked by issues of race. 46

Monitoring and ultimately reining in gangsta rap is no panacea for the problems confronting black America. But if black America is not prepared to give our children something better than violence and abuse to fantasize about, who will? 47

QUESTIONS OF CONTENT

1. What is Gartner's position with respect to banning the reading of certain books in our public schools?
2. What is McCall's attitude toward banning rap music?
3. What is the source of Gartner's information? What sources does McCall cite for the information that he presents?
4. According to Gartner, what are some books that have been recently banned from public school curricula?
5. What type of rap does McCall find particularly offensive? Why?
6. What personal experience from his adolescence does McCall feel makes him especially qualified to discuss the issue of banning rap music?

QUESTIONS OF FORM

1. Each of these arguments is essentially a claim of policy. Each begins with the description of a situation—a listing of facts or claims of facts—designed to convince the reader that a bad situation exists. Then the writer states the claim of policy, i.e., the proposed remedy. Where exactly do these steps take place in the arguments of Gartner and McCall?
2. Both Gartner and McCall make significant *qualifications* to their claims of policy—without which there would be little possibility for widespread acceptance. What exactly are those qualifications, and where do they occur?
3. Examine paragraph 14 in Gartner's essay. In it he makes a rather risky assumption that his audience has a special kind of knowledge which, in fact, many might lack. What is that risky assumption, and how might you revise the paragraph to avoid it?
4. How does McCall strengthen his essay by beginning it with his teenage experience?

SUGGESTIONS FOR WRITING

1. Can you summarize the positions taken by Gartner and McCall in such a way that they might serve as illustrations in an essay dealing with the subject of censorship?
2. You are the principal of a school who has been approached by a delegation of parents who wish to have a book named by Gartner removed from the library. Write a letter to them responding to their complaint and outlining your plan of action.

3. As a teacher in an inner-city junior high school you are disturbed by the gangsta rap that you have heard coming from the boom boxes on the playgrounds. You would like to speak at the next student assembly denouncing the playing of such music, but you are troubled about how best to present your argument to this audience. Study the Steinbeck essay, "How to Cuss" and try to discover—as he did—a warrant that both you and your audience will find readily acceptable. Once you have done that, the remainder of your argument should be fairly easy to write.

WOMEN IN COMBAT

Military Takes Equality Too Far

EDWARD SIMS

The United States is, in its form of government, the ideal for the 1
world's countless millions. Everyone is presumed equal, enjoys
equal rights under the law and there is great public and political
pressure to suppress any idea that there are sexual, racial or other
differences.

But differences exist, in sex, race and in other fields. 2

One that politicians are currently refusing to address—it would 3
lose them votes—but that should be faced is the non-selective feminization of U.S. military services.

A recent book on this subject is disturbing reading. It's titled 4
Weak Link by Brian Mitchell (Regnery Gateway). This serious study
shows that Americans are playing with fire, or worse, by playing
politics with the military services.

The commanders of all the services have in recent years been 5
under intense political pressure to introduce what's called career
equality between the sexes. At the service academies physical training is now conducted on a double standard, one for males and one
for females—much easier requirements.

This inevitably lowers the physical standard average in each 6
service. Feminists have gone so far as to demand the elimination of
some physical training activities because women were not doing
well—and they have been eliminated.

War, of course, is not the place for social engineering and abstract 7
ideology. If war comes, the nation's military will be handicapped. If
more politically inspired feminization of the military continues, national security will be even more dangerously jeopardized.

In many military jobs physical strength is highly important, de- 8
cisive as to effectiveness. Yet an Army study in 1982 showed that
while 64 percent of all men had the strength to perform heavy jobs,
only 3 percent of the women did.

But because of political pressure on the services, women have 9
been and are being assigned to jobs they can't perform. One exam-

ple is found in the Army, which assigns women to artillery supply jobs when they can't lift the shells.

In the Air Force there are women incapable of carrying their own tool kits serving as aircraft mechanics. In the Navy, where 84 percent of the jobs are considered very heavy, a majority of women are unable to close watertight doors! Etc.

Pregnancy is another growing concern in all the services—and could be crippling in wartime. Most of the service mothers, unfortunately, are single. What happens to them when an emergency rises?

Do they abandon their children and concentrate on their duty? That's asking too much. In the only test, in Korea, in the mid 1970s, when U.S. forces went to full alert, some women brought their children to their posts, others simply headed for the rear to get their children evacuated, abandoning their posts.

The "everyone must be treated the same" propaganda of the day, plus the pressure from politicians, has turned the military services and academies into social experiments. Recently a girl was selected as commandant of cadets at West Point.

That pleased the idealists. But she is exempt from combat, by law, and it's peculiar, to say the least, to idealistically promote females to be the leaders of military services in which they're barred from military combat—the purpose of the service!

U.S. military services have more females—about 20 percent already—than any other in the world. The pressure is on to get more into more jobs, even into combat infantry jobs!

In many countries, the military is limited to males. In time of war, that could be a critical factor. It's time for the service chiefs to take a firm stand (and for politicians to stop pressuring them) against non-selective feminization of the military services, before it's too late.

Vivid Images Shouldn't Alter View of Women in Combat

LOIS B. DEFLEUR

The debate in Congress over whether women should fly combat missions has more to do with images than reality.

There is the image of the hypothetical woman in the trenches, locked bayonet-to-bayonet with a stronger and deadly enemy, sketched by Gen. H. Norman Schwarzkopf when he testified recently on Capitol Hill.

There is the image of Maj. Marie T. Rossi (USA), a helicopter   3
pilot assigned to fly supplies to troops in the combat zone of the Persian Gulf War, killed in a crash the day after the cease-fire. Rossi had come to personalize the war and the role of women in it for millions of CNN viewers.

There is the image of Spc. Melissa Rathbun-Nealy (USA), only   4
20 years old, captured on a supply mission that came under fire near the Saudi Arabia border. Rathbun-Nealy, the first service woman since World War II to be made a prisoner of war, was also among the first 10 Americans released after the war by the Baghdad government.

And, finally, there were the indelible pictures that we saw on   5
magazine covers and on television of gulf-bound mothers tearfully leaving behind at home uncomprehending toddlers.

These images arouse powerful emotional reactions in all of us.   6
But, we should not permit these responses to cloud our judgment about whether women should fly Navy, Air Force and Marine warplanes in combat. This is no time to sound retreat on the gains that women have made in every one of the services since the Vietnam War.

Women have always been present on the battlefield. Some have   7
borne weapons in their own defense and that of their homes and families. Personal heroism and courage were hallmarks of generations of American nurses and other support personnel who served in field hospitals and behind the lines from the Civil War to Vietnam. What was distinctive about the gulf war was that for the first time, there were so many women whose involvement across a wide range of specialties put them where the action was.

The 35,000 women among the 540,000 troops sent to the gulf who   8
were maintaining vehicles, servicing fighter planes, carrying supplies and monitoring communications did not arrive in the gulf by accident. The armed services had recruited and trained them in unprecedented numbers throughout the '70s and '80s. A commitment by the military to equal opportunity carried with it the possibility that women would necessarily be thrust into perilous situations.

As have countless men before them, these women had chosen   9
military service as a way out of the traditional paths open to them. Like their older brothers and fathers, they were looking for technical training, money for college, medical benefits, travel and adventure. "The Army was a starting block for her," a friend of Rathbun-Nealy said in an interview when she was captured. "She had everything to look forward to."

My research and that of others supports this view. Women who 10
have served in the military have a higher self-image than do their
sisters who have remained in the pink-collar ghetto. Military service increases women's self-confidence, assertiveness and general
well-being. Self-assessments of their athletic and mechanical
abilities increase as do their assessments of their achievement
potential.

In addition, military pay and benefit structures surpass what 11
women with educational backgrounds and opportunities are able to
command in the civilian workplace. Men and women in the armed
services are paid equally for equal work—a pattern not duplicated
elsewhere.

When women complete their military service, they return to the 12
work force with training in many fields that have been traditionally
inhospitable to women. Especially in today's high-technology military, this training is very likely to open the doors to jobs in aviation,
electronics, transportation, communications, etc., that are higher
paying, even at the entry level, than those held down by women in
more traditional female jobs.

As long as promotions to leadership positions rest largely on per- 13
formance in battle, women will be at a disadvantage in achieving
high ranks. Without successful role models up and down the military hierarchy, women in the service are destined to feel like sec-
ond-class citizens.

Whether women should fly combat planes is a strategic, not a 14
political, judgment. An enemy will never know whether a man or a
woman is at the controls of an F-15 Eagle. The qualities a successful combat pilot requires today are not gender-specific. The technologically sophisticated warplanes of the '90s make far more
demands on a pilot's ability to manipulate complex computer programs and to make clear-headed tactical decisions than they do on
sheer physical strength.

As the gulf war demonstrated, not all battles are fought in the 15
trenches. If a woman can fly a helicopter filled with ammunition to
the front or pilot refueling tankers, it is difficult to see why she
could not fly an F-15 in combat. There is a very thin line between a
woman engaged in duty in the combat zone and one actually engaged in combat duty.

Women have derived significant benefits from the career and ed- 16
ucational opportunities made available to them in recent years by
the armed services. In turn, the military has been enriched by the
talent, hard work and dedication of the young women in its ranks.

The Air Force currently leads the way in utilizing women 17
throughout its ranks and among its specialties. This policy should

be continued and expanded so that women who are trained in aviation in all the service branches can fully serve the nation.

QUESTIONS OF CONTENT

1. One of Sims's reasons for opposing women being allowed in combat is that women are more often physically incapable of performing strenuous tasks. Where and how does DeFleur address this issue?
2. Why does Sims object to a woman being chosen as commandant of cadets at West Point? What do you suppose DeFleur's reaction would be to Sims's objection?
3. What are DeFleur's chief reasons for favoring combat roles for women? What are Sims's chief reasons for opposing such a move?
4. What happened during the Gulf War of 1991 that brought this discussion into sharper focus than ever before?
5. In paragraphs 11 and 12 of his essay, Sims addresses the issue of pregnancy and child care among women in the military. What does De-Fleur have to say on this subject?

QUESTIONS OF FORM

1. Sims opposes what he calls "non-selective" feminization of the military services." What does he mean by this? How does DeFleur fashion her argument to counter this position?
2. Both Sims and DeFleur cite statistics. For what purposes do they use them? What is the effect of their use?
3. How does Sims support his claim that non-selective feminization of the U.S. military is a poor policy?
4. Why, according to DeFleur, have women sought in ever-increasing number to become members of the armed forces? In making this point she is attacking a warrant to which she feels many Americans must subscribe. What is that warrant?
5. Which of these essays relies most heavily on emotional appeals? Ethical appeals?

SUGGESTIONS FOR WRITING

1. Summarize these two arguments in a paper of up to three pages. Do not take sides, but state clearly the major claims made and supported by Sims and DeFleur. Be especially careful to associate the names of the authors with their arguments.

2. Take sides with either Sims or DeFleur and point out the superiority of one person's claims over the other's by showing that support for those claims is more compelling or that the reasoning is more logical. You may find it convenient to summarize the substance of both arguments in a brief background statement before going on to take sides. Or you may wish to pattern your strategy after that used by Richard Reeves in "A Better Health Plan Goes Rejected" (p. 162), in which he compares two health care plans, taking sides with one over the other.

3. Assume that you have a seventeen-year-old sister who can meet all the admission requirements for the U.S. service academies and has indicated her desire to apply to them with the intent of making a career in one of the armed forces. Write a letter to her in which you encourage her or discourage her. Support your position by references either to Sims or to DeFleur—or to both.

SEXISM

Facing Up to Sexism

MICHAEL W. HIRSCHORN

When French playwright Jean Genet wrote *The Balcony* he noted that the best way to portray true good in the world was to force his audiences to confront true evil. Fake judges, generals, and bishops parade through a whorehouse, living out their petty hypocrisies and in the process exposing the so-called justice of the establishment as so many lies.

Genet was convinced of the immorality of the system, so he had no doubt that his audiences would react in disgust as the wanton decadence and hypocrisy of the establishment figures before them on the stage.

That point was apparently lost on those here at *The Crimson* who thought that refusing to publish a *Playboy* recruitment ad was the best way to attack immorality.

Some will argue that refusing to publish an advertisement is censorship. They are clearly wrong, for a newspaper must have control over its own pages, and it's certainly within *The Crimson's* prerogative, both legally and ethically, to refuse space to whomever it chooses.

Some will argue that refusing to publish an advertisement infringes on free speech. Not really, for advertising is not free speech, and, in any case, the *Playboy* ad is not an opinion. As one editor noted at Sunday's in-house discussion of the ad issue, one must be able to disagree with an opinion, and the counter-argument to the *Playboy* solicitation is "No, a *Playboy* photographer will *not* be at the Somerville Holiday Inn this week."

Yet, free speech is not a substanceless concept that we mouth whenever we want to prove that, yes, we really are democrats with a small "d." Free speech is the last defense of the just, for it is always the less popular, less acceptable opinion that gets quashed when freedom of expression is restricted.

This truism is not relevant to *Playboy*, for the magazine, thanks in part to news coverage generated by *The Crimson's* dispute and by prominent coverage on page one of this newspaper, is having "free

222

speech" a-plenty. The argument is relevant to those who voted not to publish the advertisement, because they failed to see their own self-interest. Put simply, they did not have enough faith in our community to believe that female students would be as repulsed by the concept of posing nude for *Playboy* (and by the magazine itself) as women at *The Crimson* were.

If, in fact, more than a handful of women do decide to pose for   8
Playboy, then there are some problems in this society whose roots lie far deeper than *The Crimson* or *Playboy* and which would make *The Crimson's* little gesture seem trivial indeed. Does *The Crimson* really believe it can or should protect society from itself?

If anything, I believe Harvard women are turned off by the ad   9
and will react strongly against the magazine and all it may stand for. Like Genet, I believe that moral goals are achieved by getting everything out in the open and allowing the people to see and react against evil.

Martin Luther King understood this dynamic when he trooped,   10
cameras rolling, into the most reactionary, racist neighborhoods in Chicago and revealed the evil of racism as it had never been seen before. Were it not for King, those neighborhoods would have continued their ways and the nation would never have been forced to face the ugliness of its people. As a result of the efforts of King and others, the social consensus was changed.

And yet, the majority at *The Crimson* believed they were fur-   11
thering a noble cause by quashing the *Playboy* ad. People who read about *The Crimson's* decision around the country—everything that happens at Harvard goes national—will get a good chuckle, as will the editors of *Playboy*, who will once again be able to make the fallacious argument that they are persisting despite the oppression of a bunch of Harvard prudes.

Meanwhile, those who argued to pull the ad, satisfied with their   12
victory, have not bothered to take their case to the rest of the Harvard population. Ironically, now that *The Crimson's* pages are pure, no one seems terribly worried about convincing women who might want to pose that what they're doing runs counter to everything for which women at Harvard and elsewhere have been fighting for decades.

Moral crusaders should never be ashamed of the truth, because   13
the truth will always work in their favor. The fight to rid society of pornography is a noble one, but it will only be won when and if enough Americans are forced to confront their own sexism.

That cause was not furthered by the actions of the majority, for   14
they took the spotlight off *Playboy* and the women of Harvard and turned it on *The Crimson*. The editors are to be congratulated on their victory, but they must realize it was only a Pyrrhic one.

Taking a Stand Against Sexism

KRISTIN A. GOSS

The Crimson's decision not to run *Playboy's* advertisement recruiting Harvard women for its October "Women of the Ivy League" issue was both the very most and the very least the newspaper could do to fight the institutionalized exploitation of women. 1

Those who claim the staff endeavored to "censor" *Playboy*, or to protect Harvard women from themselves, miss the point of the majority's intentions, just as they did seven years ago when *The Crimson* rejected the same ad. 2

The question is clearly not one of hiding information or of paternalism, but of refusing to support, either tacitly or overtly, a publication whose *raison d'être* is the objectification of women and the exploitation of womankind. It is a question of integrity. 3

Playboy editors must not expect us—a group of undergraduates who are ourselves either morally repulsed by the pornography racket or in the very least respectful of such feelings of collective degradation in our peers—to aid and abet their objectionable cause. 4

They should also not expect us to keep silent, as they attempt to make sex objects out of our classmates by offering five times as much money to those who take their clothes off as to those who remain clothed. This is not sexuality; it is sexism. 5

Those who say *The Crimson* singlehandedly stifled *Playboy's* message have no argument. *Playboy* could have spent the same amount of money that running an ad in *The Crimson* would cost to make somewhere in the neighborhood of 10,000 photocopied posters, which would have effectively reached every undergraduate, professor and administrator on this campus, and then some. It could have run an advertisement on WHRB. It did run one in the *Independent* and in the *Boston Herald.* 6

The Crimson's rejection of the ad clearly did not compromise *Playboy's* rights to freedom of expression. The newspaper has not as an institution prevented *Playboy* photographer David Chan from coming to campus. 7

Nor has it implied that Harvard women cannot decide for themselves whether to pose before him; they can and will make a proper, reasoned decision in either case. 8

Nor has *The Crimson* censored *Playboy*; the newspaper is in fact on record as supporting pornography's First Amendment right to exist. 9

The newspaper staff has used its editorial discretion to state that its toleration of pornography—by default, because the alternative 10 would be worse—does not preclude protest. It has expressed the view held by many of its editors that while *Playboy* and other forms of institutionalized sexism may be "socially acceptable," they should not be so.

Social acceptability is a function of which group controls society and to what extent minority voices can influence the spectrum of opinion. Just as racist ads of 50 years ago were socially acceptable to a white-dominated society, so are sexist ads today threatening to females who, despite the women's liberation movement, still have a long way to go to gain equality. 11

Any woman who has walked down the street and been verbally harassed, and any woman who has feared rape while walking alone in her own neighborhood at night—I might add there is not one female who has not—knows that fighting the image of woman-as-object, woman-as-silenced victim, woman-as-sex-organ remains among her most urgent tasks. 12

Sexism is most dangerous when it's subtle, when it is so deeply embedded in a culture that it becomes socially acceptable, as *Playboy* has. And so, you speak out, you yell, you rant and you rave when you recognize this subtle destruction. There is no other way to jar society out of its passive acceptance of the objectification of women, even though in this society it happens to be legal. 13

In not running the ad, *The Crimson* has taken that initiative. Seven years from now, when *Playboy* again decides to try its luck with a whole new batch of Ivy League women, we can only hope all Ivy League newspapers will decide not to extend their helping hands. It is both the most and the least they can do. 14

QUESTIONS OF CONTENT

1. Why does Hirschorn believe that *The Crimson* was wrong in denying ad space to *Playboy?*
2. Who are Jean Genet and Martin Luther King? Why does Hirschorn use them as examples?
3. What reasons does Goss give for refusing to run the *Playboy* ad?
4. In paragraphs 1 and 10 Goss claims that sexism is "institutionalized." What does she mean by that?

QUESTIONS OF FORM

1. Hirschorn begins by making two concessions. What are they, and what did he hope to gain by making them?

2. How do the examples drawn from Genet and King tend to bolster Hirschorn's argument?
3. In paragraph 11 Goss refers to the racist ads that appeared in newspapers fifty years ago. In doing so she is using an analogy. How exactly does that analogy work?
4. The majority of *The Crimson's* staff, according to Goss, chose not to support *Playboy's* sexism, despite the paper's support of "pornography's First Amendment right to exist." How does she justify that apparent contradiction? Why do you suppose she even mentions it?

SUGGESTIONS FOR WRITING

1. Briefly summarize the positions taken by Hirschorn and Goss.
2. The *Playboy* photographer has just arrived on your campus. How do you feel about his presence there? Examine your values and write a letter to your campus paper stating your attitude toward the pictorial article that will probably appear after his visit.
3. You are the editor of the campus paper, and, like Goss, you must respond to *Playboy's* request for ad space. What will your response be? Write an editorial justifying that response.

PROS AND CONS OF GAMBLING

Why I Gamble

DANIEL SELIGMAN

This article is driving me crazy. First, it is sinking in, after several days of staring at the headline above, that the issues it raises are more complex than posited when I accepted the assignment. Second, the passage of those several days has created a certain tension between two cherished goals: (1) assured manuscript delivery by vouchsafed deadline date and (2) unstinting participation in this month's poker game, only two days off as I write. Furthermore, I start out knowing that no matter what story line I come up with, a significant fraction of NR readers will unbudgingly go on thinking that gambling is bad. Several years ago, I was called by an investment-banker friend who asked if I would mind having lunch with her and a client—a conservative intellectual who happened to run a steel company, was said to admire my Fortune column, and shared my hard-line perspective on numerous issues of the day. Feeling flattered, I accepted and, until the very end of our meeting, felt I had come to know a kindred spirit. But as we were leaving La Côte Basque, my newfound friend asked a bit diffidently about the numerous references in the column to casinos and race tracks. Was it really true, he asked, that I hung around such places? I said it was, and he said, "Oh," looking embarrassed. Social conservatives tend to see gambling as a big negative on the values scorecard. Intellectuals feel it betokens a want of seriousness. Economists of every persuasion go around arguing that it is "unproductive"—that, in the words of Paul Samuelson, "it involves simple sterile transfers of money or goods between individuals, creating *no* new money or goods." The italics are Paul's, as is the familiar refusal to accept that gambling is terrific entertainment.

Gambling has been a major theme in my life since approximately age twenty, and I seem to have come by the habit honestly. My father was a heavy sports bettor for much of his life, and my mother was eternally loving and attentive—precisely the kind of mother who, according to Freud, leaves men feeling forever lucky as they march through life. Anybody wishing to observe several score characters radiating this state of grace in unison has only to board the 8 p.m. flight from Los Angeles to Las Vegas. The atmosphere features loud hoots and unconstrained hilarity. The 1:45 a.m. flight back is much more subdued; to be sure, the guys have had a long day.

There are several things to be said for gambling, the first of   3
which is: You really might win. Furthermore, you might win big. In fact, you almost certainly will win big if you hang in there and structure your bets properly. Here I am sidling up to one of my two theoretical contributions to the economics of gambling: the counterintuitive view of long-shot betting as a form of saving.

The saving process, as we all know, involves the conversion of   4
a stream of income into a lump of capital. A man who takes $100 out of his weekly paycheck and puts it under his mattress might get criticized for failing to maximize investment returns, but no economist would deny that the $5,200 he had accumulated after a year was the result of saving.

Now imagine another chap—one who also wishes to convert   5
$100 a week into $5,200 but feels he is entitled to a few kicks along the way. Since he luckily lives in downtown Las Vegas, it is convenient for him to visit Binion's Horseshoe Casino once a week. His plan on these visits is to throw $100 on the table each time, hoping eventually to get lucky and win something like $5,200. Unfortunately, no casinos offer 51 to 1 bets to low rollers, but there are a number of casino games in which you get huge long-shot payoffs by winning five or six times in a row and letting your profits ride. If you know what you are doing and elect to play blackjack with a single deck (possible at Binion's but hard to find on the Strip), you are essentially in a fair game, i.e., the house edge is minimal (and the casino depends for its profits on the inept). So if you sit down at the $100 table and win six hands in a row, you will leave the table with something like $6,400. The chance of winning an even-money bet six times in a row is only 1.56 per cent, but the chance of winning one such bet in 52 weekly visits is 56 per cent. So you are favored to win at least once a year, and if you do so, your lump will be substantially larger than that of our mattress man.

It is possible to imagine various real-world problems arising out   6
of this approach to nest-egg building, but the basic conception is rock solid. If you repetitively play a fair game, and structure your bets so as to generate frequent losses and occasional big wins, then you are converting income into capital. Indeed you are doing that even if the game is not quite fair. If your weekly savings budget was getting tossed on the craps table instead of the blackjack table, you would possibly be fighting a house edge of 0.6 per cent, but you

would still be favored (53 per cent this time) to convert $100 into $6,400 at least once a year.

My own preferred and most successful form of saving has featured ninth-race triples, also known as trifectas, at New York's Aqueduct and Belmont racetracks. A triple is a long-shot bet, requiring one to pick the first three horses to cross the finish line, in order. If you buy a "triple box," which consists of six bets featuring all combinations of your three horses, you don't have to worry about the order. A triple box costs $12, and my standard bet is four or five boxes, all on horses selected randomly by a BASIC program lovingly conceived for this purpose alone. (It prompts you for the number of horses in the race, the program numbers of any scratches, and the number of boxes you wish to buy, then spits out your selections.) If 12 steeds are running, a bettor with five boxes going has a 2.3 per cent chance of hitting a triple, and if he plays this game once a week, he has a 70 per cent chance of hitting at least once a year, and over the years he has a serious expectation of latching onto some sizable payoffs. Since 1986, when I first began putting the results of my gambling into a spreadsheet, I have had around 300 betting days that featured triples, of which only a handful were winners. But these included payoffs of $14,611, $11,225, $9,644, $3,794, and $3,394. And even though New York racetracks have a horrifying edge of 25 per cent on triple bets—i.e., payments to winners represent only about 75 per cent of the money bet—the spreadsheet shows me way ahead of the game. So it is fairly easy to view the recurrent losses of $48 or $60 as deposits into a savings account. 7

Possibly you are wondering about my other contribution to economic theory. It was built on an insight gleaned from our monthly poker game. This began in 1953 as a low-stakes limit game but soon upgraded itself to table stakes (in which a player can bet any amount up to the total of chits and chips he had in front of him when the deal started). The greybeards still in the game know there is a possibility of winning or losing as much as $1,000 in an evening, but a more likely outcome is a swing under $500. An interesting thing about those figures is that they were far larger back in the Fifties, when we were all much poorer. It was then common to win or lose over $2,500 in one session—around $14,000 in today's prices. Whatever else it was doing, the game in those years clearly served as the great monthly adventure in our lives, one that was doubly wonderful in that, unlike Antarctic exploration or rappelling in the Rockies, it came with no physical risks or material discomfort. In those days, we tended to play all night, drink quite a lot while doing so, then go out for breakfast before wandering off to a barber and the office. Once, in 1958, I personally managed to lose $1,600—at a time 8 when my annual salary was $16,000, I had no savings to speak of, and I was the sole support of a family of four. Breakfasting with the gang at a Lexington Avenue coffee shop, I did my best to feign insouciance over the night's results, but the refrain that kept rattling in my head was: How in hell do I get out of this mess?

The answer, revealed to me in the ensuing months, is at the   9
heart of my theoretical contribution, which states: Gambling has a positive effect on economic activity. A significant fraction of the winners will regard their loot as "found money" and rush to spend it, and quite a few of the losers will feel an instant, urgent need to augment earnings, which in my case meant toiling mightily in the freelance market. Please do not draw any inferences from the fact that I am still so toiling.

About the problem mentioned in the first paragraph: The guys   10
instantly agreed to postpone the March game. To be sure, they are getting old.

Gambling's Toll in Minnesota

CHRIS ISON AND DENNIS MCGRATH

Hour after hour, the blackjack cards flipped past, and still she   1
played. Friday afternoon blurred into Saturday. Through the ringing of slot machines and chattering of coins dropping into tin trays, Catherine Avina heard her name paged.

"Are you coming home tonight?" It was her 21-year-old son,   2
Joaquin, on the phone. "Probably not," she answered.

Avina didn't go to Mystic Lake Casino in Prior Lake, Minn., as   3
much as she escaped to it. That weekend in May 1994, the depressed 49-year-old mother of three was escaping the worst news yet—she was in danger of being fired after almost 11 years as an assistant state attorney general. On Monday—her fourth straight day at the casino —she dragged herself back to her St. Paul home, broke and more depressed than ever.

Two days later, Joaquin confronted his mother about her gam-   4
bling, and they argued. The next morning, when she didn't come out of her bedroom, he peeked in. Two empty bottles of anti-depressants and a suicide note were near her body. Later the family found debts of more than $7000, and Avina was still making payments for gambling-addiction therapy received a year earlier.

In less than a decade legalized gambling in Minnesota—$4.1 bil-   5
lion is legally wagered in the state each year—has created a new class

of addicts, victims and criminals whose activities are devastating families. Even conservative estimates of the social toll suggest that problem gambling costs Minnesotans more than $200 million per year in taxes, lost income, bad debts and crime.

Ten years ago only one Gamblers Anonymous group was meeting in the state; today there are 53 groups. According to research by the Center for Addiction Studies at the University of Minnesota in Duluth, nearly 38,000 Minnesota adults are probable pathological gamblers. A 1994 *Star Tribune*/WCCO-TV poll found that 128,000 adults in Minnesota—four percent—showed signs associated with problem gambling and gambling addiction. 6

Many experts agree that the potential for gambling addiction among the young—the most vulnerable group—is worse. Teens are twice as likely as adults to become addicted. 7

Jeff Copeland, a 21-year-old from suburban Minneapolis, can't go to college because he's accumulated a $20,000 gambling debt, "It ruins your life," he says. "And people don't really understand. I thought about suicide. It's the easiest way to get out of it." 8

Pawnshop Boom. Thousands of Minnesotans are burying themselves in debt because of gambling, borrowing millions they'll never be able to pay back. Bankruptcy experts estimate that more than 1000 people a year are filing for bankruptcy protection (average owed: $40,000), at an estimated cost to creditors of more than $2.5 million. "Compared with ten years ago, there are 20 times as many people who have gambling debts," says bankruptcy attorney Jack Prescott of Minneapolis. 9

One of these is Hennepin County Commissioner Sandra Hilary of Minneapolis. She filed for bankruptcy two days after admitting she was addicted to slot machines. She estimated she'd lost nearly $100,000 gambling. After counseling, Hilary is now trying to reimburse her creditors. 10

Throughout the state, at least 17 new pawnshops have sprung up near casinos, with gamblers hocking possessions for far less than real value to support their gambling habits. In or near Cass Lake (pop. 923), four miles from Palace Bingo & Casino, there are four pawnshops. That's a pawnshop for every 231 people. 11

Police near casinos note an increase in bogus reports of thefts. These from people who lie about the disappearance of a ring, video camera or other expensive item that they actually pawned to pay for their gambling. 12

Easy Credit. Minnesotans are also burning up welfare payments at casinos. Hundreds of thousands of taxpayer dollars that are meant to provide food, clothes and housing for the poor are being wagered on blackjack and in slot machines, and for residents of two Min- 13 nesota counties, the money is being made available from automated teller machines inside almost every casino in the state. During a typical month last year, welfare recipients from Hennepin and Ramsey counties withdrew $39,000 in benefits from casino ATMS.

There are few incentives for casinos to regulate the availability   14
of credit to gamblers. The casinos can't lose: they don't give the credit; they simply make the money.

Credit-card companies—there are now more than 7000—have   15
made strong profits in recent years despite increasing bankruptcy and delinquent payments nationwide. Interest rates are so high—averaging 18 percent—they still make up for losses from bankruptcy. And the issuers pass much of the loss on to consumers through higher rates, fees and penalties, says Ruth Susswein, executive director of Bankcard Holders of America, a non-profit consumer-education group.

"They're making so much money it's been worth it to them to   16
keep offering credit," Susswein adds. Some casinos also rent space to companies that cash checks and provide credit-card advances for fee.

Police Burden. It seemed to take only minutes for Carol Foley to   17
get hooked on video gambling machines. "Within two or three days." she says, "I was playing every day." To cover her losses, Foley, 43, forged $176,000 in checks at her job at the E. M. Lohmann Co, a church-goods dealer in St. Paul. Last September she was released from a correction center in Roseville, Minn., after serving eight months for forgery. She underwent counseling for her gambling addiction and is on a monthly payment plan with her former employer.

The high crime rate among problem gamblers has been well es-   18
tablished. The National Council on Problem Gambling found that 75 percent of gamblers treated at in-patient centers had committed a crime.

Between 1988—when the first of Minnesota's 17 casinos began   19
operating—and 1994, counties with casinos saw the crime rate rise twice as fast as those without casinos. The increase was the greatest for crimes linked to gambling, such as fraud, theft and forgery/counterfeiting.

Casinos are burdening local police. When Grand Casino Mille   20
Lacs opened on the Mille Lacs Indian Reservation in April 1991, county police responded to almost twice as many incidents of crime or people seeking help on the reservation.

Jean Mott, a 38-year-old mother of three, worked nights at a   21
Kmart distribution center to help pay the family bills. But the bills began backing up when Mott headed to Mystic Lake Casino, rather than her Shakopee home, at the end of her shift.

Just before dawn one day in January 1995, having lost another   22
paycheck to the casino, Mott drove to the Brooks' Food Market in
Shakopee. Wearing a ski mask and with her hand in her pocket to
simulate a gun, she stole $233. Police easily traced the holdup to
Mott because a patrol officer had run a registration check after he
saw her car parked with its lights on just south of the store that
morning. Mott was convicted of simple robbery, and served 30 days
in jail and 30 days on electronic home monitoring.

Taxpayer Tab. The list of violent gambling-related crimes is also   23
growing. Redwood Falls police officer Derek Woodford was shot by
a gambler from Gary, Ind., who had broken into a local bank after a
day of gambling at Jackpot Junction in Morton. Woodford spent 13
days in the hospital recovering from three bullet wounds.

Gambling has long been recognized, as well, as a root cause of   24
embezzlement. In most gambling-related embezzlement cases, authorities say, the court file shows the same thing: no previous criminal record.

"Prior to 1990, we had zero cases of gambling-related embezzle-   25
ments," says William Urban, president of Loss Prevention Special-
ists, Inc., a Minneapolis company that helps employers deal with
internal thefts. Since then the company has investigated gambling-
related losses of "well over $500,000."

Reva Wilkinson, of Cedar, is now in federal prison for embez-   26
zling more than $400,000 from the Guthrie Theater to support her
gambling habit. Besides the money she stole from her Minneapolis
employer, her case cost taxpayers over $100,000 to investigate, pros-
ecute and adjudicate.

In June 1993 Theresa Erdmann was charged with stealing nearly   27
$120,000 from the checking account and weekly offerings at St.
Michael's Catholic Church in Madison. She said the money was
blown on gambling, and now she's serving a three-year sentence in
a state prison.

Hidden Suicides. More and more, some problem gamblers pay   28
the ultimate price. The *Star Tribune* confirmed six gambling-related
suicides in Minnesota—five in the past three years. Almost certainly, this is only a fraction of the total.

The victims are people like 19-year-old John Lee, a St. Paul col-   29
lege student who, in a three-month period, won about $30,000 at
blackjack. Then he started losing. Down to his last $10,000, he lost
it all one night. He returned home, put a shotgun to his head and
killed himself. In addition, at least 122 Minnesota gamblers have attempted suicide, according to directors of the six state-funded gam-
bling-treatment centers.

Other deaths that may be related to depression over gambling   30
loses are not listed as suicides at all. "So often, when people talk
about suicide, they say, I'd just drive of the road. I'd drive into a
tree," says Sandi Brustuen of the Vangard Compulsive Gambling
Treatment Program in Granite Falls Minn. "They don't want anyone to know they committed suicide, and they want their families
to collect the insurance."

The suicide rate among pathological gamblers nationally is be-   31
lieved to rival that of drug addicts. Ten to 20 percent of pathological gamblers have attempted suicide, and almost 90 percent have
contemplated it.

Treatment experts, researchers and gamblers themselves say   32
states can do more to reduce the negative consequences for gamblers. Here are some of the most frequently mentioned ideas:

> *Underwrite better research.* Many efforts across the country have   33
> been criticized for failing to prove that treatment works, for
> failing to measure the social costs of gambling and for failing
> to implement a long-range plan to address problem-gambling
> issues. "We really don't know exactly how much problem
> gamblers cost society," says Henry Lesieur, editor of the *Jour-
> nal of Gambling Studies* and a criminal-justice professor at
> Illinois State University in Normal.
>
> On the federal level, the issue of gambling addiction only   34
> recently started to generate action. Last fall committees in
> the House and Senate held hearings on bills that would au-
> thorize a national commission to study the economic and so-
> cial effects of legalized gambling.
>
> *Emphasize public awareness and education—especially among*   35
> *young people—about the risks of gambling.* Some suggest
> funding more in-school efforts, perhaps in conjunction with
> math and science classes or anti-drug programs. "Let people
> know what the odds are. The longer you gamble, the more
> you're going to lose," says Alan Gilbert, solicitor general of
> Minnesota.
>
> *Train casino employees to spot—and discourage—problem gam-*   36
> *blers from betting irresponsibly.* Some casinos already do
> this. But they offer only anecdotal evidence that such efforts
> are used, and some say they've never barred a person for prob-
> lem gambling unless the person asked to be barred.

Gambling has significant social and economic impact. It results in   37
ruined lives, families and businesses, in bankruptcies and bad loans;
in suicides, embezzlements and other crimes committed to feed or

cover up gambling habits—and increases in costs to taxpayers for investigating, prosecuting and punishing those crimes.

Few of these problems have been documented as communities   38
and states across the nation instead focus on gambling as a way to boost their economies and increase tax revenues. But for Minnesota the social costs of gambling are emerging in vivid and tragic detail.

QUESTIONS OF CONTENT

1. Ison and McGrath focus almost entirely on the consequences of casino gambling in Minnesota. Name at least six undesirable consequences that they cite.
2. Seligman refers to gambling as a sort of savings. How does he justify such a claim?
3. Ison and McGrath assert that a heavier burden is laid on police departments in areas where casino gambling is legal. What are some reasons why this is so?
4. Seligman mentions several types of gambling in which he frequently indulges. Which of these, according to his article, is the most likely to prove profitable? Why?
5. Compare the direness of the situations arising from gambling losses in each of these articles. With this in mind, do you suppose that you can find some common ground on which the authors of each might agree about the dangers of gambling? What might it be?
6. What suggestions do Ison and McGrath make that might lessen the severe consequences of gambling that they describe?

QUESTIONS OF FORM

1. What type of argument is "Gambling's Toll in Minnesota"? Is it based primarily on a claim of fact, or value, or of policy? What about "Why I Gamble"?
2. At least part of the argument presented by Ison and McGrath is inductive. Where do they employ that strategy? Is it effective? Why or why not?
3. How would you characterize the *tone* of each of these articles? What effect on the reader does this difference in tone produce?
4. What sorts of appeals are being made to the audiences of these articles? Are they logical, ethical, or emotional, or some mixture? Explain your judgments with respect to each article.
5. Examine the introductions of each of these articles. What is being attempted in each; i.e., how are the authors trying to influence their audiences?

SUGGESTIONS FOR WRITING

1. Compare the positions taken in these two articles by summarizing each of them in such a way that the important contrasts of viewpoint can be clearly understood.
2. Each of you has certainly had some experience with gambling. How have your personal experiences or those of your acquaintances prompted you to take sides in this debate? Write a brief essay in which you support the position to which you feel most attracted. Or in a brief essay refute the position to which you feel most strongly opposed.
3. Your state legislature is debating a proposal that will legalize casino gambling in your county. What is your position? Write a letter in which you share that opinion with your elected representative.
4. Would your opinion be the same (as in question 3) if the bill were one to legalize a state lottery? Perhaps you would rather treat this possibility in your letter.

SHOULD COLLEGE ATHLETES BE PAID?

Cash, Check or Charge?

DOUGLAS S. LOONEY

The winds of change in college athletics aren't simply blowing. 1
They're howling.

The discussion focuses on whether collegiate athletic scholar- 2
ship recipients—primarily football and male basketball players, but
including scholarship athletes of both genders—should be able to
make or receive as much money as they can in return for their athletic talents.

That ship has sailed. That train has left the station. That lov- 3
able—yet absurd and long-violated—notion that sports in our universities are a recreational adjunct to scholarly pursuits is a dog that
won't hunt. Hellfire, it's a dog that no longer will even get off the
porch.

Make no mistake, change is coming because of cheating, ex- 4
ploitation and hypocrisy. Rules have always been put in place to address cheating. If the system is changed to legalize what has been
defined as unlawful, then opportunities for cheating will plummet.

The conclusion reached by a growing number of experts: College 5
athletes should, must and will be entitled to as much money as they
can latch onto. *Just like real students.*

Under current and archaic rules, athletes who get full scholar- 6
ships receive room, board, books, tuition and fees. All universities
estimate that the actual cost of attendance runs between $1,500 and
$2,500 a year beyond these basics—but the athletic scholarship
doesn't cover extras. Anybody who wants can give money to regular students, buy them meals, purchase plane tickets for them, give
them cars. Anything goes. But for athletes to receive the same treatment is a slam-dunk NCAA violation. It's called special benefits and
is a no-no.

Students can make money however they can, whenever they can. 7
Athletes can work only during major school vacations—mainly summer. But even that is impractical in these days of 12-month sports.
If, for example, an athlete doesn't shoot hoops all summer, he or she
won't be shooting hoops in sold-out arenas during the winter.

237

If a student wants to open a taco joint, fine; if a scholarship ath-   8
lete wants to, certainly not. Dick DeVenzio was a standout basketball
player at Duke from 1968–69 through 1970–71 and an academic All-
American. These days, he runs his Point Guard Basketball College for
young players, scheduled for 13 locations nationwide this year. He sits
in his home in Charlotte, stretches his legs, and says, "We should
treat athletes in every way like every other American student."

In sum, the current system is totally unfair to the athletes and   9
corrupt to the core. The NCAA's 500-pages-plus rulebook is testimony to folly.

DeVenzio is the nation's leading proponent of allowing players   10
to make money however they want—*just like real students*—and
that includes off athletic talents. "We are protecting a tradition that
doesn't exist," he says.

Indeed, the days of fresh-faced college youngsters playing on   11
weekends, wearing letter sweaters, swallowing goldfish and going as
a team across campus to ring the Victory Bell were wonderful. But
those times are over. Big money has ruined the ideal.

Anybody who thinks otherwise is holding on to a dream already   12
gone. In many ways, it was a dream that never was.

An exasperated DeVenzio throws up his hands as he talks of   13
those who steadfastly oppose players making money: "It's like we're
still living in the '40s and America just won the war. It's so out of
kilter."

The discussion is no longer whether, but how. Even Cedric   14
Dempsey, executive director of the NCAA, acknowledges as much.
In a lengthy interview with *The Sporting News*, Dempsey conceded:
"A lot depends on what its called. If we say we're gonna pay athletes, you're going to find huge resistance. If you talk about making
sure the student athlete has enough money to attend school, you get
great support for it. And in some ways, you are talking about the
same thing."

Most significant is that Dempsey openly talks of the develop-   15
ment of a "more realistic attitude toward a lot of our rules." That's
codespeak for big changes are certain.

At NCAA headquarters in suburban Kansas City, Steve Morgan,   16
chief of staff for Division I, says the phrase "discretionary money"
seems to go down pretty smoothly with most people.

Joe Crowley, president of the University of Nevada and, until re-   17
cently, president of the NCAA, also acknowledges the obvious: "We
have a situation that I believe is out of whack." When Crowley is
asked if it's time to reinvent the wheel rather than straighten the
spokes, he says, "I think it could be. The itch is there."

Judith Albino, who recently completed her two-year term as chair of the Presidents' Commission, says the way things are is causing "a lot of discontent" with university CEOs. The former University of Colorado president and other commission members have been focusing mightily on campus athletics.

Support for drastic change is pouring in from all corners. Most surprising is the abrupt sea change by Walter Byers. For 36 years, he was the curmudgeonly boss of the NCAA who vigorously defended what once was and supported its myriad rules with a fervor normally reserved for the Christian Right. These days, Byers is recanting and doing an enormous amount of backing and filling. He now calls the current system—of which he was a prime architect and under which huge sums of money are shared by everyone except the athletes—"economic tyranny visited on the players." He flatly concludes the long-established NCAA system has failed.

He is absolutely correct.

In a recent convention of athletic directors, the NCAA's Dempsey acknowledged that his organization is discussing the possibility of a plan by which money would be given to athletes and repaid with professional earnings, or from a trust funded by endorsements. An ad-hoc NCAA committee is studying the concepts, which could become full-fledged legislative proposals at an NCAA convention in January 1997. "The athletic grant-in-aid today is not as good as it used to be," Dempsey told the athletic directors. "It's a changing world, and we've got to change our thinking."

Everywhere, people of substance are huffing and puffing, adding dramatically—and effectively—to the velocity of the winds of change. William Gerberding, University of Washington president, last summer told a sports law symposium at Notre Dame that the current system "cannot last in this egalitarian and litigious and capitalist society. It is manifestly unfair . . . (and) we are being made to look increasingly foolish and self-serving." Tom McMillen, former Maryland basketball star, Rhodes scholar, NBA player and U.S. Congressman, predicts that "the coexistence of big-time athletics and higher education will not succeed." He thinks the system will crash when either the players "demand to be paid" or when a financial scandal of national scope erupts inside collegiate sports.

Iowa State athletic director Gene Smith says, "We have got to find a way" to change the system.

But the proof of necessity for change is not in the words but in the deeds. Dick DeVenzio asks the perfect question: "If we started over with sports at universities, would we build a system like we've got now?"

Here, gleaned from interviews with dozens of college sports   25
leaders. are 10 solid ideas to link athletes and money. Some of the
ideas will work alone. Some will work in concert with others. All
will work.

1. *Pay the athletes.* This makes so much sense that it's scary.   26
There is virtually not a single, logical reason not to.

Amateurism, whatever that was or is, is dead. Even the tradi-   27
tion-bound Olympics has given up, which is why we have Dream
Teams composed of NBA players representing the United States.

The basic reason to pay collegiate athletes is that schools and   28
boosters can't be stopped from doing it anyway. The record at trying
is abysmal. The words sting but they are true: Cheating is rampant
and can't be controlled. Father Theodore Hesburgh, former Notre
Dame president said in a recent speech that in the 1980s, 109 colleges and universities ran afoul of NCAA rules—and that includes
more than half of the 106 biggest athletic institutions. In 1989, a
University of New Haven (Conn.) sociology professor, Allen L. Sack,
conducted a survey of approximately 3,500 current and former professional athletes and heard from 1,182—an excellent return. The
responses reveal nearly one-third admitted receiving illegal payments while they were in college. These are the ones who admit to
wrongdoing. Imagine what the figure really is. Between 1985 and
'88, seven of the nine Southwest Conference schools were hit with
major NCAA violations. Walter Byers laments that "there is not as
much support for law and order in the collegiate sports community
as I thought."

That's because, says Chris Polnsky, an associate athletic director   29
at Texas, "nobody trusts each other." For good reason. Rules work
only when the governed agree to be governed. That is not the case
in college sports. We're dealing with the 90's version of Prohibition.

And it is not just going on at the Miamis and Oklahoma States   30
and Auburns and assorted other bad-boy institutions. Duke's De-
Venzio admits to receiving tainted treasure. He was given a red Ca-
maro convertible while playing for Duke, which prides itself as
pristine; Duke athletic department officials told him they could sell
his four basketball tickets for $1,000 if he wanted them to—and he
did; and DeVenzio would get "$20 to mow somebody's lawn, even
though (the man who owned the property) had done most of it himself." Meals were always free at the Holiday Inn. (Vic Bubas, Duke's
coach from 1959–60 through 1968–69 and who recruited DeVenzio,
says of DeVenzio's accusations: "If that was the case, I never, ever
knew about it I think highly of Dick DeVenzio. He's an independent
thinker and I respect his right to say it." Bucky Waters, who coached

for DeVenzio's last two seasons and who now is vice chancellor at the Duke Medical Center, says DeVenzio's charges "absolutely shock me."]

During the recent NCAA basketball tournament two Sweet 16   31
teams widely suspected of loose play with the regulations—Syracuse and Georgia—walked onto the floor. Said one onlooker, "Instead of starting this game with a whistle, they should sound a burglar alarm."

So how much should the players be paid? Whatever somebody   32
wants to pay them; whatever they can make. The bornagain Byers, in his book, *Unsportsmanlike Conduct,* writes, "I firmly believe in the incentives of capitalism, the freedom of private initiative, the human will to compete and a system wherein the more capable people receive higher rewards." Therefore, he asks, "Why not let generosity to college players happen wherever people want to be generous?"

In other words, let the cash flow begin.   33

Steve Ehrhart managing general partner of the Liberty Bowl and   34
former commissioner of the defunct USFL, remembers how people thought the early signing of Herschel Walker for big bucks by the USFL "meant the end of college football." So it will be, says Ehrhart with getting proper compensation to the players: "It will be absorbed just as the signing of undergraduates has been absorbed."

DeVenzio says athletes simply "should be free to make what-   35
ever money they can; and there is no reason whatever that educational institutions should be permitted to suppress the earning power of their athletes."

Indeed, keeping athletes poor—or trying to—invites entreaties   36
by shadowy figures, notably gamblers, who always lurk on the fringes of college sports.

Marvin Johnson was a star basketball player at the University of   37
New Mexico in 1976–77 and 1977–78 and still holds the school record for points in one game (50). He also was immersed in the epidemic cheating: "I got crumbs I'd say about $5,000. Sometimes I'd go by the coaches' offices and they'd give me cash." Once he got money when he told them his mother needed a new washer. Says Johnson, "I knew it was against the rules. I just didn't understand the rules. Any other student can get money. But with athletes, it's like we're second-class students on campus."

Johnson would eat free at the minor league Albuquerque Dukes   38
baseball park restaurant. He had a 1976 Mercury Cougar. "I was told just to go pick up a car and it will be taken care of," he says. So Johnson knows whereof he speaks when he says dramatic change regarding how players get their hands on money "instantly eliminates

the cheating and corruption that are fueling this system." (At New Mexico, spokesman Greg Remington says that "concerning something that was supposed to have happened two decades ago, it would be improper for us to make any judgment on what Mr. Johnson is saying.")

At the University of Washington, President Gerberding says he   39
has "become increasingly uncomfortable about having a largely white establishment maintaining an elaborate system of rules that deprives student/athletes, many of whom are non-white, of adequate financial support in the name of 'the ideals of amateurism.' The ghost of Avery Brundage (longtime autocratic boss of the Olympics) rattles in my memory and conscience."

What many collegiate leaders finally are coming to grips with,   40
however, is how the memory of Mr. Touchdown and raccoon coats no longer squares with anybody's conscience when attention is focused on how business is conducted today. "Who would have thought," DeVenzio says, "that we would have the Poulan/Weed Eater Independence Bowl? It's unfortunate that we should even be asking if everybody in America should be paid for their work. Of course they should. Look, a university is a wonderful place. It can handle weird artists, weapons research, experiments with animals, and athletes. It can accommodate everybody. So can it easily accommodate players getting paid? Of course. It's a university."

Asked what would happen if, for example, North Carolina   41
started paying its basketball players but Duke didn't, DeVenzio says, "That's fine. North Carolina will win."

2. *The cornerstone of democracy is free enterprise. Let it work.*   42
"The more free enterprise, as in the rest of life, the more positives you have rather than negatives and the more success stories you have rather than the problems," Ehrhart suggests. "All these rules force things underground, then you have a black market. Real life is to allow freedom."

In full agreement is Marvin Johnson, who says that "there is no   43
salary cap on the coach, the A.D., the president. America is the land of opportunity. So if the current rules aren't changed, America isn't what it says. Capitalism makes everything fair. What is more basic in our system than getting paid for your sweat and creativity?"

Admittedly, there are those who have trouble with this idea.   44
The NCAA's Dempsey says such a concept is "contrary to the amateur code of intercollegiate athletics." Nevada's Crowley calls such a possibility 'just a terrible idea" and sees it as "the last step in the commercialization of college sport." At Iowa State, A.D. Smith says

he has "a hard time" making such a jump. One logical objection to paying the players is raised by Colorado's Albino, who says it is reasonable not to if you consider the athletes' time on campus as an apprenticeship. "We all have to pay our dues before we reap the benefits," she says.

Dempsey is further concerned about the adverse effects such a 45 move might have financially because, he says, only 65 out of the 950 NCAA member institutions are generating more money on their collegiate sports than they are spending. OK, so a lot of schools need to figure out bow to run their businesses profitably. There are no more Hudsons and no more Edsels. The reason is obvious.

The solution also is obvious. We know from all the rules viola- 46 tions that there are lots of wealthy alums and boosters of various schools eager to give athletes cash and cars and stuff. They clearly care about athletic success. There's nothing wrong with that.

Therefore, it can be assumed that football behemoths will have 47 little trouble raising huge bucks, especially if the contributors don't run the risk of being publicly branded as sleazeballs if their philanthropy surfaces in the media. It also can be assumed that some football-playing schools will not be able to raise the money and will have to drop the sport. Football is not a constitutionally guaranteed right. The University of Chicago booted football and remains one of the land's premier institutions. The Ivy League flirted with bigtime sports over the years, but ultimately pulled in its horns and is content to play its games on a lower level. Harvard and Yale aren't withering.

Free enterprise also would force universities to properly focus 48 on their business, which is education, not sports. Sports are about sports and that's the end of that story. Trying to forge a tolerable marriage between education and athletics is exceptionally tricky. Asks DeVenzio, "Are all these new conferences about education? Will the athletes get a better education now that the Big Eight is becoming the Big 12?" Most telling: DeVenzio questions why the Big 12 took in Texas A&M, Texas, Texas Tech and Baylor but not Rice. After all, *US. News & World Report* last fall ranked Rice fourth academically among national universities—ahead of Princeton, Stanford, Yale, Harvard. None of the Texas schools admitted to the Big 12 made the top 24. Further, the Educational Ratings Annual named Rice one of the land's 76 most selective colleges; again, no other Texas school was mentioned. Rice, however, is a weak sister athletically.

Naysayers to the let-free-enterprise-work idea will quickly raise 49 what they see as a Title IX problem—federal legislation that dictates equal treatment for men and women athletes. This is nonsense, says a prominent Colorado attorney, Joe French, who has long represented college athletes on a variety of matters. He sees no problem with some athletes—those considered more valuable because their sports generate more revenue—receiving more money than others and suggests, "An accommodation can be achieved within the spirit of Title IX."

Indeed, French says that as long as a new system for compensating athletes is not used "as a tool" to subvert Title IX, all that's needed to make it a fair and equitable reality is "a little creativity on the part of athletic directors."

In general agreement is Val Bonnette, president of a Virginia consulting firm, Good Sports Inc., that helps institutions make sure they are in compliance with NCAA rules. For 15 years, she was employed in the Office for Civil Rights in Washington, D.C., devoting two-thirds or more of her time to Tide IX. Although Bonnette says there is "potential for concern" about equity issues should it come to paying players, she emphasizes that there is "flexibility" within Title IX legislation and that accommodation could be reached through "intelligent decisions."

At the NCAA, Janet Justus, an attorney and director of education resources, says any change would have to be "equal or equitable" under Title IX. Justus says that means it would be essential that "women receive the same kind of benefits" as men. That does not, however, necessarily require a dollar-for-dollar match for all sports, she says.

It's clear: At virtually every university, the football coach makes far more money than the golf coach. Therefore, logic sees nothing wrong with a football player getting more money than a golfer; a woman basketball player getting more than a male lacrosse player.

3. *Allow scholarship athletes the same freedoms and rights that all other students enjoy—which, among many things, includes the right to have jobs if they wish.* Indeed, athletes should be able to have employment—*just like real students.* This would be an easy one for the NCAA to adopt. It would look good but would mean little. The truth is, athletics takes up so much time and energy that there is little left for work. And this doesn't even address any academic demands.

Still, it would eliminate an obvious inequity that draws a lot of attention. The last two NCAA conventions, however, have turned down the proposal. Steve Morgan at the NCAA says there are two major concerns: that there would be far better-paying jobs in urban areas than in rural areas, which would be unfair, and that the problem of no-show jobs would again become a major problem.

Ergo, cheating.   56

But if the NCAA washed its intrusive hands of the problem, it   57
would sort itself out. It's called, drum roll, free enterprise. "Athletes," Morgan says, "need to have opportunities and benefits in order to lead a normal campus life." This is a theme on many minds. William Beauchamp, Notre Dame's executive vice president, said at the sports symposium on his campus that steps are being taken to "mainstream our student/athletes to allow them to experience college like other students. . . ."

That's laudatory and should be put into practice. Says Marvin   58
Johnson: "What has happened is that the players are barred from joining in the feast at the table, and this makes no sense because the feast is provided by the players." Johnson and others handed out flyers at an NCAA basketball tournament session in Albuquerque, in support of getting money to the players.

"The thing we most admire and want to teach the most is the   59
work ethic," Ehrhart says. "Everybody wants to recruit a high school player who had a job weekends, helped his mom make ends meet by having a paper route. The very best All-American young man. Then we get him to college and say, 'You can't work.' It's antithetical." Ehrhart says it makes sense, for example, to let players work—for pay—for the athletic department by selling ads in the game program; it makes sense, he says, to have football players tutor other football players.

The absurdity of the athletes-can't-work theory was demon-   60
strated recently when Northwestern running back Darnell Autry was told by the NCAA it was against the rules for him to play a small part in "The 18th Angel," a film being made in Italy. ("Don't blink or you'll miss me," Autry says.) The NCAA paid no attention to the fact Autry wasn't going to accept payment and that his college major is theater. There was a flurry of legal nonsense and dark threats that the NCAA would rule Autry ineligible to play any more football. Ultimately, common sense did prevail: Autry is in the film—just like any other real student could be—and he is eligible to play football this fall.

4. *Give each scholarship athlete—male and female, everything*   61
from field hockey to golf to football to basketball—50 to 100 seats
in prime locations to all home games. What do they do with them? Hey, this is America. They sell them. They give them away. They lose them. College is a learning experience. They do whatever they

want. And if sports are for the students, as is loudly proclaimed, well . . .

Certainly, it is understood that there is essentially no market 62 for field hockey tickets. So be it. What could be more fair than that? Duke's DeVenzio says this would mean that some athletes "would go to schools where his tickets would be most valuable." Universities that have successful basketball teams, for example, charge substantially more for tickets. Why shouldn't athletes be able to do the same? Athletes, like everyone else, should benefit from their abilities.

5. *Ten percent of each sport's net profits could be distributed to* 63 *the players.* New Mexico's Johnson, who went on to play extensively in Europe and beyond, says the way this works is obvious: If a sport doesn't make money, the athletes have none to share. He waves his hand across an Albuquerque restaurant and says, "If this place doesn't make money, it closes, right? Well, that's fair. That's capitalism."

Militants on this issue suggest not 10 percent of the net but 10 64 percent of the gross. That's excessive, since the schools have to pay all costs associated with athletics and the players none. The most recent "Revenues and Expenses of Intercollegiate Athletics Programs" put out by the NCAA reports that large schools spend about $29,000 a year per scholarship athlete.

6. *Dramatically increase the Special Assistance Fund.* In 1991, 65 this emergency fund was started by the NCAA with $2 million. It has now jumped to $10 million. It almost certainly is heading higher. The idea of it according to Gene Smith, who chairs an NCAA committee studying the fund, is to be able to provide needy athletes with funds for emergency trips home, dental care, eye care, necessary clothes. Smith says he hopes to find ways to "liberalize" the use of the fund. As is often the case, such thinking is laudatory, but the potential for abuse is enormous. Who truly needs the money and what truly constitutes an emergency? And is Venus made of blue cheese?

7. *Let athletes sign with agents whenever they want.* Inside the 66 blizzard of NCAA rules is one that prohibits a player from signing with an agent—normally to represent the player in negotiating a professional contract—until college eligibility is complete. Texas basketball coach Tom Penders thinks this change would go a long way toward cleaning up out-of-control skullduggery in this area. It would. That's because as things stand, agents routinely—and illegally—give money to players while they are in college; if the practice is discovered, the agent says it was a loan.

So, since agents are prime conduits for getting illegal dollars to   67
the athletes and nothing can be done about it, it obviously is time
to admit defeat and try another way. That way is to let agents become part of the solution—which is by helping fund things properly
by giving untainted money to the athlete—instead of part of the
problem.

Basically, the issue is fairness. Any other American can hire an   68
agent. College athletes are the only group so prohibited. Says Walter Byers, "The wheel of fortune is badly unbalanced in favor of the
overseers and against the players."

8. *Add substantially more money to the familiar full-ride*   69
scholarship. The NCAA's Steve Morgan says there is "a lot more
open attitude" about this idea than there used to be. This could be
where the long-discussed idea of a monthly stipend—perhaps $100
a month, maybe $200—would come in.

For his part, DeVenzio insists that there "is no justification for   70
suppressing economic opportunity. That's like giving the slaves
Sunday off. They are still slaves." University of Nevada President
Crowley says a sticky point with stipends is giving such a payment
to haves as well as have-nots. But he says, something might work in
this area depending "on how you label it."

And there are inequities depending on geography. Says Chris   71
Polnsky at Texas, "In Queens, $200 will buy a couple theater tick-
ets once a month; $200 in College Station (Texas) is a lot of trips to
Dixie Chicken."

But despite the obvious shortcomings of this idea, its strength is   72
that it would be a step—albeit a tiny, baby step—in the direction of
getting clean money into the hands of the athletes. Every worthy
journey starts with a single you-know-what.

9. *Put any money the player earns or receives while in college*   73
into a trust fund handled by the university and give it to him or her
upon graduation. If the athlete doesn't graduate, the money stays
with the university for academic purposes. This is another proposal
that makes proponents of the status quo grind their teeth. It also
makes enormous sense.

Universities have made a point of saying student/athlete, not   74
athlete/student. Fine. This makes the education a clear priority
while at the same time not preventing the athlete from making
money however he or she sees fit. This idea is not foolproof, in that
it is always difficult to uncover details of the frequent golden handshakes players receive—those handshakes that end up with $20 or
$50 or $100 or more in the player's palm. Yet, for major arrangements—endorsements, speeches, appearances, camps—it would be

easy to keep track of. DeVenzio thinks this would be a "terrific educational incentive" and would also speak to fairness because it
would help ensure that the athletes "get the education that the university offered in return for their athletic talents."

10. *Allow recruiters to offer athletes scholarships that might*   75
include graduate school, law school or medical school. Surely nobody would object to this change with its strong and serious educational bent. Currently, athletes are given scholarships one year at a
time for a maximum of five years. This idea would appeal enor-
mously to any serious student.

Beyond these 10 points that basically relate to financial concern,   76
there are a bevy of tangential issues that simply make sense when
it comes to how universities should deal reasonably, fairly and honestly with their scholarship athletes. For example:

- Stop requiring scholarship athletes to take full academic loads.   77
  No regular student is so burdened. Educators and others   78
  revel in talking about "what is best for the kids." What is
  best for an athlete is not taking a full load during the season.
  It's too much. Frankly, what is best for an athlete might well
  be taking one course each fall—in the case of a football
  player—and graduate in seven years. And, again, the full-load
  silliness invites cheating—or at least a course schedule unworthy of being called higher education. The old educational
  dodge of letting athletes major in physical education has
  largely given way to the likes of criminology, communications, sports administration, American studies. Same thing.
  Different names.

  What universities should do is tailor the academic regi-   79
  men for athletes in a proper manner. They do it all the time
  for others. Schools offer special arrangements for single mothers. They offer night and weekend classes for those whose
  work schedules prohibit weekday attendance. There is nothing wrong, and indeed, everything right with a university taking into consideration the needs of constituents.

  Structured this way, the old, tired problem of trying to get   80
  athletes to attend classes and, with luck, even learn something, becomes less onerous. Oh, yes, and why is it that in
  many if not most cases, regular students attend class only if
  they want to, but at many schools, a cadre of athletic department flunkies runs around making sure each scholarship athlete is sitting in class?

Finally, it's time to address the issue of whether a schol- 81
arship football or basketball player—who, in almost every
case is in college not for the education but to play the game—
should be made to masquerade as a student in the first place.

• In order to entice a good athlete, allow schools to offer acade- 82
mic scholarships to brothers or sisters. What a splendid opportunity to do good.

• Allow scholarship athletes to play immediately at another 83
school, if they decide to transfer.

Currently, the rule generally requires athletes to sit out a 84
year—thereby forfeiting a year of eligibility—if they transfer
between major schools. It's neither fair nor right. After all,
coaches move from school to school with impunity. Why not
athletes? Allow them to transfer once without losing any eligibility. If the athlete is lured by big bucks from another
school, that is free enterprise at work in all its glory.

University of Washington President Gerberding says that "priv- 85
ileged old orders yield slowly, but many of them finally do yield."
That's the optimistic view. Walter Byers says the larger truth is that
the powers in intercollegiate sport—about 25 football schools and
perhaps 35 in basketball—don't want to change because they "are
doing very, very well. The beneficiaries of monopoly practices don't
want to change the monopoly." And it can be argued that conversely, some weak athletic schools might fight the change for fear
a new, capitalistic system would force them out completely.

Maybe, suggests Byers, it will come down to a court case over 86
antitrust when people start disputing the old notion that the rules
are in place to ensure competitive balance when, in fact, they are in
place to ensure economic gain—a clear antitrust violation, if proved.

Those who favor the status quo will use all sorts of specious ar- 87
guments, including the one that there is not enough money. Baloney. There is plenty. But, if people who care—the university,
boosters—don't want to pay to have a good football team, then the
school won't have a good football team. Nothing wrong with that.

In addition, Cedric Dempsey suggests there is a lot of room for 88
the NCAA to grow its business, especially in the areas of licensing,
marketing and international development. And here's a real easy
source: Get on with the idea of a football championship, which
could net $80 million.

Most change is painful. Labor strikes—including the recent 89
baseball strike—are over change. Women's suffrage was over change.
Same for the Industrial Revolution, environmentalism, affirmative

action, immigration. So be it with college athletes. It is possible, suggests Marvin Johnson, that players may revolt to be treated *like real students.* They may unionize.

Meanwhile, the howling winds are picking up velocity.   90

Paying Athletes?
Colleges Do Not Need This "Cure"

RON GREEN

The current issue of The Sporting News features a cover story   1
entitled, "How We Should Pay College Athletes." It is a well-intentioned list of proposals, but it is in reality a diagram for the ruination of college athletics.

It would, for example, allow schools, primarily through well-   2
heeled boosters, to pay athletes whatever they want to pay. No limit. In all the speechmaking and editorializing that has been done on the subject over the years, and that is millions of words too many, this may be the stupidest idea ever put forth.

Here's a counterproposal—since we already have pro sports   3
teams like the NBA and NFL, why not leave college athletics as they are? Give athletes scholarships and enough money to go home two or three times a year and a little spending money, but leave the college games alone. While they aren't perfect, they aren't so terribly flawed that they should toss aside their honor.

Critics cry out about injustices. Where is the injustice in giving   4
a young person the opportunity to go to college and play on a sports team, at no cost? A great percentage of them would never step on a college campus if it weren't for those scholarships.

This astonishingly shortsighted essay in The Sporting News de-   5
serves attention because there is a movement afoot—a thoughtful movement, for the most part—to change the rules to some degree. The basic idea is to cover expenses for college athletes that are not dealt with in the scholarships, and possibly work out a plan under which athletes could work during the school year, which they are now not allowed to do.

It's time those were resolved, but not by wild-eyed change that   6
abandons the purpose and ideals of campus sports.

Critics of the present system are growing in number and decibels,   7
though. Even Walter Byers, former head of the NCAA, in a complete reversal of all he stood for in the past, asks, "Why not let generosity to college players happen where ever people want to be generous?"

I had always considered Byers a thoughtful, reasonable man, a   8
bit stuffy, perhaps, but possessed of a level head. To hear him es-
pouse such a notion, though, is like hearing a former FBI director
recommend assault weapons for one and all.

The introduction of open bidding for players would turn college   9
basketball into another NBA, college football into another NFL.
With no salary caps.

The schools with the most fat cat boosters (whose self-worth de-   10
pends on the success of his or her college's teams) would buy up top
talent. The idea is repulsive. Administrators and coaches already
have enough problems with boosters interfering. They would lose
all control if alums were buying athletes.

One advocate, asked what would happen if North Carolina paid   11
its athletes and Duke didn't, said, "That's fine. North Carolina will
win." He apparently thought that was a sensible answer.

The Sporting News story acknowledges that some football play-   12
ing schools would not be able raise the money and would have to
drop the sport. But, hey, reasons TSN, "Football is not a constitutionally guaranteed right." And apparently assumed that, too, was a
sensible answer.

Proponents of pay for collegians like to point out that schools   13
generate millions of dollars in income from athletics and that athletes don't share in that. What they don't say is that athletes receive
the scholarship for which they signed a contract, a scholarship that
is worth, on the average, $29,000 a year (the amount it costs the
school) at major colleges.

What they also fail to point out is that those millions are spent   14
on scholarships, salaries, facilities, travel, not socked away in somebody's bank account.

Salaries. There's another sticking point. The coaches and ath-   15
letic department employees make money from income generated by
the athletes, they say, why not the athletes? Because those people
are salaried employees, some of them extremely talented, and they
earn their money.

The Sporting News story also suggests giving each scholarship   16
athlete 50 to 100 seats in prime locations to all home games, to do
with as they please. Let's see now, if you gave 85 football players 100
seats each, that's 8,500 of the best seats no longer available to
alumni who donate money for the privilege of buying them. Besides,
there are laws against scalping tickets in most states.

Another TSN idea—allow football players to take only one   17
course in the fall semester and graduate in seven years. Besides, says
the paper, scholarship football and basketball players are, "in almost
every case, not in college for education but to play" and it's time to

address the issue of whether they should "be made to masquerade as a student in the first place."

Give scholarships that run all the way through doctorate degrees, says TSN, and give scholarships to athletes' brothers or sisters. Excuuuuse me? Where is all this money coming from? Oh, the fat cats. That's certainly a dependable source of income. 18

Certainly college athletics could stand some changes, could be modernized. But turning this over to boosters and abandoning the education of the athletes would ruin it. 19

Critics of the collegiate system are looking at the dark side— cheating, primarily, and there is that. They can cite many examples of athletes trying to beat the system. But we can cite millions of examples of athletes benefiting from college athletics the way those athletics have been and the way they are. 20

Surrender is what the critics advocate, but this is not something that we should surrender. 21

We've already given up too much that was good in athletics. College sports are not perfect, but they're worth saving. 22

Fix them, don't destroy them. 23

QUESTIONS OF CONTENT

1. Looney clearly does not believe that the current financial assistance programs for college athletes are working. What major flaws does he discuss? Which ones, if any, has he omitted?
2. Where and how does Green refute Looney's belief that the current programs are unjust? What adjustments in support does he suggest instead?
3. Looney lists and discusses ten ways to provide college athletes greater financial benefits than they currently receive. Which two of these seem the most reasonable to you, and why? Which seems least reasonable?
4. Looney insists his proposed changes will end the widespread cheating on financial assistance for college athletes that now occurs. What is Green's response to this claim?
5. Rather than the title for Looney's essay that actually appeared within the pages of *The Sporting News* (which we use in this book), Green refers to it by another title; how is the title that he uses a more accurate indicator of the focus of Looney's argument?

QUESTIONS OF FORM

1. Looney makes two basic claims, one of fact to begin his essay and one of policy. In which paragraphs does he present his claim of fact,

and what about his principal warrant for that claim probably makes him spend less time on that claim than on his claim of policy?

2. Looney often uses statements and interviews with presumed authorities to support his argument. What three main groups of persons does he seem to presume are authorities on college athletics, based on the quotations he uses? Has he overlooked representatives of any other groups that also have a big stake in the subject of his essay?

3. How are the last five paragraphs of Green's essay critical to his refutation of Looney?

4. Examine Looney's essay for examples of uses of language that are "slanting." (If you need help with this word, look it up in the Glossary of Useful Terms in the Appendix.) Pick out three notable examples of slanting and be prepared to discuss how they may or may not signal or contribute to some sort of "material fallacy." (These argumentative flaws are also discussed in the Appendix, in A Short Guide to Material and Formal Fallacies.)

SUGGESTIONS FOR WRITING

1. As a student yourself, you are likely to be even more aware of the realities of college financial pressures than Looney (even though for over twenty-five years he has specialized in writing about college athletics). Write a one-page letter which points out some omissions or errors in his presentation of *either* the problem *or* the solutions that he has described.

2. Assume that you are a sportswriter for your local college newspaper and, like Green, you have just read Looney's proposals for change. Choose a proposal to which Green did not respond, and prepare your own reply as if it were a sports column.

3. After you graduate from a four-year college or university, you typically will begin to receive alumni newsletters and magazines which not only keep you informed about your alma mater but also solicit your financial support. Assuming that you are ten years into significant financial success in your chosen profession, prepare your probable response to the following: an alumni association report that your college is now putting into place one of Looney's proposals for change and needs your financial help to do so.

THE DEATH PENALTY

The Deterrent Effect of the Death Penalty

ERNEST VAN DEN HAAG

Crime is going to be with us as long as there is any social order   1
articulated by laws. There is no point making laws that prohibit
some action or other (e.g., murder or theft) unless there is some
temptation to commit it. And however harsh the threats of the law,
they will not restrain some people, whether because they discount
the risk of punishment or because they are exposed to extraordinary
temptation. They may hope for an immense profit; or be passionately angry or vindictive; or be in such misery that they feel they
have nothing to lose. Thus, I repeat, the problem every society must
attempt to solve (in part by means of punishment) is not eliminating crime but controlling it.

That threats will not deter everybody all the time must be ex-   2
pected. And it must also be expected that persons committed to
criminal activity—career criminals—are not likely to be restrained
by threats; nor are persons strongly under the influence of drugs or
intoxicated by their own passions. However, if threats are not likely
to deter habitual offenders, they are likely to help deter people from
becoming habitual offenders.

People are not deterred by exactly calculating the size of the   3
threat and the actual risk of suffering punishment against the
likely benefit of the crime they consider committing. Few people
calculate at all. Rather, the effect of threats is to lead most people
to ignore criminal opportunities most of the time. One just does
not consider them—any more than the ordinary person sitting
down for lunch starts calculating whether he could have Beluga
caviar and champagne instead of his usual hamburger and beer. He
is not accustomed to caviar, and one reason he is not accustomed
to it is that it costs too much. He does not have to calculate every
time to know as much. Similarly, he is not accustomed to breaking the law, and one reason is that it costs too much. He does not
need to calculate.

It is quite a different matter if one asks, not: "Do threats deter?"   4
but rather: "How much does one threat deter compared to another?"
Does the most severe threat deter significantly more? Does the
added deterrence warrant the added severity? Thus, no one ponder-
ing the death penalty will contend that it does not deter. The question is: Does it deter more than alternative penalties proposed, such
as life imprisonment or any lengthy term of imprisonment?

In the past many attempts were made to determine whether the   5
death penalty deters the crimes for which it was threatened—capital crimes—more than other penalties, usually life imprisonment,
mitigated by parole (and amounting therefore to something like ten
years in prison in most cases). Most of these attempts led to ambiguous results, often rendered more ambiguous by faulty procedures and research methods. Frequently, contiguous states—one
with and the other without the death penalty—were compared. Or
states were compared before and after abolition. Usually these comparisons were based on the legal availability or unavailability of the
death penalty rather than on the presence or absence of executions
and on their frequency. But what matters is whether the death
penalty is practiced, not whether theoretically it is available. Finally, nobody would assert that the death penalty—or any crime-
control measure—is the only determinant of the frequency of the
crime. The number of murders certainly depends as well on the proportion of young males in the population, on income distribution,
on education, on the proportion of various races in the population,
on local cultural traditions, on the legal definition of murder, and on
other such factors.

Comparisons must take all of these matters into account if they   6
are to evaluate the effect threatened penalties may have in deterring
crimes. In contiguous states, influential factors other than the death
penalty may differ; they may even differ in the same state before and
after abolition. Hence, differences (or equalities) in capital crime
frequencies cannot simply be ascribed to the presence or absence of
the death penalty. Moreover, one does not know how soon a change
in penalties will make a difference, if it ever does, or whether
prospective murderers will know that the death penalty has been
abolished in Maine and kept in Vermont. They certainly will know
whether or not there is a death penalty in the United States. But in
contiguous states? Or within a short time after abolition or reinstatement?

Theoretically, experiments to avoid all these difficulties are pos-   7
sible. But they face formidable obstacles in practice. If, for instance,
the death penalty were threatened for murders committed on Monday, Wednesday, and Friday, and life imprisonment for murders

committed on Tuesday, Thursday, and Saturday, we would soon see which days murderers prefer, i.e., how much the death penalty deters on Monday, Wednesday, and Friday over and above life imprisonment threatened for murders committed on the other days. If we find no difference, the abolitionist thesis that the death penalty adds no deterrence over and above the threat of life imprisonment would be confirmed.

In the absence of such experiments, none of the available studies seems conclusive. Recently such studies have acquired considerable mathematical sophistication, and some of the more sophisticated studies have concluded, contrary to what used to be accepted scholarly opinion, that the death penalty can be shown to deter over and above life imprisonment. Thus, Isaac Ehrlich, in a study published in the *American Economic Review* (June 1975), concluded that, over the period 1933–1969, "an additional execution per year . . . may have resulted on the average in 7 or 8 fewer murders." 8

Other studies published since Ehrlich's contend that his results are due to the techniques and periods he selected, and that different techniques and periods yield different results. Despite a great deal of research on all sides, one cannot say that the statistical evidence is conclusive. Nobody has claimed to have *disproved* that the death penalty may deter more than life imprisonment. But one cannot claim, either, that it has been proved statistically in a conclusive manner that the death penalty does deter more than alternative penalties. This lack of proof does not amount to disproof. However, abolitionists insist that there ought to be proof positive. 9

Unfortunately, there is little proof of the sort sought by those who oppose the death penalty for the deterrent effect of any sort of punishment. Nobody has statistically shown that 4 years in prison deter more than 2, or 20 more than 10. We assume as much. But I know of no statistical proof. One may wonder why such proof is demanded for the death penalty but not for any other. To be sure, death is more serious a punishment than any other. But 10 years in prison are not exactly trivial either. . . . 10

If it is difficult, perhaps impossible, to prove statistically—and just as hard to disprove—that the death penalty deters more from capital crimes than available alternative punishments do (such as life imprisonment), why do so many people believe so firmly that the death penalty is a more effective deterrent? 11

Some are persuaded by irrelevant arguments. They insist that the death penalty at least makes sure that the person who suffered it will not commit other crimes. True. Yet this confuses incapacitation with a specific way to bring it about: death. Death is the surest way to bring about the most total incapacitation, and it is irrevoca- 12 ble. But does incapacitation need to be that total? And is irrevocability necessarily an advantage? Obviously it makes correcting mistakes and rehabilitation impossible. What is the advantage of execution, then, over alternative ways of achieving the desired incapacitation?

More important, the argument for incapacitation confuses the   13
elimination of one murderer (or of any number of murderers) with a reduction in the homicide rate. But the elimination of any specific number of actual or even of potential murderers—and there is some doubt that the actual murderers of the past are the most likely future (potential) murderers—will not affect the homicide rate, except through deterrence. There are enough potential murderers around to replace all those incapacitated. Deterrence may prevent the potential from becoming actual murderers. But incapacitation of some or all actual murderers is not likely to have much effect by itself. Let us then return to the question: Does capital punishment deter more than life imprisonment?

Science, logic, or statistics often have been unable to prove what   14
common sense tells us to be true. Thus, the Greek philosopher Zeno some 2,000 years ago found that he could not show that motion is possible; indeed, his famous paradoxes appear to show that motion is impossible. Though nobody believed them to be true, nobody succeeded in showing the fallacy of these paradoxes until the rise of mathematical logic less than a hundred years ago. But meanwhile, the world did not stand still. Indeed, nobody argued that motion should stop because it had not been shown to be logically possible. There is no more reason to abolish the death penalty than there was to abolish motion simply because the death penalty has not been, and perhaps cannot be, shown statistically to be a deterrent over and above other penalties. Indeed, there are two quite satisfactory, if nonstatistical, indications of the marginal deterrent effect of the death penalty.

In the first place, our experience shows that the greater the   15
threatened penalty, the more it deters. Ceteris paribus, the threat of 50 lashes deters more than the threat of 5; a $1,000 fine deters more than a $10 fine; 10 years in prison deter more than 1 year in prison—just as, conversely, the promise of a $1,000 reward is a greater incentive than the promise of a $10 reward, etc. There may be diminishing returns. Once a reward exceeds, say, $1 million, the additional attraction may diminish. Once a punishment exceeds, say, 10 years in prison (net of parole), there may be little additional deterrence in threatening additional years. We know hardly anything about diminishing returns of penalties. It would still seem likely, however, that the threat of life in prison deters more than any other term of imprisonment.

The threat of death may deter still more. For it is a mistake to   16
regard the death penalty as though it were of the same kind as other
penalties. If it is not, then diminishing returns are unlikely to apply.
And death differs significantly, in kind, from any other penalty. Life
in prison is still life, however unpleasant. In contrast, the death
penalty does not just threaten to make life unpleasant—it threatens
to take life altogether. This difference is perceived by those affected.
We find that when they have the choice between life in prison and
execution, 99 percent of all prisoners under sentence of death prefer
life in prison. By means of appeals, pleas for commutation, indeed
by all means at their disposal, they indicate that they prefer life in
prison to execution.

From this unquestioned fact a reasonable conclusion can be   17
drawn in favor of the superior deterrent effect of the death penalty.
Those who have the choice in practice, those whose choice has actual and immediate effects on their life and death, fear death more
than they fear life in prison or any other available penalty. If they
do, it follows that the threat of the death penalty, all other things
equal, is likely to deter more than the threat of life in prison. One
is most deterred by what one fears most. From which it follows that
whatever statistics fail, or do not fail, to show, the death penalty is
likely to be more deterrent than any other.

Suppose now one is not fully convinced of the superior deterrent   18
effect of the death penalty. I believe I can show that even if one is
genuinely uncertain as to whether the death penalty adds to deterrence, one should still favor it, from a purely deterrent viewpoint.
For if we are not sure, we must choose either to (1) trade the certain
death, by execution, of a convicted murderer for the probable survival of an indefinite number of murder victims whose future murder is less likely (whose survival is more likely)—if the convicted
murderer's execution deters prospective murderers, as it might, or
to (2) trade the certain survival of the convicted murderer for the
probable loss of the lives of future murder victims more likely to be
murdered because the convicted murderer's nonexecution might
not deter prospective murderers, who could have been deterred by
executing the convicted murderer.

To restate the matter: If we were quite ignorant about the mar-   19
ginal deterrent effects of execution, we would have to choose—like
it, or not—between the certainty of the convicted murder's death by
execution and the likelihood of the survival of future victims of other
murderers on the one hand, and on the other his certain survival and
the likelihood of the death of new victims. I'd rather execute a man
convicted of having murdered others than to put the lives of inno-
cents at risk. I find it hard to understand the opposite choice.

Rolling the Dice to Decide Who Dies

VIVIAN BERGER

Since 1984, when the Court of Appeals held unconstitutional [1]
the last vestige of the death penalty in New York State, New York
has been one of fewer than a third of the states in this country that
do not provide for capital punishment. In each of the past few years,
however, our Legislature has passed bills reauthorizing death as the
sanction for certain types of murder. Governor Cuomo, a committed opponent of capital punishment as was Governor Carey before
him, has consistently vetoed these efforts. But sooner or later the
governor will relinquish office. Surely, therefore, a time will come
when the state acquires as chief executive someone who either supports execution or declines to counter the lawmakers' wishes. Then
New Yorkers, acting through their elected officials, will have to regard the death penalty as more than a mere symbolic gesture—a
banner to wave in the war against crime.

Because that point may be in the offing, the New York Bar, [2]
whose collective opinion should weigh heavily in the final decision
whether we remain an abolitionist state, must begin to think seriously about the issues. I, like our governor, fervently oppose capital
punishment; and I do so based on considerable experience with how
it operates, not just with the rhetoric that surrounds it. I hope to persuade those of you who have no opinion on the subject and perhaps
even some who currently favor reviving the death sentence in New
York that such a course has nothing to commend it. To the contrary,
reinstatement would amount to a giant step backward in this state's
historical march toward a decent and efficient system of justice.

To plunge yourself right into the reality of capital punishment, [3]
imagine that you are sitting on a jury in Georgia or Florida or some
other death-penalty state in the following cases. Your awesome task
is to determine whether the defendant should receive life imprisonment or death. Even if you could in fact never sentence a person to
die, you must try to envision that possibility—for the prosecution
would have struck you for cause unless you had indicated on voir-
dire that you would consider the option of death. Here are the five
cases in cameo:

1. A 19-year-old man, John, and his companion stole a young [4]
   woman's purse on the street, pushed her to the ground, and
   jumped into their nearby car. A taxi driver, observing the
   theft, sought to block their getaway with his cab. The de-

fendant, John, shot and killed him. It was his first violent offense.

2. A 19-year-old man, Joe, tried to grab the purse of a 54-year-old woman in a shopping center parking lot. She resisted and began screaming. They struggled for the purse and Joe shot her once in the side, killing her. He had prior misdemeanor convictions for shoplifting and simple battery as well as a felony conviction for theft.

3. A 21-year-old man, Robert, drove up to an all-night self-service station and filled his tank. He was paying for the gas with a "hot" credit card when the attendant, a college student, became suspicious that the card was stolen. Robert then shot the attendant once, killing him instantly, in order to avoid being arrested for the credit-card theft. Robert had previous convictions for an unarmed juvenile robbery and the burglary of a store.

4. A 20-year-old man, Nickie, who was under the influence of drugs, broke into a neighbor's apartment and bludgeoned her and her 8-year-old daughter to death with a hammer. He said later that he had done it because he liked to see blood. Nickie had past convictions for robbery and attempted aggravated rape.

5. A 26-year-old man, Stephen, together with a 17-year-old friend, burglarized the home of an elderly widow for whom the friend had done yard work. They were planning to rob her. The woman ended by being raped, beaten, and strangled as well as robbed. The defendant, Stephen, admitted that the two of them had raped and robbed her. He insisted, however (and no witness supported or contradicted his story) that only the friend had killed the victim and that he, Stephen, had tried in vain to stop the murder. He had previously committed an unarmed "date rape."

Ask yourself which, if any, of these men you would have sentenced to life in prison and which to death. Next, try to guess how the actual jurors decided these cases. In fact, #1, John, the purse-snatcher who shot the cabbie, received life. #2, Joe, the other purse-snatcher who shot the 54-year-old woman, was sentenced to die. #3, Robert, the credit-card thief who shot the attendant at the gas service station, got death as well; he is one of my clients. #4, Nickie, the hammer-bludgeoner who liked to see blood, got life imprisonment. Finally, #5, Stephen, who robbed and raped and may (or may not) have strangled the widow, was sentenced to death; he is also my client.

Whether or not you called any of the cases correctly, you might   10
want to ask yourself: "Did the divergent results make sense?" If
there was a pattern, I must say it eludes me. But for the moment,
taking some liberties with the facts and treating my examples as hypothetical instead of the true accounts which they are, I want the
reader to consider the possibility that jurors in a couple of the cases
that ended in death might likelier have opted for life imprisonment
if they had received some more information. For example, suppose
the sentencing jurors had heard that Joe had been the incredibly
abused child of a violent alcoholic father and a battered, helpless, in-
competent mother? That the father had made a game of placing Joe
and his siblings in a tight circle and throwing heavy objects like
glass ashtrays into the air for the pleasure of seeing who would be
hit? That Joe had at last run away from home at the age of 12,
camped for some months in a Dempsey dumpster, and then been
taken in by a man who sheltered him in return for homosexual favors? That during his one, too-brief experience in foster care when
he was nine, Joe responded with great affection and excellent behavior to the love and attention of his foster mother? Or, to take another example, suppose the jury had known that Stephen had an IQ
in the high 50's or low 60's? That confronted once with a power
mower that wasn't running, Stephen put water from a hose inside it
because he had seen others fill the machine but never realized that
not *any* type of liquid would do?

Of course, no one knows how real jurors would have reacted to   11
the scenarios I described. But experts in capital defense work agree
that no matter how appalling the crime, twelve not unduly sentimental jurors may well decide to spare a defendant when shown
that he is a human being with some explanation if not excuse for his
horrible acts. Yet while the jurors routinely hear the worst things
about the defendant, including usually his criminal record, what is
shocking is that in so many cases they hear *nothing* else about him
that might be deemed relevant to sentence. (Why this occurs, and
what it means for the operation of capital punishment, I will explore
further shortly.) What they *do* necessarily learn is the race of both
defendant and victim. If I had recounted some more examples of the
type I asked you to judge as a juror and told you the race of the persons involved, or at least the victim's, you might have begun to detect a pattern that did not emerge from the *pertinent* data. To this
topic, too, I will soon return. But what I hope I have done thus far
is to give the reader a "slice of death." At the very least, by relating
these sadly prosaic stories, I wanted to scotch the notion which so
many people have that death is reserved for special cases: the serial

killers, the depraved torturers, the Mafia hit men. In New York we deal with the Joes and Stephens each week by the hundreds.

A bit of history sheds some light on how Capital Punishment 12 U.S.A. acquired its present salient features. The watershed came when the United States Supreme Court handed down the landmark *Furman v. Georgia* in 1972. *Furman* invalidated all existing death sentence statutes as violative of the Eighth Amendment's ban on cruel and unusual punishment and thus depopulated state death rows of their 629 occupants. Although there was no majority opinion and only Justices Brennan and Marshall would have held execution to be intrinsically cruel and unusual, Justice Stewart captured the essence of the centrist justices' view—that the death penalty *as actually applied* was unconstitutionally arbitrary—in his famous analogy between the imposition of a capital sentence and the freakishness of a strike of lightning. Being "struck" by a capital sentence was cruel and unusual in the same way as being hit by a lightning bolt: the event was utterly capricious and random.

But worse, if possible, than death sentences that are entirely ar- 13 bitrary in the sense that a strike of lightning is freakish are those imposed on invidious grounds: where the lightning rod is race, religion, gender, or class. As Justice Douglas trenchantly remarked: "The Leopolds and Loebs are given prison terms, not sentenced to death." Blacks, however, were disproportionately sentenced to die, especially for the rape of white females. Indeed, the abolitionist campaign, which culminated in the *Furman* decision, had its genesis in the effort to eliminate capital punishment for rape. So perhaps, historically, the death penalty was really less "unusual" than "cruel": an invisible hand, and clearly a white one, was sorting out whites from blacks and thereby creating a pattern of results that many decent people abhorred.

Probably the justices hoped and believed that after *Furman* the 14 death penalty in the United States would remain dead; if so, they were wrong. Many legislatures simply determined to try until they got it right. And in 1976, in *Gregg v. Georgia* and its four companion cases, a majority of the Court upheld the post-Furman capital punishment statutes of Georgia, Florida, and Texas against a challenge to their facial validity, while simultaneously nullifying the revised laws of two other states. Those states had sought to resolve the randomness problem identified in *Furman* by ensuring that lightning would strike *all* persons convicted of murder in the first degree, rather than just a hapless few. In rejecting this tack, the Court noted that mandatory death sentence laws did not really resolve the problem but instead "simply papered [it] over" since juries responded by refusing to convict certain arbitrarily chosen defendants of first-degree murder.

More importantly, though, the justices ratified the so-called guided discretion statutes at issue in three of the five cases. The Court specifically approved some features of the new statutes which it expected would reduce the capriciousness of capital punishment and at the same time further the goal of individualization in sentencing. Thus, to take Georgia's law as a sample, the *Gregg* majority endorsed its provision for separate trials on guilt and penalty and automatic appellate review of sentences of death. The bifurcated trial innovation permitted the admission of evidence relevant only to sentence (for instance, the defendant's prior convictions) in a way that would not prejudice the jury in deciding guilt or innocence. The Court also emphasized that, at the penalty trial, not only did the state have to prove some aggravating circumstances beyond the fact of the murder itself (for example, torture or a previous record of criminal violence) but also defendants had the opportunity to offer evidence in mitigation—brave-conduct medals, or thrown ashtrays and waterlogged mowers. 15

It is basically under these post-*Gregg* schemes that Capital Punishment U.S.A. has been operating for over a decade. Until recently, however, only a handful of executions occurred every year. But in the mid-80s, in the wake of four adverse Supreme Court decisions— after a period in which the Court had overturned the capital sentence in 14 out of 15 cases, the engine of death acquired new steam. In 1984 alone, there were 21 executions (almost twice as many as in all of the years following *Gregg*); 1985 and 1986 saw 18 apiece, and the body count continues to grow. Thus, *Furman II* is hardly on the horizon now. That being so, if our next governor permits the enactment of capital statutes, the Court will surely not "veto" them: members of the Bar should understand that New York will have not dead-letter laws but dying defendants. 16

Why should New Yorkers oppose this result? Some believe that capital punishment inherently violates human dignity. But because many disagree with that view and my expertise is only lawyering, not moral philosophy, I leave it to others to debate the ultimate ethical issues. I take my stand with an eminent colleague, Professor Charles L. Black, Jr. Like me, refusing to resolve the basic clash of values, he reminds us wisely that there is "no abstract capital punishment." Asked how he would feel about the death penalty if only its administration were perfected, the professor replies: "What would you do if an amoeba were taught to play the piano?" In other words, it's a silly question; capital punishment *is* as it *does*. There- 17 fore, the often high-flown rhetoric bandied about by the pros and antis assumes, in my view, second place to the homely facts that make the American "legal system not good enough to choose people to die." I end with a few of the reasons why, which I hope that those who support or are open to reviving the death sentence in New York take deeply to heart.

Consider, first, the arbitrariness of the death penalty—how, in the real world, capital punishment must be forever married to caprice. From the initial decision to charge through the determination of sentence, the criminal justice system in general is rife with unreviewable discretion. The capital setting provides all of the same opportunities (and several more) for virtually unconstrained choice: the players roll the dice in a game where the stakes consist of life or death. Non-exhaustively, the prosecutor must decide such things as whether to charge capital murder instead of a lesser degree of homicide; whether to plea bargain with the accused or, in a multi-defendant case, whether to grant one of the defendants immunity or some other concession in return for cooperating with the state; and whether, if the defendant is convicted of a potentially capital charge, to move the case to the penalty phase and attempt to obtain a verdict of death. Many of those choices and especially the likelihood of plea bargaining will be dramatically affected by factors that have little or nothing to do with the nature of the crime or the strength of the evidence. These factors include geography (district attorneys have different policies on capital punishment, not to speak of varying amounts of dollars to spend on costly capital litigation); political concerns like the proximity of an election; the perceived acumen and aggressiveness of defense counsel; and the desires of the victim's family. 18

Other players than the prosecutor occupy key roles, too, of course. These include the judge and jury and, depending on local practice, the governor, administrative board, or both, who may be requested to grant clemency. Jurors, it is worth noting, not only possess the completely unreviewable discretion to acquit or compromise on lesser charges; they are also asked, in penalty trials, to determine such intrinsically fuzzy questions as "Will the defendant kill again?" or "Was this murder especially heinous, atrocious, or cruel?" or "Do the aggravating circumstances outweigh the proof in mitigation?" The latter inquiry forces jurors to try to assess how, for instance, the fact that the murder occurred during the course of a robbery and was committed to eliminate a witness should be balanced against the facts that the defendant was high on crack, is a first offender, and has a wife and three children who love him. Could you meaningfully weigh such factors? 19

Consider, second, that these sources of arbitrariness are exacer-   20
bated by extreme variations in the performance of defense counsel.
Ineffective assistance of counsel completely permeates the penalty
phase of capital trials in the post-*Gregg* era. With regard to cases like
Stephen's and Joe's and the others with which I began this piece, I
pointed out how often the jury hears nothing personal about the defendant even when substantial mitigating proof is readily available,
yet I did not explain this phenomenon. The explanation is simply
that many defense attorneys do little or nothing by way of investigation geared to sentencing issues and hence do not themselves
learn what they should be spreading before the jury. Why do attorneys drop the ball at the penalty phase with such depressing regu-
larity? Some lack the knowledge, experience, or will to assume the
role demanded of them in the unique capital setting. Lawyers find
it easier to hunt for what one whom I know called "eyeball witnesses" than to construct a psychodrama about a protagonist who is
frequently hostile, uncommunicative, beset with mental or emotional problems, or all of the above—especially when to do so involves searching out potential witnesses (family, friends, neighbors,
teachers) who, like the client, usually hail from a different racial or
socioeconomic milieu from counsel. Others curtail their investigations on account of shockingly low compensation. Still others
"throw in the towel" once the verdict of guilt is in. Whatever the
causes of these derelictions, most or all can be expected both to
cross jurisdictional lines and to continue into the future.

Consider, finally, the last but hardly the least point in my brief   21
against the death penalty—racial discrimination in sentencing. In
its modern guise, racial bias focuses primarily on the race of the *victim*, not the defendant. Sophisticated studies by social scientists
have demonstrated that murderers of whites are much likelier to be
sentenced to death than murderers of blacks. In Georgia, for instance, Professor David Baldus's prizewinning study revealed that,
after one accounted for dozens of variables that might legitimately
affect punishment, the killer of a white stood a *4.3 times* greater
chance of receiving death than did a person who killed a black! The
reason for these results is clear and as firmly rooted in our history
as prejudice against the black defendant: white society places a pre-
mium upon white life. New Yorkers inclined to discount such division on grounds of race as a regional Southern phenomenon need
only recall the tensions evoked by the Howard Beach and Goetz trials to see how very wrong they are. In any event, capital punishment
only magnifies inequalities of race that persist in the criminal justice system and in American society generally.

Last term, the Supreme Court rejected a challenge, grounded on   22
the damning Baldus statistics, to the death penalty as applied in Georgia. Assuming the validity of the study, the Court nonetheless held
5–4 in *McCleskey v. Kemp* that unless a capital defendant could prove
that some specific actor or actors purposely discriminated in his case,
thereby causing his sentence of death, neither the Eighth Amendment
nor Equal Protection was offended. I hope, however, that New Yorkers will be offended by, and wary of, the prospect of even risking
racially tainted sentencing where a person's life is at stake.

There *is* no good reason to take that risk. The death penalty has   23
not been shown to deter murder. Administering it with even the minimum amount of decency will further increase the logjams in our
crowded courts and will likely cost more in the end than the alternative of long-term imprisonment. At worst, some innocent men and
women will be executed as time goes by. At best, the guilty we choose
to kill will be morally indistinguishable from the rest whose lives we
opt to spare. New York cannot—in any sense of the word—afford to
resurrect such a bankrupt system. Thoughtful citizens should be
proud that our last two governors have resisted the siren call of capital "justice." The Bar, therefore, should strongly support the princi-
pled and pragmatic stance of opposition to capital punishment.

QUESTIONS OF CONTENT

1. Van den Haag suggests in paragraph 5 a number of factors that determine the frequency of murders. What are these factors?
2. Van den Haag makes a distinction between the death penalty as *deterrent* and as *incapacitation.* How are these two different?
3. What effect does he believe the use of the death penalty will have on
   the crime rate? Why?
4. What is Berger's chief objection to the death penalty?
5. What does Berger mean in paragraph 17 when she says "capital punishment *is* as it *does*"?
6. In what area does Berger feel that defense counsels are generally ineffective in capital cases? Why?
7. What does Berger feel is the single most important determining factor in the administration of the death penalty in murder cases?

QUESTIONS OF FORM

1. In paragraph 14 Van den Haag admits that science, logic, and statistics are incapable of proving that capital punishment acts as a deter-

rent (what the earlier portion of his essay had examined). To what line of reasoning does he finally resort? How does that argument work?

2. Both Van den Haag and Berger use examples to illustrate their claims. How do these examples differ?

3. What does Berger's argument gain by having its readers imagine themselves as jury members on five cases in a death-penalty state?

4. Why does Berger withhold certain information from the examples that she provides (paragraphs 4 through 8)? What sort of information is she withholding? What sort of effect does that information have when she later divulges it?

5. Notice that Berger often refers to various legal authorities and to actual court cases in her essay, while Van den Haag does not. What difference, if any, does that make in the effectiveness of either argument?

SUGGESTIONS FOR WRITING

1. Summarize these two positions in a concise essay. Keep your stance as neutral as possible.

2. You are Vivian Berger, and you have just read the following statement by William Buckley:

> The business about the poor and the black suffering excessively from capital punishment is no argument against capital punishment. It is an argument against the *administration* of justice, not against the penalty. Any punishment can be unfairly or unjustly applied. Go ahead and reform the process by which capital punishment is inflicted, if you wish; but don't confuse maladministration with the merits of capital punishment.

How do you respond? Compose a letter to Buckley's magazine, *National Review*, stating your response.

3. You are convinced, like Van den Haag, that the death penalty is necessary, given the increasing crime rate in our society. Prepare a presentation, suitable for delivery at a campus forum, that supports Van den Haag's position. Here are two additional sources that you might like to use. Mention each by name as you introduce any borrowed ideas or words.

BERNS, WALTER. "For Capital Punishment." In *For Capital Punishment: Crime and Morality of the Death Penalty*. New York: Basic, 1979.

MENCKEN, H. L. "The Death Penalty." In *A Mencken Chrestomathy*. New York: Knopf, 1954.

EVOLUTION VERSUS CREATIONISM

Evolution as Fact and Theory

STEPHEN JAY GOULD

Kirtley Mather, who died last year at age eighty-nine, was a pillar of both science and the Christian religion in America and one of my dearest friends. The difference of half a century in our ages evaporated before our common interests. The most curious thing we shared was a battle we each fought at the same age. For Kirtley had gone to Tennessee with Clarence Darrow to testify for evolution at the Scopes trial of 1925. When I think that we are enmeshed again in the same struggle for one of the best documented, most compelling and exciting concepts in all of science, I don't know whether to laugh or cry.

According to idealized principles of scientific discourse, the arousal of dormant issues should reflect fresh data that give renewed life to abandoned notions. Those outside the current debate may therefore be excused for suspecting that creationists have come up with something new, or that evolutionists have generated some serious internal trouble. But nothing has changed; the creationists have not a single new fact or argument. Darrow and Bryan were at least more entertaining than we lesser antagonists today. The rise of creationism is politics, pure and simple; it represents one issue (and by no means the major concern) of the resurgent evangelical right. Arguments that seemed kooky just a decade ago have reentered the mainstream.

Creationism Is Not Science

The basic attack of the creationists falls apart on two general counts before we even reach the supposed factual details of their complaints against evolution. First, they play upon a vernacular misunderstanding of the word "theory" to convey the false impression that we evolutionists are covering up the rotten core of our edifice. Second, they misuse a popular philosophy of science to argue that they are behaving scientifically in attacking evolution. Yet the same philosophy demonstrates that their own belief is not science, and that "scientific creationism" is therefore meaningless and self-contradictory, a superb example of what Orwell called "newspeak."

In the American vernacular, "theory" often means "imperfect 4 fact"—part of a hierarchy of confidence running downhill from fact to theory to hypothesis to guess. Thus the power of the creationist argument: Evolution is "only" a theory, and intense debate now rages about many aspects of the theory. If evolution is less than a fact, and scientists can't even make up their minds about the theory, then what confidence can we have in it? Indeed, President Reagan echoed this argument before an evangelical group in Dallas when he said (in what I devoutly hope was campaign rhetoric): "Well, it is a theory. It is a scientific theory only, and it has in recent years been challenged in the world of science—that is, not believed in the scientific community to be as infallible as it once was."

Well, evolution *is* a theory. It is also a fact. And facts and theo- 5 ries are different things, not rungs in a hierarchy of increasing certainty. Facts are the world's data. Theories are structures of ideas that explain and interpret facts. Facts do not go away when scientists debate rival theories to explain them. Einstein's theory of gravitation replaced Newton's, but apples did not suspend themselves in midair pending the outcome. And human beings evolved from apelike ancestors whether they did so by Darwin's proposed mechanisms or by some other, yet to be discovered.

Moreover, "fact" does not mean "absolute certainty." The final 6 proofs of logic and mathematics flow deductively from stated premises and achieve certainty only because they are *not* about the empirical world. Evolutionists make no claim for perpetual truth, though creationists often do (and then attack us for a style of argument that they themselves favor). In science, "fact" can only mean "confirmed to such a degree that it would be perverse to withhold provisional assent." I suppose that apples might start to rise tomorrow, but the possibility does not merit equal time in physics classrooms.

Evolutionists have been clear about this distinction between fact 7 and theory from the very beginning, if only because we have always acknowledged how far we are from completely understanding the mechanisms (theory) by which evolution (fact) occurred. Darwin continually emphasized the difference between his two great and separate accomplishments: establishing the fact of evolution, and proposing a theory—natural selection—to explain the mechanism of evolution. He wrote in *The Descent of Man:* "I had two distinct objects in view; firstly, to show that species had not been separately created, and secondly, that natural selection had been the chief agent of change. . . . Hence if I have erred in . . . having exaggerated its [natural selection's] power. . . . I have at least, as I hope, done good service in aiding to overthrow the dogma of separate creations."

Thus Darwin acknowledged the provisional nature of natural selection while affirming the fact of evolution. The fruitful theoretical debate that Darwin initiated has never ceased. From the 1940s through the 1960s, Darwin's own theory of natural selection did achieve a temporary hegemony that it never enjoyed in his lifetime. But renewed debate characterizes our decade, and, while no biologist questions the importance of natural selection, many now doubt its ubiquity. In particular, many evolutionists argue that substantial amounts of genetic change may not be subject to natural selection and may spread through populations at random. Others are challenging Darwin's linking of natural selection with gradual, imperceptible change through all intermediary degrees; they are arguing that most evolutionary events may occur far more rapidly than Darwin envisioned.   8

Scientists regard debates on fundamental issues of theory as a sign of intellectual health and a source of excitement. Science is—and how else can I say it?—most fun when it plays with interesting ideas, examines their implications, and recognizes that old information may be explained in surprisingly new ways. Evolutionary theory is now enjoying this uncommon vigor. Yet amidst all this turmoil no biologist has been led to doubt the fact that evolution occurred; we are debating *how* it happened. We are all trying to explain the same thing: the tree of evolutionary descent linking all organisms by ties of genealogy. Creationists pervert and caricature this debate by conveniently neglecting the common conviction that underlies it, and by falsely suggesting that we now doubt the very phenomenon we are struggling to understand.   9

Using another invalid argument, creationists claim that "the dogma of separate creations," as Darwin characterized it a century ago, is a scientific theory meriting equal time with evolution in high school biology curricula. But a prevailing viewpoint among philosophers of science belies this creationist argument. Philosopher Karl Popper has argued for decades that the primary criterion of science is the falsifiability of its theories. We can never prove absolutely, but we can falsify. A set of ideas that cannot, in principle, be falsified is not science.   10

The entire creationist argument involves little more than a rhetorical attempt to falsify evolution by presenting supposed contradictions among its supporters. Their brand of creationism, they claim, is "scientific" because it follows the Popperian model in trying to demolish evolution. Yet Popper's argument must apply in   11 both directions. One does not become a scientist by the simple act of trying to falsify another scientific system; one has to present an alternative system that also meets Popper's criterion—it too must be falsifiable in principle.

"Scientific creationism" is a self-contradictory, nonsense phrase   12 precisely because it cannot be falsified. I can envision observations and experiments that would disprove any evolutionary theory I know, but I cannot imagine what potential data could leave creationists to abandon their beliefs. Unbeatable systems are dogma, not science. Lest I seem harsh or rhetorical, I quote creationism's leading intellectual, Duane Gish, Ph.D., from his recent (1978) book *Evolution? The Fossils Say No!* "By creation we mean the bringing into being by a supernatural Creator of the basic kinds of plants and animals by the process of sudden, or fiat, creation. We do not know how the Creator created, what processes He used, for *He used processes which are not now operating anywhere in the natural universe* [Gish's italics]. This is why we refer to creation as special creation. We cannot discover by scientific investigations anything about the creative processes used by the Creator." Pray tell, Dr. Gish, in the light of your last sentence, what then is "scientific" creationism?

The Fact of Evolution

Our confidence that evolution occurred centers upon three general   13 arguments. First, we have abundant, direct, observational evidence of evolution in action, from both the field and the laboratory. It ranges from countless experiments on change in nearly everything about fruit flies subjected to artificial selection in the laboratory to the famous British moths that turned black when industrial soot darkened the trees upon which they rest. (The moths gain protection from sharp-sighted bird predators by blending into the background.) Creationists do not deny these observations; how could they? Creationists have tightened their act. They now argue that God only created "basic kinds," and allowed for limited evolutionary meandering within them. Thus toy poodles and Great Danes come from the dog kind and moths can change color, but nature cannot convert a dog to a cat or a monkey to a man.

The second and third arguments for evolution—the case for   14 major changes—do not involve direct observation of evolution in action. They rest upon inference, but are no less secure for that reason. Major evolutionary change requires too much time for direct observation on the scale of recorded human history. All historical sciences rest upon inference, and evolution is no different from geology, cosmology, or human history in this respect. In principle, we cannot observe processes that operated in the past. We must infer them from results that still survive: living and fossil organisms for evolution, documents and artifacts for human history, strata and topography for geology.

The second argument—that the imperfection of nature reveals   15
evolution—strikes many people as ironic, for they feel that evolution should be most elegantly displayed in the nearly perfect adaptation expressed by some organisms—the chamber of a gull's wing, or butterflies that cannot be seen in ground litter because they mimic leaves so precisely. But perfection could be imposed by a wise creator or evolved by natural selection. Perfection covers the tracks of past history. And past history—the evidence of descent—is our mark of evolution.

Evolution lies exposed in the *imperfections* that record a history   16
of descent. Why should a rat run, a bat fly, a porpoise swim, and I type this essay with structures built of the same bones unless we all inherited them from a common ancestor? An engineer, starting from scratch, could design better limbs in each case. Why should all the large native mammals of Australia be marsupials, unless they descended from a common ancestor isolated on this island continent? Marsupials are not "better," or ideally suited for Australia; many have been wiped out by placental mammals imported by man from other continents. This principle of imperfection extends to all historical sciences. When we recognize the etymology of September, October, November, and December (seventh, eighth, ninth, and tenth, from the Latin), we know that two additional items (January and February) must have been added to an original calendar of ten months.

The third argument is more direct: Transitions are often found   17
in the fossil record. Preserved transitions are not common—and should not be, according to our understanding of evolution (see next section)—but they are not entirely wanting, as creationists often claim. The lower jaw of reptiles contains several bones, that of mammals only one. The nonmammalian jawbones are reduced, step by step, in mammalian ancestors until they become tiny nubbins located at the back of the jaw. The "hammer" and "anvil" bones of the mammalian ear are descendants of these nubbins. How could such a transition be accomplished? the creationists ask. Surely a bone is either entirely in the jaw or in the ear. Yet paleontologists have discovered two transitional lineages or therapsids (the so-called mammal-like reptiles) with a double jaw joint—one composed of the old quadrate and articular bones (soon to become the

hammer and anvil), the other of the squamosal and dentary bones (as in modern mammals). For that matter, what better transitional form could we desire than the oldest human, *Australopithecus afarensis,* with its apelike palate, its human upright stance, and a cranial capacity larger than any ape's of the same body size but a full 1,000 cubic centimeters below ours? If God made each of the half dozen human species discovered in ancient rocks, why did he create in an unbroken temporal sequence of progressively more modern features—increasing cranial capacity, reduced face and teeth, larger body size? Did he create to mimic evolution and test our faith thereby?

An Example of Creationist Argument

Faced with these facts of evolution and the philosophical bank- 18
ruptcy of their own position, creationists rely upon distortion and innuendo to buttress their rhetorical claim. If I sound sharp or bitter, indeed I am—for I have become a major target of these practices.

I count myself among the evolutionists who argue for a jerky, or 19
episodic, rather than a smoothly gradual, pace of change. In 1972 my colleague Niles Eldredge and I developed the theory of punctuated equilibrium [*Discover*, October]. We argued that two outstanding facts of the fossil record—geologically "sudden" origin of new species and failure to change thereafter (stasis)—reflect the predictions of evolutionary theory, not the imperfections of the fossil record. In most theories, small isolated populations are the source of new species, and the process of speciation takes thousands or tens of thousands of years. This amount of time, so long when measured against our lives, is a geological microsecond. It represents much less than 1 percent of the average life span for a fossil invertebrate species—more than 10 million years. Large, widespread, and well-established species, on the other hand, are not expected to change very much. We believe that the inertia of large populations explains the stasis of most fossil species over millions of years.

We proposed the theory of punctuated equilibrium largely to 20
provide a different explanation for pervasive trends in the fossil record. Trends, we argued, cannot be attributed to gradual transformation within lineages, but must arise from the differential success of certain kinds of species. A trend, we argued, is more like climbing a flight of stairs (punctuations and stasis) than rolling up an inclined plane.

Since we proposed punctuated equilibria to explain trends, it is 21
infuriating to be quoted again and again by creationists—whether

through design or stupidity, I do not know—as admitting that the fossil record includes no transitional forms. Transitional forms are generally lacking at the species level, but are abundant between larger groups. The evolution from reptiles to mammals, as mentioned earlier, is well documented. Yet a pamphlet entitled "Harvard Scientists Agree Evolution Is a Hoax" states: "The facts of punctuated equilibrium which Gould and Eldredge . . . are forcing Darwinists to swallow fit the picture that Bryan insisted on, and which God has revealed to us in the Bible."

Continuing the distortion, several creationists have equated the theory of punctuated equilibrium with a caricature of the beliefs of Richard Goldschmidt, a great early geneticist. Goldschmidt argued, in a famous book published in 1940, that new groups can arise all at once through major mutations. He referred to these suddenly transformed creatures as "hopeful monsters." (I am attracted to some aspects of the noncaricatured version, but Goldschmidt's theory still has nothing to do with punctuated equilibrium.) Creationist Luther Sunderland talks of the "punctuated equilibrium hopeful monster theory" and tells his hopeful readers that "it amounts to tacit admission that antievolutionists are correct in asserting there is no fossil evidence supporting the theory that all life is connected to a common ancestor." Duane Gish writes, "According to Goldschmidt, and now apparently according to Gould, a reptile laid an egg from which the first bird, feathers and all, was produced. "Any evolutionist who believed such nonsense would rightly be laughed off the intellectual stage; yet the only theory that could ever envision such a scenario for the evolution of birds is creationism—God acts in the egg. 22

Conclusion

I am both angry at and amused by the creationists; but mostly I am deeply sad. Sad for many reasons. Sad because so many people who respond to creationist appeals are troubled for the right reason, but venting their anger at the wrong target. It is true that scientists have often been dogmatic and elitist. It is true that we have often allowed the white-coated, advertising image to represent us—"Scientists say that Brand X cures bunions ten times faster than. . . ." We have not fought it adequately because we derive benefits from appearing as a new priesthood. It is also true that faceless bureaucratic state power intrudes more and more into our lives and removes choices that should belong to individuals and communities. I can understand that requiring that evolution be taught in the schools might be seen 23 as one more insult on all these grounds. But the culprit is not, and cannot be, evolution or any other fact of the natural world. Identify and fight your legitimate enemies by all means, but we are not among them.

I am sad because the practical result of this brouhaha will not be expanded coverage to include creationism (that would also make me sad), but the reduction or excision of evolution from high school curricula. Evolution is one of the half dozen "great ideas" developed by science. It speaks to the profound issues of genealogy that fascinate all of us—the "roots" phenomenon writ large. Where did we come from? Where did life arise? How did it develop? How are organisms related? It forces us to think, ponder, and wonder. Shall we deprive millions of this knowledge and once again teach biology as a set of dull and unconnected facts, without the thread that weaves diverse material into a supple unity?

But most of all I am saddened by a trend I am just beginning to discern among my colleagues. I sense that some now wish to mute the healthy debate about theory that has brought new life to evolutionary ideology. It provides grist for creationist mills, they say, even if only by distortion. Perhaps we should lie low and rally round the flag of strict Darwinism, at least for the moment—a kind of old-time religion on our part.

But we should borrow another metaphor and recognize that we too have to tread a straight and narrow path, surrounded by roads to perdition. For if we ever begin to suppress our search to understand nature, to quench our own intellectual excitement in a misguided effort to present a united front where it does not and should not exist, then we are truly lost.

A Reply to Gould

DUANE T. GISH

In his essay "Evolution as Fact and Theory" [May 1981], Stephen Jay Gould states that creationists claim creation is a scientific theory. This is a false accusation. Creationists have repeatedly stated that neither creation nor evolution is a scientific theory (and each is equally religious). Gould in fact quotes from my book, *Evolution! The Fossils Say No!*, in which I state that both concepts of origins fail the criteria of a scientific theory.

Gould uses the argument of Sir Karl Popper that the primary criterion of a scientific theory is its potential falsifiability, and then uses this sword to strike down creation as a scientific theory. Fine. Gould surely realizes, however, that this is a two-edged sword. Sir Karl has used it to strike down evolution as a scientific theory, stating that Darwinism is not a testable scientific theory, but a metaphysical research program (*Unended Quest*, 1976).

Another criterion that must apply to a scientific theory is the ability to repeatedly observe the events, processes, or properties used to support the theory. There were obviously no human witnesses to the origin of the universe, the origin of life, or in fact to the origin of a single living thing, and even if evolution were occurring today, the process would require far in excess of all recorded history to produce sufficient change to document evolution. Evolution has not and cannot be observed any more than creation.   3

Gould states, "Theories are structures of ideas that explain and interpret facts." Certainly, creation and evolution can both be used as theories in that sense. Furthermore, one or the other must be true, since ultimately they are the only two alternatives we have to explain origins.   4

Gould charges creationists with dogma. Please note, however, Gould's own dogmatism. His use of the term "fact of evolution" appears throughout his paper. Furthermore, Gould seems to have a strange view of the relationship of fact and theory. He says, "Facts do not go away when scientists debate rival theories to explain them. Einstein's theory of gravitation replaced Newton's, but apples did not suspend themselves in midair pending the outcome. And human beings evolved from apelike ancestors whether they did so by Darwin's proposed mechanism or by some other, yet to be discovered." Well, evolutionists believe indeed that both apes and hydrogen evolved into people (the latter just took longer), but neither has ever been observed. All of us, however, have seen apples fall off trees.   5

Gould's "fact of evolution" immediately deteriorates into "three general arguments," two of which quickly deteriorate further into mere inferences. Gould's only direct observational evidence for evolution (his first argument) is experiments on fruit flies and observations on peppered moths in Britain. Neither, of course, offers evidence for evolution, for from beginning to end fruit flies remain fruit flies and peppered moths remain peppered moths. The task of the evolutionist is to answer the question how moths came to be moths, tigers came to be tigers, and people came to be people. In fact, this type of evidence is what Gould himself has sought in recent years to discredit as an explanation for the origin of higher categories.   6

Gould's second argument is an inference based on *imperfections*. He mentions homologous structures as evidence for evolution from a common ancestor. Gould should know first that many, if not   7 most, homologous structures are not even possessed by the assumed common ancestor and secondly that the actual evidence (particularly that from genetics) is so contradictory to what is predicted by evolution that Sir Gavin de Beer titled his Oxford biology reader (1971) on that subject *Homology, an Unsolved Problem*. Sir Gavin, along with S. C. Harland, felt compelled to suggest that organs, such as the eye, remain unchanged while the genes governing these structures become wholly altered during the evolutionary process! The whole Darwinian edifice collapses if that is true.

Gould's third argument is based on inferences drawn from the fossil record. The fossil record, with its "explosive appearance" (the term often used by geologists) of the highly complex creatures found in Cambrian rocks, for which no ancestors have been found, and the systematic absence of transitional forms between all higher categories of plants and animals, has proven an embarrassment to evolutionists ever since Darwin. Gould's argument, however, is that "transitions are often found in the fossil record." That is surprising indeed, since he seems intent in other publications to convey just the opposite opinion. 8

For example, in his 1977 *Natural History* essay "The Return of Hopeful Monsters," after recounting the derision meted out to Richard Goldschmidt for his hopeful-monster mechanism of evolution, Gould says, "I do, however, predict that during the next decade Goldschmidt will be largely vindicated in the world of evolutionary biology." Why? Among others, "The fossil record with its abrupt transitions offers no support for gradual change." A bit later: "All paleontologists know that the fossil record contains precious little in the way of intermediate forms; transitions between major groups are characteristically abrupt." Many similar statements by Gould and others could be cited. 9

Finally, Gould assails Sunderland and me for linking him to a hopeful-monster mechanism whereby a reptile laid an egg and a bird was hatched. He says an evolutionist who believed such nonsense would rightly be laughed off the intellectual stage. Let's see, then, what Goldschmidt really did say. In *The Material Basis of Evolution*, Goldschmidt says, "I need only quote Schindewolf (1936), the most progressive investigator known to me. He shows by examples from fossil material that the major evolutionary advances must have taken place in single large steps. . . . He shows that the many missing links in the paleontological record are sought for in vain because they have never existed: 'The first bird hatched from a reptilian egg.' " By Gould's own testimony, then, Goldschmidt, Gould's hero of the next decade, should be laughed off the intellectual stage. 10

Along with thousands of other creation scientists, in view of a   11
wealth of evidence from thermodynamics, probability relationships,
biology, molecular biology, paleontology, and cosmology, I have become convinced that evolution theory is scientifically untenable
and that the concept of direct, special creation is a far more credible
explanation.

QUESTIONS OF CONTENT

1. Gould accuses his opponents of misusing the word *theory*. What
   does he mean by this word? What do his opponents mean? What
   major political figure seems to have adopted the creationists' definition of the word?
2. How can evolution be both theory and fact, as Gould claims? How
   does it differ from natural selection?
3. Gould says that scientific creationism is nonsense because it cannot
   be falsified. What does he mean by that?
4. Gould offers three arguments that support evolution. What are they?
5. Gish denies that creationism is a scientific theory and denies also
   that evolution is. How does he do this?
6. What is Gould doing in his final paragraph? How is that related to
   Gish's claim in his opening paragraph that evolution is religious?
7. In paragraphs 8–9, Gish seems to have caught Gould in a contradiction. What is that contradiction? How accurately is it stated?

QUESTIONS OF FORM

1. Gould charges that creationism "falls apart on two general counts,"
   that creationist arguments exhibit two kinds of fallacies. Consult "A
   Short Guide to Material and Formal Fallacies" in the Appendix and
   try to determine which fallacies are present in the faulty reasoning
   that Gould describes.
2. Gould makes three arguments for evolution by natural selection.
   Reduce each to its barest essentials. What is the *because*-statement
   for each?
3. Gould charges that creationists cannot produce such arguments as
   those mentioned in question 2 to support their claims; instead, they
   resort to "distortion and innuendo." He offers two examples of what
   he means by that in paragraphs 19 through 22. Compare these examples of Gould's with the arguments that Gish produces in his
   essay. How accurately has Gould described a creationist argument?
   Where, if at all, does Gish offer any claims for creationism that are
   structured like Gould's arguments for evolution?

4. How does each writer attempt to establish credibility with the portion of his audience that might be hostile?

SUGGESTIONS FOR WRITING

1. Present a summary of each of the two arguments that would be suitable for inclusion in a printed program to be distributed at a forum featuring both Gould and Gish as principal speakers.
2. You are the editor of the campus newspaper, and you have just received a letter from an irate parent, accusing the college of being godless and misguided for teaching evolution in its biology classes. Write a response to this letter in which you employ some of Gould's arguments. You plan to run your response as an editorial alongside the parent's letter. Be most careful in your response to maintain objectivity; you do not want to offend this person.
3. You have just read the exchange of letters between the antievolutionist parent and the editor of the school paper, as described in suggestion 2. You feel that the editor's reply deserves an appropriate creationist response, and you intend to use Gish's article as the basis for that response. Compose that letter, using as many of Gish's arguments as you can. You may, of course, offer additional arguments in defense of your position.

THE USEFULNESS OF STUDYING
A SECOND LANGUAGE

We Need a Nationwide Effort to Encourage, Enhance, and Expand Our Students' Proficiency in Languages

DANIEL SHANAHAN

In 1904, at a hearing on the mistreatment of immigrant laborers, the president of the Reading Railroad told a Congressional committee: "These workers don't suffer—they don't even speak English."

Working conditions in the United States have come a long way since then, but the attitude in this country toward people who do not speak English hasn't changed very much. While few of us would support the contention that non-English speakers somehow have no right to equal protection under the law, it has become more acceptable in recent years to oppose such things as bilingual education and bilingual ballots that attempt to address problems faced by speakers of languages other than English.

The issue is a relatively simple one, but it has a complex social and historical background. Before the revival of ethnic pride in the 1960's and 70's, most immigrants who came to this country tried to "launder" much of their cultural past, and their native languages were among the first things to go. For them, learning English was an act of faith in the new land they had adopted. Although the price was steeper than many of them realized at the time, most were willing, even happy, to pay it.

But in the 1960's, the civil-rights movement forced a reassessment of what was "American," and many once-acceptable means of distinguishing among groups were seen as undemocratic, to be ferreted out and eliminated wherever they were found. It is unfortunate that during that period the issue of language (largely as it applied to Hispanic Americans) became fused with the issue of civil rights.

As a result, bilingual issues were overwhelmed by emotional baggage, first the liberal guilt of the 60's and 70's and then the conservative reaction of the Reagan era. Lost in the shuffle was a much more vital issue, and one which pivots not on questions of deprivation of civil rights, but on America's ability to remain a viable actor in the increasingly global environment by becoming more competent linguistically.

The "official language" propositions that have been passed in 17 states in recent years—three in last fall's elections—are clear signs that the electorate does not understand the true effect of the language issue on the national interest. Most such propositions pass because of fear and resentment on the part of the majority language group. While the campaign advertisements run by supporters of the proposals do not overtly express resentment over money spent to serve those who do not speak English, the sentiments expressed by voters who support the initiatives often can be summed up in some variation of the statement: "My parents had to learn English when they came to this country. . . ." 6

Resentment is, of course, a more or less unacceptable basis for policy analysis, so supporters' justifications of English-only initiatives usually play on fears: of social disunity, of economic hardship, of the cost of cultural plurality. Canada is most frequently cited as an example of the way cultural plurality, maintained through linguistic plurality, can lead to social instability. Putting aside for the moment the fact that Canada not only survived Quebec's "quiet revolution" but also profited from it, as the economic boom in Quebec is now demonstrating, such analysis of the language issue ignores the extent to which the entire world is rapidly becoming a stage on which the players must speak more than one language to survive and compete economically. 7

The Japanese have led the way in learning second—and third—languages to further their economic competitiveness. It can be argued that the difficulty of their own language made it unlikely that foreigners would learn it and forced them to learn the languages of others, but it can just as easily be argued that this apparent liability simply led them to see the handwriting on the wall more quickly than others, and it thus becomes a competitive advantage. 8

Europeans have always been proficient in other languages, largely because of the high concentration of different languages in their relatively small geographic space. Being multilingual is helping them establish an economic union that looms as a powerful force in the already crowded and competitive global marketplace. 9

Even in developing countries, where one might expect lack of education to limit multilingualism, many people speak a regional dialect at home and the language of the dominant cultural group in the workplace; some also speak the European language of the colonial period as well. Against this international backdrop, the specta- 10 cle of Americans passing laws to limit the languages used in their country can only be seen as self-destructive.

Of course, there must be a standard language in a country, if only for the purpose of efficiency, but the language is designated by practice, not by law. In the United States, the standard language is and always has been English. The question should not be whether we should spend money to make it possible for immigrants to use their native languages in official situations, nor should it be whether we encourage others, children especially, to maintain a language other than English. Quite clearly, the question ought to be whether we should undertake a nationwide effort to encourage, enhance, and expand multilingual proficiency among native speakers of English, as well as among non-natives.   11

The answer to that question must be a resounding and un-equivocal Yes.   12

It is nothing less than criminal for a country so admittedly language poor and so strapped for competitive advantages in the international marketplace to be adopting myopic and regressive language laws that reinforce the naive monolingual bias that threatens to isolate and weaken it. Yet it is also understandable that Americans want clarity and perhaps a degree of reassurance in our increasingly volatile and shifting ethnic and linguistic environment.   13

A compromise addressing both sides of the issue must be found, and I believe it will not be as hard to come by as some people might imagine.   14

Let Congress pass a law designating English the "standard" language of the United States, but let the measure also include the appropriation of sufficient money to insure that 20 years from now all Americans graduating from high school will be proficient in a second language.   15

Let a high-school diploma and college admission be denied to anyone without a sufficient level of proficiency. And let proficiency in a second language—at the level of a native speaker—be required for graduation from college and entry into civil-service and private-sector white-collar employment. In other words, let us put our money where our mouths are. The price tag for instituting such requirements—including the cost of training the needed teachers over five years—would be less than the budget for the Strategic Defense Initiative for two fiscal years. Moreover, the benefits would be far greater. For only with such determined policies can we hope to calm fears about language plurality and insure that we do not become a culture of monolingual dinosaurs.   16

We have 29 years, nearly triple the time President Kennedy allowed when he committed us to reaching the moon. By comparison,   17 the expenditures required to create a linguistically proficient nation would be insignificant. The benefits, not only in economic terms but also in terms of enhancing our understanding of other cultures and of ourselves, would be beyond measure. The costs, should we fail to act decisively, could eventually prove to be catastrophic.

Importance of Studying Languages Questioned

WALTER ULRICH

I have always been puzzled by the arguments of those like Daniel Shanahan who argue that everybody should be expected to learn a foreign language.

While I agree that it is important to learn about other cultures, this could better be accomplished by requiring classes on the history, government, environment, and traditions of other countries. The learning of another language provides only indirect knowledge of a minute part of a single country's culture; the time spent in learning one language would be much better spent developing a broad understanding of a variety of cultures—an understanding that does not require an in-depth knowledge of specific languages.

The economic benefits of language study are also overclaimed. Overlooking the problem of deciding in high school or college which language a student will need to know 10 or 20 years later (knowing how to speak German will not help you if you are dealing with a Japanese client), a more serious question is why *all* students should be required to develop this skill. After all, just because we need doctors does not mean that every student should go to medical school; similarly, just because an understanding of languages is important in business does not mean that we all should know a language.

Our time and money would be best spent concentrating on developing the expertise of a limited number of language experts instead of diffusing our efforts on students who will never need or use the knowledge.

QUESTIONS OF CONTENT

1. How does Shanahan feel about the proposition that English should be adopted as the official standard language of the United States?

2. How does Shanahan feel about bilingual education, that is, the educational policy prescribing that immigrants to the United States may start learning their school subjects in their native language while they also are learning English?
3. Why does Shanahan think that Japanese and Europeans have an advantage over Americans in the business world?
4. How many years does Shanahan propose that the United States be given to develop his policy of requiring all high school graduates to be proficient in a second language? Why does he think that is a proper amount of time?
5. Instead of developing a second language proficiency, what does Ulrich propose as an alternative?
6. Why does Ulrich think that learning a second language is usually wasted effort?

QUESTIONS OF FORM

1. Shanahan does not actually state his claim of policy until paragraph 11. What was he doing before that?
2. What bad state of affairs does Shanahan's claim of policy seek to remedy? Where does he outline that state of affairs?
3. Where does Shanahan present the good effects that his policy might be expected to produce?
4. What part of Shanahan's argument does Ulrich attack: the support, the form of the argument, or the warrant?
5. What counterproposal does Ulrich offer to Shanahan? How convincing is his counterproposal?

SUGGESTIONS FOR WRITING

1. Summarize the positions taken by Shanahan and Ulrich. Be especially careful to remain neutral in your presentation.
2. Summarize the positions of Shanahan and Ulrich, but side with one against the other.
3. What middle course can you suggest that might be acceptable to both Shanahan and Ulrich? Examine possible compromises and present your best solution. Use a summary of the Shanahan and Ulrich positions as an introduction to your own notions

Varying Voices: Multiple Viewpoints on Crucial Questions

This readings section is also arranged differently from its predecessors, for it provides multiple essays on three different topics: euthanasia, gun control, and cigarette smoking. Typically, the four essays examine or present different viewpoints, so that you will get a reasonably varied view of the subject. (You will notice that the essays on gun control are an exception; while quite different in their approaches, they share essentially the same viewpoint.)

Once more we have provided questions that will direct your attention to the content and form of each essay, and that will also help you make useful comparisons and contrasts among the essays in that particular group; these questions and the related writing suggestions appear after all of that group's essays. The suggestions for writing usually will require you (unless your instructor directs otherwise) to compose your own papers or essays by drawing material from several or all of the essays in that group. Furthermore, we have provided citations for additional essays you may want to read for your research. Certainly, as before, you will find it helpful to read the questions and writing suggestions for each group of essays before you read the essays themselves.

WHO SHOULD CONTROL THE RIGHT TO DIE?

Euthanasia Is Sometimes Justified

LOWELL O. ERDAHL

Doctors, families, and patients themselves now face many choices that were not available to previous generations. The use of "artificial" life-support systems inevitably leads to situations that require choices concerning the rightness or wrongness of "pulling the plug" and raises as never before the issue of mercy killing or *euthanasia,* which literally means "good death." 1

These changes, however, did not create the problem. . . . The possibility of deliberately ending the life of a suffering person has always been present. We note that in at least two ways medical advances make consideration of mercy killing less pressing than in times past. One is that many formerly devastating illnesses and conditions of distressing disability can now be cured, corrected, or managed so that meaningful life is now possible. The other is that painkilling drugs eliminate much of the intense suffering formerly experienced by millions. The prospect of such suffering moved Mahatma Gandhi, who lived with great reverence for life and opposition to violence, to contemplate the possibility of being required by love and sacred duty to take the life of his own child as the only means of relieving the anguish of incurable rabies. We thank God that the comforts of modern medicine now offer alternatives for the relief of such suffering. 2

Difficult Cases

On the other hand, the ability to maintain biological functions that would have otherwise ceased has brought the question of euthanasia into sharper focus. The difficult cases are not those in which brain death has already occurred. When the brain is dead, the person has died. There is, therefore, no justification for maintaining the biological functions, except temporarily in order to preserve organs for transplant. The agonizing cases are those in which the person re- 3 mains alive but with little, if any, prospect of healing and meaning-ful life.

The pro-life perspective—which grants that there are tragic ex- 4
ceptional circumstances when the taking of life is justifiable, but which opposes all forms of institutionalized and established killing—also applies to mercy killing. That is, passive or even active euthanasia may sometimes be justifiable in a specific situation, but it is wrong when institutionalized in accepted practice, as, for ex-ample, under Hitler in the Nazi era. . . .

Although passive euthanasia is widely accepted, there are strong 5
emotional and legal barriers to active euthanasia. Doctors are per-mitted to refrain from treatments that would prolong their patients' lives, but are not allowed to administer drugs to kill them. Is such a distinction between passive and active euthanasia always morally justifiable? Are there circumstances in which it is right to practice active euthanasia?

Although it is tempting to take an absolute stand against active 6
euthanasia, the recognition of tragic, exceptional circumstances makes it impossible for me to do so. Just as there are situations in which it may be justifiable to kill the unborn, the enemy warrior, or the criminal intent on murder, there may be also circumstances in which active euthanasia is more compassionate than passive. Is it, for example, more kind to cause death by dehydration and starva-tion than it is to kill the patient by lethal injection? In both cases the motive and effect are exactly the same; only the method is dif-ferent. Is it possible that in some cases the sin of omission (permit-ting death by dehydration and starvation) may be greater than the sin of commission (causing death by lethal injection)?

Emotionally it is obviously much easier for the family and doc- 7
tor to permit the patient to die than to deliberately kill the patient. But is there a similar logical and moral difference? Raising such a question reminds us of the extent to which emotion, rather than logical or moral considerations, often prevails in life and death de-cisions. Many people, for example, are appalled at the thought of de-liberately killing their 95-year-old grandmother who has been in a coma for months and for whom there is no prospect of meaningful life; but at the same time they are advocates of abortion on demand. Is it not, however, more moral to deliberately act to end life's final suffering than to foreclose the possibility of life fulfillment at its be-ginning? The point of this observation is not to affirm active eu-thanasia (to me it is more of an argument against easy abortion), but to underscore the emotional rather than ethical basis of many of our decisions.

Risking the Slippery Slope

While granting that it may be morally justifiable in exceptional cir-   8
cumstances, I see great danger in the cultural and legal acceptance of
active euthanasia. Taking this step places our feet on a slippery slope
on which we can quickly slide into easy and irreverent mercy killing
for unjustifiable reasons and then on into the institutionalized and established practice of euthanasia for economic and social purposes, as
practiced by Hitler. If laws are changed to permit active euthanasia in
rare, justifiable circumstances, it will require extreme vigilance to
prevent these exceptions from becoming standard practice.

It is reported that the average age of nursing-home residents is   9
now 83 and rising. Medical costs continue to escalate, in spite of efforts to contain them. Some speak of the responsibility of the elderly
to die in order to ease the burden on the younger generation. These
signs of our times tell of increasing pressure for public acceptance of
active as well as passive euthanasia. They are small steps down a road
that could lead to provisions for the permitted, and possibly even required, elimination not only of the suffering, senile, and elderly, but
also of others of all ages who have been determined to be nonproductive members of society. Therefore, even though there may be exceptional circumstances in which active euthanasia is justified, I believe
that it is wiser public policy to continue to prohibit it altogether
rather than risk the temptations and tendencies of this slippery slope.

In summary, passive euthanasia may be justifiable (1) when it is   10
determined that the patient is irreversibly comatose, (2) when the
treatment prolongs imminent and inevitable death, and (3) when the
treatment itself is so traumatic that it is inhumane to administer it.
In addition to these criteria, active euthanasia should never be
permitted or even considered unless it is clearly inhumane to let an
illness run its course and there are no other means of ending meaningless suffering. . . .

The pro-life alternatives to euthanasia include everything pos-   11
sible to provide compassionate and often costly care of the ill, in-
firm, and elderly. The true test of a society's faithfulness to the
pro-life perspective is not only in its opposition to killing but also
in its willingness to make adequate provision for those who are suffering and nonproductive. As costs of care increase, individuals in
specific circumstances and society as a whole will be strongly
tempted to sell out both compassion and responsible reverence for
life in exchange for economic considerations. If the day comes when
euthanasia is established as an economic policy, we will have ceased
to be either fully moral or fully human. It is imperative that we oppose every step toward irresponsible euthanasia and also affirm the

reordering of the priorities and expenditures of our personal and corporate life in order to provide the compassionate care every human being deserves. If we are not vigilant in opposition to unjustifiable euthanasia, we may one day be haunted by horrors more antiseptic, but no less terrifying, than Hitler's "final solution."

We Don't Need Assisted Suicide

LINDA CHAVEZ

Has America embraced a "culture of death" as Pope John Paul   1
II warned on a visit here in 1993?

A recent USA TODAY poll showing some 75 percent of Amer-   2
icans support so-called assisted suicide suggests the pope may be
right. Most Americans who support "the right to die"—including
the ghoulish Dr. Jack Kevorkian, acquitted Tuesday of two counts
of assisted suicide, and the judges in two recent appeals court cases
in Washington and New York—claim to be motivated by compassion. After all, they are only supporting people who want to end
their own lives. But before the courts and the public get too enamored of this incipient movement, perhaps they ought to take a close
look at what's happened in the Netherlands, the only Western nation that formally endorses the idea of physicians helping patients
kill themselves.

The Dutch have nearly a quarter century of experience with   3
physician-assisted suicide and euthanasia. In 1990 a Dutch government commission conducted a survey of these practices, which
showed that euthanasia is far more widely practiced in the Netherlands than officials had believed and that it is most frequently administered without patients' consent.

According to the report of the Dutch commission, 11,800 pa-   4
tients were euthanized in 1990 through active measures, most often
by administering lethal drugs, and 5,941 of these were performed
without the patient's consent. Only 400 patients opted for assisted
suicide. The commission also reported an additional 13,506 patients
were denied "nonfutile medical treatment with intention to terminate life," a practice the Dutch call "euthanasia by omission" because it denies lifesaving treatment. And the great majority of these
cases, 64 percent, involved persons who had given no prior consent
to such a fate through a living will or other document.

The Netherlands is a tiny country, with a population of only   5
about 15 million. To put these euthanasia figures in some perspec-

tive, a comparable euthanasia rate in the United States would result in nearly 200,000 deaths from active measures and another 225,000 from euthanasia by omission. Once embarked down the path of doctor-assisted suicide, that may be where we are headed.

The Dutch didn't start out to practice euthanasia so widely, but once doctors started killing patients rather than treating them, the slide into mass murder was relatively easy. A recent article by a Dutch physician, Richard Fenigsen, in the journal "Issues in Law and Medicine" explains why. "Euthanasia is not just changing medicine; it is replacing medicine. This suppression of traditional medical thinking, medical working habits, and the medical way of reacting to events has an impact on both the emergency care and the long-term care of patients," he writes. 6

Fenigsen describes several case studies. In one teaching hospital anesthetists stopped providing anesthesia for cardiac surgery involving Down's syndrome patients. In other cases, hospitals and doctors refused to apply simple, lifesaving measures to patients whose lives they determined were "unlivable." In one case a physician did not administer insulin to a 6-year-old, mildly retarded boy who developed juvenile diabetes, thereby causing his death. In another, a doctor persuaded an elderly woman to stop taking medicine needed to treat an enlarged heart because she was living a "limited life"—she depended on several medications, needed help cleaning her house, and could walk only a few blocks at a time. 7

In all, 65 percent of Dutch doctors believe that physicians may propose active euthanasia to patients who do not ask for it themselves, according to Dutch surveys. 8

"Euthanasia has perceptibly affected the position of the individual in relation to society, society's very nature and purpose, the law, the government, the judicial system, the family, the expectations of older persons and the prospects of newborn infants, the practice of medicine, and the care of persons with disabilities," Fenigsen writes. 9

What has happened in the Netherlands could easily happen here if we allow it. 10

Is Death a Right?

PETER J. BERNARDI

A recent court decision has vindicated the suicide-rights movement and thus put in jeopardy the lives of the sick, the elderly, the 1 disabled, and the poor. On March 6 of this year the Ninth Circuit Court of Appeals struck down the state of Washington's ban on physician-assisted suicide. Judge Stephen Reinhardt, writing for the majority, declared there is a constitutional right for the "competent, terminally ill" to take their lives with a physician's help.

This momentous court decision makes expansive use of the   2 Supreme Court's abortion rulings to establish a constitutional right for some citizens to have themselves killed. It effectively reduced the terminally ill to the same legal status that *Roe* imposed on the unborn. Thus the poison of legalized abortion continues to seep through the body politic as inexorably as Dr. Jack Kevorkian's carbon monoxide.

The majority opinion for this case abounds with cavalier and ar-   3 rogant assertions. Notably, it dismisses the importance of the crucial ethical distinction between direct killing and actions that allow people to die, such as withdrawal of treatment. It reversed a previous appeals-court decision that wisely declared that the state has a valid interest "in not having physicians in the role of killers of their patients."

The Ninth Circuit Court of Appeals was not perturbed by the   4 Dutch practice of assisted suicide and euthanasia that has widened to include a large number of nonconsenting clients. This is not really surprising. Though the decision claimed to vindicate the "liberty interest" of "terminally ill, competent adults who wish to hasten their own deaths," it explicitly envisions making "assisted suicide [sic]" available to noncompetent persons.

In his dissenting opinion, Judge Robert Beezer hit the nail on the   5 head: "If physician-assisted suicide for mentally competent, terminally ill adults is made a constitutional right, voluntary euthanasia for weaker patients, unable to self-terminate, will soon follow. After voluntary euthanasia it is but a short step to a 'substituted judgment' or 'best interests' analysis for terminally ill patients who have not yet expressed their constitutionally sanctioned desire to be dispatched from this world. This is the sure and inevitable path, as the Dutch experience has amply demonstrated. It is not a path I would start down." Tragically, the Reinhardt majority concluded otherwise. And in a similar case a month later, the Second Court of Appeals struck down a New York State law that proscribed physician-assisted suicide.

Two tacit assumptions drive the suicide-rights movement: 6 (1) that the individual's autonomy is paramount, to the exclusion of other important values; and (2) that suffering is a purely negative experience to be avoided by any means.

Right To Choose, Right To Die

The first hidden engine that drives the assisted-suicide cause is embedded in the ambiguous expressions "right to choose" and "right to die." This latter slogan first won currency in the legal debate over the patient's right to refuse unwanted treatment. But now the assisted-suicide movement uses "right to die" language to include active measures to terminate life. Underlying these catch phrases is the assumption that the individual's self-determination is sovereign, severed from the realities of truth and responsibility.

7

Valuing the worth of the individual is a supreme achievement of Western culture influenced by the Greek philosophical and Judeo-Christian traditions. The human person, created in God's image, has an incomparable dignity that gives rise to rights and responsibilities. Safeguarding these rights and promoting corresponding responsibilities are the hallmarks of a just society.

8

However, as Mary Ann Glendon, professor of law at Harvard, has pointed out in *Rights Talk,* a hyper-rights rhetoric has taken hold in our society, leading to a radical individualism crowding out other fundamental values: that humans are essentially social, and that as individuals we have responsibilities to others. American rights rhetoric renders "extraordinary homage to independence and self-sufficiency, based an an image of the rights-bearer as a self-determining, unencumbered individual, a being connected to others only by choice' (p. 48). Our rights-talk recognizes the immediate and "personal dimensions of a problem, while it regularly neglects the moral, the long-term, and the social implications" (p. 171).

9

The ideal of total self-sufficiency, a radical version of individual autonomy, has become normative. Dependency is implicitly viewed as something to be avoided in oneself and disdained in others. Professor Glendon remarks: "By exalting autonomy to the degree we do, we systematically slight the very young, the severely ill or disabled, the frail elderly, as well as those who care for them" (p. 74).

10

The modern tradition of natural rights has repudiated the idea of the human person as "naturally" situated within and constituted through relationships of care and dependency. John Stuart Mill extended the domain of individual sovereignty, and he did so by virtue of a right: "the independence of the individual is, of right, absolute." Mill considered that interference with individual freedom was justified only to prevent harm to others. This principle has had a major impact on American jurisprudence, evolving into the right to privacy that served as the basis for *Roe v. Wade.* It also powers the suicide-rights movement.

11

This notion of the isolated, self-sufficient individual endowed   12
with the right to privacy is a fiction. The radical rights rhetoric pro-
motes an ethical relativism that destroys the common bonds necessary for maintaining human dignity and social order. Human beings
are not isolated monads. We urgently need to retrieve in our rights
discourse a sense of the person situated within, and partially constituted by, relationship with others. The movement to legalize assisted suicide plays on the pernicious separation between private
and public morality that corrodes our society. Physician-assisted
suicide is presented as a private affair between two consenting adults.
Proponents thus artificially isolate assisted suicide from the social
context in which physician and patient operate. But the taking of
life is never simply a private affair.

Radical autonomy is a deadly deception. Proponents of mercy   13
killing argue for the right of mentally competent, terminally ill
adults to receive a physician's assistance to commit suicide. The reality is that such autonomous requests will be subtly or not so subtly influenced by others.

A telling example of how easily the right to die can change into   14
the duty to die appeared in a letter published in the *Santa Rosa*
(Calif.) *Press Democrat* (Sept. 14, 1993) from an 84-year-old woman
who had been living with her daughter for 20 years. "Everything
went fine for many years," the woman wrote, "but when I started
to lose my hearing about three years ago, it irritated my daughter. . . . She began to question me about my financial matters and apparently feels I won't leave much of an estate for her. . . . She
became very rude to me. . . . Then suddenly, one evening, my daughter said very cautiously she thought it was o.k. for older people to
commit suicide if they cannot take care of themselves." After recounting the ways her daughter reinforced this message, the woman
commented: "So here I sit, day after day, knowing what I am expected to do when I need a little help."

It's A Sin To Suffer

The second hidden engine that drives the suicide-right movement is   15
embedded in the catch phrase "the right not to have to suffer." Implicit is the unexamined estimation that suffering is an unmitigated
evil to be avoided at all costs.

Elizabeth Kubler-Ross drew attention to the denial of death in   16
her book about the stages of death and dying. But there has been at
work in our society a more pervasive and portentous avoidance of
the distinctly human experience of suffering. Amid cultural uncer-

tainty about good and evil, suffering has come to be viewed as a secular equivalent of sin, from which we need to be saved.

There is an important distinction to be made in the use of the terms suffering and pain. Pain typically refers to a bodily sensation. Pain results from physical symptoms that usually have an objective basis, and it serves as a useful signal system.   17

The undertreatment of pain is a widespread failure of current medical practice, and there is clearly a need to enhance relief for the chronically and terminally ill. Sheer physical pain, however, seems not to be the primary reason people seek mercy killing. There is a high correlation between depression and the wish to commit suicide. Contrary to what many believe, the vast majority of individuals who are terminally ill or facing severe pain or disability are not suicidal. When the terminally ill receive appropriate treatment for depression, they usually abandon the wish to commit suicide. Perhaps the real issue is not pain, but our attitude toward suffering.   18

In contrast to pain, suffering refers to a more deeply personal experience that may or may not be concomitant with physical pain. French Catholic philosopher Gabriel Marcel's observation is useful here: suffering is a mystery and not merely a problem. It has physical, psychological, social, and spiritual aspects. Ultimately, the suffering in each of our lives is intensely personal, the depths of which we have trouble articulating or fully understanding. Eric Cassell expresses it succinctly: "Suffering is a consequence of personhood—bodies do not suffer, persons do."   19

Our society has found any sort of suffering increasingly difficult to bear, since it imperils our ideal of self-mastery and control, our pretense of self-sufficiency. However, the flights from suffering only intensify the private anguish. Suffering individuals feel isolated and stigmatized. The message in our society is that if you aren't "up," if you don't feel good, then you are an embarrassment and should have the decency to remove yourself.   20

In the last century, utilitarian philosopher and economist Jeremy Bentham formulated what has now become an operational understanding of human beings in consumer society. He held that people are basically motivated to maximize pleasure and minimize pain. Media images of human life that emanate from Hollywood studios and Madison Avenue typically perform a spiritual lobotomy on their human representations. This materialist and hedonist view of life views the experience of suffering in purely negative terms. In this climate, assisted suicide is seen as a quick fix to eliminate suffering.   21

Christian faith responds to the universal human experience of pain and suffering in a twofold manner. First, there is a humanitarian, and Christian, imperative to relieve pain and console the suf-   22 fering. Second, there is the conviction that suffering assumes redemptive and intercessory value in the light of the saving mystery of Christ's cross and resurrection. In the Cross Christ has won salvation for sinful humanity through his atoning death. In following Christ's injunction to "take up [your] cross daily and follow me," our own personal and corporate sufferings are transformed.

Christians echo the prayer of Paul: "That I may know him and 23 the power of his resurrection, and may share his sufferings, becoming like him in his death, that if possible I may attain the resurrection from the dead" (Phil. 3:10, RSV). The Letter to the Hebrews teaches us that Christ was made "perfect through sufferings," and that "because [Jesus] himself was tested by what he suffered, he is able to help those who are being tested" (Heb. 2:10, 18, NRSV). Christian faith gives meaning to our sufferings and strength to endure them and turn them into a source of spiritual good. The conviction that suffering can assume redemptive value needs to be preached and taught and, above all, witnessed to.

The suicide-rights movement poses a challenge to Christian 24 faith and witness. Christians are called to practice a renewed art of dying. This art will find a middle way between the extremes of a technologically driven dying process and the preemptory termination of life by assisted suicide. In retrieving a communal, palliative, and spiritual approach, we will humanize death and witness to "the hope that is within us."

Right to Die a Tough Call for the States

JAMES KILPATRICK

Dr. Peter Shalit's patient was in agony. The man's lower body 1 was so swollen from oozing lesions that he could not walk, his genitals so swollen that he required a catheter to drain his bladder, his fingers gangrenous from clotted arteries. He had been in the hospital for weeks. Incessantly he begged Dr. Shalit for some medication that would hasten his death.

The doctor refused to help him. Under state law (this was in 2 Washington), it is a felony to assist another in ending his life. The crime carries a prison sentence of five years and a fine of up to $10,000. Because of the law, "I could not accommodate him."

The patient eventually died, "but only after being tortured for 3 weeks by the end-phase of his disease."

In New York the same combination of law and circumstance led   4
to a lawsuit. A 76-year-old woman, having lived an active life as a
physical education instructor, was dying slowly of thyroid cancer.
The tumor had wrapped around her right cartoid artery, inhibiting
her ability to eat or to speak. The cancer was spreading to her
pleural cavity. She signed a formal declaration: "It is clear to me
that I am in the terminal phase of this disease. At the point at which
I can no longer endure the pain and suffering, I want to have drugs
available for the purpose of hastening my death in a humane and
certain manner."

Had it not been for New York's criminal law, sympathetic doc-   5
tors might have assisted the woman. But in New York, any person
who intentionally helps another person to take his own life may be
convicted of a Class C felony.

Two of the 13 U.S. Courts of Appeal have come to the same con-   6
clusion in recent weeks: The Washington and New York laws violate the 14th Amendment to the Constitution. Terminally ill
persons have a right to "death with dignity," and doctors may not
be criminally prosecuted for helping them to exercise that right.

The decisions have aroused the same moral and emotional   7
storms that accompanied Roe v. Wade 23 years ago, and for understandable reasons. Said the 9th Circuit in the Washington case:
"Like the decision to have an abortion, the decision how and when
to die is one of the most intimate and personal choices a person
may make in a lifetime, a choice central to personal dignity and
autonomy."

The 14th Amendment says a state may not deprive any person   8
of "liberty" without due process of law. Said the 9th Circuit: "A
competent terminally ill adult, having lived nearly the full measure
of his life, has a strong liberty interest in choosing a dignified and
humane death rather than being reduced at the end of his existence
to a childlike state of helplessness, diapered and incontinent."

In the New York case, the 2nd Circuit reached the same end by   9
a different path. The 14th Amendment not only protects "liberty,"
it also says that no person within a state's jurisdiction may be denied "equal protection of the laws." Under existing law, it is not a
crime for a doctor to cut off life support for a patient being kept alive
by a respirator or a gastronomical tube. The 2nd Circuit reasoned
that the equal protection clause is violated when there is one law
for the dying patient in a respirator and another law for the dying patient helpless in his bed.

Some judges and some doctors strongly disagree with the judi-   10
cial decisions. A California doctor, writing to USA Today, sees "a
huge difference between assisting a person to die and stopping a life-

prolonging treatment." The physician's duty, and the state's compelling interest, lies in "preserving life." To this argument, one may gently inquire: To preserve what kind of life?

The usually astute Wall Street Journal misses the legal point. 11
The Journal would keep the courts out of the picture and let "the people" decide. But the people can act only through their governments, and here the governments of Washington and New York have made doctor-assisted death a crime. Criminal law assuredly is a matter for judges to resolve.

It will be a long time before the judicial issues are resolved and 12
much longer before the moral and ethical issues are clearly defined. Meanwhile state legislatures have serious thinking to do about the safeguards that must be built into laws regulating a right to die. What proof of a "terminal" condition should be required?

As a conservative, I believe passionately in individual freedom 13
and responsibility, and I believe the state ought not to intrude upon our most personal decisions. But rights are not absolute, and the states are not eunuchs. These are tough calls.

The debate is just beginning, but with these two thoughtful 14
opinions the debate is well begun.

QUESTIONS OF CONTENT

1. According to Erdahl's opening paragraph, what are two phrases that serve as synonyms for the term *euthanasia?* Which term does he seem to prefer, and why do you suppose that he does so?
2. How does Erdahl differentiate between "passive" and "active" euthanasia? How are these related to "institutionalized" euthanasia, and why does he oppose that form?
3. What is Chavez's announced reason for turning to the Netherlands for all the examples in her argument?
4. What is meant by the statement by Dr. Fenigsen, quoted by Chavez: "Euthanasia is not just changing medicine; it is replacing medicine"? Where and how do the essays by Erdahl, Bernardi, and Kilpatrick bring up this same point?
5. How do Erdahl, Bernardi, and Kilpatrick relate abortion to euthanasia in their essays? Besides the "right to choose' and the "right to die," Bernardi also discusses at length yet another "right"; what is that and what is his attitude toward it?
6. Kilpatrick refers to the 14th Amendment of the Constitution as being central to the two appellate court decisions he discusses. What does that amendment say, and do you agree that it is relevant to the right to die question?

QUESTIONS OF FORM

1. Where does Erdahl refer to the use of euthanasia by Hitler, and what does his argument gain by those repeated references to the World War II Holocaust?
2. What is the "slippery slope" danger mentioned in paragraphs 8 and 9 of Erdahl's essay? How is Chavez referring to a similar danger when she describes the Netherlands' history of physician-assisted suicide and euthanasia? How is Bernardi doing the same thing in his essay's fifth paragraph, where he quotes Judge Beezer's dissenting opinion?
3. How does Chavez use statistics to bolster her argument against assisted suicide?
4. What warrant is behind Bernardi's references to Judeo–Christian traditions and especially to Christian beliefs in his essay? Since the Bible sometimes contradicts itself, and because not everyone in our culture is either a Jew or a Christian, how useful are such references in serving as an authority in an argument?
5. Kilpatrick opens his essay with two examples. How do these add both emotional and ethical appeal to his claim of fact?

SUGGESTIONS FOR WRITING

1. Using real examples from your experience or from those near you (family, friends, co-workers, and the like), and drawing upon the examples and arguments of the sample essays to any degree you wish, write a well-supported essay agreeing with or refuting the Roman philosopher Seneca's assertion that "the wise man will live as long as he ought, not as long as he can." (Feel free to convert Seneca's masculine references.)
2. Erdahl, Bernardi, and Kilpatrick all connect the ethical problems of active euthanasia to those of abortion; in a well-reasoned letter to one of these authors, agree or disagree with their contention that a relationship exists.
3. As the manager of a nursing home, you have just received a letter from the middle-aged daughter and son of a prospective resident. It explains that their parent suffers from Alzheimer's disease and no longer recognizes them; furthermore, the parent is bedridden because of a spinal injury, and thus is totally dependent upon others for feeding and hygiene. Despite these conditions, the family's physician says that the parent's heart is strong and projects a life expectancy of up to ten years. The annual cost of maintaining a patient in this condition in your facility is currently $42,000. The children say that they are seriously considering trying to find a physician who will "help end the misery" of their parent. What is your position? What sort of response will you write these people?

Additional References

Dority, Barbara. " 'In the Hands of the People': Recent Victories of the Death-with-Dignity Movement." *The Humanist* 56 (July-Aug. 1996): 6–8.

Greenhouse, Linda. "An Issue for a Reluctant High Court." *New York Times* 6 Oct. 1996, natl. ed.: E3.

Kolata, Gina. "Concerns Are Raised That Doctor-Assisted Suicide Would Leave Powerless Vulnerable." *New York Times* 20 Oct. 1996, late ed.: 14.

Lief, Jason A. "Constitution Provides No Right to be Killed." *National Law Journal* 26 Aug. 1996: A20.

Rosoff, Sidney D. "Hastening Death Is a Person's Right." *National Law Journal* 23 Sept. 1996: A19.

Verhey, Alan. "Choosing Death: The Ethics of Assisted Suicide." *Christian Century* 17 July 1996: 716–18.

Wheeler, David L. "Dignity in Death." *Chronicle of Higher Education* 22 March 1996: A8–10.

WHAT SHOULD BE DONE ABOUT GUN CONTROL?

The Right to Bear Arms

WARREN E. BURGER

Our metropolitan centers, and some suburban communities of 1
America, are setting new records for homicides by handguns. Many
of our large centers have up to 10 times the murder rate of all of
Western Europe. In 1988, there were 9000 handgun murders in
America. Last year, Washington, D.C., alone had more than 400
homicides—setting a new record for our capital.

The Constitution of the United States, in its Second Amendment, 2
guarantees a "right of the people to keep and bear arms." However,
the meaning of this clause cannot be understood except by looking to
the purpose, the setting and the objectives of the draftsmen. The first
10 amendments—the Bill of Rights—were not drafted at Philadelphia
in 1787; that document came two years later than the Constitution.
Most of the states already had bills of rights, but the Constitution
might not have been ratified in 1788 if the states had not had assur-
ances that a national Bill of Rights would soon be added.

People of that day were apprehensive about the new "monster" 3
national government presented to them, and this helps explain the
language and purpose of the Second Amendment. A few lines after
the First Amendment's guarantees—against "establishment of religion," "free exercise" of religion, free speech and free press—came
a guarantee that grew out of the deep-seated fear of a "national" or
"standing" army. The same First Congress that approved the right
to keep and bear arms also limited the national army to 840 men;
Congress in the Second Amendment then provided:

> "A well regulated Militia, being necessary to the security of a free
> State, the right of the people to keep and bear Arms, shall not be
> infringed. "

In the 1789 debate in Congress on James Madison's proposed Bill 4
of Rights, Elbridge Gerry argued that a state militia was necessary:

"to prevent the establishment of a standing army, the bane of liberty . . . Whenever governments mean to invade the rights and liberties of the people, they always attempt to destroy the militia in order to raise an army upon their ruins."

We see that the need for a state militia was the predicate of the "right" guaranteed; in short, it was declared "necessary" in order to have a state military force to protect the security of the state. That Second Amendment clause must be read as though the word "because" was the opening word of the guarantee. Today, of course, the "state militia" serves a very different purpose. A huge national defense establishment has taken over the role of the militia of 200 years ago.

Some have exploited these ancient concerns, blurring sporting guns—rifles, shotguns and even machine pistols—with all firearms, including what are now called "Saturday night specials." There is, of course, a great difference between sporting guns and handguns. Some regulation of handguns has long been accepted as imperative; laws relating to "concealed weapons" are common. That we may be "over-regulated" in some areas of life has never held us back from more regulation of automobiles, airplanes, motorboats and "concealed weapons."

Let's look at the history.

First, many of the 3.5 million people living in the 13 original Colonies depended on wild game for food, and a good many of them required firearms for their defense from marauding Indians—and later from the French and English. Underlying all these needs was an important concept that each able-bodied man in each of the 13 independent states had to help or defend his state.

The early opposition to the idea of national or standing armies was maintained under the Articles of Confederation; that confederation had no standing army and wanted none. The state militia—essentially a part-time citizen army, as in Switzerland today—was the only kind of "army" they wanted. From the time of the Declaration of Independence through the victory at Yorktown in 1781, George Washington, as the commander-in-chief of these volunteer-militia armies, had to depend upon the states to send those volunteers.

When a company of New Jersey militia volunteers reported for duty to Washington at Valley Forge, the men initially declined to take an oath to "the United States," maintaining, "Our country is New Jersey." Massachusetts Bay men, Virginians and others felt the same way. To the American of the 18th century, his state was his country, and his freedom was defended by his militia.

The victory at Yorktown—and the ratification of the Bill of Rights a decade later—did not change people's attitudes about a national army. They had lived for years under the notion that each state would maintain its own military establishment, and the seaboard states had their own navies as well. These people, and their fathers and grandfathers before them, remembered how monarchs had used standing armies to oppress their ancestors in Europe. Americans wanted no part of this. A state militia, like a rifle and powder horn, was as much a part of life as the automobile is today; pistols were largely for officers, aristocrats—and dueling.

Against this background, it was not surprising that the provision concerning firearms emerged in very simple terms with the significant predicate—basing the right on the *necessity* for a "well regulated militia," a state army. 12

In the two centuries since then—with two world wars and some lesser ones—it has become clear, sadly, that we have no choice but to maintain a standing national army while still maintaining a "militia" by way of the National Guard, which can be swiftly integrated into the national defense forces. 13

Americans also have a right to defend their homes, and we need not challenge that. Nor does anyone seriously question that the Constitution protects the right of hunters to own and keep sporting guns for hunting game any more than anyone would challenge the right to own and keep fishing rods and other equipment for fishing—or to own automobiles. To "keep and bear arms" for hunting today is essentially a recreational activity and not an imperative of survival, as it was 200 years ago; "Saturday night specials" and machine guns are not recreational weapons and surely are as much in need of regulation as motor vehicles. 14

Americans should ask themselves a few questions. The Constitution does not mention automobiles or motorboats, but the right to keep and own an automobile is beyond question; equally beyond question is the power of the state to regulate the purchase or the transfer of such a vehicle and the right to license the vehicle and the driver with reasonable standards. In some places, even a bicycle must be registered, as must some household dogs. 15

If we are to stop this mindless homicidal carnage, is it unreasonable: 16

1) to provide that, to acquire a firearm, an application be made reciting age, residence, employment and any prior criminal convictions?

2) to require that this application lie on the table for 10 days (absent a showing for urgent need) before the license would be issued?

3) that the transfer of a firearm be made essentially as with that of a motor vehicle?

4) to have a "ballistic fingerprint" of the firearm made by the manufacturer and filed with the license record so that, if a bullet is found in a victim's body, law enforcement might be helped in finding the culprit?

These are the kind of questions the American people must answer if we are to preserve the "domestic tranquility" promised in the Constitution.   17

Ban the Things.
Ban Them All.

MOLLY IVINS

Guns. Everywhere guns.   1

Let me start this discussion by pointing out that I am not anti-gun. I'm pro-knife. Consider the merits of the knife.   2

In the first place, you have to catch up with someone to stab him. A general substitution of knives for guns would promote physical fitness. We'd turn into a whole nation of great runners. Plus, knives don't ricochet. And people are seldom killed while cleaning their knives.   3

As a civil libertarian, I of course support the Second Amendment. And I believe it means exactly what it says: "A well-regulated militia being necessary to the security of a free state, the right of people to keep and bear arms shall not be infringed." Fourteen-year-old boys are not part of a well-regulated militia. Members of wacky religious cults are not part of a well-regulated militia. Permitting unregulated citizens to have guns is destroying the security of this free state.   4

I am intrigued by the arguments of those who claim to follow the judicial doctrine of original intent. How do they know it was the dearest wish of Thomas Jefferson's heart that teenage drug-dealers should cruise the cities of this nation perforating their fellow citizens with assault rifles? Channeling?   5

There is more hooey spread about the Second Amendment. It says quite clearly that guns are for those who form part of a well-regulated militia, i.e., the armed forces including the National Guard. The reasons for keeping them away from everyone else get clearer by the day.   6

The comparison most often used is that of the automobile, another lethal object that is regularly used to wreak great carnage. Obviously, this society is full of people who haven't got enough common sense to use an automobile properly. But we haven't outlawed cars yet.   7

We do, however, license them and their owners, restrict their 8
use to presumably sane and sober adults and keep track of who sells
them to whom. At a minimum, we should do the same with guns.

In truth, there is no rational argument for guns in this society. 9
This is no longer a frontier nation in which people hunt their own
food. It is a crowded, overwhelmingly urban country in which letting people have access to guns is a continuing disaster. Those who
want guns—whether for target shooting, hunting or potting rat-
tlesnakes (get a hoe)—should be subject to the same restrictions
placed on gun owners in England—a nation in which liberty has survived nicely without an armed populace.

The argument that "guns don't kill people" is patent nonsense. 10
Anyone who has ever worked in a cop shop knows how many family arguments end in murder because there was a gun in the house.
Did the gun kill someone? No. But if there had been no gun, no one
would have died. At least not without a good footrace first. Guns do
kill. Unlike cars, that is all they do.

Michael Crichton makes an interesting argument about technol- 11
ogy in his thriller *Jurassic Park.* He points out that power without
discipline is making this society into a wreckage. By the time someone who studies the martial arts becomes a master—literally able to
kill with bare hands—that person has also undergone years of training and discipline. But any fool can pick up a gun and kill with it.

"A well-regulated militia" surely implies both long training and 12
long discipline. That is the least, the very least, that should be required of those who are permitted to have guns, because a gun is
literally the power to kill. For years, I used to enjoy taunting my
gun-nut friends about their psycho-sexual hangups—always in a
spirit of good cheer, you understand. But letting the noisy minority
in the National Rifle Association force us to allow this carnage to
continue is just plain insane.

I do think gun nuts have a power hangup. I don't know what is 13
missing in their psyches that they need to feel they have the power
to kill. But no sane society would allow this to continue.

Ban the damn things. Ban them all. 14

You want protection? Get a dog. 15

Minority Report

CHRISTOPHER HITCHENS

A favorite liberal sneer at the opponents of gun control is the sug- 1
gestion that those who favor self-defense are fixated on the Old West

and the imagined tradition of the lone gunslinger. Yet the most recent piece of gun control advocacy I have read—a smug little editorial in the relaunched *New York Times Magazine*—advised all those planning to arm themselves to first go and see Clint Eastwood's *Unforgiven*. So it appears that neither side in this argument can manage without the imagery of the frontier and the cowboy. Like many immigrants to this country, I suspect, I will never cease to be surprised by certain things as long as I live here. People tell you their religious denomination when they sit next to you on United Airlines. ("Of course, we're Adventists." Of course.) People tell you about their shrink. And people believe in the right to keep and bear arms. I'll never get over the first two, but I have, gradually, come to think that there is something truly admirable in a country that codifies the responsibility for self-defense. Pity it doesn't make use of it.

If you take the Second Amendment as a whole (which the National Rifle Association and the political conservatives generally do not), it can be understood as enshrining the right, if not indeed the duty, of citizens to defend their country, and themselves, from aggression, including aggression from the government. The idea of the "well-regulated militia" arose from a hostility to the monarchic imposition of a standing army. The time might come when the people might have to muster against the state. Well, what's wrong with that? 2

At the present, the proud American citizen cowers at home, worried sick about crime and delegating, through votes and opinion polls, ever more power to "anti-crime" measures that increase statutory police power and rely upon lockdown procedures. At tax time, the same proud citizen hands over untold wealth to a titanic military bureaucracy that has usurped civilian authority in matters of foreign and defense policy. Emerging from his home, the same citizen still makes sure to put a "No Radio" sign in his car window (one of the most sickening emblems of capitulation I've ever seen) and to carry a twenty-dollar bill when jogging lest the mugger take offense at holding him up for nothing. (This piece of servility, too, is usually futile. You are more and more likely to be robbed and then shot in the face.) Meanwhile, every known civil liberty is mortgaged to a "war on drugs" that, in city after city, has meant police collusion with the drug dealers. Try calling the cops in the event of an assault on your home or your person and you risk being told in so many words that such stuff is beneath their attention. The social contract on "domestic tranquillity," at least as it exists between state and citizen, is broken. 3

The only thing wrong with this picture, as far as most liberals seem to be concerned, is that more people are tempted to go and buy a gun. On its own, of course, this is a stupid and desperate gesture 4 and, in many cases at least, increases the chance that you are handing your assailant a gun. But an equally valid conclusion to that objection would be that more people should be better instructed in the care and use of a defensive weapon. This would improve the odds, either in the case of an attack by a common criminal or in the case of an unlawful trespass by some gargoyle from the Bureau of Alcohol, Tobacco and Firearms. Better to be judged by twelve than carried by six, as they say.

The statistics on all this are inexact, but not as alarming as you might think. In cases where armed and experienced civilians have 5
intervened to challenge armed criminals, the likelihood of bystanders being hit has been several times less than in similar interventions by police. More important, though, is something that cannot be statistically quantified. People who are constantly afraid have lost their self-respect. And in an effort to get it back, they call for vicarious revenge on crime by bellowing for law and order solutions. When these fail to deliver, the talk turns to vigilantism. So one ends up with the worst of both worlds—bloated, corrupt and repressive police departments and assault weapons in the hands of gangsters, with public opinion still poisoned by fear. Instead of a confident citizenry, one has a mass of atomized opinion-poll digits, crying in vain to authority to save them, and loosing off the odd, vicious Bernhard Goetz-style fusillade. (The Black Panthers, who at least briefly taught better manners to the police, also succumbed to gangsterism and illustrated the futility of Wild West-type tactics. There is no street-theater solution to this problem.)

Thinking again about self-defense would involve reordering the 6
idea of the "well-regulated militia." In exchange for abolition of the military-industrial complex, who would not consider reporting for the occasional weekend—as in many democratic European nations—and acquiring the rudiments of weapons training, to be accompanied by a reading of the Constitution and the Bill of Rights? Utopian, you say. No more than the half-baked pacifism that, when preached by gun-controllers, has as its corollary a duopoly of force in the hands of the state and the criminal. Certainly no more utopian than the pathetic "guns for vouchers" swap meets that are now making police precincts a laughingstock as they concentrate on the disarmament of the law-abiding (and the opportunist).

Since, with about 200 million guns on the scene, a gun-free future 7
is not in the cards, and since the farce of Brady-style "registration" will have about the same effect as Prohibition has had on narcotics, what could be more revolutionary and democratic than to nationalize and socialize the arms and weapons business? Instead of being another aspect of anarchy and alienation, it could become part of the

solution. It would also cut with the American grain. Of course guns kill people. That's why the people should take control of the guns.

Kids Killing Kids Has Got to Stop

ERMA BOMBECK

If 14 children were killed in a bus accident en route to a Little League game, it would be the lead story on the 6 o'clock news. 1

If 14 children perished in a fire at a day-care center, it would make the wire services. 2

If 14 children drowned in a boating accident at a church picnic there would be a full-scale investigation. 3

Where is the outcry for the 14 children who will die today in gun accidents—the 14 who will accidentally shoot themselves or be shot by a playmate? 4

We're not taking very good care of the children we are charged to protect. And that's our job. We seem to think that after we get them through the stages of "Don't put that in your mouth!" or "Don't play with matches," we've done it. 5

But it goes on. "Don't accept rides or candy from strangers." "Don't swim alone." Don't play ball in the street." "Don't use kerosene to start a campfire." "Don't use Daddy's electrical tools." 6

Every day I hear how this generation of children is so much more advanced mentally than their parents or grandparents. Don't count on it. They're children who have not yet developed judgment and can't tell reality from make-believe. 7

By the time they have finished elementary school, they will have watched 8,000 murders on television. Bang! Bang! You're dead! And next week, the same guy gets killed again on another thriller, or he appears on a talk show to discuss his next film. 8

In the eyes of a child, he didn't really die. The gun didn't shatter his eardrums when it was fired on television. The victim didn't even bleed a lot. And there wasn't a funeral shown where people were sad the person was gone. 9

There isn't a gun made that you can hide from a child and his insatiable curiosity. The same child who can get the bell out of a ball in 20 seconds at the age of 9 months can find a handgun. He pays the price for his curiosity. 10

The cause-of-the-month is to get violence and murders off the television screens. I'd feel a lot better if we got it out of the home. 11

The purpose of this column has always been to amuse, en- 12
lighten, or say something that hasn't been said before. This one does
none of those things. It's merely an effort to call attention to 14 children whose lives ended today—and to ask, for what?

QUESTIONS OF CONTENT

1. Warren Burger insists that the main purpose of the Second Amendment was not to ensure the right to bear arms but some other, more
   fundamental right. What is that right?
2. As regards the similarities between guns and automobiles, Warren
   Burger and Molly Ivins are in agreement. What attitude do they share?
3. Ivins shares an important point of agreement with Christopher
   Hitchens. What is it?
4. Hitchens stresses the fact that a large number of American citizens
   are simply afraid, especially in urban settings. He points to two effects of this pervading sense of terror. What are those effects, and
   how do they contribute to the gun control problem?
5. What little-known fact triggered Erma Bombeck's thoughts on gun
   control?

QUESTIONS OF FORM

1. Burger argues inductively when he makes a comparison between
   guns and other things that are regulated by the government. How exactly does that induction work?
2. Burger shifts from refutation to a claim of policy at the conclusion
   of his argument. What proposal does he make?
3. Compare the tone of Ivins' essay with Burger's. Compare it also with
   Hitchens'. Which are more alike? Which do you find most effective?
   Why?
4. How does Ivins refute the argument that "guns don't kill people"?
   To which material fallacy is she appealing?
5. What claim of policy does Hitchens ultimately suggest?
6. Analyze Bombeck's use in her article of both ethical and emotional
   appeal.

SUGGESTIONS FOR WRITING

1. Summarize the major thesis of each of these gun control arguments
   in a well-organized paper. Try to arrange the argument summaries
   according to some scale of importance that you can justify.

2. Pick at least two of the strongest gun control arguments that you have examined in this section and include references to them in a letter that you send to your congressional representative who has long been a supporter of the gun lobby. In your letter be sure to give credit for the arguments that you borrow, following the guidelines in Chapter 6's section entitled "Using Sources."

3. You have been a hunter all your life, and you are more than a little offended by the selection of articles in this section, which you immediately recognized as being all on one side of the gun control controversy. You would like to mount a rebuttal but there is little in these articles that can assist you very much. Here is a brief bibliography that should provide you with some help:

Additional References

Cassiday, J. Warren. "The Case for Firearms." *Time* 29 Jan. 1990: 22.

"Gun Control Gets Readers Fired Up." *US News and World Report* 31 March 1986:74.

Hodgkins, Allen R. "Right to Bear Arms Underlies All Our Liberties." *The New York Times* 22 Dec. 1989: 22.

Kates, Don B. "Why Gun Control Won't Work." *Commonweal* 13 March 1981: 136–38.

Kopel, David. "The Untold Triumph of Concealed-Carry Permits." *Policy Review* July-Aug. 1996: 9–11.

Loftin, Colin, and others. "Mandatory Sentencing and Firearms Violence." *Law and Society Review* 17 (1983): 287–318.

SHOULD WE COMPROMISE ON CIGARETTE SMOKING?

Stop Kids from Smoking: Do We Really Want to Do It?

C. EVERETT KOOP

Three thousand young people begin to smoke every day in America. One thousand will eventually die of a tobacco-related disease. We all say that kids shouldn't smoke, but are we really serious about doing something about the problem? Or have we lost some of the zeal to save this generation of young people from addiction and death? 1

The campaign to reduce smoking has been perhaps the most dramatic public health success story of the 20th century. In 1964, about half of all adult Americans smoked. By 1989, the figure had dropped to about 26 or 27 percent. But what about kids? Tobacco use among children is at a 16-year high. And I just don't see the enthusiasm for anti-smoking campaigns directed at kids that I saw as recently as the late 1980s. 2

Why? Perhaps it's because today's generation of young people is growing up more disconnected from adults and adult guidance than any other generation in our nation's history. Many children have been left to raise themselves. Maybe it has to do with our modern preoccupation with "rights." Don't people have the "right" to do whatever they please—even kids? Or maybe it has to do with the image of smoking itself. Nicotine addiction is a stealth pediatric disease. Kids smoke, but they don't die until they're older, and we don't see the awful consequences when they're young. 3

If cigarettes were as hard to come by as dope, I think kids trying to get cigarettes would demonstrate even worse social and self-destructive behavior than kids trying to get high on heroin. 4

What can we do? I'd like to suggest two approaches. 5

Firstly, we must realize that the best way to attack smoking is to reduce demand. Left to their own devices, few young people would begin to smoke on their own. It's a behavior that's just too bizarre. Demand must be created. Young people have to be convinced to smoke, usually through the words and images of advertising. 6

Recently, President Clinton announced the first national pol- 7
icy—promulgated by the Food and Drug Administration—to restrict
tobacco advertising targeted at children. The FDA rule would also
prohibit the sale or giveaway of promotional items like caps or gym
bags that carry cigarette or smokeless tobacco brand names or logos.
Kids love this gear.

And the FDA would ban vending machines and self-service dis- 8
plays and force minors to purchase cigarettes face-to-face from re-
tailers, who would have to demand age verification.

Every state bans the sale of cigarettes to youths under the age of 9
18, but the laws have not been enforced. The FDA rule would put
some real teeth into these laws.

When I served as surgeon general, the public health community 10
was attempting to replace the single surgeon general's warning on
cigarette packs with a series of more specific warnings about a number of tobacco-related health risks.

A specific warning about nicotine addiction would also have 11
been added.

This time around, the tobacco companies are offering to agree to 12
some limitations on advertising so long as the dreaded "a" word can
be avoided once again.

Let's just say "no" to that. FDA regulation could restrict the 13
amount of nicotine in cigarettes to such small amounts that smokers would be forced to buy more and more cigarettes, making it increasingly costly. This could make it harder for kids to get cigarettes,
especially poor kids, and convince some others not to start smoking
in the first place.

Secondly, we need to get more physicians directly involved in 14
the battle. Doctors need to take advantage of every professional encounter with every patient to warn against smoking in that patient's
life or in the lives of the patient's family members.

Some people thought I was too tough on the tobacco companies 15
over 14 years ago when I called them "the most heavy-handed, ob-
tuse, impolitic, and untruthful group of corporations anywhere in
the panoply of American private enterprise."

Now I think I was too easy on them. 16

Help Kids Get Over the Hump

RICHARD HEYMAN

Kids pick up their first cigarette for a variety of different reasons. 1
Some do it for kicks, some to see how it looks and feels, some to be

cool. Sadly, of those who do it, many will continue and rapidly become addicted to nicotine. And young people addicted to nicotine have just as much trouble quitting as adults do.

As chair of the American Academy of Pediatrics Committee on   2
Substance Abuse and a specialist in adolescent medicine, I understand the terrible and growing problem of youth smoking. I not only see the problem in my practice, but also in my home. You see, my 17-year-old son smokes.

When I tell young people that cigarettes can kill them, they look   3
at me like I'm from another planet. They believe that smoking is the quickest way to become an adult, and no earthly force is going to make them quit.

To their way of of thinking, a cigarette is part of an adult uniform   4
that they can put on without having to wait to grow up. It's as much a uniform to them as the shirt and tie that I wore at the White House Rose Garden ceremony when President Clinton announced the federal government's war on children's access to and use of tobacco.

This war can be won. It must be won. When the Kathie Lee   5
Gifford child labor scandal erupted, American authorities moved quickly to protect foreign kids. How can we do any less for our own children? Make no mistakes: Just as foreign kids are enslaved to their jobs by evil bosses, American kids are enslaved to smoking by tobacco companies with nicotine that turns healthy kids into addicts.

Each day, 3,000 young Americans begin to smoke. About 1,000   6
of them will eventually die of tobacco-related diseases. Approximately 1 billion packs of cigarettes will be consumed every year in the United States by minors, and every puff will be illegal since the sale of cigarettes to anyone younger than age 18 is against the law in every state.

Worldwide, the World Health Organization has predicted that   7
between 200 to 300 million children and adolescents alive today will eventually be killed by tobacco.

Most Americans are with teenagers who smoke, but don't real-   8
ize just how successful the tobacco companies have been in targeting very young kids with their advertising and promotion.

Here's an astonishing case in point: According to a study re-   9
ported in the Journal of Marketing in 1995, more than half of all children aged 3 to 6 correctly matched the cartoon character Joe Camel with cigarettes. Our kids are hip to cigarette advertising even before they start kindergarten!

Another study, published in the Journal of the American Med-   10
ical Association, reported that Joe is more familiar to 6-year-olds than Mickey Mouse. With this kind of recognition, it's no wonder

that a recent ABC News poll found that the average smoker begins to smoke by age 12½.

Joe Camel started hawking cigarettes in 1988 with a massive advertising campaign in magazines, in billboards, and on those promotional items that kids love, like gym bags and T-shirts. The results: Between 1991 and 1994, underage smoking went through the roof. It soared by a whooping 30 percent among eighth graders, 22 percent among 10th graders, and 10 percent among 12th graders. Camel profits soared as well. Its market share among smokers soared from 0.5 percent to 32.8 percent. Salesman Joe had made his quota—and then some.   11

What caused kids to smoke? Was it the advertising or were other factors involved, such as peer pressure or natural youthful rebellion? Several factors play a role, but a landmark study published last October put the biggest blame on the ads.   12

The effectiveness of tobacco marketing was the element that triggered adolescents to begin experimenting with cigarettes, reported John Pierce, coauthor of the study and program director of the Cancer Prevention and Control Program at the University of California, San Diego. The key period when adolescents are most susceptible to smoke experimentation is between the ages of 12 and 13. It is the tobacco marketing that sends children down the slippery slope of experimentation to addiction.   13

Cigarette ads and promotion work because they ingeniously push young people's buttons just the right way and present images that have a powerful appeal to young minds. Joe is the cool dude that many kids want to be. The Marlboro Man goes wherever he likes, and doesn't have to check in with mom and dad. The people in the Newport ads are always having fun, fun, fun. Is it any wonder that 85 percent of kids who smoke choose these three brands, while only 35 percent of adults select them?   14

Tobacco companies spend more than $6 billion each year on advertising and marketing, and that breaks down to $750,000 every hour. How can kids resist this constant barrage of imagery? And how can parents bring their kids up right when kids get the wrong kinds of messages everywhere they go? We need additional tools to help us fight such an onslaught.   15

That's why the Food and Drug Administration's (FDA) proposals to restrict tobacco advertising aimed at kids, endorsed by President Clinton, can really make a difference. The FDA would remove the sexy images that hook kids so young. It would ban all outdoor advertising of tobacco products within 1,000 feet of schools and permit black-and-white text only on all other outdoor advertising. It would permit black-and-white text only in magazine ads seen by   16 significant numbers of young people. And it would prohibit tobacco advertising on promotional items.

I have another modest proposal of my own to make. Why not just raise the price of cigarettes? One study found that a 75-cent increase could cut overall youth smoking in half. Some states are already considering raising the price, and every other state should.   17

The younger smokers are hooked, the more likely it is that they'll be hooked for life. Let's give the FDA proposals a chance. They may be too late for my 17-year-old. But maybe we can save some of those 3-year-old Joe Camel fans from starting down that slippery slope to addiction.   18

Curbing Ads Won't Work and It's Unconstitutional

RICHARD BLATT

The tobacco advertising restrictions recently announced by the U.S. Food and Drug Administration (FDA) overlook both the facts and the law. They are likely to prove completely ineffective in reducing teenage smoking, and they are likely to be ruled unconstitutional as well.   1

The Freedom to Advertise Coalition, a broad alliance of advertising, publishing and media interests, agrees with the FDA's goal of reducing teenage smoking and with its proposals to strengthen enforcement of no-sales-to-minors laws and the banning of cigarette vending machines. We object strongly, however, to the FDA's cavalier attitude toward the commercial speech doctrine, which protects advertisers, media and consumers from ill-considered attempts by the government to censor non-deceptive information about legal products and services.   2

The FDA would restrict advertising in a variety of ways—permitting only black-and-white text ("tombstone") cigarette ads in magazines with a minimal level of youth readership, effectively prohibiting all point-of-purchase advertising and virtually banning all outdoor cigarette ads. These dramatic restrictions fail to meet the two key requirements the Supreme Court insists on to restrict commercial speech. The Supreme Court has said consistently that any free speech restrictions must directly and materially advance the governmental interest to be served (in this case the reduction of   3 teenage smoking) and that they be narrowly-tailored to achieve that objective.

With respect to the first of these requirements, there are numerous studies and reports on the asserted link between advertising and smoking by teenagers, but there is no persuasive evidence that advertising is a significant cause of teenage smoking. Ease of access to cigarettes, peer pressure and the example of parents and other adults are clearly more important. If tobacco advertising is not a significant cause of teenage smoking, then clearly the restrictions on advertising cannot be said to directly and materially advance the cause of reducing teenage smoking.

The experience of other countries bears this out. In countries like Finland, Sweden, Norway, Ireland, Italy, Singapore, Australia and the former Soviet Union, teenage smoking rates continued to rise even after tobacco advertising restrictions were put into place. The reason for this is simple: Teenagers in those countries were choosing to smoke for reasons that had nothing to do with advertising. Modern-day advertising for most major industries (including tobacco) is designed either to strengthen brand loyalty or encourage brand switching and thus does not affect smoking rates generally. Thus, most advertising is geared to people who *already use* the product advertised. It is not geared to encourage people to begin using the product. A 1987 study by the White House Council of Economic Advisers found that there is little evidence that advertising causes smoking because "tobacco advertising mainly shifts consumers among brands." Studies have shown that this is a much more cost-effective way to advertise. It is a lot easier to convince a soda drinker to switch brands, for example, than to convince someone to start drinking soda in the first place.

The FDA also flunks the Supreme Court's second test—these restrictions on advertising are anything but narrowly tailored. For example, the FDA would permit only "tombstone" tobacco ads in any magazine with at least 15 percent youth readership. Magazines with as little as 15 percent youth readership are primarily adult publications; yet the FDA rules would treat such magazines as though they were Boy's Life. Similarly, the FDA's effective ban on billboards and point-of-purchase ads for cigarettes would affect adults, not just teenagers.

It is almost impossible to believe that a Supreme Court that only recently greatly strengthened the commercial speech doctrine could permit these restrictions on speech to survive. As recently as May 13, the court in *44 Liquormart v. Rhode Island* unanimously struck down a Rhode Island law that banned most price advertising of alcoholic beverages. It found that the law did not "significantly" advance the cause of temperance in the state, its ultimate objective, and that it was not narrowly tailored.

The Rhode Island case is not unique. The court consistently has struck down a variety of advertising restrictions for being too broad and ineffective, including restrictions on advertisements for abortion services (*Bigelow v. Virginia*), prescription drugs (*Virginia Board of Pharmacy v. Virginia Citizens Consumer Council*), real estate yard signs (*Linmark Associates v. Township of Willingsboro*), birth control devices (the *Carey v. Population Services International* and *Bolger v. Youngs Drug Products* cases), legal services (*Aauderer v. Office of Disciplinary Counsel*) and alcoholic beverages (*Rubin v. Coors*).   8

The court's reasoning is directly applicable to the FDA restrictions on advertising. More effective enforcement of no-sales-to-minors laws, bans on vending machines and more youth-oriented education on the risks of smoking are clearly more narrowly-tailored and are likely to be more effective than the FDA's speech restrictions.   9

There is, of course, a larger question here than whether the FDA has met the test of *44 Liquormart*. The First Amendment's commercial speech doctrine exists specifically to prohibit the government from censoring truthful advertising messages. If these restrictions are enacted, it opens the door very wide for restrictions on other products which have been deemed (either by the government alone or under pressure from powerful special interest groups) to be deleterious to our well-being. Next on the hit list? Fast cars, fatty foods, cosmetics? All are likely targets if these restrictions go unchallenged.   10

The Freedom to Advertise Coalition's position is simple: The government cannot arbitrarily usurp the First Amendment rights of an entire industry, no matter how controversial that industry might be. Fortunately, the Supreme Court seems to agree with us—even if the FDA does not.   11

Thus, while the Supreme Court continues to strike down efforts to restrict nondeceptive commercial speech, the FDA marches blindly in the opposite direction. It is on the wrong track—the track of zealous, misguided censorship even though more reasonable and effective alternatives exist to achieve a widely-accepted objective. Members of the Freedom to Advertise Coalition have already challenged these misguided free speech restrictions in federal court in North Carolina. The outcome of this challenge could well determine the durability of the First Amendment for generations to come.   12

The True Toll of Cigarettes
Is Staggering

JOAN BECK

The embattled tobacco industry got a small boost recently when   1
an Indiana jury refused to award damages to the family of a smoker
who died of lung cancer at age 52.

Richard Rogers, the jury reluctantly concluded, was more re-   2
sponsible for his fatal illness than the cigarette companies that
made the product that killed him.

The legal defense that smokers have been warned about the dan-   3
gers of smoking and smoke at their own risk has served the $45 bil-
lion tobacco industry well. Tobacco companies have yet to pay even
a dollar in damages for the terrible toll of death and injury that cigarettes cause, although earlier this month, a Florida jury awarded
$750,000 to an ex-smoker and his wife. That case will be appealed.

But the terse "surgeon generals warnings" on cigarette packs   4
don't begin to tell the full dangers of tobacco. The infamous toll goes
far beyond lung cancer and heart disease, as the American Council
on Science and Health documents in a carefully researched new
book to be published in September, "Cigarettes: What the Warning
Label Doesn't Tell You." Each chapter cites scientific studies and
has been reviewed by a medical expert.

Requiring teens to read the book before they light up would do   5
a lot more good than the regulations intended to curb the marketing of cigarettes to young people that President Clinton has just
OK'd.

Here's a sample from the book: 6

Cigarette smoking is the leading preventable cause of death and   7
of early ill health and disability. It is responsible for about
500,000 deaths every year—one death in every four in the
United States, says the new book. No system of a smoker's
body is spared its harmful effects.

Smoking not only causes lung cancer, emphysema and chronic   8
bronchitis. It also makes pneumonia, tuberculosis, influenza
and the common cold worse and aggravates asthma.

Smokers have twice the death rates from cancer as non-smok-   9
ers, and almost one-third of all cancer deaths are caused by
using tobacco. Cigarettes are associated with cancer of the
mouth, pharynx, larynx, esophagus, pancreas, cervix, kid-
neys, bladder, colon and bone marrow as well as lungs.

One-fifth of all deaths from heart disease are due to smoking.   10
Smokers are more likely than non-smokers to have repeated
heart attacks and are at higher risk for angina, aortic
aneurysms and other cardiovascular diseases.

Not only does smoking do harm to the blood vessels of the   11
heart, it also injures those throughout the body, leading to
stroke and poor circulation in the legs and feel. Smoking cigarettes is one of two main risk factors for stroke.

Smokers usually look older than non-smokers because damage   12
to the skin produces wrinkles. Smoking increases the risk of
psoriasis.

The risks of surgery are higher in smokers than non-smokers.   13
They require more anesthesia, are more likely to develop res-
piratory complications, are more apt to need extra oxygen and
their wounds are slower to heal. "Many surgeons refuse to do
spinal disc surgery or any graft surgery on smokers," says the
book.   14

People who smoke have higher rates of osteoporosis and broken
bones. Their fractures take longer to heal. And they are more
likely to have back pain, which is usually more severe in
long-term, heavy smokers.   15

Women who smoke are more likely to have problems of infer-
tility, tubal pregnancies and miscarriages. They have more
complications during pregnancy and at childbirth. Their babies are at higher risk of being born premature and, on the average, weigh less than those of non-smoking mothers. A
woman's smoking also increases the risks her baby will be
stillborn or have a cleft palate. Risks are also higher for sudden infant death syndrome, infant allergies and unexplained
mental retardation and behavioral problems.   16

Living with a smoker accounts for hundreds of thousands of
cases of bronchitis, pneumonia, ear infections and worsened
asthma in young children.   17

In men, smoking decreases sperm production, deforms sperm and
reduces blood flow to the penis, sometimes causing impotence.   18

Smokers are six times more likely to snore than nonsmokers.
They have increased risk of several types of hearing loss.
They are more apt to develop cataracts and several other eye
problems. And they are at much greater risk of periodontal
diseases, loss of teeth—and bad breath.   19

Smoking affects the endocrine system, metabolism and body
chemical balance. It increases the risk of developing diabetes.
It tends to lower the age of menopause and decreases estrogen
levels, increasing the risk of osteoporosis and heart disease.

Because smoking impairs the immune system, smokers have more infections than non-smokers.

Using cigarettes increases the risk of stomach ulcers, makes ulcers harder to treat and more likely to reoccur. Smoking reduces resistance to the H. pylori bacteria that causes many ulcers, damages cells that line the stomach and duodenum and decreases the effectiveness of some medications.   20

Like the Black Death that ravaged Europe in the 14th century, the 20th century will be remembered for the tobacco plague that has killed more than 100 million people worldwide, says the book. "Smoking is now the most serious and widespread form of addiction in the world," it concludes.   21

During the 1980s, tobacco killed 5 million Americans, compared to 350,000 deaths from other addictive substances and 90,000 deaths from AIDS. Worldwide, more than 3 million people die every year from what the book calls "tobaccosis"—all the diseases caused by tobacco use.   22

"We are witnessing one of the great tragedies in human history," says the new book. And those who have pushed tobacco products for profit and promoted them with enticing skill have yet to be held accountable.   23

QUESTIONS OF CONTENT

1. What three causes does Koop name for the dramatic U. S. increase in young smokers? Which of those three causes does Heyman focus on in the opening paragraphs of his essay, and what does he say is his personal stake in this issue?

2. What two solutions to the problem of young smokers does Koop propose, and what is the connection of those to Heyman's discussion of possible solutions?

3. Blatt is president of the Point of Purchase Advertising Institute, a member of the Freedom to Advertise Coalition that he describes in paragraph 2. What sort of advertising does his group do, and why would the issue in his essay be so important to them? (Heyman provides some facts that may be useful in answering this question.)

4. Where and how does Blatt employ the material fallacy of *reductio ad absurdum* (see A Short Guide to Material and Formal Fallacies in the Appendix) late in his essay?

5. Beck provides an extensive series of statistics and other information to support the claim of fact announced in her essay's title. Where did

she get her facts? Which three of those facts about the "true toll of cigarettes" did you find most "staggering," and why?

6. Which of the four essays provides statistics about deaths linked to smoking, what one of the writers calls "tobaccosis"? Based on those numbers, how serious is this problem for today's young people?

QUESTIONS OF FORM

1. How do the essays of Beck, Heyman, and Koop differ in the degree of their use of statistics? Which of the three seems to make the most effective use of such numbers?

2. The essays of Heyman and Koop are both claims of policy. Locate the two typical components of such claims: that is, the claim of fact and then the suggested policy (or policies). What similarities and/or differences do you notice in the approaches of these two writers?

3. How does Heyman use advertising based on Joe Camel as a major target of his argument?

4. Blatt organizes his essay to contrast the attitude toward tobacco advertising of the Food and Drug Administration (FDA) with the free speech decisions of the Supreme Court; what other important contrast does he use to make his case?

5. What effect does Blatt create by his numerous references to the authority of court decisions, even though we as readers are not familiar with these cases?

6. Like Blatt, Beck also uses contrast, this time in beginning her essay; examine the first five paragraphs of her essay and be prepared to comment on the effectiveness of her introductory tactic.

7. What force is added to Beck's claim of fact by comparing the 20th-century "tobacco plague" to the Black Death of 14th-century Europe? How might she have developed this analogy further?

SUGGESTIONS FOR WRITING

1. Draw upon the essays provided in this section to warn young people about the dangers of cigarette smoking in an article for a high school, college or hometown newspaper, also using local examples if possible. In this case you should "suppress documentation," as discussed on p. 107 in Chapter 6.

2. Assume that you are either Beck, Heyman, or Koop, and had just read Blatt's essay in the *Washington Post*, where it originally appeared; now write a letter, either to him or to the newspaper (consider the different audiences involved), and use information from your own essay in creating your response.

3. Examine the brief bibliography that follows. The articles listed may aid you in preparing responses to the other two writing suggestions,

since they provide additional perspectives on the issue of cigarette smoking not addressed in the essays provided in this section. To acquire some practice in working with documentation, write a paper in which you present a consistent picture of some aspect of the controversy over cigarette smoking, drawing material from at least three sources. Your instructor may want you to use one or more of the essays printed in this section, with the others coming from the following list, or from your own library research, as she or he directs. Use the documentation methods described in Chapter 6, "Citing Your Sources," unless directed otherwise.

Additional References

"Blowing Smoke." *The New Yorker* 13 June 1994: 6–7.

Kowalski, Kathiann M. "Taking Aim at Teen Smoking." *Current Health 2* 22 (1996): 13–15.

Mangan, Katherine S. "A Collector and Critic of Cigarette Ads." *The Chronicle of Higher Education* 7 June 1996: A6.

Olson, Cheryl K. "The Lure of Lighting Up." *Parents Magazine* 71 (Nov. 1996): 125–6.

Pratt, Jane. "Smoking for the Thrill of It" *New York Times* 2 June 1996, natl. ed.: E15.

Rubenstein, Ed. "Ifs, Ands, and Butts." *National Review* 15 Aug. 1994: 16.

Zegart, Dan. "Buried Evidence: The Damaging Secret Documents and Testimony Tobacco Companies Tried to Suppress." *The Nation* 4 March 1996: 11–15.

Selected Classic Arguments

This final section of sample essays consists of arguments from distant as well as fairly recent history; some are perhaps already familiar, while undoubtedly others will be new to you. All have been reprinted often enough over the years that they may be considered "classics"; that is, they have survived the so-called "test of time." Certainly they demonstrate effective or even unique means of arguing for thought-provoking ideas, so that you should find each essay worth the effort spent to understand it.

However, you may indeed find yourself struggling somewhat to comprehend these essays, for at least three reasons. First, a couple of them, those by Plato and Machiavelli, were not only written quite long ago but also appeared originally in languages other than English, and thus they have been translated, from Greek and Italian respectively. Sometimes subtleties of thought and expressions fade under those circumstances, although we think these are accurate and accessible translations.

A more important difficulty may arise because the English language of several of the other essays is from earlier eras and in England's version of English, not America's; thus you may find yourself straining somewhat now and then to interpret those essays' older or different forms of English expression.

Finally, all these classic essays deal with relatively complex or sophisticated ideas and were composed not only for intelligent audiences but often for ones more highly educated than you are right now. However, at this point in this text and in your English course, you certainly should have had much contact with complex ideas, and indeed you are probably not only intelligent but are also moving briskly toward becoming well educated. Thus we are confident that you can handle the challenges these selections present.

Even so, we have decided to offer you a little extra help with these classic essays, in the form of short introductions to each author and the particular selection from his or her work. Also, as we did with the first group of reading selections, we have again provided you with questions of content and of form at the end of each essay, plus some suggestions for related writing (subject to modification by your instructor); review of all of these, along with reading each work's introduction, will make your study of any of these classical arguments easier and more rewarding.

The Duty of a Citizen

PLATO

A citizen of the city-state of Athens, Plato (429–347 B.C.) was one of three great philosophers of classical Greece. The second was Aristotle, who studied with Plato in his Academy, founded in 387 B. C. Plato himself had studied with the other great Greek philosopher, Socrates (469–399 B.C.), whose teachings and life are preserved in such works of Plato as The Republic *and the* Apology, Crito, *and* Phaedo. *These last three works describe the trial, imprisonment, and death of Socrates. The selection that follows is excerpted from the* Crito *and, like almost all of Plato's work, consists of a dialogue between Socrates and someone else. Unjustly condemned to death by a jury of Athenian citizens, and now in prison, Socrates has been conversing with Crito, a prosperous friend and follower.*

SOC. Let us consider the matter together, and do you either refute me if you can, and I will be convinced; or else cease, my dear friend, from repeating to me that I ought to escape against the wishes of the Athenians: for I highly value your attempts to persuade me to do so, but I may not be persuaded against my own better judgment. And now please to consider my first position, and try how you can best answer me. 1

CR. I will. 2

SOC. Are we to say that we are never intentionally to do wrong, or that in one way we ought and in another we ought not to do wrong, or is doing wrong always evil and dishonourable, as I was just now saying, and as has been already acknowledged by us? Are all our former admissions which were made within a few days to be thrown away? And have we, at our age, been earnestly discoursing with one another all our life long only to discover that we are no better than 3 children? Or, in spite of the opinion of the many, and in spite of consequences whether better or worse, shall we insist on the truth of what was then said, that injustice is always an evil and dishonour to him who acts unjustly? Shall we say so or not?

CR. Yes. 4

SOC. Then we must do no wrong? 5

CR. Certainly not. 6

SOC. Nor when injured injure in return, as the many imagine; 7
for we must injure no one at all?

CR. Clearly not. 8

SOC. Again, Crito, may we do evil? 9

CR. Surely not, Socrates. 10

SOC. And what of doing evil in return for evil, which is the 11
morality of the many—is that just or not?

CR. Not just. 12

SOC. For doing evil to another is the same as injuring him? 13

CR. Very true. 14

SOC. Then we ought not to retaliate or render evil for evil to any 15
one, whatever evil we may have suffered from him. But I would have
you consider, Crito, whether you really mean what you are saying.
For this opinion has never been held, and never will be held, by any
considerable number of persons; and those who are agreed and those
who are not agreed upon this point have no common ground, and
can only despise one another when they see how widely they differ.
Tell me, then, whether you agree with and assent to my first principle,
that neither injury nor retaliation nor warding off evil by evil
is ever right. And shall that be the premise of our argument? Or do
you decline and dissent from this? For so I have ever thought, and
continue to think; but, if you are of another opinion, let me hear
what you have to say. If, however, you remain of the same mind as
formerly, I will proceed to the next step.

CR. You may proceed, for I have not changed my mind. 16

SOC. Then I will go on to the next point, which may be put in 17
the form of a question:—Ought a man to do what he admits to be
right, or ought he to betray the right?

CR. He ought to do what he thinks right. 18

SOC. But if this is true, what is the application? In leaving the 19
prison against the will of the Athenians, do I wrong any? Or rather
do I not wrong those whom I ought least to wrong? Do I not desert
the principles which were acknowledged by us to be just—what do
you say?

CR. I cannot tell, Socrates; for I do not know. 20

SOC. Then consider the matter in this way:—Imagine that I am 21
about to play truant (you may call the proceeding by any name

which you like), and the laws and the government come and inter-
rogate me: 'Tell us, Socrates,' they say, 'what are you about? are you
not going by an act of yours to overturn us—the laws, and the whole
state, as far as in you lies? Do you imagine that a state can subsist
and not be overthrown, in which the decisions of law have no power,
but are set aside and trampled upon by individuals? What will be our
answer, Crito, to these and the like words? Any one, and especially
a rhetorician, will have a good deal to say on behalf of the law which
requires a sentence to be carried out. He will argue that this law
should not be set aside; and shall we reply, 'Yes; but the state has injured us and given an unjust sentence.' Suppose I say that?

CR. Very good, Socrates.

SOC. 'And was that our agreement with you?' the law would answer; 'or were you to abide by the sentence of the state?' And if I
were to express my astonishment at their words, the law would
probably add: 'Answer, Socrates, instead of opening your eyes—you
are in the habit of asking and answering questions. Tell us,—What
complaint have you to make against us which justifies you in attempting to destroy us and the state? In the first place did we not
bring you into existence? Your father married your mother by our aid
and begat you. Say whether you have any objection to urge against
those of us who regulate marriage?' None, I should reply. 'Or against
those of us who after birth regulate the nurture and education of
children, in which you also were trained? Were not the laws, which
have the charge of education, right in commanding your father to
train you in music and gymnastic?' Right, I should reply. 'Well then,
since you were brought into the world and nurtured and educated
by us, can you deny in the first place that you are our child and
slave, as your fathers were before you? And if this is true you are not
on equal terms with us; nor can you think that you have a right to
do to us what we are doing to you. Would you have any right to
strike or revile or do any other evil to your father or your master, if
you had one, because you have been struck or reviled by him, or received some other evil at his hands?—you would not say this? And
because we think right to destroy you, do you think that you have
any right to destroy us in return, and your country as far as in you
lies? Will you, O professor of true virtue, pretend that you are justified in this? Has a philosopher like you failed to discover that our
country is more to be valued and higher and holier far than mother
or father or any ancestor, and more to be regarded in the eyes of the
gods and of men of understanding? Also to be soothed, and gently
and reverently entreated when angry, even more than a father, and
either to be persuaded, or if not persuaded, to be obeyed? And when
we are punished by her, whether with imprisonment or stripes, the

22
23

punishment is to be endured in silence; and if she leads us to wounds or death in battle, thither we follow as is right; neither may any one yield or retreat or leave his rank, but whether in battle or in a court of law, or in any other place, he must do what his city and his country order him; or he must change their view of what is just; and if he may do no violence to his father or mother, much less may he do violence to his country.' What answer shall we make to this, Crito? Do the laws speak truly, or do they not?

CR. I think that they do.

SOC. Then the laws will say, 'Consider, Socrates, if we are speaking truly that in your present attempt you are going to do us an injury. For, having brought you into the world, and nurtured and educated you, and given you and every other citizen a share in every good which we had to give, we further proclaim to any Athenian by the liberty which we allow him, that if he does not like us when he has become of age and has seen the ways of the city, and made our acquaintance, he may go where he pleases and take his goods with him. None of us laws will forbid him or interfere with him. Any one who does not like us and the city, and who wants to emigrate to a colony or to any other city, may go where he likes, retaining his property. But he who has experience of the manner in which we order justice and administer the state, and still remains, has entered into an implied contract that he will do as we command him. And he who disobeys us is, as we maintain, thrice wrong; first, because in disobeying us he is disobeying his parents; secondly, because we are the authors of his education; thirdly, because he has made an agreement with us that he will duly obey our commands; and he neither obeys them nor convinces us that our commands are unjust; and we do not rudely impose them, but give him the alternative of obeying or convincing us;—that is what we offer, and he does neither.

'These are the sort of accusations to which, as we were saying, you, Socrates, will be exposed if you accomplish your intentions; you, above all other Athenians.' Suppose now I ask, why I rather than anybody else? They will justly retort upon me that I above all other men have acknowledged the agreement. 'There is clear proof,' they will say, 'Socrates, that we and the city were not displeasing to you. Of all Athenians you have been the most constant resident in the city, which, as you never leave, you may be supposed to love. For you never went out of the city either to see the games, except once when you went to the Isthmus, or to any other place unless when you were on military service; nor did you travel as other men do. Nor had you any curiosity to know other states or their laws: your affections did not go beyond us and our state; we were your special favourites, and you acquiesced in our government of you; and

24
25

26

here in this city you begat your children, which is a proof of your satisfaction. Moreover, you might in the course of the trial, if you had liked, have fixed the penalty at banishment; the state which refuses to let you go now would have let you go then. But you pretended that you preferred death to exile, and that you were not unwilling to die. And now you have forgotten these fine sentiments, and pay no respect to us the laws, of whom you are the destroyer; and are doing what only a miserable slave would do, running away and turning your back upon the compacts and agreements which you made as a citizen. And first of all answer this very question: Are we right in saying that you agreed to be governed according to us in deed, and not in word only? Is that true or not?' How shall we answer, Crito? Must we not assent?

CR. We cannot help it, Socrates. 27

SOC. Then will they not say: 'You, Socrates, are breaking the 28 covenants and agreements which you made with us at your leisure, not in any haste or under any compulsion or deception, but after you have had seventy years to think of them, during which time you were at liberty to leave the city, if we were not to your mind, or if our covenants appeared to you to be unfair. You had your choice, and might have gone either to Lacedaemon or Crete, both which states are often praised by you for their good government, or to some other Hellenic or foreign state. Whereas you, above all other Athenians, seemed to be so fond of the state, or, in other words, of us her laws (and who would care about a state which has no laws?), that you never stirred out of her; the halt, the blind, the maimed were not more stationary in her than you were. And now you run away and forsake your agreements. Not so, Socrates, if you will take our advice; do not make yourself ridiculous by escaping out of the city.

'For just consider, if you transgress and err in this sort of way, 29 what good will you do either to yourself or to your friends? That your friends will be driven into exile and deprived of citizenship, or will lose their property, is tolerably certain; and you yourself, if you fly to one of the neighboring cities, as, for example, Thebes or Megara, both of which are well governed, will come to them as an enemy, Socrates, and their government will be against you, and all patriotic citizens will cast an evil eye upon you as a subverter of the laws, and you will confirm in the minds of the judges the justice of their own condemnation of you. For he who is a corrupter of the laws is more than likely to be a corrupter of the young and foolish portion of mankind. Will you then flee from well-ordered cities and virtuous men? And is existence worth having on these terms? Or will you go to them without shame, and talk to them, Socrates? And what will you say to them? What you say here about virtue and justice and institutions and laws being the best things among men? Would that be decent of you? Surely not. But if you go away from well-governed states to Crito's friends in Thessaly, where there is great disorder and licence, they will be charmed to hear the tale of your escape from prison, set off with ludicrous particulars of the manner in which you were wrapped in a goatskin or some other disguise, and metamorphosed as the manner is of runaways; but will there be no one to remind you that in your old age you are not ashamed to violate the most sacred laws from a miserable desire of a little more life? Perhaps not, if you keep them in a good temper; but if they are out of temper you will hear many degrading things; you will live, but how?—as the flatterer of all men, and the servant of all men; and doing what?—eating and drinking in Thessaly, having gone abroad in order that you may get a dinner. And where will be your fine sentiments about justice and virtue? Say that you wish to live for the sake of your children—you want to bring them up and educate them—will you take them into Thessaly and deprive them of Athenian citizenship? Is this the benefit which you will confer upon them? Or are you under the impression that they will be better cared for and educated here if you are still alive, although absent from them; for your friends will take care of them? Do you fancy that if you are an inhabitant of Thessaly they will take care of them, and if you are an inhabitant of the other world that they will not take care of them? Nay; but if you who call themselves friends are good for anything, they will—to be sure they will.

'Listen, then, Socrates, to us who have brought you up. Think 30 not of life and children first, and of justice afterwards, but of justice first, that you may be justified before the princes of the world below. For neither will you nor any that belong to you be happier or holier or juster in this life, or happier in another, if you do as Crito bids. Now you depart in innocence, a sufferer and not a doer of evil; a victim, not of the laws but of men. But if you go forth, returning evil for evil, and injury for injury, breaking the covenants and agreements which you have made with us, and wronging those whom you ought least of all to wrong, that is to say, yourself, your friends, your country, and us, we shall be angry with you while you live, and our brethren, the laws of the world below, will receive you as an enemy; for they will know that you have done your best to destroy us. Listen, then, to us and not to Crito.'

This, dear Crito, is the voice which I seem to hear murmuring 31 in my ears, like the sound of the flute in the ears of the mystic; that voice, I say, is humming in my ears, and prevents me from hearing any other. And I know that anything more which you may say will be vain. Yet speak, if you have anything to say.

CR. I have nothing to say, Socrates.

SOC. Leave me then, Crito, to fulfil the will of God, and to follow whither he leads.

QUESTIONS OF CONTENT

1. What does Crito propose that Socrates do to avoid death? How is Socrates' situation analogous to that of American males subject to the draft during the Vietnam War? What were their options, besides entering the military and possibly being crippled for life or even dying because of their wounds?
2. What reasons does Socrates give for rejecting Crito's proposal? Which reason seems best to you, and why?
3. Why do you suppose Socrates feels so strongly about remaining loyal to the Athenian laws when they have been unjustly used to condemn him to death?
4. Socrates' conclusion in paragraph 30 seems to depend on a warrant stemming from a belief in an afterlife, where each person will again be judged; what does his argument lose in force if someone does not hold such a belief?

QUESTIONS OF FORM

1. What, if anything, does Plato gain by presenting this argument in dialectic (conversational) form?
2. The argument of Socrates is deductive, though not easy to pick out. What warrant serves as the major premise of his basic syllogism? What sorts of backing or support does he provide?
3. Note Socrates' use in paragraphs 28 and 29 of comparison and contrast between various city-states of his time; what does he probably hope to accomplish by that comparative approach, and how effective is it?
4. A special feature of the Socratic dialogue is the persistent use of the *rhetorical question* (see the Glossary of Useful Terms in the Appendix), where agreement by the audience is either expected or urged, thus advancing the argument. Where do you find Socrates using this device most effectively to elicit agreement from Crito?

SUGGESTIONS FOR WRITING

1. Write a concise summary of the argument of Socrates.
2. Imagine yourself, like Crito, trying to help save the life of a friend wrongly condemned to die; write out a brief argument for an alternative modern means to safety.

3. Trade papers written for suggestion 2 with a classmate and pretend you are that person's friend, and also someone who feels as strongly about his or her home area as Socrates did; try writing a refutation of your classmate's suggestion.
4. Compare Socrates ideas in paragraphs 24–26 with those expressed by Jefferson in paragraph 2 of the Declaration of Independence. Clearly Socrates and Jefferson are at odds here. With whom are you inclined to agree? May a nation's citizens rise against their government as Jefferson claims, or may they not, as Socrates claims? Make your case in an essay, providing suitable support for your opinion.

The Morals of a Prince

NICCOLO MACHIAVELLI
Translated by M. K. Marriott

A native of Florence, Italy, Niccolò Machiavelli (1469–1527) had a diverse career, typical for a Renaissance humanist such as himself. He served Florence (then a republic) and also the great Medici family as a political emissary, and sometimes as a commercial or a military one, traveling widely and observing acutely. Although also a dramatist, novelist, and historian, Machiavelli won lasting fame as the author of The Prince *(written 1513, published 1532), a political treatise on the art of governing. The fame of this small guidebook for new leaders grows from its later chapters, 15–26, which describe the personal attributes of a successful ruler. Although presenting an ideal of leadership, it is realistically grounded in Machiavelli's own direct experience of power politics. As a consequence, "Machiavellian" has become a negative term, one associated with lack of scruples, even wickedness, for* The Prince *reflects its author's pessimism about human nature and openly advises rulers to use hypocrisy and other amoral means to achieve worthwhile ends. The essay reprinted here comprises Chapters 15–18 of* The Prince.

Concerning Things for Which Men, and Especially Princes, Are Praised or Blamed

It remains now to see what ought to be the rules of conduct for a   1
prince towards subjects and friends. And as I know that many have written on this point, I expect I shall be considered presumptuous in mentioning it again, especially as in discussing it I shall depart

from the methods of other people. But, it being my intention to write a thing which shall be useful to him who apprehends it, it appears to me more appropriate to follow up the real truth of a matter than the imagination of it; for many have pictured republics and principalities which in fact have never been known or seen, because how one lives is so far distant from how one ought to live, that he who neglects what is done for what ought to be done, sooner effects his ruin than his preservation; for a man who wishes to act entirely up to his professions of virtue soon meets with what destroys him among so much that is evil.

Hence it is necessary for a prince wishing to hold his own to know how to do wrong, and to make use of it or not according to necessity. Therefore, putting on one side imaginary things concerning a prince, and discussing those which are real, I say that all men when they are spoken of, and chiefly princes for being more highly placed, are remarkable for some of those qualities which bring them either blame or praise; and thus it is that one is reputed liberal, another miserly...; one is reputed generous, one rapacious; one cruel, one compassionate; one faithless, another faithful; one effeminate and cowardly, another bold and brave; one affable, another haughty; one lascivious, another chaste; one sincere, another cunning; one hard, another easy; one grave, another frivolous; one religious, another unbelieving, and the like. And I know that everyone will confess that it would be most praiseworthy in a prince to exhibit all the above qualities that are considered good; but because they can neither be entirely possessed nor observed, for human conditions do not permit it, it is necessary for him to be sufficiently prudent that he may know how to avoid the reproach of those vices which would lose him his state; and also to keep himself, if it be possible, from those which would not lose him it; but this not being possible, he may with less hesitation abandon himself to them. And again, he need not make himself uneasy at incurring a reproach for those vices without which the state can only be saved with difficulty, for if everything is considered carefully, it will be found that something which looks like virtue, if followed, would be his ruin; whilst something else, which looks like vice, yet followed brings him security and prosperity.

Concerning Liberality and Meanness

Commencing then with the first of the above-named characteristics, I say that it would be well to be reputed liberal. Nevertheless, liberality exercised in a way that does not bring you the reputation for it, injures you; for if one exercises it honestly and as it should be exercised, it may not become known, and you will not avoid the reproach of its opposite. Therefore, anyone wishing to maintain among men the name of liberal is obliged to avoid no attribute of magnificence; so that a prince thus inclined will consume in such acts all his property, and will be compelled in the end, if he wish to maintain the name of liberal, to unduly weigh down his people, and tax them, and do everything he can to get money. This will soon make him odious to his subjects, and becoming poor he will be little valued by anyone; thus, with his liberality, having offended many and rewarded few, he is affected by the very first trouble and imperilled by whatever may be the first danger; recognising this himself, and wishing to draw back from it, he runs at once into the reproach of being miserly.

Therefore, a prince, not being able to exercise this virtue of liberality in such a way that it is recognised, except to his cost, if he is wise he ought not to fear the reputation of being mean, for in time he will come to be more considered than if liberal, seeing that with his economy his revenues are enough, that he can defend himself against all attacks, and is able to engage in enterprises without burdening his people; thus it comes to pass that he exercises liberality towards all from whom he does not take, who are numberless, and meanness towards those to whom he does not give, who are few.

We have not seen great things done in our time except by those who have been considered mean; the rest have failed. Pope Julius the Second was assisted in reaching the papacy by a reputation for liberality, yet he did not strive afterwards to keep it up, when he made war on the King of France; and he made many wars without imposing any extraordinary tax on his subjects, for he supplied his additional expenses out of his long thriftiness. The present King of Spain would not have undertaken or conquered in so many enterprises if he had been reputed liberal. A prince, therefore, provided that he has not to rob his subjects, that he can defend himself, that he does not become poor and abject, that he is not forced to become rapacious, ought to hold of little account a reputation for being mean, for it is one of those vices which will enable him to govern.

And if anyone should say: Cæsar obtained empire by liberality, and many others have reached the highest positions by having been liberal, and by being considered so, I answer: Either you are a prince in fact, or in a way to become one. In the first case this liberality is dangerous, in the second it is very necessary to be considered liberal; and Cæsar was one of those who wished to become pre-eminent in Rome; but if he had survived after becoming so, and had not moderated his expenses, he would have destroyed his government. And if anyone should reply: Many have been princes, and have done great things with armies who have been considered very liberal, I reply: Either a prince spends that which is his own or his subjects' or else that of others. In the first case he ought to be sparing, in the second he ought not to neglect any opportunity for liberality. And to the prince who goes forth with his army, supporting it by pillage, sack, and extortion, handling that which belongs to others, this liberality is necessary, otherwise he would not be followed by soldiers. And of that which is neither yours nor your subjects' you can be a ready giver, as were Cyrus, Cæsar, and Alexander; because it does not take away your reputation if you squander that of others, but adds to it; it is only squandering your own that injures you.

And there is nothing wastes so rapidly as liberality, for even   7 whilst you exercise it you lose the power to do so, and so become either poor or despised, or else, in avoiding poverty, rapacious and hated. And a prince should guard himself, above all things, against being despised and hated; and liberality leads you to both. Therefore it is wiser to have a reputation for meanness which brings reproach without hatred, than to be compelled through seeking a reputation for liberality to incur a name for rapacity which begets reproach with hatred.

Concerning Cruelty and Clemency, and Whether It Is Better to Be Loved Than Feared

Coming now to the other qualities mentioned above, I say that   8 every prince ought to desire to be considered clement and not cruel. Nevertheless he ought to take care not to misuse this clemency. Cesare Borgia was considered cruel; notwithstanding, his cruelty reconciled the Romagna, unified it, and restored it to peace and loyalty. And if this be rightly considered, he will be seen to have been much more merciful than the Florentine people, who, to avoid a reputation for cruelty, permitted Pistoia to be destroyed. Therefore a prince, so long as he keeps his subjects united and loyal, ought not to mind the reproach of cruelty; because with a few examples he will be more merciful than those who, through too much mercy, allow disorders to arise, from which follow murder or robbery; for these are wont to injure the whole people, whilst those executions which originate with a prince offend the individual only.

And of all princes, it is impossible for the new prince to avoid   9 the imputation of cruelty, owing to new states being full of dangers.

Hence Virgil, through the mouth of Dido, excuses the inhumanity of her reign owing to its being new, saying:

"Res dura, et regni novitas me talia cogunt
Moliri, et late fines custode tueri."*

Nevertheless he ought to be slow to believe and to act, nor should he himself show fear, but proceed in a temperate manner with prudence and humanity, so that too much confidence may not make him incautious and too much distrust render him intolerable.

Upon this a question arises: whether it be better to be loved than   10
feared or feared than loved? It may be answered that one should wish to be both, but, because it is difficult to unite them in one person, it is much safer to be feared than loved, when, of the two, either must be dispensed with. Because this is to be asserted in general of men, that they are ungrateful, fickle, false, cowards, covetous, and as long as you succeed they are yours entirely; they will offer you their blood, property, life, and children, as is said above, when the need is far distant; but when it approaches they turn against you. And that prince who, relying entirely on their promises, has neglected other precautions, is ruined; because friendships that are obtained by payments, and not by greatness or nobility of mind, may indeed be earned, but they are not secured, and in time of need cannot be relied upon; and men have less scruple in offending one who is beloved than one who is feared, for love is preserved by the link of obligation which, owing to the baseness of men, is broken at every opportunity for their advantage; but fear preserves you by a dread of punishment which never fails.

Nevertheless a prince ought to inspire fear in such a way that,   11
if he does not win love, he avoids hatred; because he can endure very well being feared whilst he is not hated, which will always be as long as he abstains from the property of his citizens and subjects and from their women. But when it is necessary for him to proceed against the life of someone, he must do it on proper justification and for manifest cause, but above all things he must keep his hands off the property of others, because men more quickly forget the death of their father than the loss of their patrimony. Besides, pretexts for taking away the property are never wanting; for he who has once begun to live by robbery will always find pretexts for seizing what belongs to others; but reasons for taking life, on the contrary, are

---

*Translation: "Hard times and the newness of my realm oblige me to do these things and to look to the keeping of my borders."

more difficult to find and sooner lapse. But when a prince is with his army, and has under control a multitude of soldiers, then it is quite necessary for him to disregard the reputation of cruelty, for without it he would never hold his army united or disposed to its duties.

Among the wonderful deeds of Hannibal this one is enumerated: 12
that having led an enormous army, composed of many various races of men, to fight in foreign lands, no dissensions arose either among them or against the prince, whether in his bad or in his good fortune. This arose from nothing else than his inhuman cruelty, which, with his boundless valour, made him revered and terrible in the sight of his soldiers, but without that cruelty, his other virtues were not sufficient to produce this effect. And short-sighted writers admire his deeds from one point of view and from another condemn the principal cause of them. That it is true his other virtues would not have been sufficient for him may be proved by the case of Scipio, that most excellent man, not only of his own times but within the memory of man, against whom, nevertheless, his army rebelled in Spain; this arose from nothing but his too great forbearance, which gave his soldiers more licence than is consistent with military discipline. For this he was upbraided in the Senate by Fabius Maximus, and called the corruptor of the Roman soldiery. The Locrians were laid waste by a legate of Scipio, yet they were not avenged by him, nor was the insolence of the legate punished, owing entirely to his easy nature. Insomuch that some one in the Senate, wishing to excuse him, said there were many men who knew much better how not to err than to correct the errors of others. This disposition, if he had been continued in the command, would have destroyed in time the fame and glory of Scipio; but, he being under the control of the Senate, this injurious characteristic not only concealed itself, but contributed to his glory.

Returning to the question of being feared or loved, I come to the   13
conclusion that, men loving according to their own will and fearing according to that of the prince, a wise prince should establish himself on that which is in his own control and not in that of others; he must endeavour only to avoid hatred, as is noted.

Concerning the Way in Which Princes Should Keep Faith

Everyone admits how praiseworthy it is in a prince to keep faith, and   14
to live with integrity and not with craft. Nevertheless our experience has been that those princes who have done great things have held good faith of little account, and have known how to circumvent the intellect of men by craft, and in the end have overcome those who have relied on their word. You must know there are two ways of con-

testing, the one by the law, the other by force; the first method is proper to men, the second to beasts; but because the first is frequently not sufficient, it is necessary to have recourse to the second. Therefore it is necessary for a prince to understand how to avail himself of the beast and the man. This has been figuratively taught to princes by ancient writers, who describe how Achilles and many other princes of old were given to the Centaur Chiron to nurse, who brought them up in his discipline; which means solely that, as they had for a teacher one who was half beast and half man, so it is necessary for a prince to know how to make use of both natures, and that one without the other is not durable. A prince, therefore, being compelled knowingly to adopt the beast, ought to choose the fox and the lion; because the lion cannot defend himself against snares and the fox cannot defend himself against wolves. Therefore, it is necessary to be a fox to discover the snares and a lion to terrify the wolves. Those who rely simply on the lion do not understand what they are about. Therefore a wise lord cannot, nor ought he to, keep faith when such observance may be turned against him, and when the reasons that caused him to pledge it exist no longer. If men were entirely good this precept would not hold, but because they are bad, and will not keep faith with you, you too are not bound to observe it with them. Nor will there ever be wanting to a prince legitimate reasons to excuse this non-observance. Of this endless modern examples could be given, showing how many treaties and engagements have been made void and of no effect through the faithlessness of princes; and he who has known best how to employ the fox has succeeded best.

But it is necessary to know well how to disguise this character- 15
istic, and to be a great pretender and dissembler; and men are so simple, and so subject to present necessities, that he who seeks to deceive will always find some one who will allow himself to be deceived. One recent example I cannot pass over in silence. Alexander the Sixth did nothing else but deceive men, nor ever thought of doing otherwise, and he always found victims; for there never was a man who had greater power in asserting, or who with greater oaths would affirm a thing, yet would observe it less; nevertheless his deceits always succeeded according to his wishes, because he well understood this side of mankind.

Therefore it is unnecessary for a prince to have all the good qual- 16
ities I have enumerated, but it is very necessary to appear to have them. And I shall dare to say this also, that to have them and always to observe them is injurious, and that to appear to have them is useful; to appear merciful, faithful, humane, religious, upright, and to be so, but with a mind so framed that should you require not to be so, you may be able and know how to change to the opposite.

And you have to understand this, that a prince, especially a new   17
one, cannot observe all those things for which men are esteemed,
being often forced, in order to maintain the state, to act contrary to
fidelity, friendship, humanity, and religion. Therefore it is necessary
for him to have a mind ready to turn itself accordingly as the winds
and variations of fortune force it, yet, as I have said above, not to di-
verge from the good if he can avoid doing so, but, if compelled, then
to know how to set about it.

For this reason a prince ought to take care that he never lets any-   18
thing slip from his lips that is not replete with the above-named five
qualities, that he may appear to him who sees and hears him altogether merciful, faithful, humane, upright, and religious. There is
nothing more necessary to appear to have than this last quality,
inasmuch as men judge generally more by the eye than by the hand,
because it belongs to everybody to see you, to few to come in touch
with you. Every one sees what you appear to be, few really know
what you are, and those few dare not oppose themselves to the opinion of the many, who have the majesty of the state to defend them;
and in the actions of all men, and especially of princes, which it is
not prudent to challenge, one judges by the result.

For that reason, let a prince have the credit of conquering and   19
holding his state, the means will always be considered honest, and
he will be praised by everybody; because the vulgar are always taken
by what a thing seems to be and by what comes of it; and in the
world there are only the vulgar, for the few find a place there only
when the many have no ground to rest on.

One prince of the present time, whom it is not well to name,   20
never preaches anything else but peace and good faith, and to both
he is most hostile, and either, if he had kept it, would have deprived
him of reputation and kingdom many a time.

QUESTIONS OF CONTENT

1. In his work Machiavelli blends pragmatism about princely behavior
   with cynicism about the conduct of the general public, so that he
   often argues in support of hypocrisy, for seeming rather than being;
   where do you see this tendency?
2. Machiavelli repeatedly examines alternative behaviors a prince or
   leader might choose; where does he do so, and how appropriate today
   is his advice in each place?
3. Machiavelli insists in paragraph 11 that one of the worst actions of
   a leader is confiscating property, for "men more quickly forget the

death of their father than the loss of their patrimony [inheritance from one's father]. " Assuming this was once an accurate assessment of human psychology, and also good advice, how useful is Machiavelli's advice now, and why?

4. In paragraph 18, Machiavelli suggests why hypocritical behavior is so desirable when he describes how people judge. How does he say they judge? Do you agree that his claim is an accurate reflection of many people? Why, or why not? Even if what he says is true, is this an acceptable excuse for hypocrisy?

QUESTIONS OF FORM

1. This essay is organized by comparison/contrast; what two things are being compared, and what is gained by this approach?
2. What warrant having to do with the effectiveness of a ruler seems to lie behind this whole essay?
3. Although you may not recognize many of his allusions or references to political figures of his own and earlier times, you should recognize the sort of appeal which Machiavelli employs so often. What sort is it, and why is it so useful for this particular subject?
4. In this essay's most famous section (paragraph 14), Machiavelli uses *analogy* to argue for particular kinds of princely behavior; how appropriate and useful are his comparisons of a prince to a fox and a lion?

SUGGESTIONS FOR WRITING

1. Write a summary of one of the four sections of Machiavelli's essay.
2. Write a letter to a newly-elected or appointed leader, attempting to convince her or him to read and to heed (or to avoid) the advice in one of this essay's four sections.
3. Attack or defend one of these statements by Machiavelli, remembering to provide specific support for your point of view:
   a. " . . . a man [or woman] who wishes to act entirely up to his [her] professions of virtue soon meets with what destroys him [her] among so much that is evil." (Paragraph 1)
   b. " . . . if one exercises it [liberality] honestly and as it should be exercised, it may not become known, and you will not avoid the reproach of its opposite." (Paragraph 3)
   c. " . . . friendships that are obtained by payments, and not by greatness or nobility of mind, may indeed be earned, but they are not secured, and in time of need cannot be relied upon. . . ." (Paragraph 10)
   d. "Everyone sees what you appear to be, [but] few really know what you are. . . ." (Paragraph 18)

A Modest Proposal

JONATHAN SWIFT

An English clergyman born in Ireland, Jonathan Swift (1667–1745) is best known as the author of Gulliver's Travels *(1726), certainly one of the foremost satirical works in English or any other language. A writer of political tracts, poems, and essays, Swift's satirical power is obvious in his ironic masterpiece, "A Modest Proposal" (1729). Careful readers can detect, behind his mask of calm reason and matter-of-fact language, Swift's genuine concern for the plight of the Irish poor, who were suffering mass starvation in the 1720s under oppressive British rule.*

It is a melancholy object to those who walk through this great 1
town [Dublin], or travel in the country, when they see the streets, the roads, and cabin-doors, crowded with beggars of the female sex, followed by three, four, or six children, all in rags, and importuning every passenger for an alms. These mothers, instead of being able to work for their honest livelihood, are forced to employ all their time in strolling to beg sustenance for their helpless infants; who, as they grow up, either turn thieves for want of work, or leave their dear native country to fight for the Pretender in Spain, or sell themselves to the Barbadoes.

I think it is agreed by all parties, that this prodigious number of 2
children in the arms, or on the backs, or at the heels of their mothers, and frequently of their fathers, is, in the present deplorable state of the kingdom, a very great additional grievance; and, therefore, whoever could find out a fair, cheap, and easy method of making these children sound, useful members of the commonwealth, would deserve so well of the public, as to have his statue set up for a preserver of the nation.

But my intention is very far from being confined to provide only 3
for the children of professed beggars; it is of a much greater extent, and shall take in the whole number of infants at a certain age, who are born of parents in effect as little able to support them, as those who demand our charity in the streets.

As to my own part, having turned my thoughts for many years 4
upon this important subject, and maturely weighed the several schemes of our projectors, I have always found them grossly mistaken in their computation. It is true, a child, just dropped from its dam, may be supported by her milk for a solar year, with little other nourishment; at most, not above the value of two shillings, which the mother may certainly get, or the value in scraps, by her lawful occupation of begging; and it is exactly at one year old that I pro-

posed to provide for them in such a manner, as, instead of being a charge upon their parents, or the parish, or wanting food and raiment for the rest of their lives, they shall, on the contrary, contribute to the feeding and partly to the clothing, of many thousands.

There is likewise another great advantage in my scheme, that it will prevent those voluntary abortions, and that horrid practice of women murdering their bastard children, alas, too frequent among us! sacrificing the poor innocent babes, I doubt more to avoid the expense than the shame, which would move tears and pity in the most savage and inhuman breast.

The number of souls in this kingdom being usually reckoned one million and a half, of these I calculate there may be about two hundred thousand couple whose wives are breeders; from which number I subtract thirty thousand couple, who are able to maintain their own children (although I apprehend there cannot be so many, under the present distresses of the kingdom); but this being granted, there will remain a hundred and seventy thousand breeders. I again subtract fifty thousand, for those women who miscarry, or whose children die by accident or disease within the year. There only remain a hundred and twenty thousand children of poor parents annually born. The question therefore is, How this number shall be reared and provided for? which, as I have already said, under the present situation of affairs, is utterly impossible by all the methods hitherto proposed. For we can neither employ them in handicraft, or agriculture; we neither build houses (I mean in the country,) nor cultivate land: they can very seldom pick up a livelihood by stealing, till they arrive at six years old, except where they are of towardly parts; although I confess they learn the rudiments much earlier; during which time they can, however, be properly looked upon only as probationers; as I have been informed by a principal gentleman in the county of Cavan, who protested to me, that he never knew above one or two instances under the age of six, even in a part of the kingdom so renowned for the quickest proficiency in that art.

I am assured by our merchants, that a boy or a girl before twelve years old is no saleable commodity; and even when they come to this age they will not yield above three pounds, or three pounds and a half-a-crown at most, on the exchange; which cannot turn to account either to the parents or kingdom, the charge of nutriment and rags having been at least four times that value.

I shall now, therefore, humbly propose my own thoughts, which I hope will not be liable to the least objection.

I have been assured by a very knowing American of my acquaintance in London, that a young healthy child, well nursed, is, at a year old, a most delicious, nourishing, and wholesome food,

whether stewed, roasted, baked, or boiled; and I make no doubt that
it will equally serve in a fricassee or a ragout.

I do therefore humbly offer it to public consideration, that of the
hundred and twenty thousand children already computed, twenty
thousand may be reserved for breed; whereof only one-fourth part to
be males; which is more than we allow to sheep, black-cattle, or
swine; and my reason is, that these children are seldom the fruits of
marriage, a circumstance not much regarded by our savages, therefore one male will be sufficient to serve four females. That the remaining hundred thousand may, at a year old, be offered in sale to
the persons of quality and fortune through the kingdom; always ad-
vising the mother to let them suck plentifully in the last month, so
as to render them plump and fat for a good table. A child will make
two dishes at an entertainment for friends; and when the family
dines alone, the fore or hind quarter will make a reasonable dish,
and, seasoned with a little pepper or salt, will be very good boiled
on the fourth day, especially in winter.

I have reckoned, upon a medium, that a child just born will
weigh twelve pounds, and in a solar year, if tolerably nursed, will increase to twenty-eight pounds.

I grant this food will be somewhat dear, and therefore very
proper for landlords, who, as they have already devoured most of the
parents, seem to have the best title to the children.

Infants' flesh will be in season throughout the year, but more
plentifully in March, and a little before and after: for we are told by
a grave author, an eminent French physician, that fish being a prolific diet, there are more children born in Roman Catholic countries
about nine months after Lent, than at any other season; therefore,
reckoning a year after Lent, the markets will be more glutted than
usual, because the number of Popish infants is at least three to one
in this kingdom; and therefore it will have one other collateral advantage, by lessening the number of Papists among us.

I have already computed the charge of nursing a beggar's child
(in which list I reckon all cottagers, labourers, and four-fifths of the
farmers) to be about two shillings per annum, rags included; and I
believe no gentleman would repine to give ten shillings for the carcass of a good fat child, which, as I have said, will make four dishes
of excellent nutritive meat, when he has only some particular
friend, or his own family, to dine with him. Thus the squire will
learn to be a good landlord, and grow popular among his tenants; the
mother will have eight shillings net profit, and be fit for work till
she produces another child.

Those who are more thrifty (as I must confess the times require) may flay the carcass; the skin of which, artificially dressed,

will make admirable gloves for ladies, and summer-boots for fine gentlemen.

As to our city of Dublin, shambles [slaughter houses] may be appointed for this purpose in the most convenient parts of it, and butchers, we may be assured, will not be wanting; although I rather recommend buying the children alive, then dressing them hot from the knife, as we do roasting pigs.

A very worthy person, a true lover of his country, and whose virtues I highly esteem, was lately pleased, in discoursing on this matter, to offer a refinement upon my scheme. He said, that many gentlemen of this kingdom, having of late destroyed their deer, he conceived that the want of venison might be well supplied by the bodies of young lads and maidens, not exceeding fourteen years of age, nor under twelve; so great a number of both sexes in every country being now ready to starve for want of work and service; and these to be disposed of by their parents, if alive, or otherwise by their nearest relations. But, with due deference to so excellent a friend, and so deserving a patriot, I cannot be altogether in his sentiments; for as to the males, my American acquaintance assured me, from frequent experience, that their flesh was generally tough and lean, like that of our schoolboys, by continual exercise, and their taste disagreeable; and to fatten them would not answer the charge. Then as to the females, it would, I think, with humble submission, be a loss to the public, because they soon would become breeders themselves: and besides, it is not improbable that some scrupulous people might be apt to censure such a practice (although indeed very unjustly), as a little bordering upon cruelty; which, I confess, has always been with me the strongest objection against any project, how well soever intended.

But in order to justify my friend, he confessed that this expedient was put into his head by the famous Psalmanazar, a native of the island Formosa, who came from thence to London above twenty years ago; and in conversation told my friend, that in his country, when any young person happened to be put to death, the executioner sold the carcass to persons of quality as a prime dainty; and that in his time the body of a plump girl of fifteen, who was crucified for an attempt to poison the emperor, was sold to his imperial majesty's prime minister of state, and other great mandarins of the court, in joints from the gibbet, at four hundred crowns. Neither indeed can I deny, that, if the same use were made of several plump young girls in this town, who, without one single groat to their fortunes, cannot stir abroad without a chair, and appear at playhouse and assemblies in foreign fineries which they never will pay for, the kingdom would not be the worse.

Some persons of a desponding spirit are in great concern about that vast number of poor people, who are aged, diseased, or maimed; and I have been desired to employ my thoughts, what course may be taken to ease the nation of so grievous an encumbrance. But I am not in the least pain upon that matter, because it is very well known, that they are every day dying, and rotting, by cold and famine, and filth and vermin, as fast as can be reasonably expected. And as to the young labourers, they are now in almost as hopeful a condition: they cannot get work, and consequently pine away for want of nourishment, to a degree, that if at any time they are accidentally hired to common labour, they have not strength to perform it; and thus the country and themselves are happily delivered from the evils to come. 19

I have too long digressed, and therefore shall return to my subject. I think the advantages by the proposal which I have made are obvious and many, as well as of the highest importance. 20

For first, as I have already observed, it would greatly lessen the number of Papists, with whom we are yearly over-run, being the principal breeders of the nation, as well as our most dangerous enemies; and who stay at home on purpose to deliver the kingdom to the Pretender, hoping to take their advantage by the absence of so many good Protestants, who have chosen rather to leave their country than stay at home and pay tithes against their conscience to an Episcopal curate. 21

Secondly, The poorer tenants will have something valuable of their own, which by law may be made liable to distress, and help to pay their landlord's rent; their corn and cattle being already seized, and money a thing unknown. 22

Thirdly, Whereas the maintenance of a hundred thousand children, from two years old and upward, cannot be computed at less than ten shillings a piece per annum, the nation's stock will be thereby increased fifty thousand pounds per annum, beside the profit of a new dish introduced to the tables of all gentlemen of fortune in the kingdom, who have any refinement in taste. And the money will circulate among ourselves, the goods being entirely of our own growth and manufacture. 23

Fourthly, The constant breeders, beside the gain of eight shillings sterling per annum by the sale of their children, will be rid of the charge of maintaining them after the first year. 24

Fifthly, This food would likewise bring great custom to taverns; where the vintners will certainly be so prudent as to procure the best receipts for dressing it to perfection, and, consequently, have their houses frequented by all the fine gentlemen, who justly value themselves upon their knowledge in good eating; and a skilful cook, 25 who understands how to oblige his guests, will contrive to make it as expensive as they please.

Sixthly, This would be a great inducement to marriage, which all wise nations have either encouraged by rewards, or enforced by laws and penalties. It would increase the care and tenderness of mothers toward their children, when they were sure of a settlement for life to the poor babes, provided in some sort by the public, to their annual profit or expense. We should see an honest emulation among the married women, which of them could bring the fattest child to the market. Men would become as fond of their wives during the time of their pregnancy as they are now of their mares in foal, their cows in calf, their sows when they are ready to farrow; nor offer to beat or kick them (as is too frequent a practice) for fear of a miscarriage. 26

Many other advantages might be enumerated. For instance, the addition of some thousand carcasses in our exportation of barrelled beef; the propagation of swine's flesh, and improvement in the art of making good bacon, so much wanted among us by the great destruction of pigs, too frequent at our table; which are no way comparable in taste or magnificence to a well-grown, fat, yearling child, which, roasted whole, will make a considerable figure at a lord mayor's feast, or any other public entertainment. But this, and many others, I omit, being studious of brevity. 27

Supposing that one thousand families in this city would be constant customers for infants' flesh, beside others who might have it at merry-meetings, particularly at weddings and christenings, I compute that Dublin would take off annually about twenty thousand carcasses; and the rest of the kingdom (where probably they will be sold somewhat cheaper) the remaining eighty thousand. 28

I can think of no one objection, that will possibly be raised against this proposal, unless it should be urged, that the number of people will be thereby much lessened in the kingdom. This I freely own, and it was indeed one principal design in offering it to the world. I desire the reader will observe, that I calculate my remedy for this one individual kingdom of Ireland, and for no other that ever was, is, or I think ever can be, upon earth. Therefore let no man talk to me of other expedients: of taxing our absentees at five shillings a pound: of using neither clothes, nor household furniture except what is our own growth and manufacture: of utterly rejecting the materials and instruments that promote foreign luxury: of curing the expensiveness of pride, vanity, idleness, and gaming in our women: of introducing a vein of parsimony, prudence, and temperance: of learning to love our country, in the want of which we differ even from Laplanders, and the inhabitants of Topinamboo: of quitting our animosities and factions, nor acting any longer like the Jews, who were murder- 29 ing one another at the very moment their city was taken: of being a little cautious not to sell our country and conscience for nothing: of teaching landlords to have at least one degree of mercy toward their tenants: lastly, of putting a spirit of honesty, industry, and skill into our shopkeepers; who, if a resolution could now be taken to buy only our native goods, would immediately unite to cheat and exact upon us in the price, the measure, and the goodness, nor could ever yet be brought to make one fair proposal of just dealing, though often and earnestly invited to it.

Therefore I repeat, let no man talk to me of these and the like   30
expedients, till he has at least some glimpse of hope, that there will be ever some hearty and sincere attempt to put them in practice.

But, as to myself, having been wearied out for many years with   31
offering vain, idle, visionary thoughts, and at length utterly de-spairing of success, I fortunately fell upon this proposal; which, as it is wholly new, so it has something solid and real, of no expense and little trouble, full in our own power, and whereby we can incur no danger in disobliging England. For this kind of commodity will not bear exportation, the flesh being of too tender a consistence to admit a long continuance in salt, although perhaps I could name a country, which would be glad to eat up our whole nation without it.

After all, I am not so violently bent upon my own opinions as to   32
reject any offer proposed by wise men, which shall be found equally innocent, cheap, easy, and effectual. But before something of that kind shall be advanced in contradiction to my scheme, and offering a better, I desire the author, or authors, will be pleased maturely to consider two points. First as things now stand, how they will be able to find food and raiment for a hundred thousand useless mouths and backs. And, secondly, there being a round million of creatures in human figure throughout this kingdom, whose whole subsistence put into a common stock would leave them in debt two millions of pounds sterling, adding those who are beggars by profession, to the bulk of farmers, cottagers, and labourers, with the wives and children who are beggars in effect; I desire those politicians who dislike my overture, and may perhaps be so bold as to attempt an answer, that they will first ask the parents of these mortals, whether they would not at this day think it a great happiness to have been sold for food at a year old, in the manner I prescribe, and thereby have avoided such a perpetual scene of misfortunes, as they have since gone through, by the oppression of landlords, the impossibility of paying rent without money or trade, the want of common sustenance, with neither house nor clothes to cover them from the inclemencies of the weather, and the most inevitable prospect of entailing the like, or greater miseries, upon their breed for ever.

I profess, in the sincerity of my heart, that I have not the least 33
personal interest in endeavouring to promote this necessary work,
having no other motive than the public good of my country, by advancing our trade, providing for infants, relieving the poor, and giving some pleasure to the rich. I have no children by which I can
propose to get a single penny; the youngest being nine years old, and
my wife past child-bearing.

QUESTIONS OF CONTENT

1. This satirical essay uses understatement as its principal ironic device to focus attention on the desperate poverty of many Irish people in the 1720s. Who might be among Swift's intended audience for
   this essay, and how can you tell?
2. What is the particular problem Swift sees, and how does he propose
   to solve it?
3. What benefits of his proposal does Swift point out?
4. Why do you suppose Swift, who never married, included facts about
   a fictitious family in his final paragraph?

QUESTIONS OF FORM

1. Swift has obviously made a claim of policy, but it is pretty clearly an
   outrageous and exaggerated proposal, and thus is not modest at all.
   Why might he have chosen this ironic approach?
2. How is his entire argument at the same time both serious and an example of one kind of material fallacy?
3. Swift's tone of calm reason masks the murderous reality of his proposal; where are there particularly effective instances of this artfully
   ironic language?
4. Note how often Swift provides specific calculations or statistics;
   what does his essay gain by this practice? Similarly, what does he
   gain by carefully enumerating the probable benefits of his proposal
   in paragraphs 21 through 27?

SUGGESTIONS FOR WRITING

1. Examine carefully the six advantages of Swift's proposal that he describes in paragraphs 21 through 26, and then write a logical refutation of one of those, making clear why you find fault with it.
2. Using a tone of calm reason similar to Swift's, compose your own
   outrageous satirical proposal for curing some current social malady.

3. Now, in the form of a straightforward claim of policy, write your denunciation and proposed solution of the same problem satirized in suggestion 2, citing first the claim of fact (the deplorable situation), followed by the proposed solution. Which of these efforts seems to you to be the more effective approach—or the one most worth pursuing?

An Argument Against Payment of Salaries to Executive Officers of the Federal Government

BENJAMIN FRANKLIN

A native of Boston, Benjamin Franklin (1706–1790) moved as a teenager to Philadelphia, where he eventually became a leading citizen by living the sensible precepts he outlined in the many editions of Poor Richard's Almanack, *which he compiled and published. By his fortieth year, his writing, printing, and publishing ventures had made him wealthy enough to retire from business, but his active mind and bodily vigor impelled him into other arenas, including science and technology (where he was constantly experimenting and inventing) and public service. He was one of the signers of the Declaration of Independence, the first American ambassador to France, and a delegate to the new republic's Constitutional Convention, where he made the following speech on June 2, 1787.*

Sir, it is with reluctance that I rise to express a disapprobation of any one article of the plan, for which we are so much obliged to the honorable gentleman who laid it before us. From its first reading, I have borne a good will to it, and, in general, wished it success. In this particular of salaries to the executive branch, I happen to differ; and, as my opinion may appear new and chimerical, it is only from a persuasion that it is right, and from a sense of duty, that I hazard it. The Committee will judge of my reasons when they have heard them, and their judgment may possibly change mine. I think I see inconveniences in the appointment of salaries; I see none in refusing them, but on the contrary great advantages.

Sir, there are two passions which have a powerful influence in the affairs of men. These are *ambition* and *avarice:* the love of power and the love of money. Separately, each of these has great force in prompting men to action; but when united in view of the same object, they have in many minds the most violent effects. Place before the eyes of such men a post of honor, that shall at the same time be a place of *profit,* and they will move heaven and earth to obtain it. The vast number of such places it is that renders the British government so tempestuous. The struggles for them are the true source of all those factions which are perpetually dividing the nation, distracting its councils, hurrying it sometimes into fruitless and mischievous wars, and often compelling a submission to dishonorable terms of peace.

And of what kind are the men that will strive for this profitable pre-eminence, through all the bustle of cabal, the heat of contention, the infinite mutual abuse of parties, tearing to pieces the best of characters? It will not be the wise and moderate, the lovers of peace and good order, the men fittest for the trust. It will be the bold and violent, the men of strong passions and indefatigable activity in their selfish pursuits. These will thrust themselves into your government, and be your rulers. And these, too, will be mistaken in the expected happiness of their situation; for their vanquished competitors, of the same spirit, and from the same motives, will perpetually be endeavoring to distress their administration, thwart their measures, and render them odious to the people. 3

Besides these evils, sir, though we may set out in the beginning with moderate salaries, we shall find that such will not be of long continuance. Reasons will never be wanting for proposed augmentations, and there will always be a party for giving more to the rulers, that the rulers may be able in return to give more to them. Hence, as all history informs us, there has been in every state and kingdom a constant kind of warfare between the governing and the governed; the one striving to obtain more for its support, and the other to pay less. And this alone has occasioned great convulsions, actual civil wars, ending either in dethroning of the princes or enslaving of the people. 4

Generally, indeed, the ruling power carries its point, and we see the revenues of princes constantly increasing, and we see that they are never satisfied, but always in want of more. The more the people are discontented with the oppression of taxes, the greater need the prince has of money to distribute among his partisans, and pay the troops that are to suppress all resistance and enable him to plunder at pleasure. There is scarce a king in a hundred, who would not, if he could, follow the example of Pharaoh—get first all the people's money, then all their lands, and then make them and their children servants forever. 5

It will be said that we do not propose to establish kings. I know it. But there is a natural inclination in mankind to kingly govern- 6 ment. It sometimes relieves them from aristocratic domination. They had rather have one tyrant than five hundred. It gives more of the appearance of equality among citizens; and that they like. I am apprehensive, therefore—perhaps too apprehensive—that the government of these states may in future times end in a monarchy. But this catastrophe, I think, may be long delayed, if in our proposed system we do not sow the seeds of contention, faction, and tumult, by making our posts of honor places of profit. If we do, I fear that, though we employ at first a number and not a single person, the number will in time be set aside; it will only nourish the foetus of a king (as the honorable gentleman from Virginia very aptly expressed it), and a king will the sooner be set over us.

It may be imagined by some that this is an utopian idea, and that we can never find men to serve us in the executive department, without paying them well for their services. I conceive this to be a mistake. Some existing facts present themselves to me, which incline me to a contrary opinion. The High Sheriff of a county in England is an honorable office, but it is not a profitable one. It is rather expensive, and therefore not sought for. But yet it is executed, and well executed, and usually by some of the principal gentlemen of the country. In France, the office of Counsellor, or member of their judiciary parliaments, is more honorable. It is therefore purchased at a high price; there are indeed fees on the law proceedings, which are divided among them, but these fees do not amount to more than three per cent on the sum paid for the place. Therefore, as legal interest is there at five per cent, they in fact pay two per cent for being allowed to do the judiciary business of the nation, which is at the same time entirely exempt from the burden of paying them any salaries for their services. I do not, however, mean to recommend this as an eligible mode for our judiciary department. I only bring the instance to show that the pleasure of doing good and serving their country, and the respect such conduct entitles them to, are sufficient motives with some minds to give up a great portion of their time to the public, without the mean inducement of pecuniary satisfaction. 7

Another instance is that of a respectable society, who have made the experiment, and practiced it with success, now more than a hundred years. I mean the Quakers. It is an established rule with them that they are not to go to law, but in their controversies they must apply to their monthly, quarterly, and yearly meetings. Committees of these sit with patience to hear the parties, and spend much time in composing their differences. In doing this, they are supported by a sense of duty and the respect paid to usefulness. It is honorable to be so employed, but it was never made profitable by salaries, fees, 8 or perquisites. And indeed, in all cases of public service, the less the profit the greater the honor.

To bring the matter nearer home, have we not seen the greatest   9
and most important of our offices, that of General of our Armies, executed for eight years together, without the smallest salary, by a patriot whom I will not now offend by any other praise; and this, through fatigues and distresses, in common with the other brave men, his military friends and companions, and the constant anxieties peculiar to his station? And shall we doubt finding three or four men in all the United States, with public spirit enough to bear sitting in peaceful council, for perhaps an equal term, merely to preside over our civil concerns, and see that our laws are duly executed? Sir, I have a better opinion of our country. I think we shall never be without a sufficient number of wise and good men to undertake, and execute well and faithfully, the office in question.

Sir, the saving of the salaries, that may at first be proposed, is   10
not an object with me. The subsequent mischiefs of proposing them are what I apprehend. And therefore it is that I move the amendment. If it is not seconded or accepted, I must be contented with the satisfaction of having delivered my opinion frankly, and done my duty.

QUESTIONS OF CONTENT

1. When Franklin says he wants to avoid paying salaries to three or four persons in the executive branch of our government, whom does he probably mean? Who would be the equivalent persons at the state and the city or county levels?
2. What government does Franklin indicate is already flawed because it has posts whose holders receive both power and money? Why is this probably a useful point to bring up with his fellow delegates to the Constitutional Convention?
3. Why, for his audience, are Franklin's references in paragraphs 5 and 6 to princes and kings, and also to the Egyptian Pharoah, particularly apt?
4. The delegates to the Constitutional Convention did not accept Franklin's amendment. What, if anything, has happened since that time to make American citizens wish that the vote had been in favor of his idea? What, on the other hand, are some practical limitations to Franklin's proposal, both in terms of the current size and complexity of our government and of the strength of patriotic impulses in our time, especially when weighed against personal financial situations?

QUESTIONS OF FORM

1. Originally a speech, Franklin's argument has a rather formal tone and is clearly organized to present his claim of policy in a straightforward fashion. How does he use cause–effect analysis to urge his point, beginning in paragraph 2?
2. Why, given America's recent history at the time of this speech, did Franklin apparently feel in paragraph 4 that he did not need to provide specific examples in support of his discussion of the "warfare between the governing and the governed" and the results of that warfare?
3. Particularly considering his audience, which of the four analogies he uses in paragraphs 7 through 9 do you think are the most appropriate ones to choose in supporting his claim of value, that his idea is not a Utopian one? Why does he probably save the example of General Washington for last?
4. Notice that Franklin, like Swift in "A Modest Proposal," at the end of his essay also denies one obvious reason for making his proposal. Why might that be placed so late?

SUGGESTIONS FOR WRITING

1. Arguments similar to Franklin's are heard across our country every time the U.S. Congress or a state legislature proposes to raise its salary. Using Franklin's essay as your inspiration and starting place, compose a hypothetical letter to the editor of a local paper in which you argue for or against increasing the salary of an office holder who represents you.
2. Franklin is a man of varied experience, able to see both the bad and good in humans. Take one of Franklin's statements regarding human behavior and write an essay in which you demonstrate that his assertion is either correct or incorrect; try using an analogy or a current example, as he did, in support of your case.
3. Consider some famous scandals in American politics, as well as local or state ones that you may know about. Could any of these have been lessened or avoided if Franklin's proposal had been adopted for all levels of government? Write an essay in which you illustrate the truth or falsity of such a claim in reference to one such scandal involving an elected executive leader.

Declaration of Sentiments

ELIZABETH CADY STANTON

One of the earliest and most able proponents of women's rights in America was Elizabeth Cady Stanton (1815–1902). Married to the abolitionist leader Henry B. Stanton and the mother of five children, she still found time to join Susan B. Anthony in founding the National Women's Suffrage Group and to serve as its president, to write extensively for magazines of her era, and to help write the History of Woman Suffrage *(1881–1886). In 1848 Mrs. Stanton was a leader in organizing the first women's rights convention in America. The convention, with her guidance, used* The Declaration of Independence *as a model in creating its own declaration, reprinted here.*

When, in the course of human events, it becomes necessary for one portion of the family of man to assume among the people of the earth a position different from that which they have hitherto occupied, but one to which the laws of nature and of nature's God entitle them, a decent respect to the opinions of mankind requires that they should declare the causes that impel them to such a course. 1

We hold these truths to be self-evident: that all men and women are created equal; that they are endowed by their Creator with certain inalienable rights; that among these are life, liberty, and the pursuit of happiness; that to secure these rights governments are instituted, deriving their just powers from the consent of the governed. Whenever any form of government becomes destructive of these ends, it is the right of those who suffer from it to refuse allegiance to it, and to insist upon the institution of a new government, laying its foundation on such principles, and organizing its powers in such form, as to them shall seem most likely to effect their safety and happiness. Prudence, indeed, will dictate that governments long established should not be changed for light and transient causes; and accordingly all experience hath shown that mankind are more disposed to suffer, while evils are sufferable, than to right themselves by abolishing the forms to which they were accustomed. But when a long train of abuses and usurpations, pursuing invariably the same object, evinces a design to reduce them under absolute despotism, it is their duty to throw off such government, and to provide new guards for their future security. Such has been the patient sufferance of the women under this government, and such is now the necessity which constrains them to demand the equal station to which they are entitled. 2

The history of mankind is a history of repeated injuries and usurpations on the part of man toward woman, having in direct object the establishment of an absolute tyranny over her. To prove this, let facts be submitted to a candid world. 3

He has never permitted her to exercise her inalienable right to the elective franchise. 4

He has compelled her to submit to laws, in the formation of 5
which she had no voice.

He has withheld from her rights which are given to the most ig- 6
norant and degraded men—both natives and foreigners.

Having deprived her of this first right of a citizen, the elective 7
franchise, thereby leaving her without representation in the halls of
legislation, he has oppressed her on all sides.

He has made her, if married, in the eye of the law, civilly dead. 8

He has taken from her all right in property, even to the wages 9
she earns.

He has made her, morally, an irresponsible being, as she can 10
commit many crimes with impunity, provided they be done in the
presence of her husband. In the covenant of marriage, she is compelled to promise obedience to her husband, he becoming, to all in-
tents and purposes, her master—the law giving him power to
deprive her of her liberty, and to administer chastisement.

He has so framed the laws of divorce, as to what shall be the 11
proper causes, and in case of separation, to whom the guardianship
of the children shall be given, as to be wholly regardless of the happiness of women—the law, in all cases, going upon a false supposition of the supremacy of man, and giving all power into his
hands.

After depriving her of all rights as a married woman, if single, 12
and the owner of property, he has taxed her to support a government
which recognizes her only when her property can be made profitable
to it.

He has monopolized nearly all the profitable employments, and 13
from those she is permitted to follow, she receives but a scanty re-
muneration. He closes against her all the avenues to wealth and distinction which he considers most honorable to himself. As a teacher
of theology, medicine, or law, she is not known.

He has denied her the facilities for obtaining a thorough educa- 14
tion, all colleges being closed against her.

He allows her in Church, as well as State, but a subordinate po- 15
sition, claiming Apostolic authority for her exclusion from the ministry, and, with some exceptions, from any public participation in
the affairs of the Church.

He has created a false public sentiment by giving to the world a 16
different code of morals for men and women, by which moral delin-
quencies which exclude women from society are not only tolerated,
but deemed of little account in man.

He has usurped the prerogative of Jehovah himself, claiming it 17
as his right to assign for her a sphere of action, when that belongs to
her conscience and to her God.

He has endeavored, in every way that he could, to destroy her   18
confidence in her own powers, to lessen her self-respect, and to
make her willing to lead a dependent and abject life.

Now, in view of this entire disenfranchisement of one-half the   19
people of this country, their social and religious degradation—in
view of the unjust laws above mentioned, and because women do
feel themselves aggrieved, oppressed, and fraudulently deprived of
their most sacred rights, we insist that they have immediate admission to all the rights and privileges which belong to them as citizens of the United States.

In entering upon the great work before us, we anticipate no small   20
amount of misconception, misrepresentation, and ridicule; but we
shall use every instrumentality within our power to effect our object.
We shall employ agents, circulate tracts, petition the State and National legislatures, and endeavor to enlist the pulpit and the press in
our behalf. We hope this Convention will be followed by a series of
Conventions embracing every part of the country.

QUESTIONS OF CONTENT

1. Thomas Jefferson's villain in 1776 was King George III of England,
   but who is Mrs. Stanton's? Who is her probable audience?
2. Which one of the "repeated injuries and usurpations" listed in paragraphs 4 through 18 seems the worst to you? Which ones, if any, still
   take place?
3. In paragraph 20 Stanton and her peers make clear their intent to
   make their grievances widely known. What difficulties did they apparently face, as made implicit in the list of "injuries and usurpations" and explicit in this concluding paragraph?

QUESTIONS OF FORM

1. Compare Stanton's Declaration with Jefferson's, reprinted earlier in
   this book. Where are they identical in content? In form? What basis
   can you see for any important changes in content or in form?
2. Why do you think Stanton chose the denial of the right to vote as the
   first grievance to list? Which other grievance might also have been a
   good choice to head up the list?
3. Select three examples of words or phrases with emotional appeal,
   and be prepared to explain their appeal; then pick out at least one
   word or phrase that you think could be changed for the better, and
   be prepared to justify your recommendation.

4. Stanton is making a claim of policy, but she has not provided information on any benefits that would result from the changes she desires. What might be some of the benefits and why do you suppose she didn't name any?

SUGGESTIONS FOR WRITING

1. Write a letter to Mrs. Stanton as if she were still able to receive it, and describe the current state of one of the grievances she originally listed.
2. Assume you are an adult American male in 1848, the editor of the local newspaper in an area similar to the one where you now live; write a brief editorial in which you explain why you are agreeing to or refusing Mrs. Stanton's request to reprint her "Declaration of Sentiments" in your newspaper.

Ain't I a Woman?

SOJOURNER TRUTH

Born a slave in New York State, Sojourner Truth (1797–1883), escaped to freedom in 1827 and eventually became a fiery speaker (she was illiterate) on behalf of Christian, racial, and women's causes. Originally called Isabella Van Wagener, in 1843 Truth gave herself the symbolic names by which she is now known, and she began to travel and speak widely, focusing especially on abolitionist causes in the decade before the Civil War. After the war, under the influence of Elizabeth Cady Stanton, she turned her oratorical powers more fully to the cause of women's rights; but she had begun that crusade much earlier, as can be seen in her most famous speech, first given in 1851 and presented below in essay form. "Ain't I a Woman?" has been adapted here from the version that first appeared in The History of Woman Suffrage *(1881–1886), edited by Mrs. Stanton and others.*

Well, children, where there is such a racket there must be something out of kilter. I think that between the Negroes of the South and the women of the North, all talking about rights, the white men will be in a fix pretty soon. But what's all this here talking about?

That man yonder says that women need to be helped into carriages, and lifted over ditches, and to have the best place everywhere. But nobody ever helps me into carriages, or over ditches, or gives me any best place! And ain't I a woman? Look at me! Look at my arm! I have ploughed and planted, and gathered into barns, and no man could head me! And ain't I a woman? I could work as much and eat as much as a man—when I could get it—and bear the lash as well! And ain't I a woman? I have borne thirteen children, and seen most of them sold off to slavery, and when I cried out with my mother's grief, none but Jesus heard me! And ain't I a woman?

Then they talk about this thing in the head. What's this that they call it? ["Intellect," someone in the crowd whispers.] That's it, honey. What's that got to do with women's rights or with Negro's rights? If my cup won't hold but a pint, and yours holds a quart, wouldn't you be mean not even to let me have my little half-measure full? 3

Then that little man in black there, he says women can't have as much rights as men, because Christ wasn't a woman! Where did your Christ come from? Where did your Christ come from? From God—and a *woman!* Man had nothing to do with Him. 4

If the first woman God ever made was strong enough to turn the world upside down all alone, then these women together ought to be able to turn it back, and to get it right side up again! And now that they are asking to do it, men better let them! 5

I'm obliged to you for hearing me, and now old Sojourner ain't got nothing more to say. 6

QUESTIONS OF CONTENT

1. How can you tell this work was first presented as a speech? What in the speech suggests Truth's amount of formal education?
2. Where do you see evidence of Truth's age? Of her religion? Of her background as a slave? As a mother?
3. Paragraphs 2, 3, and 4 focus on different aspects of an individual human; what are those three aspects?
4. What does the "little man in black" represent? Who is the woman that turned the world upside down by herself? How is she related to whatever the little man in black represents?

QUESTIONS OF FORM

1. Probably the most important features of Truth's speech are her constant use of rhetorical questions and her use of repetition. How do those work in tandem to give her message extra force?
2. This brief speech is clearly organized, with an introduction, a conclusion, and four paragraphs that form the work's main body. How

are the four central paragraphs linked by subject? What claims does she make in each? What is the special connection between paragraphs 4 and 5?

3. How is comparison used to support Truth's claims in each of the four body paragraphs?

4. Only in paragraph 2 does Truth use examples to support her claim; why do you suppose that might be so, and how effective are they?

5. Truth makes appeals to pity in two of her body paragraphs. What are those appeals and how effective are they in advancing her argument?

SUGGESTIONS FOR WRITING

1. Although this speech by Truth is focused on equal rights for women, it also touches on the question of equal rights for black Americans. Try rewriting her work to focus on equal rights for some group other than women, using essentially her same organization and approach. As an alternative, try modernizing her examples in paragraph 2 for any group, including women.

2. Presumably there are descendants of Truth all across America. Write a letter to one of them, describing your honest reaction to his or her ancestor's speech; be specific about what you see as its strengths and/or weaknesses.

3. Assume you are either of the two men that Truth points to in paragraphs 2 and 4, and write a concise refutation of her charge against you.

Crime and Criminals

CLARENCE DARROW

Considered the most brilliant criminal lawyer of his day, Clarence Darrow (1857–1938) is probably most famous for the so-called Monkey Trial in Dayton, Tennessee. There he defended John Scopes against a charge of teaching evolution in the local high school. Though Scopes was found guilty and fined, objective onlookers agree that Darrow had actually outdone William Jennings Bryan, an equally famous lawyer, orator, and politician. Darrow's numerous publications include two books: Crime: Its Cause and Treatment *(1922) and* The Story of My Life *(1932). However, the essay below was originally presented in 1902 as a speech to the inmates of the Cook County Jail in Chicago.*

If I looked at jails and crimes and prisoners in the way the ordinary person does, I should not speak on this subject to you. The rea-   1 son I talk to you on the question of crime, its cause and cure, is because I really do not in the least believe in crime. There is no such thing as a crime as the word is generally understood. I do not believe there is any sort of distinction between the real moral condition of the people in and out of jail. One is just as good as the other. The people here can no more help being here than the people outside can avoid being outside. I do not believe that people are in jail because they deserve to be. They are in jail simply because they can not avoid it on account of circumstances which are entirely beyond their control and for which they are in no way responsible.

I suppose a great many people on the outside would say I was   2
doing you harm if they should hear what I say to you this afternoon, but you can not be hurt a great deal anyway, so it will not matter. Good people outside would say that I was really teaching you things that were calculated to injure society, but it's worthwhile now and then to hear something different from what you ordinarily get from preachers and the like. These will tell you that you should be good and then you get rich and be happy. Of course we know that people do not get rich by being good, and that is the reason why so many of you people try to get rich some other way, only you do not understand how to do it quite as well as the fellow outside.

There are people who think that everything in this world is an   3
accident. But really there is no such thing as an accident. A great many folk admit that many of the people in jail ought not to be there, and many who are outside ought to be in. I think none of them ought to be here. There ought to be no jails, and if it were not for the fact that the people on the outside are so grasping and heartless in their dealings with the people on the inside, there would be no such institution as jails.

I do not want you to believe that I think all you people here are   4
angels. I do not think that. You are people of all kinds, all of you doing the best you can, and that is evidently not very well—you are people of all kinds and conditions and under all circumstances. In one sense everybody is equally good and equally bad. We all do the best we can under the circumstances. But as to the exact things for which you are sent here, some of you are guilty and did the particular act because you needed the money. Some of you did it because you are in the habit of doing it, and some of you because you are born to it, and it comes as natural as it does, for instance, for me to be good.

Most of you probably have nothing against me, and most of you   5
would treat me the same as any other person would; probably better than some of the people on the outside would treat me, because you think I believe in you and they know I do not believe in them.

While you would not have the least thing against me in the world, you might pick my pockets. I do not think all of you would, but I think some of you would. You would not have anything against me, but that's your profession, a few of you. Some of the rest of you, if my doors were unlocked, might come in if you saw anything you wanted—not out of any malice to me, but because that is your trade. There is no doubt there are quite a number of people in this jail who would pick my pockets. And still I know this, that when I get outside pretty nearly everybody picks my pocket. There may be some of you who would hold up a man on the street, if you did not happen to have something else to do, and needed the money; but when I want to light my house or my office the gas company holds me up. They charge me one dollar for something that is worth twenty-five cents, and still all these people are good people; they are pillars of society and support the churches, and they are respectable.

When I ride on the streetcars, I am held up—I pay five cents for a ride that is worth two-and-a-half cents, simply because a body of men have bribed the city council and legislature, so that all the rest of us have to pay tribute to them. 6

If I do not want to fall into the clutches of the gas trust and choose to burn oil instead of gas, then good Mr. Rockefeller holds me up, and he uses a certain portion of his money to build universities and support churches which are engaged in telling us how to be good. 7

Some of you are here for obtaining property under false pretenses—yet I pick up a great Sunday paper and read the advertisements of a merchant prince—"Shirtwaists for 39¢, marked down from $3." 8

When I read the advertisements in the paper I see they are all lies. When I want to get out and find a place to stand anywhere on the face of the earth, I find that it has all been taken up long ago before I came here, and before you came here, and somebody says, "Get off, swim into the lake, fly into the air; go anywhere, but get off." That is because these people have the police and they have the jails and the judges and the lawyers and the soldiers and all the rest of them to take care of the earth and drive everybody off that comes in their way. 9

A great many people will tell you that all this is true, but that it does not excuse you. These facts do not excuse some fellow who reaches into my pocket and takes out a five-dollar bill; the fact that the gas company bribes the members of the legislature from year to year, and fixes the law, so that all you people are compelled to be "fleeced" whenever you deal with them; the fact that the streetcar companies and the gas companies have control of the streets and the 10 fact that the landlords own all the earth, they say, has nothing to do with you.

Let us see whether there is any connection between the crimes of   11
the respectable classes and your presence in jail. Many of you people are in jail because you have really committed burglary. Many of you, because you have stolen something: in the meaning of the law, you have taken some other person's property. Some of you have entered a store and carried off a pair of shoes because you did not have the price. Possibly some of you have committed murder. I can not tell what all of you did. There are a great many people here who have done some of these things who really do not know themselves why they did them. I think I know why you did them—every one of you; you did these things because you were bound to do them. It looked to you at the time as if you had a chance to do them or not, as you saw fit, but still after all you had no choice. There may be people here who had some money in their pockets and who still went out and got some more money in a way society forbids. Now you may not yourselves see exactly why it was you did this thing, but if you look at the question deeply enough and carefully enough you would see that there were circumstances that drove you to do exactly the thing which you did. You could not help it any more than we outside can help taking the positions that we take. The reformers who tell you to be good and you will be happy, and the people on the outside who have property to protect—they think that the only way to do it is by building jails and locking you up in cells on weekdays and praying for you Sundays.

I think that all of this has nothing whatever to do with right con-   12
duct. I think it is very easily seen what has to do with right conduct. Some so-called criminals—and I will use this word because it is handy, it means nothing to me—I speak of the criminals who get caught as distinguished from the criminals who catch them—some of these so-called criminals are in jail for first offenses, but nine-tenths of you are in jail because you did not have a good lawyer and of course you did not have a good lawyer because you did not have enough money to pay a good lawyer. There is no very great danger of a rich man going to jail.

Some of you may be here for the first time. If we would open the   13
doors and let you out, and leave the laws as they are today, some of you would be back tomorrow. This is about as good a place as you can get anyway. There are many people here who are so in the habit of coming that they would not know where else to go. There are people who are born with the tendency to break into jail every chance they get, and they can not avoid it. You can not figure out your life and see why it was, but still there is a reason for it, and if we were all wise and knew all the facts we could figure it out.

In the first place, there are a good many more people who go to   14
jail in the winter time than in the summer. Why is this? Is it because
people are more wicked in winter? No, it is because the coal trust
begins to get in its grip in the winter. A few gentlemen take possession of the coal, and unless the people will pay $7 or $8 a ton for
something that is worth $3, they will have to freeze. Then there is
nothing to do but to break into jail, and so there are many more in
jail in the winter than in summer. It costs more for gas in the winter because the nights are longer, and people go to jail to save gas
bills. The jails are electric-lighted. You may not know it, but these
economic laws are working all the time, whether we know it or do
not know it.

There are more people who go to jail in hard times than in good   15
times—few people comparatively go to jail except when they are
hard up. They go to jail because they have no other place to go. They
may not know why, but it is true all the same. People are not more
wicked in hard times. That is not the reason. The fact is true all over
the world that in hard times more people go to jail than in good
times, and in winter more people go to jail than in summer. Of
course it is pretty hard times for people who go to jail at any time.
The people who go to jail are almost always poor people—people
who have no other place to live first and last. When times are hard
then you find large numbers of people who go to jail who would not
otherwise be in jail.

Long ago, Mr. Buckle, who was a great philosopher and histo-   16
rian, collected facts and he showed that the number of people who
are arrested increased just as the price of food increased. When they
put up the price of gas ten cents a thousand I do not know who will
go to jail, but I do know that a certain number of people will go.
When the meat combine raises the price of beef I do not know who
is going to jail, but I know that a large number of people are bound
to go. Whenever the Standard Oil Company raises the price of oil, I
know that a certain number of girls who are seamstresses, and who
work night after night long hours for somebody else, will be compelled to go out on the streets and ply another trade, and I know that
Mr. Rockefeller and his associates are responsible and not the poor
girls in the jails.

First and last, people are sent to jail because they are poor. Some-   17
times, as I say, you may not need money at the particular time, but
you wish to have thrifty forehanded habits, and do not always wait
until you are in absolute want. Some of you people are perhaps ply-
ing the trade, the profession, which is called burglary. No man in his
right senses will go into a strange house in the dead of night and
prowl around with a dark lantern through unfamiliar rooms and

take chances of his life if he has plenty of good things of the world in his own home. You would not take any such chances as that. If a man had clothes in his clothes-press and beefsteak in his pantry, and money in the bank, he would not navigate around nights in houses where he knows nothing about the premises whatever. It always requires experience and education for this profession, and people who fit themselves for it are no more to blame than I am for being a lawyer. A man would not hold up another man on the street if he had plenty of money in his own pocket. He might do it if he had one dollar or two dollars, but he wouldn't if he had as much money as Mr. Rockefeller has. Mr. Rockefeller has a great deal better holdup game than that.

The more that is taken from the poor by the rich, who have the   18
chance to take it, the more poor people there are who are compelled to resort to these means for a livelihood. They may not understand it, they may not think so at once, but after all they are driven into that line of employment.

There is a bill before the Legislature of this State to punish kid-   19
naping children with death. We have wise members of the Legislature. They know the gas trust when they see it and they always see it—they can furnish light enough to be seen, and this Legislature thinks it is going to stop kidnaping children by making a law punishing kidnapers of children with death. I don't believe in kidnaping children, but the Legislature is all wrong. Kidnaping children is not a crime, it is a profession. It has been developed with the times. it has been developed with our modern industrial conditions. There are many ways of making money—many new ways that our ancestors knew nothing about. Our ancestors knew nothing about a billion-dollar trust; and here comes some poor fellow who has no other trade and he discovers the profession of kidnaping children.

This crime is born, not because people are bad; people don't kid-   20
nap other people's children because they want the children or because they are devilish, but because they see a chance to get some money out of it. You cannot cure this crime by passing a law punishing by death kidnapers of children. There is only one way to cure it. There is one way to cure all the offenses, and that is to give the people a chance to live. There is no other way, and there never was any other way since the world began, and the world is so blind and stupid that it will not see. If every man and woman and child in the world had a chance to make a decent, fair, honest living, there would be no jails, and no lawyers and no courts. There might be some persons here or there with some peculiar formation of their brain, like Rockefeller, who would do these things simply to be doing them; but they would be very, very few, and those should be sent to a hos-

pital and treated, and not sent to jail; and they would entirely disappear in the second generation, or at least in the third generation.

I am not talking pure theory. I will just give you two or three illustrations. 21

The English people once punished criminals by sending them 22
away. They would load them on a ship and export them to Australia.
England was owned by lords and nobles and rich people. They
owned the whole earth over there, and the other people had to stay
in the streets. They could not get a decent living. They used to take
their criminals and send them to Australia—I mean the class of
criminals who got caught. When these criminals got over there, and
nobody else had come, they had the whole continent to run over,
and so they could raise sheep and furnish their own meat, which is
easier than stealing it; these criminals then became decent, respectable people because they had a chance to live. They did not
commit any crimes. They were just like the English people who sent
them there, only better. And in the second generation the descendants of those criminals were as good and respectable a class of people as there were on the face of the earth, and then they began
building churches and jails themselves.

A portion of this country was settled in the same way, landing 23
prisoners down on the southern coast; but when they got here and
had a whole continent to run over and plenty of chances to make a
living, they became respectable citizens, making their own living
just like any other citizen in the world; but finally these descendants of the English aristocracy, who sent the people over to Australia, found out they were getting rich, and so they went over to get
possession of the earth as they always do, and they organized land
syndicates and got control of the land and ores, and then they had
just as many criminals in Australia as they did in England. It was
not because the world had grown bad; it was because the earth had
been taken away from the people.

Some of you people have lived in the country. It's prettier than 24
it is here. And if you have ever lived on a farm you understand that
if you put a lot of cattle in a field, when the pasture is short they
will jump over the fence; but put them in a good field where there
is plenty of pasture, and they will be law-abiding cattle to the end
of time. The human animal is just like the rest of the animals, only
a little more so. The same thing that governs in the one governs in
the other.

Everybody makes his living along the lines of least resistance. A 25
wise man who comes into a country early sees a great undeveloped
land. For instance, our rich men twenty-five years ago saw that
Chicago was small and knew a lot of people would come here and

settle, and they readily saw that if they had all the land around here it would be worth a good deal, so they grabbed the land. You cannot be a landlord because somebody has got it all. You must find some other calling. In England and Ireland and Scotland less than 5 percent own all the land there is, and the people are bound to stay there on any kind of terms the landlords give. They must live the best they can, so they develop all these various professions—burglary, picking pockets and the like.

Again, people find all sorts of ways of getting rich. These are diseases like everything else. You look at people getting rich, organizing trusts, and making a million dollars, and somebody gets the disease and he starts out. He catches it just as a man catches the mumps or the measles; he is not to blame, it is in the air. You will find men speculating beyond their means, because the mania of money-getting is taking possession of them. It is simply a disease; nothing more, nothing less. You can not avoid catching it; but the fellows who have control of the earth have the advantage of you. See what the law is; when these men get control of things, they make the laws. They do not make the laws to protect anybody; courts are not instruments of justice; when your case gets into court it will make little difference whether you are guilty or innocent; but it's better if you have a smart lawyer. And you can not have a smart lawyer unless you have money. First and last it's a question of money. Those men who own the earth make the laws to protect what they have. They fix up a sort of fence or pen around what they have, and they fix the law so the fellow on the outside can not get in. The laws are really organized for the protection of the men who rule the world. They were never organized or enforced to do justice. We have no system for doing justice, not the slightest in the world. 26

Let me illustrate: Take the poorest person in this room. If the community had provided a system of doing justice the poorest person in this room would have as good a lawyer as the richest, would he not? When you went into court you would have just as long a trial, and just as fair a trial as the richest person in Chicago. Your case would not be tried in fifteen or twenty minutes, whereas it would take fifteen days to get through with a rich man's case. 27

Then if you were rich and were beaten, your case would be taken to the Appellate Court. A poor man can not take his case to the Appellate Court; he has not the price; and then to the Supreme Court, and if he were beaten there he might perhaps go to the United States Supreme Court. And he might die of old age before he got into jail. If you are poor, it's a quick job. You are almost known to be guilty, else you would not be there. Why would any one be in the criminal court if he were not guilty? He would not be there if he could be any- 28 where else. The officials have no time to look after all these cases. The people who are on the outside, who are running banks and building churches and making jails, they have no time to examine six hundred or seven hundred prisoners each year to see whether they are guilty or innocent. If the courts were organized to promote justice the people would elect somebody to defend all these criminals, somebody as smart as the prosecutor—and give him as many detectives and as many assistants to help, and pay as much money to defend you as to prosecute you. We have a very able man for State's Attorney, and he has many assistants, detectives and policemen without end, and judges to hear the cases—everything handy.

Most of all our criminal code consists in offenses against property. People are sent to jail because they have committed a crime against property. It is of very little consequence whether one hundred people more or less go to jail who ought not to go—you must protect property, because in this world property is of more importance than anything else. 29

How is it done? These people who have property fix it so they can protect what they have. When somebody commits a crime it does not follow that he has done something that is morally wrong. The man on the outside who has committed no crime may have done something. For instance: to take all the coal in the United States and raise the price two dollars or three dollars when there is no need of it, and thus kill thousands of babies and send thousands of people to the poorhouse and tens of thousands to jail, as is done every year in the United States—this is a greater crime than all the people in our jails ever committed, but the law does not punish it. Why? Because the fellows who control the earth make the laws. If you and I had the making of the laws, the first thing we would do would be to punish the fellow who gets control of the earth. Nature put this coal in the ground for me as well as for them, and nature made the prairies up here to raise wheat for me as well as for them, and then the great railroad companies came along and fenced it up. 30

Most of all, the crimes for which we are punished are property crimes. There are a few personal crimes, like murder—but they are very few. The crimes committed are mostly those against property. If this punishment is right the criminals must have a lot of property. How much money is there in this crowd? And yet you are all here for crimes against property. The people up and down the Lake Shore have not committed crimes, still they have so much property they don't know what to do with it. It is perfectly plain why those people have not committed crimes against property; they make the laws and therefore do not need to break them. And in order for you to get some property you are obliged to break the rules of the game. 31

I don't know but what some of you may have had a very nice chance to get rich by carrying the hod for one dollar a day, twelve hours. Instead of taking that nice, easy profession, you are burglar. If you had been given a chance to be a banker you would rather follow that. Some of you may have had a chance to work as a switchman on a railroad where you know, according to statistics, that you can not live and keep all your limbs more than seven years, and you can get fifty dollars or seventy-five dollars a month for taking your lives in your hands, and instead of taking that lucrative position you choose to be a sneak thief, or something like that. Some of you made that sort of choice. I don't know which I would take if I was reduced to this choice. I have an easier choice.

I will guarantee to take from this jail, or any jail in the world, 32 five hundred men who have been the worst criminals and law-breakers who ever got into jail, and I will go down to our lowest streets and take five hundred of the most abandoned prostitutes, and go out somewhere where there is plenty of land, and will give them a chance to make a living, and they will be as good as the average in the community.

There is a remedy for the sort of condition we see here. The world 33 never finds it out, or when it does find out it does not enforce it. You may pass a law punishing every person with death for burglary, and it will make no difference. Men will commit it just the same. In England there was a time when one hundred offenses were punishable with death, and it made no difference. The English people strangely found out that so fast as they repealed the severe penalties and so fast as they did away with punishing men by death, crime decreased instead of increased; that the smaller the penalty the fewer the crimes.

Hanging men in our county jails does not prevent murder. It 34 makes murderers.

And this has been the history of the world. It's easy to see how to 35 do away with what we call crime. It is not so easy to do it. I will tell you how to do it. It can be done by giving the people a chance to live— by destroying special privileges. So long as big criminals can get the coal fields, so long as the big criminals have control of the city council and get the public streets for streetcars and gas rights, this is bound to send thousands of poor people to jail. So long as men are allowed to monopolize all the earth, and compel others to live on such terms as these men see fit to make, then you are bound to get into jail.

The only way in the world to abolish crime and criminals is to 36 abolish the big ones and the little ones together. Make fair conditions of life. Give men a chance to live. Abolish the right of private ownership of land, abolish monopoly, make the world partners in production, partners in the good things of life. Nobody would steal if he could get something of his own some easier way. Nobody will commit burglary when he has a house full. No girl will go out on the streets when she has a comfortable place at home. The man who owns a sweatshop or a department store may not be to blame himself for the condition of his girls, but when he pays them five dollars, three dollars, and two dollars a week, I wonder where he thinks they will get the rest of their money to live. The only way to cure these conditions is by equality. There should be no jails. They do not accomplish what they pretend to accomplish. If you would wipe them out there would be no more criminals than now. They terrorize nobody. They are a blot upon any civilization, and a jail is an evidence of the lack of charity of the people on the outside who make the jails and fill them with the victims of their greed.

QUESTIONS OF CONTENT

1. According to Darrow, what is the basic cause for the existence of prisons and prisoners? Do you agree, or not?
2. Why does Darrow believe more people go to jail in winter than in any other season, and in hard economic times rather than in good? How convincing are his explanations for the causes?
3. Several of Darrow's examples show their age; which ones do so? What might you put in their places? Which examples are still appropriate, indicating that the problem seen by Darrow still exists?
4. How does Darrow use the early history of Australia in his argument?
5. What is the relationship between property and crime, according to Darrow?
6. How does Darrow propose to solve the problem of crime? How well do you think his solution might have worked in his time? In ours?

QUESTIONS OF FORM

1. Who was Darrow's original audience? What influence does that audience have on the examples he uses?
2. What is Darrow's apparent tone? Why do you suppose he adopted it? How does he achieve it?
3. Darrow's argument is essentially an extended claim of policy; where and how does he use comparisons and cause–effect analyses to illustrate the situation his policy would correct?
4. Darrow states in paragraph 20 that there would be no criminals if everyone were given the chance to make a decent living; how does he support this proposition?

5. How effective is the analogy he provides in paragraph 24?
6. Where in his argument does Darrow announce his solution to the problem of crime and criminals? How wise was he to place it there?

SUGGESTIONS FOR WRITING

1. Summarize Darrow's basic argument.
2. Take one of Darrow's supporting examples and rewrite it for a modern audience of law-abiding citizens rather than jailed criminals.
3. Attack or defend one of these assertions by Darrow:
   a. "When I read the advertisements in the papers I see they are all lies." (Paragraph 9)
   b. "There is no very great danger of a rich man going to jail." (Paragraph 12)
   c. "First and last, people are sent to jail because they are poor." (Paragraph 17)
   d. "Everybody makes his living along the lines of least resistance." (Paragraph 25)
   e. "Nobody will commit burglary when he has a house full." (Paragraph 36)

The Indispensable Opposition

WALTER LIPPMANN

A prolific journalist and political commentator, Walter Lippmann (1889–1974) published over 4000 newspaper columns and 20 books in a distinguished career that stretched from World War I to the Vietnam War. An acute critic and accomplished prose stylist, his writing and reasoning powers are fully apparent in the essay below, which first appeared in the August 1939 issue of The Atlantic Monthly.

Were they pressed hard enough, most men would probably confess that political freedom—that is to say, the right to speak freely and to act in opposition—is a noble ideal rather than a practical necessity. As the case for freedom is generally put today, the argument lends itself to this feeling. It is made to appear that, whereas each man claims his freedom as a matter of right, the freedom he accords to other men is a matter of toleration. Thus, the defense of freedom of opinion tends to rest not on its substantial, beneficial, and indispensable consequences, but on a somewhat eccentric, a rather vaguely benevolent, attachment to an abstraction.

It is all very well to say with Voltaire, "I wholly disapprove of what you say, but will defend to the death your right to say it," but as a matter of fact most men will not defend to the death the rights of other men: if they disapprove sufficiently what other men say, they will somehow suppress those men if they can. 2

So, if this is the best that can be said for liberty of opinion, that a man must tolerate his opponents because everyone has a "right" to say what he pleases, then we shall find that liberty of opinion is a luxury, safe only in pleasant times when men can be tolerant because they are not deeply and vitally concerned. 3

Yet actually, as a matter of historic fact, there is a much stronger foundation for the great constitutional right of freedom of speech, and as a matter of practical human experience there is a much more compelling reason for cultivating the habits of free men. We take, it seems to me, a naïvely self-righteous view when we argue as if the right of our opponents to speak were something that we protect because we are magnanimous, noble, and unselfish. The compelling reason why, if liberty of opinion did not exist, we should have to invent it, why it will eventually have to be restored in all civilized countries where it is now suppressed, is that we must protect the right of our opponents to speak because we must hear what they have to say. 4

We miss the whole point when we imagine that we tolerate the freedom of our political opponents as we tolerate a howling baby next door, as we put up with the blasts from our neighbor's radio because we are too peaceable to heave a brick through the window. If this were all there is to freedom of opinion, that we are too good-natured or too timid to do anything about our opponents and our critics except to let them talk, it would be difficult to say whether we are tolerant because we are magnanimous or because we are lazy, because we have strong principles or because we lack serious convictions, whether we have the hospitality of an inquiring mind or the indifference of an empty mind. And so, if we truly wish to understand why freedom is necessary in a civilized society, we must begin by realizing that, because freedom of discussion improves our own opinions, the liberties of other men are our own vital necessity. 5

We are much closer to the essence of the matter, not when we quote Voltaire, but when we go to the doctor and pay him to ask us the most embarrassing questions and to prescribe the most disagreeable diet. When we pay the doctor to exercise complete freedom of speech about the cause and cure of our stomachache, we do not look upon ourselves as tolerant and magnanimous, and worthy to be admired by ourselves. We have enough common sense to know that if we threaten to put the doctor in jail because we do not like 6 the diagnosis and the prescription it will be unpleasant for the doctor, to be sure, but equally unpleasant for our own stomachache. That is why even the most ferocious dictator would rather be treated by a doctor who was free to think and speak the truth than by his own Minister of Propaganda. For there is a point, the point at which things really matter, where the freedom of others is no longer a question of their right but of our own need.

The point at which we recognize this need is much higher in   7
some men than in others. The totalitarian rulers think they do not need the freedom of an opposition: they exile, imprison, or shoot their opponents. We have concluded on the basis of practical experience, which goes back to Magna Carta and beyond, that we need the opposition. We pay the opposition salaries out of the public treasury.

In so far as the usual apology for freedom of speech ignores this   8
experience, it becomes abstract and eccentric rather than concrete and human. The emphasis is generally put on the right to speak, as if all that mattered were that the doctor should be free to go out into the park and explain to the vacant air why I have a stomachache. Surely that is a miserable caricature of the great civic right which men have bled and died for. What really matters is that the doctor should tell me what ails me, and that I should listen to him; that if I do not like what he says I should be free to call in another doctor; and that then the first doctor should have to listen to the second doctor; and that out of all the speaking and listening, the give-and-take of opinions, the truth should be arrived at.

This is the creative principle of freedom of speech, not that it is   9
a system for the tolerating of error, but that it is a system for finding the truth. It may not produce the truth, or the whole truth all the time, or often, or in some cases ever. But if the truth can be found, there is no other system which will normally and habitually find so much truth. Until we have thoroughly understood this principle, we shall not know why we must value our liberty, or how we can protect and develop it.

Let us apply this principle to the system of public speech in a   10
totalitarian state. We may, without any serious falsification, picture a condition of affairs in which the mass of the people are being addressed through one broadcasting system by one man and his chosen subordinates. The orators speak. The audience listens but cannot and dare not speak back. It is a system of one-way communication; the opinions of the rulers are broadcast outwardly to the mass of the people. But nothing comes back to the rulers from the people except the cheers; nothing returns in the way of knowledge of forgotten facts, hidden feelings, neglected truths, and practical suggestions.

But even a dictator cannot govern by his own one-way inspira-   11
tion alone. In practice, therefore, the totalitarian rulers get back the
reports of the secret police and of their party henchmen down
among the crowd. If these reports are competent, the rulers may
manage to remain in touch with public sentiment. Yet that is not
enough to know what the audience feels. The rulers have also to
make great decisions that have enormous consequences, and here
their system provides virtually no help from the give-and-take of
opinion in the nation. So they must either rely on their own intu-
ition, which cannot be permanently and continually inspired, or, if
they are intelligent despots, encourage their trusted advisers and
their technicians to speak and debate freely in their presence.

On the walls of the houses of Italian peasants one may see in-   12
scribed in large letters the legend, "Mussolini is always right." But
if that legend is taken seriously by Italian ambassadors, by the Italian General Staff, and by the Ministry of Finance, then all one can
say is heaven help Mussolini, heaven help Italy, and the new Emperor of Ethiopia.

For at some point, even in a totalitarian state, it is indispensable   13
that there should exist the freedom of opinion which causes opposing opinions to be debated. As time goes on, that is less and less easy
under a despotism; critical discussion disappears as the internal opposition is liquidated in favor of men who think and feel alike. That
is why the early successes of despots, of Napoleon I and of Napoleon
III, have usually been followed by an irreparable mistake. For in listening only to his yes men—the others being in exile or in concentration camps, or terrified—the despot shuts himself off from the
truth that no man can dispense with.

We know all this well enough when we contemplate the dicta-   14
torships. But when we try to picture our own system, by way of contrast, what picture do we have in our minds? It is, is it not, that
anyone may stand up on his own soapbox and say anything he
pleases, like the individuals in Kipling's poem who sit each in his
separate star and draw the Thing as they see it for the God of Things
as they are. Kipling, perhaps, could do this, since he was a poet. But
the ordinary mortal isolated on his separate star will have an hallu-
cination, and a citizenry declaiming from separate soapboxes will
poison the air with hot and nonsensical confusion.

If the democratic alternative to the totalitarian One-way broad-   15
casts is a row of separate soapboxes, then I submit that the alternative is unworkable, is unreasonable, and is humanly unattractive. It
is above all a false alternative. It is not true that liberty has developed among civilized men when anyone is free to set up a soapbox,
is free to hire a hall where he may expound his opinions to those

who are willing to listen. On the contrary, freedom of speech is established to achieve its essential purpose only when different opinions are expounded in the same hall to the same audience.

For, while the right to talk may be the beginning of freedom, the necessity of listening is what makes the right important. Even in Russia and Germany a man may still stand in an open field and speak his mind. What matters is not the utterance of opinions. What matters is the confrontation of opinions in debate. No man can care profoundly that every fool should say what he likes. Nothing has been accomplished if the wisest man proclaims his wisdom in the middle of the Sahara Desert. This is the shadow. We have the substance of liberty when the fool is compelled to listen to the wise man and learn; when the wise man is compelled to take account of the fool, and to instruct him; when the wise man can increase his wisdom by hearing the judgment of his peers. 16

That is why civilized men must cherish liberty—as a means of promoting the discovery of truth. So we must not fix our whole attention on the right of anyone to hire his own hall, to rent his own broadcasting station, to distribute his own pamphlets. These rights are incidental; and though they must be preserved, they can be preserved only by regarding them as incidental, as auxiliary to the substance of liberty that must be cherished and cultivated. 17

Freedom of speech is best conceived, therefore, by having in mind the picture of a place like the American Congress, an assembly where opposing views are represented, where ideas are not merely uttered but debated, or the British Parliament, where men who are free to speak are also compelled to answer. We may picture the true condition of freedom as existing in a place like a court of law, where witnesses testify and are cross-examined, where the lawyer argues against the opposing lawyer before the same judge and in the presence of one jury. We may picture freedom as existing in a forum where the speaker must respond to questions; in a gathering of scientists where the data, the hypothesis, and the conclusion are submitted to men competent to judge them; in a reputable newspaper which not only will publish the opinions of those who disagree but will re-examine its own opinion in the light of what they say. 18

Thus the essence of freedom of opinion is not in mere toleration as such, but in the debate which toleration provides: it is not in the venting of opinion, but in the confrontation of opinion. That this is the practical substance can readily be understood when we remember how differently we feel and act about the censorship and regulation of opinion purveyed by different media of communication. We find then that, in so far as the medium makes difficult the confrontation of opinion in debate, we are driven towards censorship and regulation. 19

There is, for example, the whispering campaign, the circulation 20
of anonymous rumors by men who cannot be compelled to prove
what they say. They put the utmost strain on our tolerance, and
there are few who do not rejoice when the anonymous slanderer is
caught, exposed, and punished. At a higher level there is the moving picture, a must powerful medium for conveying ideas, but a
medium which does not permit debate. A moving picture cannot be
answered effectively by another moving picture; in all free countries
there is some censorship of the movies, and there would be more if
the producers did not recognize their limitations by avoiding political controversy. There is then the radio. Here debate is difficult: it
is not easy to make sure that the speaker is being answered in the
presence of the same audience. Inevitably, there is some regulation
of the radio.

When we reach the newspaper press, the opportunity for debate 21
is so considerable that discontent cannot grow to the point where
under normal conditions there is any disposition to regulate the press.
But when newspapers abuse their power by injuring people who have
no means of replying, a disposition to regulate the press appears.
When we arrive at Congress we find that, because the membership of
the House is so large, full debate is impracticable. So there are re-
strictive rules. On the other hand, in the Senate, where the conditions
of full debate exist, there is almost absolute freedom of speech.

This shows us that the preservation and development of free- 22
dom of opinion are not only a matter of adhering to abstract legal
rights, but also, and very urgently, a matter of organizing and arranging sufficient debate. Once we have a firm hold on the central
principle, there are many practical conclusions to be drawn. We
then realize that the defense of freedom of opinion consists primarily in perfecting the opportunity for an adequate give-and-take of
opinion; it consists also in regulating the freedom of those revolu-
tionists who cannot or will not permit or maintain debate when it
does not suit their purposes.

We must insist that free oratory is only the beginning of free 23
speech; it is not the end, but a means to an end. The end is to find the
truth. The practical justification of civil liberty is not that self-ex-
pression is one of the rights of man. It is that the examination of opinion is one of the necessities of man. For experience tells us that it is
only when freedom of opinion becomes the compulsion to debate that
the seed which our fathers planted has produced its fruit. When that
is understood, freedom will be cherished not because it is a vent for
our opinions but because it is the surest method of correcting them.

The unexamined life, said Socrates, is unfit to be lived by man. 24
This is the virtue of liberty, and the ground on which we may best

justify our belief in it, that it tolerates error in order to serve the truth. When men are brought face to face with their opponents, forced to listen and learn and mend their ideas, they cease to be children and savages and begin to live like civilized men. Then only is freedom a reality, when men may voice their opinions because they must examine their opinions.

The only reason for dwelling on all this is that if we are to preserve democracy we must understand its principles. And the principle which distinguishes it from all other forms of government is that in a democracy the opposition not only is tolerated as constitutional but must be maintained because it is in fact indispensable.   25

The democratic system cannot be operated without effective opposition. For, in making the great experiment of governing people by consent rather than by coercion, it is not sufficient that the party in power should have a majority. It is just as necessary that the party in power should never outrage the minority. That means that it must listen to the minority and be moved by the criticisms of the minority. That means that its measures must take account of the minority's objections, and that in administering measures it must remember that the minority may become the majority.   26

The opposition is indispensable. A good statesman, like any other sensible human being, always learns more from his opponents than from his fervent supporters. For his supporters will push him to disaster unless his opponents show him where the dangers are. So if he is wise he will often pray to be delivered from his friends, because they will ruin him. But, though it hurts, he ought also to pray never to be left without opponents; for they keep him on the path of reason and good sense.   27

The national unity of a free people depends upon a sufficiently even balance of political power to make it impracticable for the administration to be arbitrary and for the opposition to be revolutionary and irreconcilable. Where that balance no longer exists, democracy perishes. For unless all the citizens of a state are forced by circumstances to compromise, unless they feel that they can affect policy but that no one can wholly dominate it, unless by habit and necessity they have to give and take, freedom cannot be maintained.   28

QUESTIONS OF CONTENT

1. Lippmann begins his argument by describing the usual rationale for the political right of freedom of speech; what is that rationale?

2. Lippmann says freedom of speech is not a noble ideal but a practical necessity; for whom is it a necessity, the speaker or the listener? Why is that so?

3. As he describes it, what does freedom of speech help us find or reach? Why is reaching or finding that worthwhile?

4. What sorts of places or circumstances does Lippmann think best represent freedom of speech in the sense he most values? Which house of the U.S. Congress best represents that preferred kind of freedom of speech?

5. Read paragraphs 23 through 28 carefully; what do you think Lippmann's opinion would be regarding those who burn the American flag? Would he probably condemn or would he defend their right to do so?

QUESTIONS OF FORM

1. Lippmann presents both a claim of value and a claim of policy in his argument; how might you concisely state each one?

2. Notice Lippmann's several uses of analogy. Why is his use of the analogy of a doctor in paragraphs 6 through 9 particularly effective in explaining what he means by real freedom of speech?

3. Where and how does Lippmann use comparisons other than analogy to support his claim?

4. What seems to be the warrant that is behind Lippmann's argument, and where is it expressed most obviously?

SUGGESTIONS FOR WRITING

1. Find out the basic facts of the backgrounds of Voltaire and Socrates, and after presenting that information in an orderly fashion, also explain why they are appropriate authorities for Lippmann to allude to in a discussion of the right of freedom of speech.

2. Look again at paragraph 18. Besides the places or circumstances listed by Lippmann, what others are likely forums for freedom of speech in the best sense of that right? In an organized paper, explain why a forum he lists, or one you name, is especially valuable as a place where the truth can be sought and debated.

3. Examine some recent political or business scandals in America in light of Lippmann's claims about the value of the opposition. Do the facts of such debacles bear out or do they refute Lippmann's contentions? Write an essay in which you deal with the appropriateness of his argument with regard to one of these events that you know about. (Your instructor may ask you to do limited library research in order to make sure that your essay is well supported with accurate facts regarding the scandal you choose.)

How to Mark a Book

MORTIMER J. ADLER

A longtime (1930–1952) professor of philosophy at the University of Chicago, Mortimer J. Adler (1902–) was then for decades associated with the Great Books of the Western World series of Encyclopaedia Britannica. Over thirty books have his name on them, as author, coauthor, or editor. The essay below is an important section of Dr. Adler's best-known work, How to Read a Book: The Art of Getting a Liberal Education *(1940; revised edition 1972).*

You know you have to read "between the lines" to get the most out of anything. I want to persuade you to do something equally important in the course of your reading. I want to persuade you to "write between the lines." Unless you do, you are not likely to do the most efficient kind of reading. 1

I contend, quite bluntly, that marking up a book is not an act of mutilation but of love. 2

You shouldn't mark up a book which isn't yours. Librarians (or your friends) who lend you books expect you to keep them clean, and you should. If you decide that I am right about the usefulness of marking books, you will have to buy them. Most of the world's great books are available today, in reprint editions, at less than a dollar. 3

There are two ways in which one can own a book. The first is the property right you establish by paying for it, just as you pay for clothes and furniture. But this act of purchase is only the prelude to possession. Full ownership comes only when you have made it a part of yourself, and the best way to make yourself a part of it is by writing in it. An illustration may make the point clear. You buy a beefsteak and transfer it from the butcher's ice-box to your own. But you do not own the beefsteak in the most important sense until you consume it and get it into your bloodstream. I am arguing that books, too, must be absorbed in your bloodstream to do you any good. 4

Confusion about what it means to *own* a book leads people to a false reverence for paper, binding, and type—a respect for the physical thing—the craft of the printer rather than the genius of the author. They forget that it is possible for a man to acquire the idea, to possess the beauty, which a great book contains, without staking his claim by pasting his bookplate inside the cover. Having a fine library doesn't prove that its owner has a mind enriched by books; it proves nothing more than that he, his father, or his wife, was rich enough to buy them. 5

There are three kinds of book owners. The first has all the stan-   6
dard sets and best-sellers—unread, untouched. (This deluded individual owns woodpulp and ink, not books.) The second has a great
many books—a few of them read through, most of them dipped into,
but all of them as clean and shiny as the day they were bought. (This
person would probably like to make books his own, but is restrained
by a false respect for their physical appearance.) The third has a few
books or many—every one of them dog-eared and dilapidated,
shaken and loosened by continual use, marked and scribbled in from
front to back. (This man owns books.)

Is it false respect, you may ask, to preserve intact and unblem-   7
ished a beautifully printed book, an elegantly bound edition? Of
course not. I'd no more scribble all over the first edition of *Paradise
Lost* than I'd give my baby a set of crayons and an original Rembrandt!
I wouldn't mark up a painting or a statue. Its soul, so to speak, is in-
separable from its body. And the beauty of a rare edition or of a richly
manufactured volume is like that of a painting or a statue.

But the soul of a book *can* be separated from its body. A book is   8
more like the score of a piece of music than it is like a painting. No
great musician confuses a symphony with the printed sheets of
music. Arturo Toscanini reveres Brahms, but Toscanini's score of
the C-minor Symphony is so thoroughly marked up that no one but
the maestro himself can read it. The reason why a great conductor
makes notations on his musical scores—marks them up again and
again each time he returns to study them—is the reason why you
should mark up your books. If your respect for magnificent binding
or typography gets in the way, buy yourself a cheap edition and pay
your respects to the author.

Why is marking up a book indispensable to reading it? First, it   9
keeps you awake. (And I don't mean merely conscious; I mean wide
awake.) In the second place, reading, if it is active, is thinking, and
thinking tends to express itself in words, spoken or written. The
marked book is usually the thought-through book. Finally, writing
helps you remember the thoughts you had, or the thoughts the author expressed. Let me develop these three points.

If reading is to accomplish anything more than passing time, it   10
must be active. You can't let your eyes glide across the lines of a
book and come up with an understanding of what you have read.
Now an ordinary piece of light fiction, like say, *Gone with the
Wind*, doesn't require the most active kind of reading. The books
you read for pleasure can be read in a state of relaxation, and nothing is lost. But a great book, rich in ideas and beauty, a book that
raises and tries to answer great fundamental questions, demands the
most active reading of which you are capable. You don't absorb the

ideas of John Dewey the way you absorb the crooning of Mr. Vallee. You have to reach for them. That you cannot do while you're asleep.

If, when you've finished reading a book, the pages are filled with 11 your notes, you know that you read actively. The most famous *active* reader of great books I know is President Hutchins, of the University of Chicago. He also has the hardest schedule of business activities of any man I know. He invariably reads with a pencil, and sometimes, when he picks up a book and pencil in the evening, he finds himself, instead of making intelligent notes, drawing what he calls "caviar factories" on the margins. When that happens, he puts the book down. He knows he's too tired to read, and he's just wasting time.

But, you may ask, why is writing necessary? Well, the physical 12 act of writing, with your own hand, brings words and sentences more sharply before your mind and preserves them better in your memory. To set down your reaction to important words and sentences you have read, and the questions they have raised in your mind, is to preserve those reactions and sharpen those questions.

Even if you wrote on a scratch pad, and threw the paper away 13 when you had finished writing, your grasp of the book would be surer. But you don't have to throw the paper away. The margins (top and bottom, as well as side), the end-papers, the very space between the lines, are all available. They aren't sacred. And, best of all, your marks and notes become an integral part of the book and stay there forever. You can pick up the book the following week or year, and there are all your points of agreement, disagreement, doubt, and inquiry. It's like resuming an interrupted conversation with the advantage of being able to pick up where you left off.

And that is exactly what reading a book should be: a conversa- 14 tion between you and the author. Presumably he knows more about the subject than you do; naturally, you'll have the proper humility as you approach him. But don't let anybody tell you that a reader is supposed to be solely on the receiving end. Understanding is a two-way operation; learning doesn't consist in being an empty receptacle. The learner has to question himself and question the teacher. He even has to argue with the teacher, once he understands what the teacher is saying. And marking a book is literally an expression of your differences, or agreements of opinion, with the author.

There are all kinds of devices for marking a book intelligently 15 and fruitfully. Here's the way I do it:

1. *Underlining:* Of major points, of important or forceful state- 16 ments.
2. *Vertical lines at the margin:* To emphasize a statement al- 17 ready underlined.

3. *Star, asterisk, or other doo-dad at the margin:* To be used   18
sparingly, to emphasize the ten or twenty most important
statements in the book. (You may want to fold the bottom
corner of each page on which you use such marks. It won't
hurt the sturdy paper on which most modern books are
printed, and you will be able to take the book off the shelf at
any time and, by opening it at the folded-corner page, refresh
your recollection of the book.)

4. *Numbers in the margin:* To indicate the sequence of points   19
the author makes in developing a single argument.

5. *Numbers of other pages in the margin:* To indicate where   20
else in the book the author made points relevant to the point
marked; to tie up the ideas in a book, which, though they
may be separated by many pages, belong together.

6. *Circling of key words or phrases.*   21

7. *Writing in the margin, or at the top or bottom of the page,*   22
for the sake of: Recording questions (and perhaps answers)
which a passage raised in your mind; reducing a complicated
discussion to a simple statement; recording the sequence of
major points right through the book. I use the end-papers at
the back of the book to make a personal index of the author's
points in the order of their appearance.

The front end-papers are, to me, the most important. Some peo-   23
ple reserve them for a fancy bookplate. I reserve them for fancy
thinking. After I have finished reading the book and making my personal index on the back endpapers, I turn to the front and try to outline the book, not page by page, or point by point (I've already done
that at the back), but as an integrated structure, with a basic unity
and an order of parts. This outline is, to me, the measure of my understanding of the work.

If you're a die-hard anti-book-marker, you may object that the   24
margins, the space between the lines, and the end-papers don't give
you room enough. All right. How about using a scratch-pad slightly
smaller than the page-size of the book—so that the edges of the
sheets won't protrude? Make your index, outlines, and even your
notes on the pad, and then insert these sheets permanently inside
the front and back covers of the book.

Or, you may say that this business of marking books is going to   25
slow up your reading. It probably will. That's one of the reasons for
doing it. Most of us have been taken in by the notion that speed of
reading is a measure of our intelligence. There is no such thing as the
right speed for intelligent reading. Some things should be read
quickly and effortlessly, and some should be read slowly and even la-

boriously. The sign of intelligence in reading is the ability to read different things differently according to their worth. In the case of good books, the point is not to see how many of them you can get through, but rather how many can get through you—how many you can make your own. A few friends are better than a thousand acquaintances. If this be your aim, as it should be, you will not be impatient if it takes more time and effort to read a great book than it does a newspaper.

You may have one final objection to marking books. You can't lend them to your friends because nobody else can read them without being distracted by your notes. Furthermore, you won't want to lend them because a marked copy is a kind of intellectual diary, and lending it is almost like giving your mind away.   26

If your friend wishes to read your *Plutarch's Lives*, "Shakespeare," or *The Federalist Papers*, tell him, gently but firmly, to buy   27
a copy. You will lend him your car or your coat—but your books are as much a part of you as your head or your heart.

QUESTIONS OF CONTENT

1. Why does Adler think it is fine to mark up a book of your own?
2. How many kinds of book owners are there? Which kind does Adler clearly think is best? What is your opinion?
3. What are three useful results of marking in a book when reading it? Which do you think matters most?
4. How can writing in a book result in a "conversation" with its author, as Adler claims? Why is such a conversation useful?
5. Beginning with paragraph 16, Adler describes how he marks a book; which one of his techniques seems most useful to you, and why?

QUESTIONS OF FORM

1. Which of his examples or allusions indicate that Adler wrote this essay over fifty years ago? What changes would you make to update the essay?
2. How does the classification and comparison/contrast of book owners in paragraph 6 advance Adler's argument?
3. Adler uses analogies in paragraphs 4 and 8; what does he compare and how successful are these analogies in clarifying and supporting his points?
4. Adler's essay is clearly a claim of policy; how would you summarize his claim, and what warrant related to reading books lies behind his claim?

5. Adler makes three concessions, where he admits to two drawbacks of marking up a book when reading it; what are they and how appropriate is his placement of them in his essay?

SUGGESTIONS FOR WRITING

1. Write an essay in which you discuss the value of Adler's advice for a student in a subject or course other than English.
2. Choose one of the other essays in this Classic Arguments section and show, using specific references to that essay, how it "demands the most active reading of which you are capable" (paragraph 10).
3. Choose some type of reading material that does not need to be marked, in your opinion, and write a well-supported persuasive essay demonstrating why it doesn't.

Letter from Birmingham Jail

MARTIN LUTHER KING, JR.

An ordained Baptist minister who received a Ph.D. in theology from Boston University, the Reverend Martin Luther King, Jr., (1929–1968) was the foremost leader of the civil rights movement of the 1960s. But Dr. King's efforts to secure civil liberties and fair treatment for black Americans actually began in the 1950s, first in organizing a boycott of public buses with segregated seating in Montgomery, Alabama, and then as the director and one of the founders of the Southern Christian Leadership Conference. Jailed repeatedly for his civil rights efforts, Dr. King wrote this essay in 1963, in response to criticism of his work in Birmingham, Alabama, by local white clergy. An advocate of nonviolence, he is following the path of Thoreau and Gandhi when he argues here for civil disobedience as a reasonable means, under the circumstances, for advancing the cause of integration. The next year he was awarded the Nobel Peace Prize for his work. Ironically, four years later, violence, in the form of an assassin's bullet, cut short Dr. King's efforts on behalf of equality and justice.

April 16, 1963

My Dear Fellow Clergymen:

While confined here in the Birmingham city jail, I came across your recent statement calling my present activities "unwise and un-   1 timely." Seldom do I pause to answer criticism of my work and ideas. If I sought to answer all the criticisms that cross my desk, my secretaries would have little time for anything other than such correspondence in the course of the day, and I would have no time for constructive work. But since I feel that you are men of genuine good will and that your criticisms are sincerely set forth, I want to try to answer your statement in what I hope will be patient and reasonable terms.

I think I should indicate why I am here in Birmingham, since   2
you have been influenced by the view which argues against "outsiders coming in." I have the honor of serving as president of the Southern Christian Leadership Conference, an organization operating in every southern state, with headquarters in Atlanta, Georgia. We have some eighty-five affiliated organizations across the South, and one of them is the Alabama Christian Movement for Human Rights. Frequently we share staff, educational and financial resources with our affiliates. Several months ago the affiliate here in Birmingham asked us to be on call to engage in a nonviolent direct-action program if such were deemed necessary. We readily consented, and when the hour came we lived up to our promise. So I, along with several members of my staff, am here because I was invited here. I am here because I have organizational ties here.

But more basically, I am in Birmingham because injustice is   3
here. Just as the prophets of the eighth century B.C. left their villages and carried their "thus saith the Lord" far beyond the boundaries of their home towns, and just as the Apostle Paul left his village of Tarsus and carried the gospel of Jesus Christ to the far corners of the Greco-Roman world, so am I compelled to carry the gospel of freedom beyond my own home town. Like Paul, I must constantly respond to the Macedonian call for aid.

Moreover, I am cognizant of the interrelatedness of all commu-   4
nities and states. I cannot sit idly by in Atlanta and not be concerned about what happens in Birmingham. Injustice anywhere is a threat to justice everywhere. We are caught in an inescapable network of mutuality, tied in a single garment of destiny. Whatever affects one directly, affects all indirectly. Never again can we afford to live with the narrow, provincial "outside agitator" idea. Anyone who lives inside the United States can never be considered an outsider anywhere within its bounds.

You deplore the demonstrations taking place in Birmingham.   5
But your statement, I am sorry to say, fails to express a similar concern for the conditions that brought about the demonstrations. I am sure that none of you would want to rest content with the superficial kind of social analysis that deals merely with effects and does

not grapple with underlying causes. It is unfortunate that demonstrations are taking place in Birmingham, but it is even more unfortunate that the city's white power structure left the Negro community with no alternative.

In any nonviolent campaign there are four basic steps: collection of the facts to determine whether injustices exist; negotiation; self-purification; and direct action. We have gone through all these steps in Birmingham. There can be no gainsaying the fact that racial injustice engulfs this community. Birmingham is probably the most thoroughly segregated city in the United States. Its ugly record of brutality is widely known. Negroes have experienced grossly unjust treatment in the courts. There have been more unsolved bombings of Negro homes and churches in Birmingham than in any other city in the nation. These are the hard, brutal facts of the case. On the basis of these conditions, Negro leaders sought to negotiate with the city fathers. But the latter consistently refused to engage in good-faith negotiation.

Then, last September, came the opportunity to talk with leaders of Birmingham's economic community. In the course of the negotiations, certain promises were made by the merchants—for example, to remove the stores' humiliating racial signs. On the basis of these promises, the Reverend Fred Shuttlesworth and the leaders of the Alabama Christian Movement for Human Rights agreed to a moratorium on all demonstrations. As the weeks and months went by, we realized that we were the victims of a broken promise. A few signs, briefly removed, returned; the others remained.

As in so many past experiences, our hopes had been blasted, and the shadow of deep disappointment settled upon us. We had no alternative except to prepare for direct action, whereby we would present our very bodies as a means of laying our case before the conscience of the local and the national community. Mindful of the difficulties involved, we decided to undertake a process of self-purification. We began a series of workshops on nonviolence, and we repeatedly asked ourselves: "Are you able to accept blows without retaliating?" "Are you able to endure the ordeal of jail?" We decided to schedule our direct-action program for the Easter season, realizing that except for Christmas, this is the main shopping period of the year. Knowing that a strong economic-withdrawal program would be the by-product of direct action, we felt that this would be the best time to bring pressure to bear on the merchants for the needed change.

Then it occurred to us that Birmingham's mayoral election was coming up in March, and we speedily decided to postpone action until after election day. When we discovered that the Commissioner of Public Safety, Eugene "Bull" Connor, had piled up enough votes to be in the run-off, we decided again to postpone action until the day after the run-off so that the demonstrations could not be used to cloud the issues. Like many others, we waited to see Mr. Connor defeated, and to this end we endured postponement after postponement. Having aided in this community need, we felt that our direct action program could be delayed no longer.

You may well ask: "Why direct action? Why sit-ins, marches   10
and so forth? Isn't negotiation a better path?" You are quite right in calling for negotiation. Indeed, this is the very purpose of direct action. Nonviolent direct action seeks to create such a crisis and foster such a tension that a community which has constantly refused to negotiate is forced to confront the issue. It seeks so to dramatize the issue that it can no longer be ignored. My citing the creation of tension as part of the work of the nonviolent-resister may sound rather shocking, But I must confess that I am not afraid of the word "tension." I have earnestly opposed violent tension, but there is a type of constructive, nonviolent tension which is necessary for growth. Just as Socrates felt that it was necessary to create a tension in the mind so that individuals could arise from the bondage of myths and half-truths to the unfettered realm of creative analysis and objective appraisal, so must we see the need for nonviolent gadflies to create the kind of tension in society that will help men rise from the dark depths of prejudice and racism to the majestic heights of understanding and brotherhood.

The purpose of our direct-action program is to create a situation   11
so crisis-packed that it will inevitably open the door to negotiation. I therefore concur with you in your call for negotiation. Too long has our beloved Southland been bogged down in a tragic effort to live in monologue rather than dialogue.

One of the basic points in your statement is that the action that   12
I and my associates have taken in Birmingham is untimely. Some have asked: "Why didn't you give the new city administration time to act?" The only answer that I can give to this query is that the new Birmingham administration must be prodded about as much as the outgoing one, before it will act. We are sadly mistaken if we feel that the election of Albert Boutwell as mayor will bring the millennium to Birmingham. While Mr. Boutwell is a much more gentle person than Mr. Connor, they are both segregationists, dedicated to maintenance of the status quo. I have hope that Mr. Boutwell will be reasonable enough to see the futility of massive resistance to desegregation. But he will not see this without pressure from devotees of civil rights. My friends, I must say to you that we have not made a single gain in civil rights without determined legal and nonviolent

pressure. Lamentably, it is an historical fact that privileged groups seldom give up their privileges voluntarily. Individuals may see the moral light and voluntarily give up their unjust posture; but, as Reinhold Niebuhr has reminded us, groups tend to be more immoral than individuals.

We know through painful experience that freedom is never vol- 13
untarily given by the oppressor; it must be demanded by the oppressed. Frankly, I have yet to engage in a direct-action campaign that was "well timed" in the view of those who have not suffered unduly from the disease of segregation. For years now I have heard the word "Wait! " It rings in the ear of every Negro with piercing familiarity. This "Wait" has almost always meant "Never." We must come to see, with one of our distinguished jurists, that "justice too long delayed is justice denied."

We have waited for more than 340 years for our constitutional 14
and God-given rights. The nations of Asia and Africa are moving with jetlike speed toward gaining political independence, but we still creep at horse-and-buggy pace toward gaining a cup of coffee at a lunch counter. Perhaps it is easy for those who have never felt the stinging darts of segregation to say, "Wait." But when you have seen vicious mobs lynch your mothers and fathers at will and drown your sisters and brothers at whim; when you have seen hate-filled policemen curse, kick and even kill your black brothers and sisters; when you see the vast majority of your twenty million Negro brothers smothering in an airtight cage of poverty in the midst of an affluent society; when you suddenly find your tongue twisted and your speech stammering as you seek to explain to your six-year-old daughter why she can't go to the public amusement park that has just been advertised on television, and see tears welling up in her eyes when she is told that Funtown is closed to colored children, and see ominous clouds of inferiority beginning to form in her little mental sky, and see her beginning to distort her personality by developing an unconscious bitterness toward white people; when you have to concoct an answer for a five-year-old son who is asking: "Daddy, why do white people treat colored people so mean?"; when you take a cross-country drive and find it necessary to sleep night after night in the uncomfortable corners of your automobile because no motel will accept you; when you are humiliated day in and day out by nagging signs reading "white" and "colored"; when your first name becomes "nigger," your middle name becomes "boy" (however old you are) and your last name becomes "John," and your wife and mother are never given the respected title "Mrs."; when you are harried by day and haunted by night by the fact that you are a Negro, living constantly at tiptoe stance, never quite knowing what to ex-

pect next, and are plagued with inner fears and outer resentments; when you are forever fighting a degenerating sense of "nobodiness"—then you will understand why we find it difficult to wait. There comes a time when the cup of endurance runs over, and men are no longer willing to be plunged into the abyss of despair. I hope, sirs, you can understand our legitimate and unavoidable impatience.

You express a great deal of anxiety over our willingness to break   15
laws. This is certainly a legitimate concern. Since we so diligently urged people to obey the Supreme Court's decision of 1954 outlawing segregation in the public schools, at first glance it may seem rather paradoxical for us consciously to break laws. One may well ask: "How can you advocate breaking some laws and obeying others?" The answer lies in the fact that there are two types of laws: just and unjust. I would be the first to advocate obeying just laws. One has not only a legal but a moral responsibility to obey just laws. Conversely, one has a moral responsibility to disobey unjust laws. I would agree with St. Augustine that "an unjust law is no law at all."

Now, what is the difference between the two? How does one de-   16
termine whether a law is just or unjust? A just law is a man-made code that squares with the moral law or the law of God. An unjust law is a code that is out of harmony with the moral law. To put it in the terms of St. Thomas Aquinas: An unjust law is a human law that is not rooted in eternal law and natural law. Any law that uplifts human personality is just. Any law that degrades human personality is unjust. All segregation statutes are unjust because segregation distorts the soul and damages the personality. It gives the segregator a false sense of superiority and the segregated a false sense of inferiority. Segregation, to use the terminology of the Jewish philosopher Martin Buber, substitutes an "I-it" relationship for an "I-thou" relationship and ends up relegating persons to the status of things. Hence segregation is not only politically, economically and sociologically unsound, it is morally wrong and sinful. Paul Tillich has said that sin is separation. Is not segregation an existential expression of man's tragic separation, his awful estrangement, his terrible sinfulness? Thus it is that I can urge men to obey the 1954 decision of the Supreme Court, for it is morally right; and I can urge them to disobey segregation ordinances, for they are morally wrong.

Let us consider a more concrete example of just and unjust laws.   17
An unjust law is a code that a numerical or power majority group compels a minority group to obey but does not make binding on itself. This is *difference* made legal. By the same token, a just law is a code that a majority compels a minority to follow and that it is willing to follow itself. This is *sameness* made legal.

Let me give another explanation. A law is unjust if it is inflicted   18
on a minority that, as a result of being denied the right to vote, had
no part in enacting or devising the law. Who can say that the legislature of Alabama which set up that state's segregation laws was democratically elected? Throughout Alabama all sorts of devious
methods are used to prevent Negroes from becoming registered voters, and there are some counties in which, even though Negroes
constitute a majority of the population, not a single Negro is registered. Can any law enacted under such circumstances be considered
democratically structured?

Sometimes a law is just on its face and unjust in its application.   19
For instance, I have been arrested on a charge of parading without a
permit. Now, there is nothing wrong in having an ordinance which
requires a permit for a parade. But such an ordinance becomes unjust when it is used to maintain segregation and to deny citizens the
First-Amendment privilege of peaceful assembly and protest.

I hope you are able to see the distinction I am trying to point out.   20
In no sense do I advocate evading or defying the law, as would the
rabid segregationist. That would lead to anarchy. One who breaks an
unjust law must do so openly, lovingly, and with a willingness to accept the penalty. I submit that an individual who breaks a law that
conscience tells him is unjust, and who willingly accepts the penalty
of imprisonment in order to arouse the conscience of the cornmunity
over its injustice, is in reality expressing the highest respect for law.

Of course, there is nothing new about this kind of civil disobe-   21
dience. It was evidenced sublimely in the refusal of Shadrach, Me-
shach and Abednego to obey the laws of Nebuchadnezzar, on the
ground that a higher moral law was at stake. It was practiced su-
perbly by the early Christians, who were willing to face hungry lions
and the excruciating pain of chopping blocks rather than submit to
certain unjust laws of the Roman Empire. To a degree, academic
freedom is a reality today because Socrates practiced civil disobedience. In our own nation, the Boston Tea Party represented a massive
act of civil disobedience.

We should never forget that everything Adolf Hitler did in Ger-   22
many was "legal" and everything that Hungarian freedom fighters
did in Hungary was "illegal." It was "illegal" to aid and comfort a
Jew in Hitler's Germany. Even so, I am sure that, had I lived in Germany at the time, I would have aided and comforted my Jewish
brothers. If today I lived in a Communist country where certain
principles dear to the Christian faith are suppressed, I would openly
advocate disobeying that country's antireligious laws.

I must make two honest confessions to you, my Christian and   23
Jewish brothers. I must confess that over the past few years I have

been gravely disappointed with the white moderate. I have reached the regrettable conclusion that the Negro's great stumbling block in his stride toward freedom is not the White Citizen's Counciler or the Ku Klux Klanner, but the white moderate, who is more devoted to "order" than to justice; who prefers a negative peace which is the absence of tension to a positive peace which is the presence of justice; who constantly says: "I agree with you in the goal you seek, but I cannot agree with your methods of direct action"; who paternalistically believes he can set the timetable for another man's freedom; who lives by a mythical concept of time and who constantly advises the Negro to wait for a "more convenient season." Shallow understanding from people of good will is more frustrating than absolute misunderstanding from people of ill will. Lukewarm acceptance is much more bewildering than outright rejection.

I had hoped that the white moderate would understand that law 24 and order exist for the purpose of establishing justice and that when they fail in this purpose they become the dangerously structured dams that block the flow of social progress. I had hoped that the white moderate would understand that the present tension in the South is a necessary phase of the transition from an obnoxious negative peace, in which the Negro passively accepted his unjust plight, to a substantive and positive peace, in which all men will respect the dignity and worth of human personality. Actually, we who engage in nonviolent direct action are not the creators of tension. We merely bring to the surface the hidden tension that is already alive. We bring it out in the open, where it can be seen and dealt with. Like a boil that can never be cured so long as it is covered up but must be opened with all its ugliness to the natural medicines of air and light, injustice must be exposed, with all the tension its exposure creates, to the light of human conscience and the air of national opinion before it can be cured.

In your statement you assert that our actions, even though 25 peaceful, must be condemned because they precipitate violence. But is this a logical assertion? Isn't this like condemning a robbed man because his possession of money precipitated the evil act of robbery? Isn't this like condemning Socrates because his unswerving commitment to truth and his philosophical inquiries precipitated the act by the misguided populace in which they made him drink hemlock? Isn't this like condemning Jesus because his unique God-consciousness and never-ceasing devotion to God's will precipitated the evil act of crucifixion? We must come to see that, as the federal courts have consistently affirmed, it is wrong to urge an individual to cease his efforts to gain his basic constitutional rights because the quest may precipitate violence. Society must protect the robbed and punish the robber.

I had also hoped that the white moderate would reject the myth concerning time in relation to the struggle for freedom. I have just received a letter from a white brother in Texas. He writes: "All Christians know that the colored people will receive equal rights eventually, but it is possible that you are in too great a religious hurry. It has taken Christianity almost two thousand years to accomplish what it has. The teachings of Christ take time to come to earth." Such an attitude stems from a tragic misconception of time, from the strangely irrational notion that there is something in the very flow of time that will inevitably cure all ills. Actually, time itself is neutral; it can be used either destructively or constructively. More and more I feel that the people of ill will have used time much more effectively than have the people of good will. We will have to repent in this generation not merely for the hateful words and actions of the bad people but for the appalling silence of the good people. Human progress never rolls in on wheels of inevitability; it comes through the tireless efforts of men willing to be co-workers with God, and without this hard work, time itself becomes an ally of the forces of social stagnation. We must use time creatively, in the knowledge that the time is always ripe to do right. Now is the time to make real the promise of democracy and transform our pending national elegy into a creative psalm of brotherhood. Now is the time to lift our national policy from the quicksand of racial injustice to the solid rock of human dignity.

You speak of our activity in Birmingham as extreme. At first I was rather disappointed that fellow clergymen would see my nonviolent efforts as those of an extremist. I began thinking about the fact that I stand in the middle of two opposing forces in the Negro community. One is a force of complacency, made up in part of Negroes who, as a result of long years of oppression, are so drained of self-respect and a sense of "somebodiness" that they have adjusted to segregation; and in part of a few middle-class Negroes who, because of a degree of academic and economic security and because in some ways they profit by segregation, have become insensitive to the problems of the masses. The other force is one of bitterness and hatred, and it comes perilously close to advocating violence. It is expressed in the various black nationalist groups that are springing up across the nation, the largest and best-known being Elijah Muhammad's Muslim movement. Nourished by the Negro's frustration over the continued existence of racial discrimination, this movement is made up of people who have lost faith in America, who have absolutely repudiated Christianity, and who have concluded that the white man is an incorrigible "devil."

I have tried to stand between these two forces, saying that we need emulate neither the "do-nothingism" of the complacent nor the hatred and despair of the black nationalist. For there is the more excellent way of love and nonviolent protest. I am grateful to God that, through the influence of the Negro church, the way of nonviolence became an integral part of our struggle.

If this philosophy had not emerged, by now many streets of the South would, I am convinced, be flowing with blood. And I am further convinced that if our white brothers dismiss as "rabble-rousers" and "outside agitators" those of us who employ nonviolent direct action, and if they refuse to support our nonviolent efforts, millions of Negroes will, out of frustration and despair, seek solace and security in black-nationalist ideologies—a development that would inevitably lead to a frightening racial nightmare.

Oppressed people cannot remain oppressed forever. The yearning for freedom eventually manifests itself, and that is what has happened to the American Negro. Something within has reminded him of his birthright of freedom, and something without has reminded him that it can be gained. Consciously or unconsciously, he has been caught up by the *Zeitgeist,* and with his black brothers of Africa and his brown and yellow brothers of Asia, South America and the Caribbean, the United States Negro is moving with a sense of great urgency toward the promised land of racial justice. If one recognizes this vital urge that has engulfed the Negro community, one should readily understand why public demonstrations are taking place. The Negro has many pent-up resentments and latent frustrations, and he must release them. So let him march; let him make prayer pilgrimages to the city hall; let him go on freedom rides—and try to understand why he must do so. If his repressed emotions are not released in nonviolent ways, they will seek expression through violence; this is not a threat but a fact of history. So I have not said to my people: "Get rid of your discontent." Rather, I have tried to say that this normal and healthy discontent can be channeled into the creative outlet of nonviolent direct action. And now this approach is being termed extremist.

But though I was initially disappointed at being categorized as an extremist, as I continued to think about the matter I gradually gained a measure of satisfaction from the label. Was not Jesus an extremist for love: "Love your enemies, bless them that curse you, do good to them that hate you, and pray for them which despitefully use you, and persecute you." Was not Amos an extremist for justice: "Let justice roll down like waters and righteousness like an ever-flowing stream." Was not Paul an extremist for the Christian gospel: "I bear in my body the marks of the Lord Jesus." Was not Martin Luther an extremist: "Here I stand; I cannot do otherwise, so help me God." And John Bunyan: "I will stay in jail to the end of my days before I make a butchery of my conscience. " And Abraham Lincoln "This nation cannot survive half slave and half free." And Thomas Jefferson: "We hold these truths to be self-evident, that all men are created equal . . . ." So the question is not whether we will be extremists, but what kind of extremists we will be. Will we be extremists for hate or for love? Will we be extremists for the preservation of injustice or for the extension of justice? In that dramatic scene on Calvary's hill three men were crucified. We must never forget that all three were crucified for the same crime—the crime of extremism. Two were extremists for immorality, and thus fell below their environment. The other, Jesus Christ, was an extremist for love, truth and goodness, and thereby rose above his environment. Perhaps the South, the nation and the world are in dire need of creative extremists.

I had hoped that the white moderate would see this need. Perhaps I was too optimistic; perhaps I expected too much. I suppose I should have realized that few members of the oppressor race can understand the deep groans and passionate yearnings of the oppressed race, and still fewer have the vision to see that injustice must be rooted out by strong, persistent and determined action. I am thankful, however, that some of our white brothers in the South have grasped the meaning of this social revolution and committed themselves to it. They are still all too few in quantity, but they are big in quality. Some—such as Ralph McGill, Lillian Smith, Harry Golden, James McBride Dabbs, Ann Braden and Sarah Patton Boyle—have written about our struggle in eloquent and prophetic terms. Others have marched with us down nameless streets of the South. They have languished in filthy, roach-infested jails, suffering the abuse and brutality of policemen who view them as "dirty nigger-lovers." Unlike so many of their moderate brothers and sisters, they have recognized the urgency of the moment and sensed the need for powerful "action" antidotes to combat the disease of segregation. 32

Let me take note of my other major disappointment. I have been so greatly disappointed with the white church and its leadership. Of course, there are some notable exceptions. I am not unmindful of the fact that each of you has taken some significant stands on this issue. I commend you, Reverend Stallings, for your Christian stand on this past Sunday, in welcoming Negroes to your worship service on a nonsegregated basis. I commend the Catholic leaders of this state for integrating Spring Hill College several years ago. 33

But despite these notable exceptions, I must honestly reiterate   34
that I have been disappointed with the church. I do not say this as
one of those negative critics who can always find something wrong
with the church. I say this as a minister of the gospel, who loves the
church; who was nurtured in its bosom; who has been sustained by
its spiritual blessings and who will remain true to it as long as the
cord of life shall lengthen.

When I was suddenly catapulted into the leadership of the bus   35
protest in Montgomery, Alabama, a few years ago, I felt we would
be supported by the white church. I felt that the white ministers,
priests and rabbis of the South would be among our strongest allies.
Instead, some have been outright opponents, refusing to understand
the freedom movement and misrepresenting its leaders; all too
many others have been more cautious than courageous and have remained silent behind the anesthetizing security of stained-glass
windows.

In spite of my shattered dreams, I came to Birmingham with the   36
hope that the white religious leadership of this community would
see the justice of our cause and, with deep moral concern, would
serve as the channel through which our just grievances could reach
the power structure. I had hoped that each of you would understand.
But again I have been disappointed.

I have heard numerous southern religious leaders admonish   37
their worshipers to comply with a desegregation decision because it
is the law, but I have longed to hear white ministers declare: "Follow this decree because integration is morally right and because the
Negro is your brother." In the midst of blatant injustices inflicted
upon the Negro, I have watched white churchmen stand on the side-
line and mouth pious irrelevancies and sanctimonious trivialities.
In the midst of a mighty struggle to rid our nation of racial and economic injustice, I have heard many ministers say: "Those are social
issues, with which the gospel has no real concern." And I have
watched many churches commit themselves to a completely other-
worldly religion which makes a strange, un-Biblical distinction between body and soul, between the sacred and the secular.

I have traveled the length and breadth of Alabama, Mississippi   38
and all the other southern states. On sweltering summer days and
crisp autumn mornings I have looked at the South's beautiful
churches with their lofty spires pointing heavenward. I have beheld
the impressive outlines of her massive religious-education build-
ings. Over and over I have found myself asking: "What kind of people worship here? Who is their God? Where were their voices when
the lips of Governor Barnett dripped with words of interposition and
nullification? Where were they when Governor Wallace gave a clar-

ion call for defiance and hatred? Where were their voices of support when bruised and weary Negro men and women decided to rise from the dark dungeons of complacency to the bright hills of creative protest?"

Yes, these questions are still in my mind. In deep disappointment I have wept over the laxity of the church. But be assured that my tears have been tears of love. There can be no deep disappointment where there is not deep love. Yes, I love the church. How could I do otherwise? I am in the rather unique position of being the son, the grandson and the great-grandson of preachers. Yes, I see the church as the body of Christ. But, oh! How we have blemished and scarred that body through social neglect and through fear of being nonconformists. 39

There was a time when the church was very powerful—in the time when the early Christians rejoiced at being deemed worthy to suffer for what they believed. In those days the church was not merely a thermometer that recorded the ideas and principles of popular opinion; it was a thermostat that transformed the mores of society. Whenever the early Christians entered a town, the people in power became disturbed and immediately sought to convict the Christians for being "disturbers of the peace" and "outside agitators." But the Christians pressed on, in the conviction that they were "a colony of heaven," called to obey God rather than man. Small in number, they were big in commitment. They were too God-intoxicated to be "astronomically intimidated." By their effort and example they brought an end to such ancient evils as infanticide and gladiatorial contests. 40

Things are different now. So often the contemporary church is a weak, ineffectual voice with an uncertain sound. So often it is an archdefender of the status quo. Far from being disturbed by the presence of the church, the power structure of the average community is consoled by the church's silent—and often even vocal—sanction of things as they are. 41

But the judgment of God is upon the church as never before. If today's church does not recapture the sacrificial spirit of the early church, it will lose its authenticity, forfeit the loyalty of millions, and be dismissed as an irrelevant social club with no meaning for the twentieth century. Every day I meet young people whose disappointment with the church has turned into outright disgust. 42

Perhaps I have once again been too optimistic. Is organized religion too inextricably bound to the status quo to save our nation and the world? Perhaps I must turn my faith to the inner spiritual church, the church within the church, as the true *ekklesia* and the hope of the world. But again I am thankful to God that some noble 43 souls from the ranks of organized religion have broken loose from the paralyzing chains of conformity and joined us as active partners in the struggle for freedom. They have left their secure congregations and walked the streets of Albany, Georgia, with us. They have gone down the highways of the South on tortuous rides for freedom. Yes, they have gone to jail with us. Some have been dismissed from their churches, have lost the support of their bishops and fellow ministers. But they have acted in the faith that right defeated is stronger than evil triumphant. Their witness has been the spiritual salt that has preserved the true meaning of the gospel in these troubled times. They have carved a tunnel of hope through the dark mountain of disappointment.

I hope the church as a whole will meet the challenge of this decisive hour. But even if the church does not come to the aid of justice, I have no despair about the future. I have no fear about the outcome of our struggle in Birmingham, even if our motives are at present misunderstood. We will reach the goal of freedom in Birmingham and all over the nation, because the goal of America is freedom. Abused and scorned though we may be, our destiny is tied up with America's destiny. Before the pilgrims landed at Plymouth, we were here. Before the pen of Jefferson etched the majestic words of the Declaration of Independence across the pages of history, we were here. For more than two centuries our forebears labored in this country without wages; they made cotton king; they built the homes of their masters while suffering gross injustice and shameful humiliation—and yet out of a bottomless vitality they continued to thrive and develop. If the inexpressible cruelties of slavery could not stop us, the opposition we now face will surely fail. We will win our freedom because the sacred heritage of our nation and the eternal will of God are embodied in our echoing demands. 44

Before closing I feel impelled to mention one other point in your statement that has troubled me profoundly. You warmly commended the Birmingham police force for keeping "order" and "preventing violence." I doubt that you would have so warmly commended the police force if you had seen its dogs sinking their teeth into unarmed, nonviolent Negroes. I doubt that you would so quickly commend the policemen if you were to observe their ugly and inhumane treatment of Negroes here in the city jail; if you were to watch them push and curse old Negro women and young Negro girls; if you were to see them slap and kick old Negro men and young boys; if you were to observe them, as they did on two occasions, refuse to give us food because we wanted to sing our grace together. I cannot join you in your praise of the Birmingham police department. 45

It is true that the police have exercised a degree of discipline in   46
handling the demonstrators. In this sense they have conducted
themselves rather "nonviolently" in public. But for what purpose?
To preserve the evil system of segregation. Over the past few years
I have consistently preached that nonviolence demands that the
means we use must be as pure as the ends we seek. I have tried to
make clear that it is wrong to use immoral means to attain moral
ends. But now I must affirm that it is just as wrong, or perhaps even
more so, to use moral means to preserve immoral ends. Perhaps Mr.
Connor and his policemen have been rather nonviolent in public, as
was Chief Pritchett in Albany, Georgia, but they have used the
moral means of nonviolence to maintain the immoral end of racial
injustice. As T. S. Eliot has said: "The last temptation is the greatest treason: To do the right deed for the wrong reason."

I wish you had commended the Negro sit-inners and demon-   47
strators of Birmingham for their sublime courage, their willingness
to suffer and their amazing discipline in the midst of great provoca-
tion. One day the South will recognize its real heroes. They will be
the James Merediths, with the noble sense of purpose that enables
them to face jeering and hostile mobs, and with the agonizing lone-
liness that characterizes the life of the pioneer. They will be old, oppressed, battered Negro women, symbolized in a seventy-two-year-
old woman in Montgomery, Alabama, who rose up with a sense of
dignity and with her people decided not to ride segregated buses, and
who responded with ungrammatical profundity to one who inquired
about her weariness: "My feets is tired, but my soul is at rest." They
will be the young high school and college students, the young ministers of the gospel and a host of their elders, courageously and nonviolently sitting in at lunch counters and willingly going to jail for
conscience's sake. One day the South will know that when these
disinherited children of God sat down at lunch counters, they were
in reality standing up for what is best in the American dream and
for the most sacred values in our Judaeo-Christian heritage, thereby
bringing our nation back to those great wells of democracy which
were dug deep by the founding fathers in their formulation of the
Constitution and the Declaration of Independence.

Never before have I written so long a letter. I'm afraid it is much   48
too long to take your precious time. I can assure you that it would
have been much shorter if I had been writing from a comfortable
desk, but what else can one do when he is alone in a narrow jail cell,
other than write long letters, think long thoughts and pray long
prayers?

If I have said anything in this letter that overstates the truth and   49
indicates an unreasonable impatience, I beg you to forgive me. If I

have said anything that understates the truth and indicates my havi-
iig a patience that allows me to settlc for anything less than brotherhood, I beg God to forgive me.

I hope this letter finds you strong in the faith. I also hope that   50
circumstances will soon make it possible for me to meet each of
you, not as an integrationist or a civil-rights leader but as a fellow
clergyman and a Christian brother. Let us all hope that the dark
clouds of racial prejudice will soon pass away and the deep fog of
misunderstanding will be lifted from our fear-drenched communities, and in some not too distant tomorrow the radiant stars of love
and brotherhood will shine over our great nation with all their scin-
tillating beauty.

Yours for the cause of Peace and Brotherhood,

Martin Luther King, Jr.

QUESTIONS OF CONTENT

1. In responding to his fellow clergymen's charge that he is an outsider,
   what three reasons does King give for his presence? What point does
   he make about *any* person living in the United States? How realistic
   or idealistic is his statement there?
2. What are the four basic steps in a nonviolent campaign against injustices, according to King? How carefully had King and his follow-
   ers apparently adhered to those steps in Birmingham in 1963?
3. How does King respond to the suggestion that the Birmingham direct-action campaign was not "well timed," and that he and his fol-
   lowers should "Wait"?
4. How does King differentiate between "just" and "unjust" laws?
   What historical examples does he use for support, and how appropriate are they?
5. King says that he is disappointed with white moderates (paragraphs
   23 through 32) and with the white church and its leaders (33 through
   44); why do you suppose he focuses on these two groups, and by what
   varied means does he support his claims of value regarding them?

QUESTIONS OF FORM

1. You will notice that King frequently refers to the Bible and to religious authorities. Which of his allusions did you find most valuable
   or convincing? Why are such uses especially appropriate in terms of

his primary intended audience? What effect(s) might they have on his general audience?

2. After listing the four basic steps in a nonviolent campaign, where and how does King show that his group fulfilled those in Birmingham? What does his argument gain from this support?

3. What is the value of the rhetorical effect created in paragraph 14 by King's repetition of phrases beginning with "when you"? Where else do you notice his use of repetition for rhetorical effect?

4. King often uses figurative language to heighten the appeal of his argument. Where are three such uses, and how effective are they?

5. King's argument is long and complex, making a variety of claims, supporting those in many ways, and using all three sorts of appeals. Which appeal seems most prominent: logical, ethical, or emotional? Be prepared to point out an effective example of each of the three sorts in this essay.

6. Why do you suppose King included his essay's last three paragraphs? How do they fit into his overall argument?

SUGGESTIONS FOR WRITING

1. Argue for or against one of King's assertions listed below. Use a news event or (events) to support your claim.
   a. "Injustice anywhere is a threat to justice everywhere." (Paragraph 4)
   b. " . . . groups tend to be more immoral than individuals. " (Paragraph 12—attributed to the theologian Reinhold Niebuhr)
   c. "Sometimes a law is just on its face and unjust in its application." (Paragraph 19)
   d. " . . . the time is always ripe to do right." (Paragraph 26)
   e. "Oppressed people cannot remain oppressed forever." (Paragraph 30)

2. Choose the paragraph in King's essay which appeals to you the most, and in an organized paper discuss the key factors in its appeal for you, with particular attention to the accuracy of his language and the strength of his examples.

3. Assume you are one of the white Birmingham religious leaders to whom King's letter was directed. Respond to him in a letter of your own, being sure to identify your assumed religion. (Your instructor may want you to do some background research, especially in newspapers and magazines of the time, so that you can manage this assignment better.)

APPENDIX

A Short Guide to Material and Formal Fallacies

Fallacies are various types of deceptive or erroneous or false reasoning; they cause an argument to be logically flawed, even though that argument may be emotionally persuasive and may appear to be true. A fallacious argument may contain one or several fallacies.

The value of being able to recognize fallacies may already be clear, even before you read the brief descriptions that appear below. For instance, since all of us are consumers, we are confronted every day with fallacious media advertisements and salespersons' propositions. As citizens, we must often consider explanations from officials, pronouncements from government agencies, and speeches from politicians; any of these may contain fallacies. Finally, we can expect, as employees and employers, to have to contend with fallacies in the public and private communications that help business, industry, and professions operate. Therefore, at home and at work, we need to be alert for and ready to resist conscious or unconscious fallacies, in others' arguments or our own. After all, fallacies hinder or even prevent honest, rational discussions and the making of correct, logical decisions.

As an aid to understanding, fallacies are often divided into two broad categories: material and formal. *Material fallacies* (sometimes called informal fallacies) result from errors in the content or wording of arguments, and thus could be separated into two groups (although they overlap in places): emotional and language. These sorts of fallacies tend to be present in arguments that we intuitively recognize as wrong but whose flaws we have trouble explaining.

Formal fallacies (sometimes called structural fallacies) result from errors in the form or structure of deductive arguments. Their conclusions are unacceptable because of those flaws in reasoning, and you should be able to learn to pick out those flaws.

You will see in what follows that some fallacies have several names. They may also be best known by their traditional Latin names, dating from an earlier time when fallacies were a familiar part of rhetorical study in schools. You will need to learn the various names and definitions for fallacies in order to understand and to participate in class discussions and other course exercises.

Material Fallacies

Material fallacies result either from: (1) imprecise or improper use of language, or from (2) appeals to emotion rather than to reason. Here are short discussions, with examples, of some of the most common material fallacies.

Appeal to Force.   This emotion-based fallacy can cause people to act in inappropriate ways, or not to act in appropriate ways. Either real force or the threat of force is used in an attempt to cause the acceptance of a conclusion. The threat may be veiled and non-physical, as in a threat to withhold votes from one politician or to deliver them to an opponent, based on government actions that the politician may influence or control. In contrast, an open threat might include beatings, the brandishing of weapons, kidnappings, bombings, or even war. Appeals to force are the staples of gang warfare and revolutions.

This fallacy is very closely related to another emotion-based fallacy, the *appeal to fear,* which plays upon its audience's sense of danger; you may have seen useful but still fallacious examples in anti-drug and anti-drunk driving public service advertisements. The appeal to fear is a particular favorite of insurance companies, which capitalize upon our legitimate worries concerning potential losses of property, health, or even life itself.

Appeal to the People (ad Populum).   This fallacy is the "my friends and fellow Americans" (or New Yorkers or teachers or Presbyterians or whatever group is being addressed) approach especially favored by some politicians, who hope to hide the flimsiness of an idea or an argument behind a verbal screen that emphasizes attitudes or beliefs that are presumably shared. But emotional language will not suffice as supporting evidence.

Appeal to Pity (ad Misericordiam).   This emotional approach tries to arouse the sympathy or pity of a person or group in order to influence a decision. For instance, a defense attorney may put her client's family prominently on display in the courtroom in an attempt to persuade the jury or judge that the future welfare and happiness of that family depends wholly on lenient treatment of the accused. A student might be using a similar approach when, having missed a class—or wanting to miss one—she or he tells an instructor about the illness, accident, or death of a relative or close friend. If the story is false, the student is both lying and appealing to pity; if the student is telling the truth, then this would be an instance of an appeal to pity only if the student was actually unmoved by the other person's misfortune and was merely using it as an excuse.

Appeal to Tradition. This rather transparent fallacy is based on the assumption that whatever has existed for a long time, or has been repeated fairly regularly for a number of times, is somehow made legitimate by its history. But historical maltreatment of others, for instance as members of a minority group, certainly cannot justify continuation of that bad behavior; it should be easy enough to think of examples of the appearance of this fallacy in arguments involving civil rights, women's rights, animal rights, and the like. The person proposing to maintain a tradition that is dangerous or oppressive should be made to provide reasons or backing, beyond the mere fact of historical precedent, as support for the continuation of that tradition.

Argument ad Hominem (at the Person). This emotional fallacy occurs when someone attacks an adversary's character in the course of an argument. One familiar and open form of the fallacy involves *name calling*, which occurs when a person's ideas are criticized because she or he has some apparent background flaw, such as being a reformed alcohol or drug abuser, or having flunked out of college, or even having served a prison sentence. At other times the fallacy may be more subtle, for instance through the use of familiar psychological labels for neuroses, such as inferiority complex, compulsive behavior, Oedipus complex, and so forth. However, such criticisms, even if true (frequently they are not, or else they are overstated), are generally irrelevant to the points at issue, to which attention must be directed to neutralize this fallacy.

The *genetic* or *stereotypical fallacy* is closely related. In this case, a person's ideas are criticized because of his or her race, sex, religion, nationality, and the like. But even if suspect because of possible self-interest, a feminist's ideas about abortion or a police officer's ideas on capital punishment may be perfectly sound. Certainly in fairness we ought to try to keep the background of a person separate from the ideas she or he supports, and ought to accept or reject any idea on logical, not emotional, grounds.

A pernicious subvariety of these two fallacies is labeled *poisoning the well.* In this case, an attack is made on a person's background or character, or on a person or group originating an idea, before the argument has actually begun.

Bandwagon. This familiar fallacy is really a variety of the appeal to fear, for it profits from our desire to be part of a group, or "in the parade." Thus, because we don't want to be left out, we "jump on the bandwagon." Accordingly, we are often fallaciously encouraged to buy a product because it is the most popular (or so its commercials claim), or we may be urged to support a candidate that polls show is ahead in a political race. Yet we should depend first on logical, not emotional, reasons for the choices we make. The teenager's familiar claim, "Everyone else has one," is not a logical reason; "Everyone else" can be wrong again, just as they have often been before.

Begging the Question (Circular Reasoning). This fallacy might be classed as formal rather than material, for in it the conclusion of a deductive argument is contained among the deductive argument's premises: "Of course cocaine users lack will power. That's why they're cocaine users." This fallacy is very difficult to detect when buried in a lengthy argument or when it is expressed in difficult language, as in this example: "To allow every person unrestricted freedom of speech must always be, on the whole, advantageous to the state; for it is highly conducive to the interests of the society at large when each individual citizen enjoys the liberty, perfectly unlimited, of expressing his or her sentiments." In simpler words: "Free speech is good for the state because it's good for the state when there is free speech." Taking an argument through a full circle does not prove anything.

Dicto Simpliciter (Unqualified Generalization). This fallacy results when an argument is based upon a generalization that is completely inclusive and presented as unequivocally true in all circumstances. "Milk is good for you" is simply not true for everybody; neither is "Alcohol is bad for your health" (physicians sometimes recommend an occasional glass of beer for nursing mothers, to aid their milk flow, and may suggest a daily moderate amount of alcohol for some aged patients).

Either/or (False Dilemma). This fallacy denies that there is any intermediate possibility between two extremes. Examples include:

"Ms. Franklin must be a communist; she won't join the other local business owners in the Chamber of Commerce." "Mary has become an atheist since she went off to college; she hasn't been to church all semester." "Jason wants to become a killer; he just enlisted in the Army." Unfortunately, because such statements too often appeal to our prejudices and ignorance, we sometimes accept them as true without considering any probable alternative explanations.

Equivocation. This language fallacy is produced by accidental or deliberate misuse of two or more meanings of the same word or phrase in a statement. The ambiguous results may be amusing, sometimes in a grim way, as in these sample newspaper headlines: "Mass Murderer Receives Last Rights Before Execution," "Airlines Drop Union Pilots From Flights," "Doctors to Offer Poor Examinations." Equivocation can also occur in serious contexts, thereby causing critical disagreements. This is particularly so when abstract words such as "right," "guarantee," and "natural" are involved. Consider, for instance, the commonly used phrase "lifetime warranty." Without any qualifying information, how can you tell what either word means? Whose "lifetime"? What is covered by the "warranty"? The best policy in such cases is to be sure that all equivocal words are explained or defined, thus greatly reducing the possibility of misunderstandings that may be personally or financially damaging.

Faulty Analogy. This fallacy results when two subjects are compared, and while the two share certain similarities, their differences may be so important that they negate the value of the comparison; a familiar statement used to point out faulty analogy is "You're comparing apples and oranges." Of course, comparing the current world political situation to one 20, 50, or 100 years back may be interesting and even enlightening. But many factors have changed in the intervening time spans, so any conclusions based on this analogy are liable to be imperfect.

A related fallacy is *faulty metaphor*, which makes a comparison based on a few resemblances (or just one), usually to criticize. The language is sometimes lively and colorful, as in this example: "Knee-jerk, milktoast-eating liberals always want to confiscate our guns, leaving us red-blooded American patriots nothing but our teeth and nails as protection for the living treasures of our homes against a host of drug-crazed perverts." But such metaphor-laden statements offer little basis for rational understanding or logical choice.

Hasty (Faulty, Sweeping) Generalization. This fallacy occurs when a proposed inductive conclusion is based on either a too limited sample or number of examples or else is based on unrepresentative examples. For instance, while you and most of your neighbors may prefer a certain presidential candidate or brand of soft drink, that sample is so small and localized that it is of questionable value; neither the candidate or the soft drink company would be wise to use the results as the basis for important decisions about the success of the candidate's campaign or the likelihood that Pepsi and Coke can be displaced as leading brands.

Hypostatization. This language fallacy results from the failure to differentiate between abstract and concrete words, speaking of abstractions such as *nature, justice, science,* and the like as though they were concrete. Although such abstract words can convey and create emotion, they are not specific enough to convey useful, precise information that will help in reaching a rational decision. "Have you thanked nature today?" is one example of hypostatization, as are "Love conquers all" and "Science puts industry to work."

Hypothesis Contrary to Fact. In this fallacy a hypothesis (a proposition offered as an explanation for the occurrence of some event or phenomenon) that is not true is used as the starting place for a deductive argument. "If Albert Einstein had stayed in Germany, the Nazis would have had an atomic bomb before the United States did" is one such fallacious argument, for Einstein did not stay in Germany, and even if he had, various other factors might well have prevented the Nazis from producing an atomic bomb before the United States did.

Irrelevance (Red Herring). This fallacy results when the argument or discussion deliberately or accidentally strays off the subject and begins to deal with another, even an unrelated, subject, just as dragging smoked (red) herring across a trail will divert hunting dogs from following their prey and lead them off in another direction. Thus, opponents of gun registration may display bumper stickers which read "If guns are outlawed, only outlaws will have guns." This slogan has emotional appeal (its ending assertion uses the *appeal to fear* fallacy), but it has fallaciously changed the point of contention from *registering* guns to *outlawing* them, thus misrepresenting the gun registration supporters' position.

Labored Hypothesis. This fallacy results when a hypothesis drawn from one body of evidence is more complex, unlikely, or unusual than an alternative one; for example, "Dozens of laboratory animals were released from their cages at University Medical Center during the night, and they escaped through an outside door whose lock was broken; there were no witnesses, but Medical Center personnel must have done it in order to get the local animal rights activist group in trouble with the police."

Non Sequitur.   This fallacy's Latin phrase means "It does not follow." The conclusion in such an argument lacks a connection to the premises: "I grew up in Miami; therefore I have always wanted to be a movie star." This example is clearly nonsense, but sometimes the argument may go astray in a less obvious way: "Free enterprise is being undermined by the federal government, which tells all companies how to operate, has taken over management of our farms, and even forces managers to cooperate with union organizers. Democracy is almost extinct in the United States." Perhaps this argument has quite a bit of emotional appeal for you and seems convincing. But you then must not have noticed how the argument shifted, for free enterprise is an economic system and democracy is a political system; thus there is no connection between the premises and the conclusion.

Post Hoc, Ergo Propter Hoc (False Cause).   Latin words that translate as "after this, therefore because of this" commonly identify this fallacy. The problem occurs when a person assumes that a cause and effect relationship exists just because one event follows another. But there must be a demonstrable causal link between the two events before such reasoning can be considered sound. An example familiar to us all is assuming that bad luck will occur if a black cat crosses our path. It's clear here that we are being led astray by our superstitious natures, but all too often we resort to similar fallacious reasoning, assigning our good and bad experiences to some questionably-related prior causes.

Reductio ad Absurdum.   This is another fallacy with a Latin name, here meaning "reduction to absurdity." An effective means of refuting another argument, frequently with a satirical effect, this approach, though fallacious, makes an idea or an attitude seem to be irrational by exaggerating or extending its logical consequences, sometimes to the point of ridiculousness. The classic example of this approach is Jonathan Swift's essay, "A Modest Proposal," reprinted in the "Selected Classic Arguments" section of this book. Swift ironically recommends that, to solve the terrible poverty in eighteenth century Ireland, the poor should sell their children to be used as food.

Slippery Slope (Domino Theory). This fallacy, like *post hoc, ergo propter hoc,* has its basis in the fallacious linking of causes and effects. A slippery slope argument hypothetically links a series of events, asserting that if the first event takes place, then the others will follow, just as one false step on an icy hill may result in an injured person at the hill's bottom, and just as a row of closely spaced dominoes placed on their ends will topple, one after another, if the first one in the row is pushed over. But often events are not as closely linked as those carefully placed dominoes (a *faulty analogy* is also present here), and therefore bans on automatic weapons and cheap handguns need not lead inevitably to the confiscation of Great Grandpa's hunting rifle that has been passed down in the family for generations. Stopping places usually exist along the way, and pointing those out is one appropriate way to refute such fallacies.

Special Pleading (Card Stacking). This inductive fallacy results when certain evidence, generally numerical or statistical, is emphasized, while other evidence, equally or even more pertinent, is suppressed or minimized. When we are told by the local power company's news release that its coal-burning smokestack has new pollution control devices that have reduced its sulphur dioxide emissions (the key ingredient in acid rain) to one-half of one percent, that may seem commendable; but then we realize we haven't been told what that "percent" is part of. Eventually we learn that the percent is of the total volume of emissions, which amount to 10 tons per day, so that annually the plant is still producing over 18 tons of sulphur dioxide, or enough to form quite a few railroad tank cars of sulfuric acid. Twain indirectly referred to just this fallacy when he said, "There are three kinds of lies: lies, damn lies, and statistics." News media can be guilty of this fallacy in a modified form if they feature the activities of certain political figures or government programs that they favor and ignore or give abbreviated coverage to those that they do not.

Syntactic Ambiguity. This language fallacy is the result of faulty sentence structure. Sometimes parts are misplaced: "Sam cut firewood with his best friend"; "The students couldn't understand why Shakespeare was so well liked in high school"; "The professor explained why plagiarism is wrong on Monday." Sometimes multiple or complex questions are phrased so they are self-incriminating whether answered yes or no: "Have you stopped spending all of your money on beer?" or "Are you still cheating on tests?" Similarly, because pauses and emphasis on words can create different meanings, they can result in deliberate or accidental misunderstandings. If you repeat this short sentence, "She slapped him," three times and emphasize a different word each time, the potential for ambiguity will be obvious.

Transfer (False Authority).   This fallacy is based on the principle of favorable association, even though there may be little or no logical connection. In one variety, the subject is identified with some idea or entity that is inherently pleasing or attractive. Any viewer of television or reader of popular magazines is constantly bombarded with advertisements or commercials that use transfer. The association may be with having a good time (see soft drink, liquor, and cigarette ads) or with pleasant memories (food and telephone) or with looking better (clothing and personal care products, always featuring attractive models).

Another variety of transfer, also favored by advertisers, is related to the use of authority in an argument, except here the prestige or reputation of a respected or admired person or institution is used to support an idea or product. This *false authority* fallacy occurs when the person featured is removed from his or her area of expertise; thus while persons may be great stars in fields like popular music and professional sports, their claims of value regarding soft drinks are not likely to be any more accurate than the average person's—and furthermore they are being paid sizable sums for their promotional efforts. In a related way, Biblical references may be used fallaciously to support political or other ideas. In any case, the association or identification should certainly be examined for a logical connection; if there is none, the fallacy of transfer or false authority is present.

Tu Quoque.   This Latin term for "you also" or "you're another" identifies a fallacy that avoids the subject or deflects questions or accusations by making similar accusations against an opponent. For instance, a person being criticized for eating a second candy bar might reply to the critic, "Well, you're *already* too fat or you'd take a *third* one!" or "If you weren't on a diet, you'd be reaching for a Snickers yourself!" Neither of these responses provides logical reasons for eating a second candy bar, but each instead attempts to divert attention elsewhere.

Formal Fallacies

Formal fallacies result from the improper construction of syllogisms, which form the frameworks of deductive arguments. Such fallacies are therefore errors of structure or form. In order to understand formal fallacies, you will also need to have a working knowledge of the simple syllogism. A *syllogism* is a series of three statements arranged according to this formula:

All humans are mortal.   (First or major premise)
Jill is a human.   (Second or minor premise)

_____

Therefore, Jill is mortal.   (Conclusion)

The syllogism must meet certain standards of construction and arrangement in order to be *valid,* or logically consistent. First, the syllogism must consist of three two-term statements: two propositions (*premises*) and a *conclusion,* as in the example just given.

Second, it must consist of three different *terms* ("humans," "mortal," and "Jill" in the above example); one term must appear in both premises but not in the conclusion, and each of the other two terms must appear in one premise and in the conclusion. The term that appears in both premises but not in the conclusion ("human") is called the *middle term;* the other terms ("mortal" and "Jill") are called *end terms.*

Third, in order to be valid a syllogism must conform to three simple rules, the first and most important being that the middle term must be *distributed* only once. To be distributed, a term, whether middle or end, must appear *either* as the subject of a universal statement (one that by means of such words as "every," "all," or "no" totally includes or totally excludes all members of a class or group) *or* as the predicate term of a negative statement. (For our purposes, a predicate term is one that completes either the verb "to be" or some other linking verb—as, for example, "eater of plants" does in this negative statement: "Fido is not an eater of plants.")

A term is *undistributed* if it is the subject of a particular statement or the predicate term of a positive statement. For instance, in this syllogism,

All Italians are fans of opera.   (First premise)
Susie is not a fan of opera.   (Second premise)

_____

Susie is not an Italian.   (Conclusion)

the middle term, "fan(s) of opera," is undistributed in the first premise, since it is the predicate term of a positive statement, and distributed in the second premise as the predicate term of a negative statement. The end term "Susie" is undistributed in both of its positions, being the subject of a particular statement, while "Italians" is distributed twice, once as the subject of a universal statement ("*All* Italians . . . ") and once as the predicate term of a negative statement (" . . . is *not* an Italian").

The case of the end term "Italian" also illustrates rule two: No end term may be distributed only once in a valid syllogism. The third and final rule, as you will see demonstrated later, is that no valid syllogism can have two negative premises.

Either to understand why this last rule is necessary or to determine the validity of any syllogism, you will probably find it useful to draw circles to represent the various classes or groups and individuals named. For example, draw a large circle to represent the class consisting of fans of opera. Then, since all Italians are fans of opera, draw a small circle within the large circle to represent all Italians (you must, of course, leave room for fans of opera from other countries). Now, where does Susie's small individual circle go? Outside both larger circles, of course (see Figure A.1).

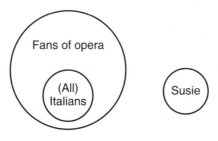

FIGURE A.1

But what happens if you then give the syllogism two negative premises, like this:

No Italians are fans of opera.
Susie is not a fan of opera.

What can you conclude? By drawing the circles you will see the you cannot really say anything exclusively and positively about Susie's nationality, for you do not know exactly where to place her circle (see Figure A.2). Susie may or may not be an Italian, which is not a useful conclusion. Now you should understand why rule three is important. By using the circles you should also be able to determine why the rest of the standards and rules for validity are important.

So far we have been concentrating on the question of the *validity* of the deductive syllogism. A quick glance at the sample syllogisms and circles, however, will suggest that the question of *truth* in a de-

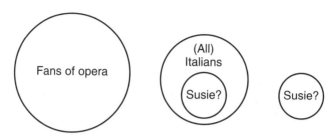

FIGURE A.2

ductive syllogism is a separate one, for while it is commonly known that many Italians are indeed fans of opera, we can also be reasonably sure that at least some Italians prefer rock, jazz, or other musical entertainment. However, and this is a point that you must understand about deductive arguments, *if* a syllogism meets the standards of *validity*, and *if* the premises are accepted as true propositions, whether intuitively, inductively, or even deductively as conclusions of other syllogisms, then the conclusion of the syllogism in question is logically and undeniably true. Of course, few of us consciously use deductive syllogisms in the formal sense, although we do use deductive logic daily, often in an abbreviated form called an enthymeme.

An *enthymeme* is a syllogism with one of its three statements missing or unstated, and perhaps with its conclusion preceding its premise(s), as in this case: "Susie's not Italian. She doesn't like opera." Clearly the first premise, "All Italians are fans of opera," is absent, perhaps because the speaker thinks it is too obvious to need mentioning. Yet the speaker's audience, if they are critical thinkers, might realize the problem with the *truth* of the unstated first premise and reject the speaker's conclusion about Susie's nationality. (They could also reject the conclusion without really knowing exactly why, perhaps on the basis of "common sense.") Similarly, another speaker might state, "Dr. Green probably eats meat, since she is a veterinarian." But this conclusion might also be false, perhaps because the syllogism is invalid:

Most veterinarians eat meat.
Dr. Green is a veterinarian.

———————————

Dr. Green eats meat.   X

Here the middle term ("veterinarian") is not distributed, for "most" is not a word that includes or excludes all of a class or group. Or even if in valid form, with "all" substituted for "most," the first premise or proposition could be rejected as inductively false by a person who knows of one or more veterinarians who are vegetarians.

This is not to suggest, though, that all enthymemes are either invalid or false. Instead, you should be aware when they are being used and examine the total syllogism for validity and for true, acceptable propositions before you agree with or reject any deductive conclusion.

The five most common formal fallacies are discussed below. If you care to do so, you can use scratch paper to draw and appropriately label circles for each argument, in order to determine its invalidity.

1. *The four-term argument.*

All persons who drink to excess are alcoholics.
Sandra drinks beer.

Therefore, Sandra is an alcoholic.

The four terms here are "persons who drink to excess," "Sandra," "drinkers of beer," and "alcoholics." To make the argument a valid one, it must be shown that Sandra drinks to excess, thus eliminating the fourth term and providing a properly distributed middle term, "persons who drink to excess."

2. *Improperly distributed middle term.* This fallacy results when the middle term of a deductive syllogism is distributed more or less than once. For instance, in this invalid syllogism the middle term, "fans of opera," is not distributed at all:

All Italians are fans of opera.
Wolfgang is a fan of opera.

Wolfgang is an Italian.   X

Nothing prevents people of other nationalities from joining the class of fans of opera, since the middle term is not distributed. So Wolfgang may well be of some nationality other than Italian. If the middle term is distributed more than once, this invalid syllogism results:

All Italians are fans of opera.
All Italians are friendly.

?

When the middle term drops out, as it always does in a valid syllogism, we are left with no conclusion at all, for some fans of opera are not Italian and some friendly people are not Italians; we can assert nothing validly or positively about the friendliness of non-Italian fans of opera.

3. *Unequal distribution.* In this fallacy, an end term is distributed only once, as in this example:

All Italians are fans of opera.
No Germans are Italians.

No Germans are fans of opera.   X

Here, since the end term "fans of opera" is distributed in the conclusion (as the predicate of a negative statement) yet not distributed in the premise (as the predicate of a universal statement), it violates the basic rule of deduction that no end term may be distributed only once.

4. *Two particular premises.* No valid conclusion may be drawn from two particular premises. Consider this example:

Some tall persons are awkward.
Jim is a tall person.

Therefore, Jim is awkward.

Maybe he is, and maybe he isn't; no positive or negative conclusion can be reached.

5. *Two negative premises.* This fallacy results because no valid syllogism may have two negative premises, for then no exclusive and no positive conclusion can be drawn. For example,

No Australians have ever lived in my neighborhood.
Kathleen has never lived in my neighborhood.

?

Kathleen may be an Australian or not; we can't say for sure either way.

You have now finished this short discussion of material and formal fallacies. You will probably find it useful to turn back now and then to this section and to review it, just to maintain your ability to detect fallacies in arguments created by you and by others.

Glossary of Useful Terms

The following list provides brief definitions of key logical, rhetorical, and stylistic terms arranged alphabetically. Italics show that a word or phrase found in a definition also has its own definition in this glossary.

abstract words: Words expressing intangible feelings, ideas, or generalities (anger, religion, summer), as opposed to *concrete words*, which stand for tangible objects or things.

allusion: A brief reference to a person, place, thing, or event, or to a literary work or passage. Sometimes classified as historical, literary, or topical, allusions are comparisons used by writers to expand upon or to clarify ideas.

analogy: A comparison of two things which share some but not all qualities. By helping an *audience* comprehend the unfamiliar in terms of the familiar, analogy is one useful means of supporting a *claim*.

argument: The systematic process of providing proof to support a *conclusion*; the support for a *claim*.

argumentation: One of the basic modes of *prose* discourse, the others being *description, narration,* and *exposition. Purpose* is a key determinant in differentiating between these modes, with the writer of argumentative prose setting out to change the minds of the intended *audience*.

assertion: A specific declarative statement *(claim, proposition)* expressing a belief or opinion which the writer or speaker must support with *evidence* in order to gain the approval of an *audience*.

assumption: A statement or idea accepted or supposed true without demonstration or substantial proof.

414

audience: The person(s) who will read or hear an *argument*. The best writers have a particular audience in mind as they compose their work, taking into account the intended audience's knowledge of the subject, its opinions or biases, and the like. Although the real audience may differ from the intended one, the writer seeking success must select and organize the material, determine *purpose*, and adjust *tone* with his or her perceived audience in mind.

authority: A person or a source of information presumed or known to be reliable. An appeal to authority, made by referring to such a person, or to that person's findings or work, is one way to support a *claim.*

backing: The support for a *warrant* or *assertion.*

bibliography: A list of works, usually on a specific subject or by a specific person or group of persons, normally appearing at the end of a research paper, scholarly article, or book.

cause and effect: An important *method of development* used in supporting a *claim* by analyzing the connection(s) between the effects (results) and the causes of (reasons for) those effects.

claim: A statement or *assertion* that the writer of an *argument* must successfully support or prove. These can be classified as one of three types: claims of fact, claims of policy, claims of value.

classification: A *method of development* that can be used to support a *claim* by showing the connections between classes or types of ideas, persons, and things because of shared features or attributes.

cliché: A worn-out idea or expression, usually a comparison, which is so familiar that it no longer causes thought or calls to mind a visual image. "Good as gold," "beginner's luck," "happy as a lark" are examples; their use by a writer suggests mental dullness or laxity.

coherence: One desired goal of effective prose composition, wherein all of the parts of the written piece fit together clearly and logically. (Also see *transition* and *unity.*)

comparison/contrast: A *method of development* used to support a *claim* by focusing on the similarities (comparison) and/or differences (contrast) of two or more members of the same group of ideas or things.

concession: A rhetorical tactic whereby the writer acknowledges conflicting or differing views, *claims, warrants,* and the like on a subject, thereby attempting not only to neutralize those opposing points but also to indicate that the subject has been considered fully.

conclusion: (1) Structurally, the closing sentence, paragraph, or other section of a piece of writing, whose function is to add a sense of unity and finality to the composition; (2) in an *argument,* the specific statement or *assertion* being proven by a line of reasoning.

concrete words: Words which stand for tangible objects or things, ones which can be perceived by the human senses. Due to their sensory appeal, concrete words (in contrast to *abstract words*) help a writer's *audience* to imagine the object or thing, thereby adding clarity of expression while reducing ambiguity.

connotation: The secondary or associational meanings that most words have, due either to their contexts or to their emotional overtones for readers. (Compare to *denotation.*)

deduction: A traditional method of *logical argument* in which a *conclusion* (specific statement or *assertion*) is derived from *premises* (general or inclusive statement or *assertions*). (Compare to *induction.*)

definition: Normally, a synonym for or a statement of the exact meaning(s) of a word, such as can be found in a dictionary. Also a *method of development* used to support a *claim* by clarifying or demonstrating the meaning of a word or concept.

denotation: The literal or dictionary meaning of a word, as opposed to its *connotation.*

description: A form of writing relying mainly on *concrete words* to convey exact sensory impressions of persons, places, and things, and therefore often valuable in supporting a *claim*; frequently used in conjunction with *narration.*

diction: The selection of words in writing or speaking, with emphasis on accuracy, appropriateness, and level *of usage.* (See also *tone.*)

documentation: The references a writer provides in order to show the source(s) of any borrowed or adapted information. (See also *bibliography.*)

editing: The process of correcting writing problems of *diction*, grammar, or phrasing. (See also *proofreading, revising.*)

enthymeme: A *syllogism* with an unstated or implied *premise.*

essay: A *prose* composition that attempts to explain something, discuss a topic, express an attitude, or persuade an *audience* to accept a *proposition.*

evidence: Facts, statistics, or other data used to support a *claim* or *thesis.*

exemplification: The most important *method of development*, especially useful for supporting a *claim*, it is based on the use of examples to clarify a subject or support a *thesis.*

exposition: One of the basic *modes of discourse* or forms of *prose*, which are classified according to *purpose.* The writer of exposition attempts to explain a subject, or to inform the intended *audience* about it.

fact: Something accepted as true based on experience or observation, and which all reasonable persons normally will accept as true (wood comes from trees; seat belts save lives; milk contains calcium). A *claim* of fact is usually not debatable. Contrary to fact is *opinion.*

fallacy: Any of various types of deceptive, erroneous, or false reasoning that cause an *argument* to be logically flawed, even though the fallacy may be psychologically persuasive and seem to be true. (A complete discussion is provided in "A Short Guide to Material and Formal Fallacies," beginning on p. 399.)

figurative language: Writing or speaking that includes brief comparisons (figures of speech) based on the purposeful departure from the literal or common meanings of words in order to create clarity, freshness, or additional special meanings. Familiar figures of speech include *allusion, metaphor,* and *simile.*

focus: Confining a subject to a single point of view. In order to provide appropriate and steady focus, a writer must especially keep in mind the intended *audience,* the *purpose,* and the *subject.*

hypothesis: A *claim* presented as an explanation for some event or set of phenomena; also the *premise* for an *argument.*

induction: A method of *logical argument* in which a *hypothesis* or generalization is proposed, based on observation of representative actions, specific instances, statistical data, or other evidence.

introduction: The beginning of a piece of writing, varying in length from a single sentence to several pages or even a chapter, depending on the complexity of the subject and approach and on the work's length. An effective introduction identifies the subject, limits the subject, interests the *audience,* and may indicate the work's overall organization.

invalid: Not following the rules of *logical argument,* especially in the case of *deduction.* An invalid *argument* is not in the proper form, so its *conclusion* does not necessarily follow from its *premises.*

irony: A manner of writing or speaking so as to present one surface meaning while also presenting one or more veiled, contrasting meanings. Sometimes used quite effectively for argumentation, as in the case of Jonathan Swift's "A Modest Proposal," it may use such specific techniques as exaggeration, sarcasm, or understatement.

level of usage: The kind of language, especially in terms of *diction* and *syntax,* most suitable for the intended *audience.* The normal categories are these: (1) general; (2) informal; (3) formal; (4) nonstandard. Most undergraduate academic writing is done at the general level, a blend of the formal and informal.

logical argument: A kind of *argumentation* relying on appeals to reason, it features a reserved and detached *tone* and tends to avoid or limit appeals to emotion.

metaphor: A figure of speech suggesting an unstated comparison between one object and another, basically different object.

method of development: Those organizational techniques (sometimes called modes) used in *paragraphs* or larger pieces of *prose*, especially *argumentation* and *exposition*, with the intent of achieving the best rhetorical effect on the intended *audience*. The most common methods are *cause and effect, classification, comparison/contrast, definition, exemplification*, and *process analysis*; several or even all of these methods may be used at once in a piece of writing.

modes of discourse: The three *prose* forms, *argumentation, description–narration, exposition*, which may appear separately or in various combinations in a piece of writing.

narration: The process of telling about events, as in story form. Combined with *description*, this is one of the three basic *prose* forms (or *modes of discourse*). Often used for purposes of *argumentation* or *exposition*, it may also exist separately for its own sake.

objective: Expressing opinions or ideas based on detached observation, undistorted by personal feelings. (See *subjective*.)

opinion: A belief confidently held but not necessarily shared by other reasonable persons (city life is better than rural life; no dessert tastes better than blueberry cheesecake; skydiving is fun). Compare to *fact*.

paradox: A statement that on its face seems self-contradictory or in conflict with general belief, yet nevertheless contains some truth. "No news is good news" is a familiar example.

paragraph: A separate portion of a composition, usually marked by indentation of its first written line, it expresses a thought or point related to the whole work but is essentially complete by itself. Varying in length from one sentence to many, paragraphs may function as *introduction, conclusion*, and *transition* elements of an *essay*; other paragraphs form the main body of the essay and are used to develop or present the subject.

paraphrase: Restating another person's words either (1) to make them more understandable or concise or else (2) to show how those words are understood. In contrast with a *summary*, a paraphrase more closely approximates the length of the original version.

persuasion: A kind of *argumentation* that relies primarily on appeal to the emotions of an *audience* (compare to *logical argument*). Featuring a personal, even a friendly, *tone*, persuasion depends minimally, if at all, on *fact* and other elements of logical argument.

plagiarism: Presenting the words or ideas of another person as one's own, or without proper *documentation.*

premise: The *claim* or *proposition* on which an *argument* is based.

process analysis: A *method of development* that can be used to support a *claim* by showing the sequence of steps involved in doing or making something.

proofreading: The correcting of a piece of writing for errors of mechanics (spelling, punctuation, capitalization, and the like) and of typing and transcription. (See also *editing, revising.*)

proposition: A statement or *claim* that is to be proven or disproven.

prose: Written (or spoken) language that lacks metrical structure (as opposed to poetry or verse). It appears in three basic forms (or *modes of discourse*): argumentation, description–narration, and *exposition.*

purpose: A writer's intended goal, which may be to describe (*description*), to tell a story (*narration*), to explain (*exposition*), to change the *audience's* opinion (*argumentation*), or some combination of these.

qualifier: A word or words used to limit a *claim* or *assertion,* indicating that it may not always be true as stated. Familiar examples of qualifying words include "often," "normally," "in general," "with few exceptions," and the like.

refutation: Examining *arguments* or any of their parts and showing logical reasons for rejecting them.

revising: The major reworking of a piece of writing, including changes in organization, development, approach to the subject, point of view, and the like. (See also *editing* and *proofreading.*)

rhetoric: Written or spoken language consciously composed to influence the thought and conduct of an *audience.*

rhetorical question: A question posed mainly for effect, with either no answer expected or an obvious answer implied. Usually a rhetorical question is presented to gain the agreement of the *audience* to something the writer assumes is obvious.

simile: A figure of speech in which a similarity between two things is directly expressed, most often by using *like, as,* or *than* to create the comparison.

slanting: Using *diction* (especially the *connotation* of words) and choosing *facts* so as to make the writer's *argument* seem better than it is. This practice may result in a *fallacy.*

style: The distinctive features of a piece of writing, especially as created by the writer's *diction, syntax, tone,* and arrangement of material.

subjective: Expressing opinions or ideas based on personal feelings or interests rather than on detached, disinterested observation. (See *objective.*)

summary: A concise statement of the major points or ideas of a piece of writing.

support: Anything used to prove a *claim,* including not only *evidence* but also appeals to the values and emotions of the *audience.*

syllogism: The basic formula or pattern of *deduction,* consisting of a major premise (general proposition), a minor premise (specific proposition), and a conclusion drawn from terms or parts of each premise. (See also *enthymeme.*)

syntax: The arrangement and relationship of words, phrases, and sentences.

thesis: A writer's assumption or specific statement, usually expressed in the *introduction,* which he or she then attempts to validate. A thesis statement or sentence (in a paragraph, called a topic sentence) often reveals the writer's *purpose.*

tone: The apparent attitude of the writer toward both subject and *audience,* especially as revealed by *diction,* selection of details and examples, and *syntax.* (See also *style.*)

transition: Any of various means of linking one topic (or aspect of a topic) to another. The most basic means of achieving effective transitions is logical organization, but a writer may also use such tactics as transitional words and phrases, repetition of key words and phrases, and repetition of sentence structure.

unity: The desirable quality found in a piece of writing that is limited to and focused on a single idea or topic.

valid: Following the rules of *logical argument.* A valid deductive argument adheres to the correct form, and thus its *conclusion* necessarily follows from its *premises.*

warrant: An underlying assumption or general principle that provides a connection between the *claim* and its *support.*

Acknowledgments

Dyer, Wayne W., "Your Erroneous Zones." Excerpt from *Your Erroneous Zones* by Wayne W. Dyer (New York: Funk and Wagnalls, 1976, pp. 164–165). Copyright © 1976 by Wayne W. Dyer. Reprinted by permission of HarperCollins Publishers, Inc.

Gorman, James, "Fight Sleepism Now," *New York Times Magazine*, August 8, 1993. Copyright © 1993 by The New York Times Company. Reprinted by permission.

Murphy, Cullen, "No, Let's Keep Them," *The Atlantic Monthly*, December 1989. Copyright © 1989 by The Atlantic Monthly. Reprinted by permission.

Eiseley, Loren, "An Evolutionist Looks at Modern Man," *The Saturday Evening Post*, April 26, 1958. Reprinted from *The Saturday Evening Post* © 1958.

McGinley, Phyllis, "Women Are Better Drivers." Reprinted from *The American Weekly*, © 1959 by Hearst Publishing Co., Inc., by permission of King Features Syndicate Division.

Jackson, Jesse, "Why Blacks Need Affirmative Action." Excerpted from "Why Blacks Need Affirmative Action," *Regulation*, Sept./Oct. 1978. Reprinted with the permission of the American Enterprise for Public Policy Research, Washington, D.C.

King, Martin Luther, Jr., "Letter from Birmingham Jail" from *Why We Can't Wait* by Martin Luther King, Jr. Copyright © 1963, 1964 by Martin Luther King, Jr. Reprinted by permission of Harper & Row, Publishers, Inc.

Steinbeck, John, "How to Cuss," *The Virginian Pilot*, May 22, 1966, p. C5. Copyright © 1966 by John Steinbeck. Reprinted by permission of McIntosh and Otis, Inc.

Warner, James H., "Freedom—Even for Those Who Burn the Flag." Originally entitled "When They Burned the Flag Back Home: Thoughts of a Former POW," *The Washington Post*, July 11, 1989. © *The Washington Post*.

Phillips, B. J., "Irresponsible to Allow Companies to Push Credit Cards at the Young," *Asheville (NC) Citizen-Times*, August 30, 1996. Copyright © 1996 by Knight-Ridder/Tribune News Service. Reprinted by permission.

Gartner, Michael, "Right and Wrong Way to Get Involved," *Asheville Citizen-Times,* September 11, 1996. Copyright © 1996 by Michael G. Gartner. Reprinted by permission.

McCall, Nathan, "My Rap Against Rap," *The Washington Post,* November 14, 1993. Copyright © 1993 The Washington Post. Reprinted by permission.

Sims, Edward. "Military Takes Equality Too Far," *Asheville Citizen-Times,* Nov. 5, 1989, p. 3D. Copyright © 1989 by Editor's Copy Syndicate. Reprinted by permission.

DeFleur, Lois B., "Vivid Images Shouldn't Alter View of Women in Combat," *Air Force Times,* July 15, 1991. Copyright © by Lois B. DeFleur. Reprinted by permission.

Hirschorn, Michael W., "Facing Up to Sexism," *The Harvard Crimson,* March 5, 1986. Copyright © 1986 by *The Harvard Crimson.* Reprinted by permission.

Goss, Kristin A., "Taking a Stand Against Sexism," *The Harvard Crimson,* March 5, 1986. Copyright © 1986 by *The Harvard Crimson.* Reprinted by permission.

Seligman, Daniel, "Why I Gamble," *National Review,* May 1, 1995, pp. 59–62. © 1995 by National Review, Inc., 150 East 35th Street, New York, NY 10016. Reprinted by permission.

Ison, Chris, and Dennis J. McGrath, *Reader's Digest,* April 1996, pp. 101–105. Reprinted with permission from the April 1996 *Reader's Digest.* Originally published in the *Minneapolis Star Tribune* (Dec. 3, 4, 5, 6, 1995). Copyright © 1995 by Star Tribune. Condensation copyright ©1996 by The Reader's Digest Assn., Inc.

Looney, Douglas S., "Cash, Check or Charge?" *The Sporting News,* July 1, 1996. Copyright © 1996 by The Sporting News Publishing Company. Reprinted courtesy of *The Sporting News.*

Green, Ron, "Paying Athletes? Colleges Do Not Need this 'Cure,'" *Asheville (NC) Citizen-Times,* July 9, 1996. Copyright © 1996 by Knight-Ridder/Tribune News Service. Reprinted by permission.

van den Haag, Ernest, "The Deterrent Effect of the Death Penalty," from Ernest van den Haag and John Conrad, *The Death Penalty Pro and Con: A Debate* (New York: Plenum Press, 1983, pp. 67–69). Copyright © 1983 by Ernest van den Haag and John P. Conrad. Reprinted by permission of Plenum Press and the author.

Berger, Vivian, "Rolling the Dice to Decide Who Dies," *New York State Bar Journal,* Oct. 1988. Copyright © 1988 by New York State Bar Association. Reprinted with permission.

Gould, Stephen Jay, "Evolution as Fact and Theory." From *Discover Magazine,* May 1981, pp. 34–37. Copyright © 1981 by Stephen Jay Gould. Reprinted by permission of the author.

Gish, Duane T., "A Creationist's Reply to Gould." From *Discover Magazine,* July 1981. Copyright © 1981, Discover Magazine, Inc. Reprinted by permission of the author, Duane T. Gish.

Shanahan, David, "We Need a Nationwide Effort to Encourage, Enhance, and Expand Our Students' Proficiency in Language," *The Chronicle of Higher Education,* May 31, 1989, p. A40. Copyright © 1989 by *The Chronicle of Higher Education.* Reprinted by permission.

Ulrich, Walter, "Importance of Studying Languages Questioned." From *The Chronicle of Higher Education*, July 5, 1989, p. B4. Copyright © 1989, *The Chronicle of Higher Education*. Reprinted by permission of the author.

Erdahl, Lowell O., "Euthanasia Is Sometimes Justified." Reprinted from *Pro-Life/Pro-Peace* by Lowell O. Erdahl, copyright © 1986 Augsburg Publishing House. Used by permission of Augsburg Fortress.

Chavez, Linda, "We Don't Need Assisted Suicide," from *Asheville (NC) Citizen-Times*, May 16, 1996. Copyright © 1996 by Linda Chavez. Used with permission.

Bernardi, Peter J., "Is Death a Right?" Loyola University of New Orleans, from *Christianity Today*, May 20, 1996. Copyright © 1996 by Peter J. Bernardi. Reprinted by permission.

Kilpatrick, James, "Right to Die a Tough Call for the States," Taken from the James J. Kilpatrick column by James J. Kilpatrick, *Asheville Citizen-Times*, April 20, 1996. Copyright ©, Universal Press Syndicate, Inc. Reprinted with permission. All rights reserved.

Burger, Warren, "The Right to Bear Arms," *Parade*, Jan. 14, 1990, pp. 4–6. Reprinted with permission from *Parade*, copyright © 1990.

Ivins, Molly, "Ban the Things. Ban Them All," the *Fort Worth Star-Telegram*, March 11, 1993. By permission of Molly Ivins and Creators Syndicate.

Hitchens, Christopher, "Minority Report," *The Nation*, January 24, 1994. Copyright © 1994 *The Nation* magazine/The Nation Company, Inc. Reprinted by permission.

Bombeck, Erma, "Kids Killing Kids Has Got to Stop," Copyright © 1996, Universal Press Syndicate, Inc. Reprinted with permission.

Koop, C. Everett, M. D., "Stopping Kids from Smoking: Do We Really Want to Do It?" *Asheville (NC) Citizen-Times*, September 3, 1996. Copyright © 1996 by C. Everett Koop and by the Citizen-Times Publishing Company. Reprinted by permission.

Heyman, Richard, "Help Kids Get Over the Hump," *Raleigh (NC) News and Observer*, October 2, 1996. Copyright © 1996 by Knight-Ridder/Tribune Information Services. Reprinted by permission.

Blatt, Richard, "Curbing Ads Won't Work and It's Unconstitutional," *The Washington Post*, September 8, 1996. Copyright © 1996 by Richard Blatt. Reprinted by permission.

Beck, Joan, "The True Toll of Cigarettes Is Staggering," *Asheville (NC) Citizen-Times*, September 1, 1996. Copyright © 1996 by Chicago Tribune Corporation. All rights reserved. Reprinted with permission of Knight-Ridder/Tribune Information Services.

Lippmann, Walter, "The Indispensable Opposition." *The Atlantic Monthly*, Aug. 1939, pp. 186–190. Copyright © 1939 ® 1967 by The Atlantic Monthly Co., Boston, Mass. Reprinted with permission of the President and Fellows of Harvard College.

Adler, Mortimer J., "How to Mark a Book," *Saturday Review of Literature*, July 6, 1940. Copyright © 1940 by Mortimer J. Adler; copyright © renewed 1967 by Mortimer J. Adler. Reprinted by permission of the author.

King, Martin Luther, Jr., "Letter from Birmingham Jail," from *Why We Can't Wait* by Martin Luther King, Jr. Copyright © 1963, 1964 by Martin Luther King, Jr. Reprinted by permission of Harper & Row, Publishers, Inc.

Index of Authors and Titles